Innovation in Responsible Management Education

Innovation in Responsible Management Education: Preparing the Changemakers of Tomorrow

EDITED BY

REGINA OBEXER
MCI | The Entrepreneurial School, Austria

DESIREE WIESER
MCI | The Entrepreneurial School, Austria

CHRISTIAN BAUMGARTNER
FHGR University of Applied Sciences of the Grisons in Chur, Switzerland

ELISABETH FRÖHLICH
ISPIRA Think Tank for Sustainable Supply Chains, Germany

ALFRED ROSENBLOOM
Dominican University, USA
AND

ANITA ZEHRER
MCI | The Entrepreneurial School, Austria

United Kingdom – North America – Japan – India – Malaysia – China

Emerald Publishing Limited
Emerald Publishing, Floor 5, Northspring, 21-23 Wellington Street, Leeds LS1 4DL

First edition 2024

Reprints and permissions service
Contact: www.copyright.com

British Library Cataloguing in Publication Data
A catalogue record for this book is available from the British Library

ISBN: 978-1-83549-465-3 (Print)
ISBN: 978-1-83549-464-6 (Online)
ISBN: 978-1-83549-466-0 (Epub)

Printed and bound by CPI Group (UK) Ltd, Croydon, CR0 4YY

INVESTOR IN PEOPLE

Contents

List of Abbreviations

CBR	Community-Based Research
ESD	Education for Sustainable Development
PRME	Principles for Responsible Management Education
RME	Responsible Management Education
RMERC	Responsible Management Education, Research Conference
SDGs	Sustainable Development Goals
SL	Service-Learning
UN	United Nations

About the Editors

Desiree Wieser did her PhD in Management at the University of Innsbruck, Austria in 2022. She is an Assistant Professor in the department of Non-profit, Social & Health Care Management. Desiree's teaching activities focus on entrepreneurship, social entrepreneurship (2022 Ars Docendi Recognition Award for Excellent Teaching in Austrian Universities), responsible management, and research ethics. Her research interests are diverse and stretch from higher education management to education, including online, entrepreneurship and responsible management education. She was a member of the program committee and coordinator of the ninth Responsible Management Education Research Conference.

Regina Obexer is a university Lecturer and the Head of the Center for Responsible Management & Social Impact at MCI | The Entrepreneurial School. She coordinates activities and initiatives in the field of responsibility, sustainability, and ethics across MCI and is the Head of the PRME Task Force. She is also a member of the steering group of the PRME Chapter DACH, and she serves as the Vice Chair of the MCI Research Ethics Committee. In 2022, she led the program committee and coordinated the ninth Responsible Management Education Research Conference. Her research interests are at the intersection of digital education, change management, education for sustainable development, and responsible management education. She is a doctoral candidate at Lancaster University, researching collective transformative agency in sustainability change laboratory settings.

Alfred Rosenbloom is a Professor Emeritus and was the first John and Jeanne Rowe Distinguished Professor at Dominican University. His research interests include case writing, the application of the case method in management education, global branding, marketing in countries with emerging and subsistence markets, and the challenge of integrating the topic of poverty into the management education. Al coleads the Anti-Poverty Working Group, Principles of Responsible Management Education (PRME), and participates broadly within PRME. He was a Fulbright Scholar in Nepal and Bulgaria and was twice honored with the Teaching Excellence Award from Brennan School of Business students.

Anita Zehrer holds the position of Professor and serves as the Head of the Family Business Center at MCI The Entrepreneurial School ®. Concurrently, she also assumes the role of Head of Research in the domain of Management and Society within the institution. Her scholarly pursuits are characterized by a breadth of research interests, with a primary emphasis on the landscape of family business management and entrepreneurial behavior in small- and medium-sized Enterprises (SMEs). The scholarly impact of Dr Zehrer's work is evidenced by publications in leading business management and tourism journals.

Christian Baumgartner studied Landscape Ecology and is a Professor for Sustainable Tourism at the University of Applied Sciences Graubünden (Switzerland) and the owner of Response and Ability (www.responseandability.com). He specializes in the development and implementation of sustainable tourism and sustainable regional development and has led specific tourism development projects in Europe, Central and Southeast Asia. He is passionate about working and researching in the field of labeling and monitoring and is an Auditor and Certification Councilor in several European certification schemes. He has taught at several universities in Europe and Asia.

Prof Dr Elisabeth Fröhlich served as the President of CBS International Business School, Germany, until 2022. She holds a full professorship in Sustainable Procurement and Supply Chains and is an internationally recognized expert in sustainable supply chain management. She is highly engaged in the field of Responsible Management Education. She serves as a board member of the PRME, she chairs the PRME Nomination and Governance Committee, and is PRME DACH Chapter Chair. She is also leading the AOM MED Ambassador Program as the Vice Chair. She is leading the Board of JARO Institute and offering online trainings in the field of sustainable procurement. Her research focuses on sustainable supply chain management and green procurement, qualification in purchasing, Procurement 4.0, and strategic supplier relationship management. Innovative teaching formats of Responsible Management Education are further main areas of her research. She has published several books and articles on the above-mentioned topics and supports several journals as an external reviewer.

About the Contributors

Antje Bierwisch is a Professor and Study Coordinator for Innovation, Entrepreneurship and Foresight in "Business Administration Online" at MCI in the Department of Business Administration Online since 2018 (https://www.mci.edu/de/faculty/antje.bierwisch). Prior to that, she worked for 10 years as a Project Manager/Senior Researcher at the Fraunhofer Institute for Systems and Innovation Research, ISI in Karlsruhe. Her research focuses on futures literacy, strategic foresight, innovation management, and sustainable innovation. Based on her experience gained from more than 50 applied research projects, she is a consulting expert on strategic foresight at both the economic level for different industries, and the policy level for several national and federal governments, in Germany, Vietnam, Lithuania, and Romania. Since 2023, she has held the "UNESCO Chair in Futures Capability for Innovation and Entrepreneurship," established at the MCI. The Chair deals with the promotion of future skills and the strengthening of students' innovative ability and entrepreneurial spirit (https://research.mci.edu/de/unesco-chair-futures-capability).

Since October 2018, **Prof Bernd Ebersberger** has been the Head of the Department for Innovation Management at the University of Hohenheim, Stuttgart, Germany. He also leads the InnoGreenhouse, the University's entrepreneurship hub. Formerly, Prof Ebersberger held a professorship at the Management Center Innsbruck (MCI). He also held positions at Fraunhofer ISI in Karlsruhe, the Technical Research Center of Finland in Espoo, Statistics Finland, and the University of Augsburg. Prof Ebersberger's research focuses on innovation management, systems, business strategies, entrepreneurship, and the nexus between innovation and sustainability. He is an author, coauthor, and editor of numerous books and scientific publications in renowned journals such as the Journal of Applied Economics, Research Policy, Regional Studies, *Journal of Economic Geography, Journal of Business Research, European Management Review, Entrepreneurship and Regional Development, Journal of Evolutionary Economics, and Journal of Technology Transfer and Structural Change & Economic Dynamics.*

Lois Fearon is an Assistant Professor and the intellectual lead for international marketing courses for the Faculty of Management at Royal Roads University. She has also served as the Head of the MBA Program, and the Business School Director where she led significant curriculum advancements. Throughout her academic career, Dr. Fearon has taught, managed, and developed numerous courses and programs. Prior to becoming a full time academic, she worked in industry for over 20 years, gaining extensive leadership and consulting experience. Her recent research focuses on assessing the impact of integrating sustainability into business school curricula, reflecting her commitment to advancing sustainable business practices through education.

Gundula Glowka is a Distinguished Researcher affiliated with the MCI | The Entrepreneurial School. Her primary research focus revolves around unraveling the intricate dynamics of risk behavior within small and medium enterprises, studying family-related, SME-specific, strategic, tourism-specific, and external risks. Gundula Glowka was an active contributor to the Erasmus + EU Project titled "Entrepreneurial and Intrapreneurial Competences Assessment Alliance" adding her expertise to the development of teaching and training materials designed to promote entrepreneurial competences.

Alexandra Grammenou is a Lecturer and Research Associate in the Center for Corporate Responsibility, Department International Business in the ZHAW School of Management and Law, Switzerland. Along teaching and research, she is PRME Coordinator in the ZHAW School of Management and Law. She is currently a PhD Candidate in Organizational and Cultural Studies in the University of St. Gallen, Switzerland. Her research focuses on business and human rights, governance, and CSR. In the past she worked as Research Assistant in CSR in South Africa and in the Institute of Marketing and Communication in the University of Lugano, Switzerland. She holds an MA in Economics and Communication from the University of Lugano and a Licentiate in Law from the Aristotle University, Greece.

Rebecca Chunghee Kim is a Professor of NUCB Business School in Japan. She was a British Chevening scholar and a visiting scholar of University of California, Berkeley. Rebecca received her PhD degree (2009) from The University of Strathclyde Business School. Previously, she taught at Ritsumeikan Asia Pacific University, University of Nottingham, University of Strathclyde, and University of Edinburgh. Rebecca is particularly interested in research on comparative and international CSR, ESG, and capitalism through active collaboration with scholars/practitioners from around the world. As a discussion-loving scholar, Rebecca has delivered speeches on comparative CSR in various nations including Japan, Korea, Malaysia, India, Indonesia, Vietnam, Philippines, Mongolia, the United Kingdom, and the United States.

Marcus Kreikebaum, European Business School, Wiesbaden, Germany, has been teaching Service-Learning and promoting PRME at EBS University since 2008. He has coached many cohorts of students in local and global Service-Learning projects and published several papers, some of them together with his father Hartmut, with whom he founded the Center of Business Ethics at EBS in 2007. Through field studies in Mexico and Guatemala during his studies in Cognitive Sciences, Philosophy, Literature, and Linguistics in Germany and Oregon, Marcus developed a deep interest in the potential of encounters of the social other. This is also the main thread in his work as a dramatist for several theaters. Marcus got his doctoral degree in 2002 for a dissertation on the Poems of Heiner Müller. He is currently the Director of Business Ethics Center at EBS University and a Senior Lecturer for Service-Learning at the Business School of University of Business and Law, Wiesbaden, Germany.

Louisa Mach is a research associate and a PhD candidate at the University of Hohenheim in Stuttgart, Germany. With her background in teaching business administration and economics in vocational business schools, she is passionate about competence-based learning. While working for the Department of Innovation Management at the University of Hohenheim, she focuses her work on competences for sustainable innovation. Moreover, as part of the Entrepreneurial and Intrapreneurial Competences Assessment Alliance (EICAA), she gained valuable insight into the learning and assessment of competences.

Lisa Marx is a Product Manager at a Tyrolean SME in the cosmetics industry. Before that, she studied part time (International Business and Management with a focus on Marketing and Digital Business) at the Management Center Innsbruck while working part time. Her great interest for digging into the human mind and understanding specific behaviors but also bringing attention to the importance of mental health led to the topic of this study. Moreover, putting research focus on the business context where this topic is often outmissed.

Helga Mayr is working in the Department of Digitalization, Education for Sustainable Development (ESD) and Quality Management at the University College of Teacher Education Tyrol (PHT). She coordinates the implementation of ESD at the PHT, teaches in ESD-relevant teacher training courses, and is involved in several research projects. Her research interest is in integrating ESD in teacher training as well as teaching practice. The focus of her PhD project is on ESD and Design Thinking. Helga studied international economics and business education.

Avvari V. Mohan is a Professor and Deputy Head (Engagement & Impact) at the School of Business, Monash University Malaysia. He received his doctorate in Management of Innovation from the Department of Management Studies, Indian Institute of Science (IISc), Bangalore, following which he visited South Korea on a Research Fellowship at the Korea Advanced Institute of Science and Technology (KAIST). Prior to joining Monash University, he served as a member of the faculty at Nottingham University Business School (Malaysia campus). His teaching and research interests are broadly in strategy and innovation with special interests in sustainability-related/responsible business strategies. His research focuses on innovations systems (interorganizational linkages) that help organizations to develop innovations and contribute to sustainable development. He has published his work in international journals and in reports for international agencies. He is on the editorial panels of international journals in the area of innovation and policy.

Marina Schmitz serves as a Researcher and a Lecturer at the Coca-Cola Chair of Sustainable Development at IEDC-Bled School of Management in Bled, Slovenia, as well as a CSR expert/senior consultant at Polymundo AG in Heilbronn, Germany. She draws on several years of work experience as a Lecturer, Research Associate, and Project Manager at the Center for Advanced Sustainable

Management (CASM) at the CBS International Business School in Cologne, Germany, as well as the University of Göttingen (Chair of Human Resources Management and Asian Business). Marina is passionate about challenging the status quo of how we understand and teach economy and management-related content to our students. She uses experiential learning to foster meaningful and critical reflection, envisioning alternative futures, and learning to embrace complexity and uncertainty. Additionally, she is currently involved in various international research projects dedicated to innovative higher education pedagogy, involving gamification, theater, and other methods informing arts-based management.

Yoshiki Shinohara is an Associate Professor at the College of International Management, Ritsumeikan Asia Pacific University. He is also the Director of the Center for Inclusive Leadership (CIL). His research focuses on corporate sustainability, corporate social performance and financial performance, and diversity and inclusion in organizations. He is the President of Intellectual Partners Ltd and engages in consulting. He holds a PhD in Business and Commerce from Keio University.

Pratibha Singh, European Business School, Wiesbaden, Germany, has dedicated close to a decade of her career working with NGOs, think tanks, and associations in India, Thailand, and Germany on issues such as gender equality, climate change, migration, conflict management, and sustainable development. Adept in content creation and storytelling, she has published around 40 articles, book chapters, issue briefs, and papers. She holds two Master's degrees in Gender and Development Studies and Public Policy. Currently, she aims to maximize positive impact of financial institutions in consonance with Agenda 2030 at Agents for Impact where she is working as an SDG Rating Analyst. Simultaneously, she is pursuing her PhD from EBS University of Business and Law on sustainability transitions in small- and medium-sized cities of the Global South.

Kristina Steinbiß holds a full professorship for Management with a focus on Marketing at the ESB Business School at Reutlingen University, where she teaches primarily in the Industrial Engineering programs. Her current research focuses on sustainable marketing, how to influence consumer behavior, and the implementation of new business models. She is the author of numerous publications in the above-mentioned fields, including the textbook "Marketing," the second edition of which has just been published. Next to her university activities, she is also enthusiastic about the TRIZ innovation methodology. As a trainer and coach, she likes to combine this methodology with her marketing approach.

Wayne Visser is a Fellow and Head Program Instructor at the University of Cambridge Institute for Sustainability Leadership. He is also a Visiting Professor at Antwerp Management School's Sustainable Transformation Lab, which he established in 2017. He is the Director of the think tank and media company, Kaleidoscope Futures, through which he coproduced and presented the award-winning documentary film on the circular economy called *Closing the Loop*. In addition, he is the Founder of CSR International and a Board Member of the Globally Responsible Leadership Initiative (GRLI). Dr Visser previously served as the Director of Sustainability Services for KPMG and a Strategy Analyst for Capgemini in South Africa. His work as a Strategy Analyst, Sustainability Advisor, CSR Expert, Futurist, and Professional Speaker has taken him to 78 countries in the past 30 years to work with over 230 clients. He is the author of 44 books, including *Thriving*, an Amazon bestseller in 17 countries. He is also the recipient of the Global CSR Excellence and Leadership Award, the Emerald Literati Outstanding Author Contribution Award.

Foreword

By Wayne Visser
Management education has come a long way since I first did my business studies around 35 years ago. Back then, sustainable development had just been coined, and the 1992 Rio Earth Summit had not yet taken place. Subjects like business ethics and social responsibility were already on the academic research agenda but had not yet made their way onto most curricula. In contrast, if my experience was anything to go by, business students and business leaders were already actively engaging with social and environmental challenges.

What we have witnessed in the intervening decades is an incremental process of mainstreaming sustainability in business education. One key landmark was undoubtedly the launch of the UN Principles for Responsible Management Education (PRME) in 2007, which now has around 850 signatories. This is progress, but there are approximately 16,000 business schools, according to an AACSB estimate, so there is still a long way to go. Of course, even among PRME signatory schools, the progress is not even.

My experience of working with over 50 universities and business schools around the world is that there are stages of maturity in the implementation of responsible management education, from ad hoc engagement on sustainability topics, such as through seminars or volunteer activities (stage 1), to a *pick-and-mix* offering of sustainability elective courses or research projects, sometimes called a saddle-bag approach (stage 2). Then, there's *embedding* of compulsory business ethics, CSR, ESG or sustainability courses or projects into curricula (stage 3), and *mainstreaming* sustainability by ensuring that it features in all taught subjects, research programs, and campus operations (stage 4).

Many believe that mainstreaming is the ultimate goal of responsible management education, but I would add a fifth stage, *transforming*, which is qualitatively different. Here, sustainability is mainstreamed, but there is also critical reflection on the unsustainability of underlying economic systems and business models, and a conscious focus on innovation to transition from systemic breakdown in nature, society, and the economy to breakthrough solutions and market opportunities. In this mode of engagement, through teaching, research, and outreach, responsible management education becomes a driver of systems change and a catalyst for positive tipping points.

The focus of this collection is exactly what we need right now to shake management education out of its complacency. Educational institutions – and especially those that are developing our current and future leaders – need to move from being human capital factories that perpetuate the status quo to creative incubators of a radically different economy in which both nature and humans thrive. This is the essence of my book, *Thriving: The Breakthrough Movement to Regenerate Nature, Society and the Economy*, and the takeaway message from my poem, Change the World, with which I will end this Foreword.

Change the World

Part 1

> Let's change the world, let's shift it
> Let's shake and remake it
> Let's rearrange the pieces
> The patterns in the maze
> The reason for our days
> In ways that make it better
> In shades that make it brighter
> That make the burden lighter
> Because it's shared, because we dared
> To dream and then to sweat it
> To make our mark and not regret it
> Let's plant a seed and humbly say:
> I changed the world today!

> Let's change the world, let's lift it
> Let's take it and awake it
> Let's challenge every leader
> The citadels of power
> The prisoner's in the tower
> The hour of need's upon us
> It's time to raise our voices
> To stand up for our choices
> Because it's right, because we fight
> For all that's just and fair
> For a planet we can share
> Let's join the cause and boldly say:
> We'll change the world today!

> Let's change the world, let's love it
> Let's hold it and unfold it
> Let's redesign the future
> The fate of earth and sky
> The existential why
> Let's fly to where there's hope
> To where the world is greener
> Where air and water's cleaner

Because it's smart to make a start
To fix what we have broken
Our children's wish unspoken
Let's be the ones who rise and say:
We changed the world today!

Part 2

Let's change the world, let's move it
Let's chance it and free dance it
Let's feel its sliding rhythms
The echoes of its rhymes
The calling of our times
With signs of stars aligning
With mimes of joy and madness
Of syncopated sadness
Because we bend, because we tend
To lose the beat, then find it
To live life forward, not rewind it
Let's stamp our feet, link arms and say:
We'll change the world today!

Let's change the world, invoke it
Let's weave it and conceive it
Let's sing our songs of freedom
The myths of heroes' quests
The trial-by-fire tests
With rests to ease our struggle
With crests that draw us onward
Because we roam, because we've shown
With tears and wide-eyed wonder
These days are not for squander
Let's choose our narrative to say:
We changed the world today!

Let's change the world, let's heed it
Let's hear it and not fear it
Let's place our finger on life's pulse
Where mountain rivers flow
Where ancient forests grow
We know, for elders tell us
We grow by seeing what can be
Because within we find our jinn
And rub each deep desire
From sparks into bright flames of fire
Let's wish for every chance to say:
I changed the world today!

Introduction

Regina Obexer[a], Desiree Wieser[a], Christian Baumgartner[b], Elisabeth Fröhlich[c], Alfred Rosenbloom[d] and Anita Zehrer[a]

[a]MCI | The Entrepreneurial School, Austria
[b]FHGR University of Applied Sciences of the Grisons in Chur, Switzerland
[c]ISPIRA Think Tank for Sustainable Supply Chains, Germany
[d]Dominican University, USA

Abstract

Despite long-standing efforts, higher education's transformation to meet the challenges of the 21st century and foster sustainable development remains elusive, particularly in management education. responsible management education (RME) emphasizes sustainability, ethics, and responsibility in business, yet progress is slow. This book, stemming from the 9th Responsible Management Education Research Conference, explores innovative approaches to RME. The book is divided into three parts, delving into curriculum design and policy directives, teaching methods, and insights from business practice. The book advocates for a paradigm shift in education, emphasizing the need for higher education institutions to embrace sustainable development principles. It provides inspiration for educators and practitioners to incorporate responsible management education into various contexts, aiming to drive positive societal change and shape future leaders with a social impact.

Keywords: Innovation; responsible management education; sustainable development; social impact; entrepreneurship

Despite several decades of efforts at policy and institutional level, the transformation of higher education required to prepare learners to tackle the pressing challenges of the 21st century and accelerate sustainable development remains fragmented and illusive. This is particularly problematic in the field of management education (García-Feijoo et al., 2020), where learners represent business leaders, managers, and decision makers of the future. Responsible management

Innovation in Responsible Management Education, 1–5
Copyright © 2024 Regina Obexer, Desiree Wieser, Christian Baumgartner, Elisabeth Fröhlich, Alfred Rosenbloom and Anita Zehrer
Published under exclusive licence by Emerald Publishing Limited
doi:10.1108/978-1-83549-464-620241001

education (RME) is concerned with responsibility, sustainability and ethics in business and represents a growing field of research and practice (Laasch et al., 2020), but progress in implementation is still too slow and incremental to engender the fundamental economic and societal changes required (Maloni et al., 2021). The UN Sustainable Development Goals (SDGs) represent a useful framework for a holistic approach, but adopting and implementing SDGs in higher education is known to be a fuzzy project, which is demanding, intricate, and fragmented (Beddewela et al., 2021). What is required is no less than a paradigm shift (Pirson, 2020), where creative and innovative approaches to curriculum design and teaching and learning methods are implemented within a learning environment that recognizes and addresses real world challenges and is cognizant of the context within which these occur. A paradigm shift is not based on established pathways and pre-existing modi operandi. Instead, it calls for innovative and novel ideas, radical rethinking of existing practices and knowledge, and an entrepreneurial spirit that wants to invent new ways of doing things, and new things to do.

The book addresses new developments and approaches in the field of responsible management education, with a focus on the role of innovation. The chapters are based on contributions presented at the 9th RMER Conference on "Societal Impact through Entrepreneurship & Innovation: Responsible Leadership Education for the Change Makers of Tomorrow" and have been selected carefully to provide diverse and innovative perspectives. The volume is divided into three parts, with each part shedding light on a specific level of responsible leadership education from curricular to pedagogical to contextual aspects.

Part 1, Innovation in curriculum design and institutional policy, describes innovations and new approaches in the design and development of educational programs in business and related areas that aim to develop future change makers. Starting with a critical perspective on prevailing business models, the part includes discussions relating to learning goals with responsible management principles, impact of RME programs, and the question of policy directives for responsible research and innovation in the context of higher education.

In chapter 1, *Kim and Shinohara* seek to generate inclusive insights into the educational embeddedness of management and leadership members, and the consequences of such embeddedness on managerial processes, structures, and outcomes under contemporary capitalism.

In chapter 2, *Mach and Ebersberger* analyze 72 further education programs in Southern Germany (Baden-Württemberg) and relate them to the six Principles for Responsible Management Education (PRME), identifying a gap in higher-level learning goals for sustainable and ethical thinking among tertiary educational offers in this region.

In chapter 3, *Fearon* takes a closer look at business school curriculum to develop sustainable change agents. Her study applies a multi-case approach, investigating two different undergraduate business programs at Royal Roads University in Canada to find out how including sustainability in the curriculum contributed to changes in students' conceptualization of sustainability and their sustainability-related attitudes and behavior.

Finally, *Grammenou* introduces responsible research and innovation (RRI) as a new policy framework for universities to handle the systemic change in higher education in chapter 6. The article describes drivers, barriers, best practices, and monitoring of this new approach, drawing on the case of Zurich University of Applied Sciences (ZHAW).

New designs at curricular level and the competences required for responsible management as discussed in Part 1 demand innovative and novel teaching and learning methods.

Part 2, Innovation in teaching and learning methods, provides descriptions of creative approaches for responsible management education at the level of individual courses. This part seeks to motivate educators to experiment with unconventional methods and formats to sensitize students for sustainable development in management, laying the foundation for future responsible leaders.

Bierwisch and Schmitz focus on fostering anticipatory and futures (thinking) skills in Chapter 5. The authors plead for the integration of the arts into management education (theater, visual arts, design) by introducing solarpunk-inspired role plays (inspired by sociodrama and improvisation in theater studies), visioning exercises, prototyping based on world-building, foresight, and forecasting-related tools as examples how to train futures literacy in students.

The next chapter by *Kreikebaum and Singh* puts the issues of food security, consumption, access, and poverty on the table by examining students' food consumption habits and attitudes. The authors qualitatively analyze student learning diaries and essays that have been created as part of an experiential service learning format at the food banks. Results reveal that students do not only enhance their knowledge about the community and food-related issues, but also develop a higher sense of purpose and empathy.

Avvari describes the Sustainable Decision and Organization (SDO) module in Chapter 7, which has been developed by and implemented at the Nottingham University Business School (NUBS) UK first and was later adapted for delivery in Malaysia and Singapore campuses. Using a stakeholder approach, MBA students are challenged to develop business strategies with limited resources, that lead to more sustainable value creation. The module is based on action learning and includes the transfer of conceptual and practical knowledge through the involvement of academic and business experts, including site visits, as well as group works and role plays.

Part 2 concludes with *Mayr and Baumgartner* introducing the Global Goals Design Jam as a playful, participatory, and creativity-enhancing learning format based on design thinking that can be used in different contexts. Following the principle of becoming active, students not only discuss challenges and opportunities, but also develop solutions in the form of prototypes. In addition, they are given the opportunity to pursue their projects in the further course of their studies, ideally also in cooperation with actors outside the university.

Part 3, Inspiration from innovative business practices, provides different perspectives on the business contexts and practices that learners will find when they enter the world of work. The business world forms an important background to the educational programs designed and delivered and can be seen as both an ingredient and at the same time an outcome of responsible management education. The specific business contexts considered in the chapters in this part embrace problematic and critical business issues at different levels. The cases described serve to illustrate current business developments driven by and impacting on responsible management, thus building a direct bridge to practice and contributing significantly to the development of a holistic understanding of the competencies needed for future changemakers.

Steinbiß and Fröhlich address the topic of waste generation in the fast-fashion industry in chapter 9. Based on a quantitate analysis of consumer behavior and attitudes on sharing fashion platforms, the authors discuss the sharing economy as one possible business model of circular economy to solve the challenge of waste reduction and overconsumption in the fast-fashion industry.

In chapter 10, *Zehrer, Marx, and Glowka* discuss the importance of personal resilience in terms of SME change, crisis, well-being, and job performance. Conducting an exploratory study, they provide a framework of personal resilience of SME owners, building a basis for identifying stress triggers, sharpen self-awareness, and strengthen their own resources. This framework is a reference point to develop leadership programs that help foster resilience of future changemakers.

The concluding chapter by *Wieser, Obexer, and Rosenbloom* is a creative synthesis of various paths along which positive action can be taken in RME. The authors highlight, discuss, and further develop aspects of social impact and innovation in RME as they are enacted through institutional policies, curriculum designs, teaching and learning methods, competence frameworks, and business practices described in the preceding chapters.

To make a paradigm shift happen, we believe that higher education institutions and business schools must adopt a role model function in terms of sustainable development and responsible management by embedding associated values and principles deeply into their missions, curricula, educational models, and organizational practice. It is time for innovation, disruption, and action in education (Borland et al., 2022).

The present edition raises various aspects of these challenges and provides an information base as well as source of inspiration for further research for the academic and scientific audience, including scholars and researchers. More importantly, however, the various examples and cases serve as orientation points and outlooks for educators and practitioners to move forward and to incorporate responsible management education along different ways and within various settings.

With this book, we aim to provide innovative answers to the question of where management education needs to go and how to educate changemakers and leaders with social impact. By sharing visions of what RME could look like, this volume aims to raise awareness of the changes our society is facing and ideas of how we can address them in education for the future we want.

References

Beddewela, E., Anchor, J., & Warin, C. (2021). Institutionalising intra-organisational change for responsible management education. *Studies in Higher Education, 46*(12), 2789–2807. https://doi.org/10.1080/03075079.2020.1836483

Borland, H., Butler, M., Elliott, C., Ormrod, N., & Traczykowski, L. (2022). *Embedding sustainability, corporate social responsibility and ethics in business education.* Edward Elgar Publishing.

García-Feijoo, M., Eizaguirre, A., & Rica-Aspiunza, A. (2020). Systematic review of sustainable-development-goal deployment in business schools. *Sustainability, 12*(1), 440.

Laasch, O., Moosmayer, D., Antonacopoulou, E., & Schaltegger, S. (2020). Constellations of transdisciplinary practices: A map and research agenda for the responsible management learning field. *Journal of Business Ethics, 162*, 735–757.

Maloni, M. J., Palmer, T. B., Cohen, M., Gligor, D. M., Grout, J. R., & Myers, R. (2021). Decoupling responsible management education: Do business schools walk their talk? *International Journal of Management in Education, 19*(1), 100456. https://doi.org/10.1016/j.ijme.2021.100456

Pirson, M. (2020). A humanistic narrative for responsible management learning: An ontological perspective. *Journal of Business Ethics, 162*, 775–793.

Part 1

Innovation in Curriculum Design and Institutional Policy

Chapter 1

Reinventing Responsible Management Education Under New Capitalism

Rebecca Chunghee Kim[a] and Yoshiki Shinohara[b]

[a]NUCB Business School, Nagoya University of Commerce & Business, Japan
[b]Ritsumeikan Asia Pacific University, Japan

Abstract

Capitalism is under siege (Porter & Kramer, 2011), and business schools are under fire (Amann et al., 2013). So, management and leadership education in higher education institutions should be reinvented under the more challenging era of capitalism. How then can business schools cope with these challenges and contribute to global endeavor for making sustainable capitalism? In this context, there is thus reason for the following *three* core concerns that new understanding of management and leadership education is required. First, shortcomings of contemporary capitalism lead to failures of responsible management. Second, ethical failure of management leadership is a pressing issue. Third, academic responsibility under the new capitalism remains unexamined. Based on these three core concerns, we seek to generate inclusive insights into the educational embeddedness of management and leadership members and the consequences of such embeddedness on managerial processes, structures, and outcomes under contemporary capitalism.

Keywords: Responsible management education; capitalism; corporate social responsibility; ethical leadership; inclusive education

Less Attention Is Devoted to Responsible Management Education

Corporations are struggling, under the pressure of the global society, to contribute to the sustainable development of the world (Kim, 2018). In this regard, we can observe the rise (and rediscovery) of the responsible business (Thomson & Bates, 2022). Never before has there been such intense discussion on responsible

Innovation in Responsible Management Education, 9–25
Copyright © 2024 Rebecca Chunghee Kim and Yoshiki Shinohara
Published under exclusive licence by Emerald Publishing Limited
doi:10.1108/978-1-83549-464-620241003

management and the role of business *in* and *for* a global society by pursuing the themes of United Nations Sustainable Development Goals (UN SDGs). However, it is fair to say that business schools around the globe devote less attention to responsible management education despite this being where future business leaders and managers are raised. For example, in a survey of researchers in the area of business ethics in Japan, Nakano et al. (2012) found that approximately 60% were teaching specialized course of business ethics. However, the remaining 40% only handled business ethics-related content as part of broader courses such as management, modern business, strategic management, marketing, or human management. In addition, the majority of business ethics-related courses were elective courses, with very few universities placing these subjects on compulsory courses (Nakano et al., 2012). Consequently, business schools are far behind the discussion of responsible management. Why has this happened and what is the fundamental responsibility of management education in contemporary capitalism?

Capitalism is under siege (Porter & Kramer, 2011). The capitalism system is often the target of attack and complaint of the global society. From the mass of criticism concerning the dominant version of stock market capitalism, many global leaders propose a new lens through which to look at capitalism (i.e., beyond the rich man's game). In this light, corporations nowadays are struggling to find their genuine leadership identity whether they pursue a single bottom line (economic), double bottom line (economic and social), or triple bottom line (economic-social-environmental). For instance, Porter and Kramer (2011) highlight chronic problems in contemporary capitalism by addressing the idea of creating shared view (CSV). CSV stems from the notion of contemporary business limits, that is, the legitimacy problem of contemporary capitalism and corporate responsibility management. It argues that CSV is not corporate social responsibility or corporate donation but, rather, a new way to achieve economic success. The core idea is that corporations can simultaneously benefit society and boost their economic competitiveness. This appealing concept has emerged to address the debate between two incompatible positions – shareholder and stakeholder value – and the current business task of regaining legitimacy and sustainability in an era of contemporary capitalism. For contemporary business, how to cope with society's pressure and how to be a smart, socially conscious, for-profit business by pursuing responsible management is the key to gaining a competitive advantage. However, there is limited endeavor to teach responsible management in higher educational management institutions around the globe. There is a gap within business education, especially concerning how to tackle the legitimacy and sustainability issue confronting contemporary businesses.

The above phenomenon provokes the debate that business schools are under fire (Amann et al., 2013). Management education, today, lacks a noble purpose. Traditional education approaches to make graduates respond to demands for a more responsible way of managing a business has failed (Haertle et al., 2017). This is related to poor understanding of the role and responsibility of the business school in the vulnerable global market context. We must be careful not to fall into the trap of assuming that students already have the resources to meet the myriad challenges in the modern workplace surrounding ethics and responsibility.

Sensitizing business students to the importance of individual and inclusive actions seems increasingly warranted (Kolodinsky et al., 2010). Particularly in this era of globalization, too many teachers are inadequately prepared to include responsible management education to culturally and ethnically diverse students. In this regard, management education in higher education institutions should be reinvented under the more challenging era of capitalism. To address these recognized gaps, the present study is built around three critical research questions:

(1) How can business schools cope with challenges in global markets and society and contribute to the endeavor for making sustainable capitalism?
(2) How can business schools develop leading management professionals capable of building a sustainable global society?
(3) Do business schools have a plan to grow their efforts in pursuit of societal impact?

Raising future responsible global leaders is a key priority in responsible management education. It is necessary for international business education to develop a relevant education policy and pedagogy that is able to cover demanding topics and institutional dynamics and pressures in contemporary capitalism. More research is necessary to analyze the embeddedness of responsibility-related variables of the other management subjects in order to develop tools and to train responsible business leaders. In particular, responsible management teaching should cultivate business leaders who have a depth of understanding to challenge the nature of the new capitalism and who are capable of solving a wide range of problems while addressing the challenges of business and society in an inclusive and ethical way.

In this context, there is thus reason for considering the *three* core concerns that new perspectives of responsible management education are required. The present article focusses on generating new insights into consideration of the three issues concerning responsible management education by proposing that an inclusive business school education can be beneficial by systematically ingraining the demanding topics (e.g., reinventing capitalism; ethical failure of management; academic responsibility of business schools), outlined below, into international management teaching. Before proceeding, we would like to clarify that the purpose of the article is not to judge the failure of responsible management or responsible management education. Rather, it seeks to indicate some lessons for future responsible management education by critically observing the limits of current business education in tackling the pressures of new capitalism.

Issue #1: Shortcomings of Capitalism Lead to Gaps in Responsible Management

Skepticism toward capitalism is increasing. Creating high-performance capitalism is questioned nowadays. The main purpose of business, "maximizing shareholder value" and "a profit-and-loss mindset", have been severely criticized as not being sustainable, democratic, or ethical (Thomson & Bates, 2022; Vogel, 2005; Young, 2003). Moreover, the current capitalism idea is not enough to contribute toward pursuing a sustainable global society and capitalism. The poor outcomes of responsible management are frequently the result of the "shortcomings" of contemporary capitalism.

While capitalism is an unparalleled vehicle for creating jobs, building wealth, improving efficiency, and meeting human needs, the narrow and selfish approach of current capitalism has prevented business from harnessing its full potential to meet society's broader challenges (Porter & Kramer, 2011). In this regard, we often observe that contemporary capitalism has many errors and distortions. For instance, there are a range of chronic byproducts of the capitalistic system such as business misbehavior, corruption, bankruptcy, and scandal, which are regularly found in capitalist economies, in addition to inequality, societal exclusion, institutional collapse, environmental destruction including global warming issues, and more.

In particular, capitalism introduces the so-called financialization dilemma to business (Thomson & Bates, 2022). Business tends to monetize people, nature, and society according to myopic profit-and-loss ideas, and this stream has been narrowly valuing each critical component of the global society which especially challenges its sustainable development. In this regard, critics argue that capitalism corrodes values. Kim (2022) highlights five shortcomings of contemporary capitalism: runaway self-interest, quarterly focus, elite orientation, volume orientation, and one-pattern capitalism, which lead to the shortcomings of responsible management as well.

First, the idea of "self-interest" is one of the most compelling moral justifications for capitalism: as long as business creates the greatest good for the greatest number of people, it is ethical (Henderson & Ramanna, 2015). Yet, when we look at the real world, it is difficult to make the case that capitalism creates the greatest good for the greatest number of people. The argument that pursuit of self-interest benefits society is grounded in the idea that competition among profit-seeking firms in free markets results in an "efficient" allocation of scarce resources and distributional outcomes that benefit society at large. One outcome of the pursuit of self-interest by individuals and corporations is that it encourages business leaders to take a utilitarian view of corporate social responsibility (CSR) and responsible management, to see it as a means to tackle organizational inertia, to foster public relations (PR) such as company image and social reputation, or to conceal the unethical behavior of business leaders and corporations (Marques & Mintzberg, 2015; Pope & Wæraas, 2016). This often leads to CSR that not only fails to contribute to societal goals and global sustainable development, but that is questionable business performance, such as "window dressing" CSR around the global economic society.

Second, "quarterly capitalism" forests on the short-term operational and fiscal approach of capitalism which, Barton (2011) insists, is one of the greatest weaknesses, or misuses, of modern-day capitalism. The pressures on business leaders and managers to meet quarterly earnings targets are strong, and undoubtedly contribute to efficiency and productivity. However, focusing on quarterly earnings consumes an extraordinary amount of business leaders' time and attention, and excessive focus on short-term financials can adversely affect the long-term health of the business itself. These are the focal problems of business, especially business leadership in a contemporary economic society. The tyranny of short-termism (Govindarajan & Srivastara, 2020; Kotler, 2015) negatively affects the sustainability of companies, investors' consideration obsessed with short-term results, and the broader global economic system (Henderson, 2020; Kramer, 2020). New generations of young people are asking businesses to step up.

Third, a global economic system mainly for the rich and the elite is one of the important shortcomings of capitalism. There is little moral justification for the extraordinary concentration of capital and wealth by the rich and the elite. Elitist capitalism often results in "elitist" management initiatives, communications, and outcomes, designed by/for exclusive groups, which miss the mark because they do not incorporate, reflect, and respond to the needs of nonelite stakeholders. Billionaires and large corporations have become caricatures of capitalism's failures (Lane, 2019), as many feel that capitalism has left them behind as only the privileged and the richest benefit. Ostry et al. (2019) call for an economic system for inclusive growth that delivers a more equitable, humane, and democratic distribution of wealth. Under contemporary capitalism, economic inequality feeds and is fed by a wide range of discriminatory practices based on such things as race, religion, and status which, like economic inequality, are self-perpetuating. In this light, trying to implement a responsible management agenda created exclusively by management leaders or a CSR department is misguided. As the actions of businesses affect a broad array of stakeholders, including employees, NGOs, customers and the local and global communities, representatives of these groups should be consulted and involved in the conception and design of CSR programs. Elite-designed CSR is likely to be viewed with skepticism by many stakeholders, who are apt to doubt the sincerity of the initiatives or may interpret them as indications the company is hiding something.

Fourth, "volume-oriented capitalism", meaning that size and quantity (i.e., economies of scale) matter in capitalism, is regarded as one of the most powerful engines driving capitalism: the larger the company, the larger the volume of production, and the greater the cost savings and resulting profits. This utilitarian concept began as a solution to the pressing problem of how to allocate resources for production. Obviously, capitalism provides advantages of scale in the output of goods and services and maximizing profit is, perhaps, the singular normative principle embodied in contemporary competitive capitalist economies (Henderson & Ramanna, 2015). However, there is a shortcoming to the value of volume and size, and the value of maximizing profit; today's world demands that firms move beyond maximizing economic value to also creating social value that benefits stakeholders (Meyer & Kirby, 2012; Rocha et al., 2020). Under a system of volume-oriented capitalism aimed at maximizing profits, corporations' endeavor toward responsible management tends to be co-opted into the single objective of maximizing shareholder value. In fact, the most popular claim made for CSR among managers is that companies can do well by doing good, that is, that engaging in CSR is profitable. The "bigger is better" dynamic is often reflected in a corresponding volume-oriented approach to CSR, with corporations evaluating their CSR efforts by the yardstick of how much money is spent (e.g., volume in social contribution) and how CSR is linked to maximizing financial performance. Scholars' heavy focus on the financial impact of CSR has meant that limited attention has been given to its value and social impact.

Fifth, de Soto (2021) argues that capitalism triumphs in the west and fails everywhere else. There is no single capitalism phenomenon. Different nations practice different forms of capitalism, which are culturally and institutionally diverse. Therefore, the idea of "one-pattern capitalism" (i.e., shareholder focus American capitalism) has limits when exploring the diverse management system of the global economy. For instance, Vogel (2019) introduces Japan's ambivalent version of shareholder capitalism, which does not converge on the US model of shareholder capitalism but preserves the characteristics – some would say strengths – of traditional Japanese business models, such as prioritizing stake-holders over shareholders and long-term growth over short-term profits. Other Asian countries likewise exhibit strong tensions between the free-market capitalism model and more closed Asian cultural dynamics. The Asian variety of capitalism that grafts traditional Confucian values onto Western capitalism has been a driving force of Asian economic development. In this light, the initiatives and performances of responsible management are diverse beyond streams of global CSR ranking and environmental, social, and governance (ESG) standards since CSR could be the particular assets and competencies that the firm possesses and that match the particular business practices, consumer expectations, form of capitalism, and institutional dynamics of the location where they are carried out.

Furthermore, the economic system has been dynamic and, especially, the COVID-19 pandemic suggested us the necessity of rethinking capitalism for the truly sustainable global society. This suggests that "the moment for a new conception of capitalism is now" through reinventing capitalism. Nevertheless, there is limited attention for searching solutions to conceptualize, design, and implement this unavoidable phenomenon in the global business society. How then can business schools bring this inconvenient truth into classrooms and discuss with students, frankly, by exploring the under-researched linkages among responsible management, contemporary capitalism, and global institutional contexts?

Issue #2: Ethical Failure of Management Is One of the Pressing Issues in Capitalism

Why do many companies and business leaders fail ethically? The crisis in ethical failures in capitalist markets has been highlighted more than ever. Many unethical leaders have remained in power on the strength of seductive "hero" images in the current capitalist society, while many leaders have been caught up in cases of fraud, corruption, and unethical and irresponsible behaviors. People, especially the young generation such as millennials and Gen Z, do not want to continue to be patient with and accept unethical business leadership in times of new capitalism, especially when business and its leaders' decisions profoundly affect their everyday lives, and may even cause their deaths, as in the case of, for example, the COVID-19 pandemic.

Many corporations pursue a business strategy to tackle social and environmental problems, but the main reason for this strategic decision is not potential win–wins but to address ethical dilemmas (Davis et al., 2000). Corporate wrongdoings in relation to ethically questionable performances of business and business leaders have been continuous. More demanding issues of business are how to react after the wrongdoings, especially in response to the pressures of multi-stakeholders, in the current global society. The frequent pitfall of a business following a risk is that they tend to find a way to escape from the tricky situation by seeking ways to hide misdeeds (often by using CSR-wash techniques such as green-washing, pink-washing, etc.). There might be the risk of CSR-wash – that is, businesses only utilize CSR as a PR tool without adapting their responsible business strategy or measuring their societal impact. In this regard, one of the main reasons why CSR or businesses' demonstration of responsible behavior has been criticized by the public is closely concerned with adaptability and genuineness in general. Therefore, how to maintain the credibility of CSR and encourage genuine commitment through developing efficient and fair enforcement and measurement mechanisms is the key to stimulate businesses' actual engagement in the responsible management phenomenon.

For instance, Kim et al. (2018) investigates how the corporation interprets and communicates with stakeholders' demands following the recent viral business scandal – Korea Airline Nut Rage Scandal – and detects the importance of business's sense of urgency and response to ethical pressures (such as how to "ethically" treat victims and account for wrongdoings). It is observed that there is increasing recognition of the divergence and complexity in public views toward business's ethical and sustainable management (Eagle & Dahl, 2015). Beyond domestic stakeholders, managing ethically with global stakeholders is a significant challenge for business.

Importantly, responsible management cannot be separated from ethics in other aspects of daily life, so it is rather difficult to easily extract business terms from general terms. We should understand the diverse ethical roots (i.e., religion, culture, and society) of diverse societies and seek to explore how these are conveyed as business usage. In this regard, a great deal of literature discusses popular religiosity and culture and people's tendency to treat religion and culture within a view of everyday life embracing moral codes, ethical norms, institutional contexts, and economic systems that go beyond religiosity and ritual (Bouckaert & Zsolnai, 2011).

It is admitted that no single ethical theory, especially from the western advanced capitalist society (such as Kant's deontological ethics or Mill's utilitarianism), can fully explore how and why business should perceive and perform in responsible ways in a contemporary capitalist society. For instance, Kant's view of business ethics often uses the theory in a way that is contrary to its own conditions. His account of how we are bound by the *categorical imperative* depends on a particular conception of moral agency that precludes collective responsibility and, more specifically, corporate responsibility. Although a business can act, its actions can only be judged morally with reference to the reasons held by particular businesspeople. Thus, the applicability of Kant's philosophy to business ethics is limited, because it cannot make sense of the moral obligations that constrain the corporation as a whole (Altman, 2007). Meanwhile, the deontological approach to ethics denies the utilitarian claim that the morality of an action depends on its consequences. Deontologists maintain that actions are morally right or wrong independent of their consequences. One's duty is to do what is morally right and to avoid what is morally wrong regardless of the consequences of so doing (De George, 1995, pp. 83–84).

Whereas there are clear, dominant, ethical traditions in the West, Asia's ethical traditions are myriad and often in tension. Moreover, while the effects of Judeo-Christian ethics have been considerably secularized, the hold of Asian ethical institutions, often ancient and entirely historic, remains strong on society and business alike. The West is dominated by democratic political design, with some variation among forms of government, election systems, and locus of authority. Asian political design not only varies by form of government, electoral system, and dispersal of authority, but also some of these procedurally democratic systems vary in the assurance of the processes being "fair and free", and are overlain by dynastic, military, or clientelist forms of power (see Hague & Harrop, 2013). Also, state roles in Western economic systems have been broadly similar (with variations in the role of government as an owner and director, and in ownership and control of business) (see Hall & Soskice, 2001). Again, there has been great variety in Asia, reflecting the extent and nature of the state as an economic actor. This Asian picture is compounded by greater diversity in economic activity, particularly regarding the size of the agricultural sectors therein. Moreover, while it would be appropriate to claim that each Western system is homogeneous (and federal and decentralized systems not only reflect but also drive heterogeneity), the internal variation of business systems is much more profound, prompting Witt and Redding (2013) to apply the term "multiplexity" to Asian business systems.

In the West, CSR has been promoted as having strategic value for firms, on which basis firms are encouraged to better understand their social and political environment. However, the discussion of the CSR-strategy link should be more cautious in Asia. Porter and Kramer (2006, 2011) argue that CSR is a vital means of gaining social legitimacy and may be linked to the creation of competitive advantage in a firm and shared value. This is predominantly suggestive of an ethical market dichotomy in the Western context. This dichotomy sits rather strangely from an Asia perspective, where business and moral values tend to be seen as overlapping; some have even argued that ethical/moral values are ahead of business values (Kim et al., 2013; Zhu, 2015). Ethical foundations have always appeared on the business agenda in Asian business history, although not always discussed in the vocabularies of CSR (Yin & Zhang, 2012). In this regard, Asia is more demanding toward ethical behavior of corporations and business leaders. In Asian nations, where the influence of Confucianism is strongly felt, questions have long been raised about money-making business activities versus business morality and market ethics (Kim & Moon, 2015). Companies have always taken care to justify their profit-making in these ethic-demanding capitalist societies. Therefore, building trust in business and business leaders as ethical is a critical value-generating strategy in the Asian market.

Confucianism, the dominant religion in China but also important in Korea and Japan and in the other successful "Small Tigers", stresses the importance of controlling our "passionate nature". According to classical Chinese teaching one should not be involved in profit seeking activities. Mencius, a Confucian teacher says "One's act never should be motivated by what profits him or her nor be motivated by what profits one's family or even one's state." Seeking profit will endanger the harmony of the state, and the state for Confucius is the most important ideal (Romar, 2004). What is most important is that it emphasizes one's traditional social obligations and advocates high moral standards – diligence, loyalty, reliability, and reciprocity. It is politically conservative and emphasizes deference to authority, but supports self-reliance, even entrepreneurial activity. Confucianism is a theory of moral leadership where an individual cannot become a complete person without living a moral life. Furthermore, the leadership of the moral person is critical to organizational and social success and a central concept in Confucianism. It is especially important that moral people fill high offices. In early Confucian Classics, there are many examples of the importance of leadership in the development of a moral person and the just and moral society.

Buddhism also has a great impact on CSR in Asian countries. For example, Buddhism is significantly positively associated with corporate environmental responsibility in China (Du et al., 2014). Xu et al. (2022) also found that the percentage of Buddhist entrepreneurs in a region is positively associated both with the level of charity and the probability of establishing businesses in a less developed region. These results suggest that Buddhism value can promote CSR activities and ethical decision making by evoking the consciousness of social responsibility (Du et al., 2014) and curb materialism because of compassion, loving kindness, empathetic joy, and equanimity (Pace, 2013). Japanese traditional business value – Sanpo-yoshi, which stands for three-way satisfaction beyond individual benefit, also has a root of Buddhism (Shinohara & Kim, 2022). The Ohmi merchants of Japan's Edo Period (1603–1867) respected the idea of Sanpo-yoshi and conducted their business based on altruism, not just their own profit. Therefore, they conducted their business with consideration for the contribution they made to the communities to which they belonged as well as the people with whom they did business (Shinohara & Kim, 2022; Warnell & Umeda, 2019). These examples suggest the relationship between Buddhism and CSR in Asian countries.

In addition, one of the main reasons for failures of CSR strategies in Asia is a widespread suspicion toward companies' unethical motivation for adopting CSR; many believe it is simply to improve the business's image as an alternative communication strategy. This distrust places more pressure on businesses to be "ethical" in Asia. For example, even though many leading corporations have poured money into so-called CSR expenditures as a way of contributing to society, people distrust corporations because of their record of unethical behavior, which is closely coupled with the corrupt systems of institutions. One corporation's CSR budget was interpreted by the public and the courts as bribery, which resulted in the CEO being arrested (see the Samsung case, Chun, 2017). These suggest that merely performing CSR-type "good deeds" is not enough to gain public trust; business strategy, to be effective, and business operations must be ethical as well. In general, it can be said that Asian society pays greater attention to business leaders' ethical or unethical decision-making and behavior toward stakeholders.

In sum, theory-focused discussions somewhat ignore the significance of moral intent and dynamic influences for ethical decision-making in a diverse capitalist society. It is suggested that teaching of wise understanding of ethical issues and ethical judgment could be significantly related to facilitating the ethical behavior of future talent in international business. Although it would be unwise to discount teaching the understanding and judgment of ethical issues, Kim (2016) advocates that more care needs to be taken in facilitating students' moral motivation and whether or not they may contribute to the sustainable development of the global society and, more importantly, the generations to come.

Issue #3: The Academic Responsibility of Business Schools Has Been Insufficiently Examined

To what extent can management education contribute to the highlighted defective phenomenon of responsible management in contemporary capitalism? The business school becomes a social context which binds individual ethos and an ethically engaged community (Akrivou & Bradbury-Huaang, 2015). Discussion regarding teaching responsible management to future global talents who will be at the business stage soon is scant and underdeveloped although business schools' penetration of ethical decision-making in international business has become increasingly more apparent. High impact business scandals which continue to occur around the globe are explicit evidence of this oxymoronic situation. In addition, various misinterpretations by business leaders on what constitutes a responsible and sustainable decision and strategy are major reasons in relation to irresponsible decisions and behaviors.

In these contradictory situations, teaching students ethical and responsible decision-making and how to treat ethical dilemmas in their future business life is challenging. Although there are questions concerning teaching ethics and responsible management in professional schools (e.g., ethics could not be or should not be taught; faculty are ill-equipped to teach responsible management; CSR is a part of the "hidden curriculum"; interdisciplinary affairs between moral philosophy, psychology and education), teaching responsibility and ethics is essential to promote students' moral development and character formation. Each student has a different cultural and institutional background and, hence, different priorities regarding decision-making. Issues in responsible management and ethical dilemmas emerge from individuals' perceptions and stances on the ethical climate of society, culture, and organizational environments (Jones et al., 2007). Ethical dilemmas and solutions need to be investigated as a context-dependent phenomenon (Pimentel et al., 2010). In this sense, teaching responsible and ethical decision-making needs to have a holistic approach which covers various issues of society and the complex interactions of individuals.

Students will play a critical role in international business in the near future. Their ethical decision-making will contribute to the efficient rule of the game in the new capitalist society. However, the teaching on it is admittedly limited and, hence, we argue the transformation of the teaching focus: from moral awareness and judgment to facilitation of moral motivation. Since there is no single answer concerning moral reasoning and judgment, we should refrain from imposing or teaching certain universal theoretical constraints on people (Vauclair, 2014) and, rather, encourage people to be motivated by ethical decision-making through teaching about the complexity and dynamics of ethical decision-making (Kim, 2016). In this light, business schools should play a leading role in accelerating the sustainability transition in global society through the promotion of responsibility management-related teaching and research. However, to be fair, educational institutions lag far behind the global movement of sustainable development. Therefore, what are the main problems of business schools?

Business schools exacerbate the problem by hiring and promoting individuals who are incapable of conducting research relevant to practicing managers. The irresponsible and insensitive behavior of business leaders worldwide shows that business is an under-professionalized occupation today (Zsolnai, 2009). Who has the biggest responsibility of business's unethical incidents in current capitalist systems? Business school faculties are, at best, guilty! (Mitroff, 2004). For instance, who has the biggest responsibility for the fake news items that are mass produced by Facebook; platforms, reporters, management, or users who do not have the capability of filtering? Is vaccine mandate ethical in private enterprise? There are continuously emerging questions, which students should ponder and seek to answer in order to find solutions for better leadership of the future. How is education in business schools reflective and responsive to the needs of challenging economic systems?

Management educators should improve holistic skills that pay more attention to responsibility and sustainability and especially complex interaction and dynamics of contemporary business society. Recently, a wide range of responsible management issues have been theoretically and empirically analyzed in relation to management strategy. Nonetheless, many studies tend to represent a rather anecdotal and fragmented approach. We argue that it is not sufficient to explain the holistic picture of responsible management, which is embedded in all management paradigms, firms' performance, institutional environments, and individual needs and values. People's decisions are systematically interrelated as a set of reasons, rather than as an independent single matter.

For instance, rather than simply considering the paycheck, future global talents need to search for jobs that offer a strong sense of meaning, purpose, and the worth of moral values and work ethics (Vesty, 2016; Weber, 2017). Therefore, if a business school seeks to help students better find purpose at work along with responsible leadership and a friendly working environment, then the business society may benefit from having more responsible and successful human assets. In this light, responsible management should not be treated as a fragmented responsibility or sustainability-related phenomenon but should require more of a holistic view which critically concerns interaction with many management themes as contributors for future global talents' business life. If it is to be admitted that an understanding of a large fraction of tomorrow's workers ought to be of paramount importance, then a more holistic approach by business schools is required to enable this within the views of the firm's sustainable strategy and implementation process in a future global society. In this light, business schools should adapt to challenging global realities. Accordingly, leadership and business schools' systems should be ready for all changes such as cultural change, structural change, changes in curricula, changes in research approach and activities and changes in industry relations.

In conclusion, there must be more active commitment from business schools in order to foster positive societal change through leadership, curricula, and scholarship. Recently, leading higher educational institutions have started to emphasize their impact toward a global society beyond teaching and research. Societal impacts are the ways in which a school's mission and strategic plan guide actions that positively impact society at the local, regional, national, or international level. It is suggested that schools can be important drivers for business as a force for good by making impact an explicit part of their strategic management and school activities and priorities. There needs to be well-balanced school policies and programs among research, teaching, and societal impact.

In this light, there should be encouragement for faculty to broaden their research focus to be more impactful, which needs to be closely linked to research-led teaching and pedagogical impact. More faculty should be connected with international experts and policy makers. Overall, all these kinds of endeavors, carried out by school and faculty members, are related to foster students' responsible business mindset, thereby fostering the understanding of the complexity and dynamics of contemporary capitalism and that a business is deeply inter-connected with the society and environment in which it operates (Rimanoczy, 2020). Consequently, teaching and research on responsible management should be explored from multidisciplinary and interdisciplinary perspectives.

The Way Forward

The goal of the present article is to detect three key emerging factors in searching for developing successful and responsible management education, which are interconnected and mutually reinforcing. Based on the three core concerns on the education of responsible management, we seek to generate inclusive insights into the management's education embeddedness, and the consequences of such embeddedness on managerial processes, structures, and outcomes under contemporary capitalism. Furthermore, we suggest responsible paths of future research, practice, and education toward the endeavor of a sustainable global economy.

Importantly, we insist that today's business schools need to take a strong stand on responsibility issues in their education programs. However, few appear to have made responsibility-related topics an essential part of the management curriculum in higher education institutions. In order to tackle this gap, the present study delved into three complex reasons behind this phenomenon. There have been limited discussions of how and the extent to which the variables of responsible management interact and how responsibility matters for decisions of higher educational institutions in the contemporary global market. Through the discussion above, the content of determinants for global responsible management are enriched. We also note that this result comes from diversity and various institutional and cultural interactions and changes in this global era, which affect the perceptions and ways of thinking and behaving both in businesses and business schools. In this regard, we insist that future responsible management needs to consider these complex interactions with care in this emerging era of sustainable development.

It is noteworthy that a lack of attention has been paid to responsible management. In this regard, the above discussions have some key implications for responsible management researchers, practitioners, and educators. First, the study contributes to the discussion on curriculum improvement. Management educators should be able to integrate responsible management-related issues into functional topics in an inclusive way by considering institutional dynamics and contexts in pursuing a global capitalist society. The study suggests the need for an inclusive curriculum of management education along with the dynamics of capitalism and the ethical business dilemma. That is, while responsibility and sustainability-related education is increasingly placing importance in higher educational institutions (Macheridis & Paulsson, 2021), it is challenging as it remains a hidden curriculum; furthermore, it seems to play alone, without a systematic approach and, often, conflicting with other management subjects (Weber et al., 2021).

To tackle this phenomenon, as the way forward, we suggest the potential of integration of responsibility into overall management subjects that are currently rather fragmented. At first sight, responsible management and other management-related topics might be regarded as completely different fields and, hence, we found somewhat ignored educational endeavor in linking those subjects. Moreover, limited research attends to how and the extent to which sustainability-related subjects can be systematically embedded in other fields such as Human Resource Management (HRM), finance, and marketing. We reinsist the importance of interdisciplinarity in higher education. In this work, we suggest many alternatives for handling management subjects, through the lenses of various responsible management and sustainability issues. We believe that the outcome fosters enhancing the curriculum of responsible management education by extending endeavors to incorporating responsible management-related factors into international management.

To reiterate, it is noteworthy from this study that responsible management and other management subjects are closely involved and interact within the capitalist system and, hence, management educators can bring the suggested ideas to future global management curricula and advance the understanding of related theories and ideas in relation to capitalism and the institutional context. It is expected that by holistically incorporating responsible management issues into the other topics provides a turning point to the strategic angle of business and management in focusing on responsible business matters rather than only as an important feature of work-related issues. Through this insightful approach, we suggest that the fundamental problems of a myopic approach to management teaching in higher business educational institutions on separation between responsibility with other subjects could be improved in an inclusive and innovative way.

To conclude, business schools should adapt to changing global realities (Jack, 2022). We admit that responsible management remains a hidden curriculum in higher education and should be massively improved. We believe that embeddedness of responsibility into an international management curriculum holds substantial potential for improvement of international management education. It is our hope that the study can inspire more efficient international management teaching in higher education institutions and stimulate efforts to link the dignified workplace via the emerging angles of sustainability and responsibility to attract/ retain future global talent.

Acknowledgment

The first author acknowledges the support of the Japan Society for the Promotion of Science (Grant no. 23K01601) and Center for Inclusive leadership.

References

Akrivou, K., & Bradbury-Huang, H. (2015). Educating integrated catalysts: Transforming business schools toward ethics and sustainability. *The Academy of Management Learning and Education, 14*(2), 222–240. https://doi.org/10.5465/amle.2012.0343

Altman, M. C. (2007). The decomposition of the corporate body: What Kant cannot contribute to business ethics. *Journal of Business Ethics, 74*(3), 253–266. https://doi.org/10.1007/s10551-006-9233-z

Amann, W., Pirson, M., Dierksmeier, C., Kimakowitz, E. V., & Spitzeck, H. (2013). *Business schools under fire: Humanistic management education as the way forward.* Palgrave Macmillan.

Barton, D. (2011). Capitalism for the long term. *Harvard Business Review, 89*(3), 84–91.

Bouckaert, L., & Zsolnai, L. (2011). *The Palgrave handbook of spirituality and business.* Palgrave Macmillan.

Chun, R. (2017). Samsung, shame, and corporate atonement. *Harvard Business Review Digital Articles*, 2–5. https://hbr.org/2017/05/samsung-shame-and-corporate-atonement

Davis, J. H., Schoorman, F. D., Mayer, R. C., & Tan, H. H. (2000). The trusted general manager and business unit performance: Empirical evidence of a competitive advantage. *Strategic Management Journal, 21*(5), 563–576. https://doi. org/10.1002/(sici)1097-0266(200005)21:5<563::aid-smj99>3.0.co;2-0

De George, R. T. (1995). *Business ethics* (4th ed.). Prentice Hall.

de Soto, H. (2021). *The mystery of capital: Why capitalism triumphs in the west and fails everywhere else.* Basic Books.

Du, X. Q., Jian, W., Zeng, Q., & Du, Y. J. (2014). Corporate environmental responsibility in polluting industries: Does religion matter? *Journal of Business Ethics, 124*(3), 485–507. https://doi.org/10.1007/s10551-013-1888-7

Eagle, L., & Dahl, S. (2015). *Marketing ethics & society.* Sage Publications.

Govindarajan, V., & Srivastara, N. (2020). We are nowhere near stakeholder capitalism. *Harvard Business Review Digital Articles,* 2–5. https://hbr.org/2020/01/we-are-nowhere-near-stakeholder-capitalism

Haertle, J., Parkes, C., Murray, A., & Hayes, R. (2017). PRME: Building a global movement on responsible management education. *International Journal of Management in Education, 15*(2), 66–72. https://doi.org/10.1016/j.ijme.2017.05.002

Hague, R., & Harrop, M. (2013). *Comparative politics: An introduction.* Palgrave Macmillan.

Hall, P. A., & Soskice, D. (2001). *Varieties of capitalism.* Oxford University Press.

Henderson, R. (2020). *Reimaging capitalism in a world on fire.* PublicAffairs.

Henderson, R., & Ramanna, K. (2015). Do managers have a role to play in sustaining the institutions of capitalism? *Center for Effective Public Management at Brookings,* 1–20. https://www.brookings.edu/wp-content/uploads/2016/06/BrookingsInstitutions ofCapitalismv5.pdf

Jack, A. (2022, October 17). *Business schools adapt to changing global realities.* Financial Times. https://www.ft.com/content/95c62782-a3d8-4227-b1fe-8637388 b39cb

Jones, T. M., Felps, W., & Bigley, G. A. (2007). Ethical theory and stakeholder-related decisions: The role of stakeholder culture. *Academy of Management Review, 32*(1), 137–155. https://doi.org/10.5465/amr.2007.23463924

Kim, R. C. (2016). Ethical decision making in international business: A study of challenge in teaching to future global talents. *Business and Management Studies, 2*(2), 1–13. https://doi.org/10.11114/bms.v2i2.1469

Kim, R. C. (2018). Can creating shared value (CSV) and the United Nations Sustainable Development Goals (UN SDGs) collaborate for a better world? Insights from East Asia. *Sustainability, 10*(11), 4128. https://doi.org/10.3390/su10114128

Kim, R. C. (2022). Rethinking corporate social responsibility under contemporary capitalism: Five ways to reinvent CSR. *Business Ethics, the Environment & Responsibility, 31*(2), 346–362. https://doi.org/10.1111/beer.12414

Kim, C. H., Amaeshi, K., Harris, S., & Suh, C. J. (2013). CSR and the national institutional context: The case of South Korea. *Journal of Business Research, 66*(12), 2581–1591. https://doi.org/10.1016/j.jbusres.2012.05.015

Kim, R. C., & Moon, J. (2015). Dynamics of corporate social responsibility in Asia: Knowledge and norms. *Asian Business & Management, 14*(5), 1–34. https://doi.org/ 10.1057/abm.2015.15

Kim, R. C., Yoo, I., & Uddin, H. (2018). The Korean Air nut rage scandal: Domestic versus international responses to a viral incident. *Business Horizons, 61*(4), 533–544. https://doi.org/10.1016/j.bushor.2018.03.002

Kolodinsky, R. W., Madden, T. M., Zisk, D. S., & Henkel, E. T. (2010). Attitudes about corporate social responsibility: Business student predictors. *Journal of Business Ethics, 91*(2), 67–181. https://doi.org/10.1007/s10551-009-0075-3

Kotler, P. (2015). *Confronting capitalism: Real solutions for a troubled economic system.* Amacom.

Kramer, M. R. (2020). Coronavirus is putting corporate social responsibility to the test. *Harvard Business Review Digital Articles,* 2–4. https://hbr.org/2020/04/coronavirus-is-putting-corporate-social-responsibility-to-the-test

Lane, R. (2019, March 4). Reimagining capitalism: How the greatest system ever conceived (and its billionaires) need to change. *Forbes.* https://www.forbes.com/sites/randalllane/2019/3/4/reimagining-capitalism-how-the-greatest-system-ever-conceivedand-its-billionairesneed-to-change/?sh=a81eba364c83

Macheridis, N., & Paulsson, A. (2021). Tracing accountability in higher education. *Research in Education, 110*(1), 78–97. https://doi.org/10.1177/0034523721993143

Marques, J. C., & Mintzberg, H. (2015). Why corporate social responsibility isn't a piece of cake. *MIT Sloan Business Review, 56*(4), 7–11.

Meyer, C., & Kirby, J. (2012). Runaway capitalism. *Harvard Business Review, 90*(1–2), 66–75.

Mitroff, I. I. (2004). An open letter to the deans and the faculties of American business schools. *Journal of Business Ethics, 54*(2), 185–189. https://doi.org/10.1007/s10551-004-9462-y

Nakano, C., Umeda, T., Ohno, M., Teramoto, K., Tanaka, T., & Yokota, R. (2012). Japan. In D. Rossouw & C. Stückelberger (Eds.), *Global survey of business ethics: In training, teaching and research* (pp. 329–344). Globethics.net.

Ostry, J. D., Loungani, P., & Berg, A. (2019). *Confronting inequality: How societies can choose inclusive growth.* Columbia University Press.

Pace, S. (2013). Does religion affect the materialism of consumers? An empirical investigation of Buddhist ethics and the resistance of the self. *Journal of Business Ethics, 112*(1), 25–46. https://doi.org/10.1007/s10551-012-1228-3

Pimentel, J. R. C., Kuntz, J. R., & Elenkov, D. S. (2010). Ethical decision-making: An integrative model for business practice. *European Business Review, 22*(4), 359–376. https://doi.org/10.1108/09555341011056159

Pope, S., & Wæraas, A. (2016). CSR-washing is rare: A conceptual framework, literature review, and critique. *Journal of Business Ethics, 137*(1), 173–193. https://doi.org/10.1007/s10551-015-2546-z

Porter, M., & Kramer, M. R. (2006). Strategy & society: The link between competitive advantage and corporate social responsibility. *Harvard Business Review, 84*(12), 78–92.

Porter, M., & Kramer, M. R. (2011). Creating shared value. *Harvard Business Review, 89*(1–2), 62–77.

Rimanoczy, I. (2020). *The sustainability mindset principles: A guide to develop a mindset for a better world.* Routledge.

Rocha, H., Pirson, M., Suddaby, R., Miles, R., Felber, C., Sisodia, R., Adler, P., & Wookey, C. (2020). Business with purpose and the purpose of business schools: Re-Imagining capitalism in a post pandemic world: A conversation with Jay Coen Gilbert. *Journal of Management Inquiry, 30*(3), 354–367. https://doi.org/10.1177/1056492620970279

Romar, E. J. (2004). Managerial harmony: The Confucian ethics of Peter F. Drucker. *Journal of Business Ethics, 51*(2), 199–210. https://doi.org/10.1023/B:BUSI. 0000033613.11761.7b

Shinohara, Y., & Kim, R. C. (2022). Sanpo-yoshi and corporate social responsibility in Japan. *Strategic Analysis, 46*(4), 403–415. https://doi.org/10.1080/09700161. 2022.2111763

Thomson, I., & Bates, D. (2022). *Urgent business: Five myths business needs to overcome to save itself and the planet.* Bristol University Press.

Vauclair, C. M. (2014). Cultural conceptions of morality: Examining laypeople's associations of moral character. *Journal of Moral Education, 43*(1), 54–74. https:// doi.org/10.1080/03057240.2013.873365

Vesty, L. (2016, September 14). Millennials want purpose over paychecks. So why can't we find it at work. *The Guardian.*

Vogel, D. (2005). *The market for virtue: The potential and limits of corporate social responsibility.* Brookings Institution Press.

Vogel, S. K. (2019). Japan's ambivalent pursuit of shareholder capitalism. *Politics & Society, 47*(1), 117–144. https://doi.org/10.1177/0032329218825160

Warnell, J. M., & Umeda, T. (2019). Perspectives on business ethics in the Japanese tradition: Implications for global understanding of the role of business in society. *Asian Journal of Business Ethics, 8*(1), 25–51. https://doi.org/10.1007/s13520-019-00087-2

Weber, J. (2017). Discovering the millennials' personal values orientation: A comparison to two managerial populations. *Journal of Business Ethics, 143*(3), 517–529. https://doi.org/10.1007/s10551-015-2803-1

Weber, J. M., Lindenmeyer, C. P., Liò, P., & Lapkin, A. A. (2021). Teaching sustainability as complex systems approach: A sustainable development goals workshop. *International Journal of Sustainability in Higher Education, 22*(8), 25–41. https://doi.org/10.1108/ijshe-06-2020-0209

Witt, M. A., & Redding, G. (2013). Asian business systems: Institutional comparison, clusters and implications for varieties of capitalism and business systems theory. *Socio-Economic Review, 11*(2), 265–300. https://doi.org/10.1093/ser/mwt002

Xu, Z. H., Liu, Z. Y., & Wu, J. (2022). Buddhist entrepreneurs, charitable behaviors, and social entrepreneurship: Evidence from China. *Small Business Economics, 59*(3), 1197–1217. https://doi.org/10.1007/s11187-021-00570-w

Yin, J., & Zhang, Y. (2012). Institutional dynamics and corporate social responsibility (CSR) in an emerging country context: Evidence from China. *Journal of Business Ethics, 111*(2), 301–316. https://doi.org/10.1007/s10551-012-1243-4

Young, S. (2003). *Moral capitalism: Reconciling private interest with the public good.* Berrett-Koehler Publishers.

Zhu, Y. (2015). The role of *Qing* (positive emotions) and *Li* (rationality) in Chinese entrepreneurial decision-making: A Confucian *Ren-Yi* wisdom perspective. *Journal of Business Ethics, 126*(4), 613–630. https://doi.org/10.1007/s10551-013-1970-1

Zsolnai, L. (2009). Business as a profession. In L. Zsolnai & A. Tencati (Eds.), *The future international manager: A vision of the roles and duties of management* (pp. 1–8). Palgrave Macmillan. https://doi.org/10.1057/9780230274068_1

Chapter 2

Competences for a Great, Big, and Beautiful Tomorrow? Sustainability Competences Within Innovation Dedicated Further Education

Louisa Mach and Bernd Ebersberger

University of Hohenheim, Germany

Abstract

This chapter delves into sustainability-related competences in innovation management for further education as part of the European lifelong learning initiative. Despite extensive research in primary and secondary education, adult education often remains overlooked. Competence-based learning is a favored approach to integrating knowledge, skills, and attitudes across various domains. Through thematic analysis and deductive coding, the study examines 72 innovation management-related further education programs conducted in Baden-Württemberg, Germany, between June and December 2022. The findings unequivocally demonstrate the inclusion of sustainability competences in innovation-related further education. Notably, Strategic Competence emerges as the most prevalent, while Normative Competence appears least frequently. This research significantly advances the convergence of further education in innovation management, responsible management education, and competence-based learning, emphasizing the importance of sustainability competences in adult learning contexts. By shedding light on this underexplored domain, the study prompts further exploration and development of sustainable educational practices for lifelong learning.

Keywords: Sustainability competence; adult education; lifelong learning; thematic analysis; competence-based learning; knowledge-based view

Innovation in Responsible Management Education, 27–62
Copyright © 2024 Louisa Mach and Bernd Ebersberger
Published under exclusive licence by Emerald Publishing Limited
doi:10.1108/978-1-83549-464-620241004

Introduction

Back in 1964, the New York World's Fair featured a remarkable attraction created by Walt Disney: the Carousel of Progress. In just 21 minutes, while following an idyllic "all-American" family, the audience was taken on a journey through the 20th and 21st centuries, witnessing technological advancements. As time progressed, the family's technological environment underwent significant changes. As time within the attraction progressed, the animatronic family's technological environment underwent significant changes. The mother's responsibilities in running the household diminish, and the children become proficient in using computers (formerly black and white TVs), while the grandparents even engage in video games. The journey through time showcased society's achievements including air and space travel, incorporating new technology into daily life, and a continuous commitment to enhance our lives. This all was backed by the Sherman Brothers' optimistic tune: "There's a Great, Big, Beautiful Tomorrow Shining at the End of Every Day...".

We can draw inspiration from the animatronic family's ability to learn from the past, adapt to changes, and grow; the message is clear: building competence requires constant adaptation, continuous learning, and developing proficient skills and attitudes. As we observe the changes in the animatronic family, we are reminded of our capacity to learn, adapt, and thrive in the face of change, building competence to navigate and tackle the challenges of our dynamic world. In the current landscape, sustainability challenges have grown increasingly complex and multifaceted, encompassing global warming, poverty, and desertification. This complexity raises the question of how to cultivate competences that changemakers need to effectively address these ever-evolving wicked sustainability problems (Rittel & Webber, 1973). Addressing these challenges demands collective action, with various stakeholders being called upon to embrace norms and values that foster responsible behavior in tackling sustainability-related issues (Blok et al., 2016). Individuals, firms, and individuals within firms as the "key factor for sustainable development" (Carneiro, 2000, p. 90) need to act responsibly to tackle sustainability-related problems. The learning activities of individuals and the development of human capital within a firm can significantly contribute to its overall performance and innovation endeavors (Coopey, 1995; Hatch & Dyer, 2004; Senge, 1990; Sinkula, 1994).

The term sustainable development is coined in the United Nations (UN) Brundtland report. Sustainable actions should always consider "meeting the needs of the present without compromising the ability of future generations to meet their own needs" (Brundtland, 1987, p. 292). With the continuous development and production of new products, services, and processes, importance of environmental and social concerns for innovation rise (Ketata et al., 2015; Verloop, 2006).

Sustainable innovation is defined as "innovation that improves environmental performance" (Carrillo-Hermosilla et al., 2010, p. 1075). Their primary goal is to extend the product lifecycle and enhance usability while mitigating environmental hazards, pollution, and adverse consequences associated with resource consumption (Kemp & Pearson, 2007). This necessitates a shift in behavior and a novel approach to innovation. To support this transformative shift in thinking, companies or their employees frequently participate in further education programs.

These educational initiatives provide participants with new knowledge and insights, establishing, developing, and reinforcing competence. This is important because the knowledge-based view of the firm hypothesizes that organizations that have cultivated specific skills and competences can achieve innovation (Cohen & Levinthal, 1990; Grant, 1996) and sustainable innovation in particular. This knowledge management process is essential for "exploit(ing) technological advances, competitors' failure, (and) industry opportunities" (Carneiro, 2000, p. 90) and building competent knowledge workers that sustain the concept of the learning organization (Brewer & Brewer, 2010; Carneiro, 2000).

Sustainable innovation is commonly acknowledged as a more intricate undertaking compared to other forms of innovation activities, introducing additional dimensions of complexity (Hall & Vredenburg, 2003; Ketata et al., 2015) and hence requiring special sustainability competences. While sustainability competences have been formulated within a general context, their identification in further education settings remains underexplored (Bianchi, 2020).

Hence, there is a need to delve deeper into the application and effectiveness of sustainability competences within further education, giving rise to the following research question: *Which sustainability competences are taught in innovation-related further education?*

To accomplish this objective, we analyzed secondary data from all innovation-related staff training offerings occurring between June and December 2022 in the Baden-Württemberg region in Germany. Our approach systematically compares the course content and mission statements provided by further education institutions with the sustainability competence framework we developed. Through this process, we sought to gain comprehensive insights into the landscape of adult education within the context of sustainability competences.

Theoretical Background

Competences and Learning

Learning is "a result of critical reflection on one's own experiences" (Drejer, 2000, p. 211) in contrast to recalling theories and remembering facts. In staff training, the aim of the training intervention should be to improve practice. Based on different experiences and educational prerequisites, staff training aims at different proficiency levels for competence development (Drejer, 2000; Marsick & Watkins, 1990). By completing one full learning cycle (passing every level of apprehension in learning objectives), employees improve their level of competence step-by-step. The usual individual starts off as a novice, then an advanced beginner, becomes proficient, develops expert-level competence, and finishes as a world-class (Drejer, 2000). To develop competence, employees start formal training and develop a sense of reflection and judgment. They participate in projects to use their new knowledge to practice their skills. Thereby, holistic competence development is achieved (Drejer, 2000; Marsick & Watkins, 1990). Lifelong learning (LLL) is a term coined by the European Union (EU) to appeal to all types of education in different learning settings. Before LLL became a "cradle-to-grave approach"

(Volles, 2016, p. 344), learning initiatives concentrated on secondary education. By introducing a holistic approach to education, the EU integrates all education levels and education institutions. Learning refers to more than education alone – education is seen as a standardized process conducted by formal institutions, whereas learning is rather informal and can be undertaken at any point in life (Borg & Mayo, 2005; European Parliament & Council of Europe, 2006). Since the introduction of the "new skills agenda for Europe" (European Commission, 2016, p. 1), European Member States and the European Commission are committed to LLL in training, formal, non-formal, and informal education settings. This put staff training back on the agenda as staff training is intended to result in competence development as an outcome of learning.

Scholars use the term "competence" to describe somebody's ability to do something or to conquer a given task (Klemp, 1980; Komarkova et al., 2015; Mitchelmore & Rowley, 2010). Deeply rooted in its Latin origin (com-petere = strive in common), competences are learnable on an individual and group level. Not to be confused with the term competency, competence describes clear observable actions or behavior (= what one is doing), while competency rather refers to the performance of said competence (= how well one is doing it). The European Qualification Framework (EQF) defines competence as the "proven ability to use knowledge, skills, and personal, social, and/or methodological abilities in work or study situations and professional and personal development" (European Parliament & European Council, 2008, p. 4). Competence-based learning (CBL) concentrates on teaching transversal (interpersonal, systemic, and instrumental) and generic competences, skills, and knowledge for a specific job. Aiming at integrating values and attitudes that are appropriate for the professional and personal life of learners, the teaching approach focuses on relating competences from different areas to one another, as well as reflecting on their learning journey. CBL integrates the principles of lifelong learning to add value to the social, cultural, and economic development of society as a whole (Sanchez et al., 2008).

Learning and education are not only beneficial for companies and their competitiveness. Also, employees need to continue training to remain productive and competitive on the labor market. To do so, they must acquire new knowledge, learn new skills, and develop new attitudes – in short, they must develop new competences.

Sustainability Competences in the Literature

Sustainability competence should equip individuals to internalize the principles of sustainability and navigate intricate systems, enabling them to initiate or advocate for actions with an impact on people, the planet, and prosperity. Sustainability competence also fosters the creation of visions for sustainable futures and innovations (Bianchi et al., 2022). Therefore, we specifically look at the integration within the context of innovation management.

Within their GreenComp framework, the EU differentiates between four competence areas grounded in the systematic review by Bianchi (2020). Although their naming differs from the competence names in this chapter, the content is the same. Later in the empirical analysis we derive the six key aspects for sustainability which are rooted in the work of Bianchi (2020) and Bianchi et al. (2022). The literature about sustainability competences is methodically rather diverse, yet only a few studies investigate sustainability with an empirical research design. We observe that conceptual studies (Glasser & Hirsh, 2016; Lozano et al., 2017; Rieckmann, 2018), literature reviews (Dimante et al., 2016; Pacis & VanWynsberghe, 2020; Trad, 2019), and studies relying on expert insights (Giangrande et al., 2019; Rieckmann, 2012) are rather prominent among the influential contributions on the topic. Studies with a strong empirical basis consist of research based on survey data (Lozano et al., 2022; Quendler & Lamb, 2016) and curricula review (Trad, 2019).

Wiek et al. (2011) form the basis for the GreenComp Framework with *Systems-Thinking Competence, Anticipatory Competence, Normative Competence, Strategic Competence*, and *Interpersonal Competence*. In a subsequent study, authors also added "Integrated Problem-Solving Competence" (Wiek et al., 2016, p. 251), which is defined as the application of diverse problem-solving frameworks to address complex sustainability challenges and develop actionable solutions. The practice of this competence enables the effective combination of problem analysis, sustainability assessment, visioning, and strategy development in a meaningful way (Wiek et al., 2016). Furthermore, Brundiers et al. (2021) underline the importance of "a normative orientation for all other competences" (p. 20), as sustainability values must be rooted in every argument and action. They then derive the "Values-Thinking Competence" (Wiek et al., 2016, p. 246), which is a more goal-oriented approach to the *Normative Competence*. Furthermore, the authors relate the key sustainability competences to a base of foundational competences and specific knowledge. Nevertheless, the essential competences in sustainability do not rely on specific knowledge domains, implying that the framework can be applied to sustainability-related courses in various academic and non-academic programs (Bianchi, 2020; Brundiers et al., 2021).

Cörvers et al. (2016) offer a new angle on comprehensive sustainability competences: five key aspects in "Systems-thinking", "Anticipatory", "Normative", "Strategic", and "Interpersonal" (Cörvers et al., 2016, p. 352) as dynamic competences for solving sustainability problems. Based on the broad body of literature we distill the following sustainability competences:

Systems-Thinking competence: Being able to deal with (organizational as well as systems) complexity, commit to learning from (past) experiences, and being able to change perspectives were possible (Adomßent & Hoffmann, 2013; Cörvers et al., 2016; Lozano et al., 2017; Senge, 2006; Wiek et al., 2011).

Anticipatory competence: Being able to examine, assess, and develop comprehensive future scenarios while also taking quantitative and qualitative information into account and dealing with ambiguity, uncertainty, and risk (Adomßent & Hoffmann, 2013; Cörvers et al., 2016; Lozano et al., 2017; Wiek et al., 2011).

Normative competence: Being able to define, apply, and negotiate (sustainability) values, principles, and goals, acquire and process normative knowledge and encompass concepts of ethics, justice, and equity, and make decisions based on learned concepts and knowledge (Cörvers et al., 2016; Dlouhá et al., 2019; Evans, 2019; Lozano et al., 2017; Wiek et al., 2011).

Strategic competence: Being able to develop and execute interventions toward sustainability (sometimes also referred to as intervention competence), a deep comprehension of historical influences, barriers, feasibility, and efficiency of the intervention, also keeping consequences for stakeholders in mind (Cörvers et al., 2016; Dlouhá et al., 2019; Pérez Salgado et al., 2012, 2018; Wiek et al., 2011).

Interpersonal competence: Being able to motivate others and collaborate with them. This includes social and leadership skills and empathy. Interpersonal Competence is crucial for persuasion (Adomßent & Hoffmann, 2013; Ayers, 2020; Cörvers et al., 2016; Lozano et al., 2017; Martínez Valdivia et al., 2023; Shephard et al., 2019; Wiek et al., 2011).

Some studies (de Haan, 2006, 2008, 2010) add the German concept of "Gestaltungskompetenz" (*shaping competence*) to the portfolio of sustainability competences. It refers to applying knowledge about sustainable and unsustainable development. In essence, drawing conclusions from present analyses and future studies regarding ecological, economic, and social developments and their interdependence. Based on these conclusions, decisions should be made, understood, and balanced at an individual, communal, and political level, enabling the realization of sustainable development processes (Adomßent & Hoffmann, 2013; de Haan, 2008; Dlouhá et al., 2019).

Adomßent and Hoffmann (2013) reference shaping competence as an initial step for sustainable development that needs underlying knowledge, skills, and attitudes. This competence requires planning and management competences and taking the initiative to actively change/transform current systems. Therefore, it is a meta-competence that people acquire while developing other sustainability competences (Bianchi, 2020).

Methodology

To analyze the research question, *Which sustainability competences are taught in innovation-related further education?* We employ a qualitative research design.

Sample

In 2020, the Federal State of Baden-Württemberg started a large-scale further education initiative. We use the descriptions of innovation-related training offers as data to identify sustainability competences taught in further education offerings utilizing thematic analysis and deductive coding.

The Chambers of Commerce and Industry and the Ministry of Economics, Labour, and Tourism maintain freely available databases of continuing education offers. Given that companies that invest more into employee education are more likely to produce a sustainable innovation (Ketata et al., 2015), the relevance of knowledge and learning to address sustainability challenges serves as the basis for our analysis. We searched both databases using the keywords *innovation, knowledge management, organizational culture, organizational learning, leadership, collaboration, creativity, idea management,* and *innovation strategy* (Hero et al., 2017; Iddris, 2016; Mention, 2012; Smith et al., 2011), time frame (June 1–Dec 31, 2022), and location of training (Baden-Württemberg or online). This leads to a total of 72 continuing education offerings in the form of secondary data. A brief overview of the educational offerings in the sample is provided in Table 2.1 in the Appendix. We also identified the mission statement for every provider of the courses to be included in the thematic analysis.

Thematic Analysis and Deductive Coding

Thematic analysis is the most frequently used method within qualitative research. It is a useful tool that does not require theoretical or technological knowledge to identify, analyze, organize, and describe patterns (themes) in qualitative data (Braun & Clarke, 2006, 2019; Nowell et al., 2017). Braun and Clarke (2006) note that rigorously applied thematic analysis can generate reliable results. In our analysis, we follow the six-phase model by Braun and Clarke (2006), which we sketch in more detail in A1.

We analyze the descriptions of the educational offers and learning outcomes to show the overall goal of the program, as the learning outcomes should be "clearly observable and measurable" (Keinänen et al., 2018, p. 31). The learning outcomes describe how a competence is expressed (qualitatively) using action verbs. Ideally, learning outcomes describe what the learner should know, understand, or be able to do after successful completion of the course. Instead of starting this process with a blank slate, we align competences in the training offerings with the already identified competences in the theoretical background section of this chapter (systems-thinking competence, anticipatory competence, normative competence, strategic competence, interpersonal competence, and shaping competence). We code deductively. This allows for a better understanding, operationalization, and validation of the competences. An extensive codebook is provided in the appendix (see A2).

Results

The following section presents the results of analyzing the 72 further training programs about their coverage of sustainability competences. The systematic analysis was conducted with MAXQDA to find connections within competence areas and across the sample. The subsequent part will give information on descriptive as well as thematic parts.

Description of the Sample

Thirteen education programs can be attributed to the database of the Ministry of Economics, Labor, and Tourism Baden-Württemberg, and 59 programs can be tracked back to the WIS platform (IHK DIGITAL GmbH, 2022; Stengele, 2022). Most education programs are offered by the Chambers of Commerce and

Industry (13 programs in total, 18.06%).[1] As part of the *IHK Akademie*, subsidiaries of the Chambers of Commerce and Industry offer further staff training as part of the lifelong learning initiative. In addition, courses are offered in various delivery modes (completely online, blended learning, or only in-person) to enable a more flexible reconciliation of further education, family, and career.

Using the provider's location, the offerings in this sample are spread across Germany, as most courses were still offered online due to COVID-19 restrictions (IHK Akademie, 2022). The second most programs are offered by a local continuing education provider.[2] Located in Ostfildern near Stuttgart, the training provider offers courses in various areas of engineering, management, and healthcare. Six of the education providers are publicly funded, as they are departments of public universities or closely linked to the Chambers of Commerce and Industry. Most courses in our sample are offered by private education suppliers.

In addition, the education programs last about 13 days on average (with a working day standard of 8 hours a day). The average is skewed due to three programs spanning over one or two semesters.[3] When eliminating these three programs for the calculation, we got an average of 6.38 days with an average fee of € 256.05 per day. Table 2.1 (see appendix) provides an overview of the sample.

Based on our search query, the 72 innovation courses cover seven broad learning fields. We assigned only one learning field per course to capture the field that the course focuses on. More than 45% of the courses in this sample cover innovation and innovation management-related topics only. They range from classic innovation management to innovation culture and business model innovation.[4] The subject of digitalization in innovation management is another emerging topic. Courses offered within this context are management of the digitalization process, development of digital competences, and digitalization of specific business segments.[5] Design thinking is the third most popular topic in innovation-related training. Overall, six courses title their program just "design thinking". Two courses only cover design thinking and the ability to create user-friendly solutions in their courses, despite not mentioning it in the title.[6] Furthermore, working agile and implementing agile methods is frequent in the sample. Further staff training focuses on agile leadership and agile project management within the innovation management field.[7] The fifth most offered theme within the sample is project management. Despite already being partly covered in "agile working", project management in innovation projects offers more than just agility. Classic project management methods as well as project-specific approaches are covered.[8] At last, sustainability, change, and artificial intelligence (AI) are covered

---

[1](ID 2, 4, 24, 27, 28, 30, 31, 33, 54, 57, 59).
[2](ID 9, 11, 12, 16, 56, 60, 61, 62, 63, 64).
[3](ID 42, 65, 69).
[4](ID 6, 7, 9, 10, 14, 18, 19, 24, 26, 27, 28, 29, 30, 31, 36, 37, 38, 39, 41, 42, 43, 44, 45, 46, 47, 48, 54, 56, 58, 63, 64, 65, 68).
[5](ID 5, 33, 34, 35, 57, 69, 70, 71, 72).
[6](ID 17, 19, 20, 21, 22, 23, 24, 25).
[7](ID 1, 2, 3, 11, 51, 52, 59).
[8](ID 49, 50, 59, 60, 61, 63).

with five and four courses, respectively. The topic sustainability and change focuses on all aspects connected to environmental change, resource scarcity, and mobilizing the staff toward sustainable actions within innovation management.[9] AI courses cover basics of AI, machine learning, and how to successfully implement AI in the company or innovation management.[10] Table 2.2 (see appendix) depicts the emerging themes of the courses and their frequency.

Content Analysis

Overall, 334 coded segments were distributed among the six competences (see Fig. 2.1). The most frequently found competence is Strategic Competence, with 80 coded segments among 45 courses. Interpersonal Competence was found in 68 segments among 34 courses, followed by Anticipatory Competence with 67 coded segments among 40 courses. The remaining competences were found with similar percentages in Shaping Competence, with 43 coded segments in 17 courses and in 17 mission

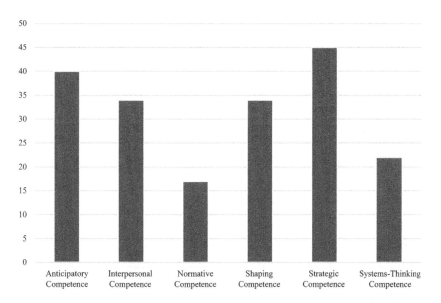

Fig. 2.1.   Distribution of Sustainability Competences Among Further Education Courses. *Note:* This chart demonstrates the frequency of the identified sustainability competences among the innovation-related education courses. The frequency is determined by the coded segments in MAXQDA.

---

[9](ID 12, 15, 40, 55, 67).
[10](ID 4, 8, 53, 66).

statements, Systems-Thinking Competence with 41 coded segments among 22 courses, and Normative Competence with 35 coded segments among 17 courses. Derived from the number of coded segments, innovation-related further education mostly incorporates aspects of Strategic Competence. The contents will be explored in the following sub-sections. The normative formulation in the section below takes up the tone of the empirical material.

Strategic Competence

In today's dynamic business environment, strategic competence is pivotal for organizational resilience. This competence involves recognizing and overcoming challenges, fostering innovative business models, and embracing sustainable digital transformation. Within the context of sustainability and innovation, teaching strategic competence requires a careful consideration of its impact on stakeholders, society, and the environment, emphasizing a balanced and sustainable approach. Operating at the environment level, strategic competence navigates the complexities of changing economic, social, and ecological conditions, including factors like climate change's impact on manufacturing and the demand for fair working conditions.[11] Decisions made at this level significantly shape firm- and individual-level dynamics. On the firm level, strategic competence involves overcoming internal and external barriers, implementing sustainable business model changes, fostering agile learning, and managing organizational values. Overcoming these barriers fosters adaptability, growth, and identifies innovation opportunities.[12] At the individual level, effective communication during the change process is essential. Understanding the psychology of change and committing to individual development enhances performance, with reflection contributing to more sustainable decision-making.[13] A holistic approach to strategic competence integrates business model analysis, strategic alignment, agile development, innovation management, leadership in the digital realm, and sustainability.

Interpersonal Competence

Interpersonal competence, a critical facet in the contemporary academic landscape, encompasses communication and soft skills, emphasizing diverse stakeholder interactions and personal engagements within innovative learning environments. The communication dimension is bifurcated into innovation-related communication and change management communication. Innovation-related communication underscores the importance of global collaboration and teamwork, particularly in the digital realm, as pivotal for future work success. Courses within this framework strive to establish effective communication channels for the innovation process, cultivating partnerships and alliances essential for successful market entry. The promotion of

---

[11](ID 62, 71).
[12](ID 5, 9).
[13](ID 49).

teamwork and an innovation culture serves to enhance creative flows and foster open communication dynamics.[14] Tailoring communication strategies to different stakeholders is imperative; internal stakeholders require attributes such as curiosity, a willingness to learn, and enthusiasm for innovation, while external stakeholders necessitate engaging in dialogue and adopting a measured approach. Noteworthy projects may demand citizen dialogue and adept public relations management.[15] Change management communication assumes a vital role in conveying transitions, particularly in dual transformations such as sustainability and digitalization. The fusion of learning with change management becomes indispensable for the success of change initiatives. In corporate settings, higher level management positions often spearhead change communication efforts.[16] Soft skills, intricately woven into course curricula, address the challenges posed by digitalization. Enhanced presentation techniques, adept conversation management, self-awareness, self-management, self-motivation, and self-organization are deemed indispensable in innovation education. Interactive components during instructional sessions facilitate the practical application of these skills. Moreover, fostering curiosity, a willingness to learn, and an innovative spirit are considered foundational for digital advancement, frequently nurtured through coaching and role models.[17]

Anticipatory Competence

Within the academic discourse, anticipatory competence emerges as a multifaceted construct, incorporating two interconnected perspectives: the anticipation of external push and pull factors and the discernment of internal drivers shaping unforeseeable futures. Courses across disciplines seamlessly integrate both perspectives, emphasizing their symbiotic relationship. External pull factors encapsulate the identification of opportunities and risks in burgeoning markets, the trajectory of digital transformation, and the growth of AI. Courses underscore the pivotal role of AI in driving innovation, acknowledging concurrently the associated risks and impacts on established structures.[18] The evolving landscape of digitalization, influencing market dynamics and leadership competences, underscores the imperative for organizational adaptability and resilience.[19] Notably, design thinking emerges as a method frequently cited for cultivating anticipatory competence, offering teams a framework to address intricate problems with solutions centered on customer needs.[20] Internally, within organizational contexts, readiness and competence-building for future requirements and market changes are deemed indispensable. Programmatic interventions encompass diverse methods and workshops aimed at fostering innovative thinking, creativity,

---

[14](ID 5, 9, 12, 33, 44, 50, 52, 54, 69).
[15](ID 27, 52, 54, 67).
[16](ID 9, 12, 14, 55).
[17](ID 63, 72).
[18](ID 4, 13, 20, 26, 66, 69).
[19](ID 28, 33, 39, 41, 72).
[20](ID 1, 13).

leadership, and change management. Learning environments are purposefully adapted to confront challenges posed by digital transformation and internal resistances, fostering a pervasive culture of continuous learning.[21] Encouraging open-minded thinking, holistic learning, and systemic thinking is paramount for comprehending intricate systems and their far-reaching consequences.[22] The cultivation of creativity and receptivity to novel ideas is recognized as foundational in navigating unforeseen challenges and generating innovative solutions.[23] In synthesizing these elements, anticipatory competence serves as a linchpin, aligning sustainability imperatives with the demands of an innovative future.

Systems-Thinking Competence

Systems-Thinking competence entails adeptly managing complexity, drawing insights from historical experiences, and adaptively shifting perspectives as necessitated by evolving circumstances. The curricula comprehensively address systems-thinking and understanding, encompassing facets such as change and innovation management, agile and transformative processes, decision-making and empowerment, reflection and learning processes, and organizational structures and innovation. Within the realm of systemic thinking, an appreciation of interconnectedness within organizational frameworks is underscored, recognizing that alterations in one segment reverberate across the entire system. This systemic perspective equips individuals to discern interdependencies, feedback loops, and unintended consequences, thereby facilitating informed decision-making and effective interventions. Conflict management, the embracement of diverse perspectives, and the application of systemic thinking collectively contribute to adept navigation of complexity, drawing valuable lessons from experiences, and facilitating adaptive shifts in perspectives.[24] The integration of innovation and implementation methodologies, coupled with change management practices, constitutes a pivotal dimension in managing innovation initiatives. Innovation methodology delineates systematic processes for generating, evaluating, and implementing innovative ideas, while implementation methodology guides the execution and integration of these ideas into practice.[25] Change management interventions address resistance and foster mindset and behavioral shifts conducive to successful organizational change.[26] In the context of agile project organization and management, an iterative and collaborative approach is adopted, conscientiously considering system interdependencies, stakeholder engagement, and feedback incorporation. The agile development of digital products and services similarly embraces systems-thinking, acknowledging their intricate interactions with stakeholders, processes, and technologies.[27] Agile

---

[21](ID 42, 69, 72).
[22](ID 45, 51, 62).
[23](ID 23).
[24](ID 10, 14, 33, 48, 51).
[25](ID 10, 51, 68).
[26](ID 14, 42, 55, 70).
[27](ID 1, 11, 27, 28, 30, 31, 33, 42, 45, 68, 70).

transformations, guided by a systems-thinking lens, concentrate on reshaping structures and processes, identifying opportunities for improvement, redesigning processes, and optimizing structures to foster collaboration, innovation, and adaptability in alignment with overarching organizational goals.

Normative Competence

Within the academic discourse, normative competence signifies a profound grasp and implementation of sustainability values, ethical considerations, and principles of justice and equity, all converging to inform discerning decision-making processes. The curricula meticulously address this competence through dedicated courses focusing on agile methodologies, innovation and project management, systems transformation, and the ethical dimensions of change management. A central tenet in further education seems to be the emphasis on agility, with courses designed to instil agile routines and normative thinking. The instructional framework incorporates agile learning, agile reporting, and agile project management approaches, highlighting their relevance in navigating the intricate intersections of sustainability and innovation.[28] The multifaceted concept of innovation is approached through diverse lenses, advocating deliberate planning and structured methodologies to foster successful innovative endeavors. Employing tools such as the Business Model Canvas, Pitch Desk, and assessment instruments, the courses facilitate the alignment of innovation initiatives with organizational objectives and the cultivation of customer-centric innovation.[29] Furthermore, predefined methods and normative thinking are underscored to augment innovation capabilities and facilitate adaptability in the face of a dynamically changing business landscape.[30] This integration of normative competence into the realms of sustainability and innovation substantiates its pivotal role in fostering ethically informed and strategically aligned decision-making within contemporary organizational contexts.

Shaping Competence

Shaping competence, a multifaceted construct, comprises distinct components rooted in anticipatory, interpersonal, and strategic competence. Interpersonal competence emphasizes open-mindedness, incorporating new perspectives, conflict management, and innovative learning approaches.[31] Interdisciplinary thinking, linked to anticipatory competence, is vital for anticipating trends and planning innovation initiatives.[32] Strategic competence involves developing and implementing innovation strategies, modernizing equipment, and bridging scientific insights with practical

---

[28](ID 14, 21, 34, 49, 51, 52).
[29](ID 3, 5, 6, 7, 16, 32, 67).
[30](ID 32, 34, 35, 42, 49, 50).
[31](ID 14, 68).
[32](ID 68, 70).

concepts.[33] Normative competence, demonstrated through values and personal development,[34] aligns with ethical considerations in sustainability and innovation. Systems-thinking competence is evident in agile learning, knowledge management, and agile project management approaches.[35] Further education providers emphasize the significance of shaping competence in innovation-related education, highlighting its comprehensive nature. This integrative approach prepares individuals for the dynamic challenges at the intersection of sustainability and innovation.

Co-Occurrence of Competences

During the analysis process, each one of the courses can be assigned one or more competences that it addresses. The analysis of the co-occurrences investigates which ones of the competences tend to occur together in the analyzed courses. Fig. 2.2 shows the co-occurrence of competences within the sample as a network,

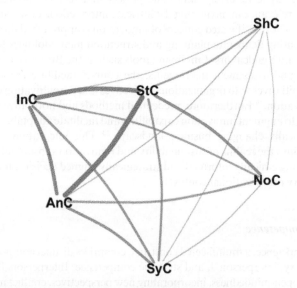

Fig. 2.2.   Co-Occurrence of Sustainability Competences in the Sample. Abbreviations: AnC = Anticipatory Competence; InC = Interpersonal Competence; NoC = Normative Competence; ShC = Shaping Competence; StC = Strategic Competence; SyC = Systems-Thinking Competence.

---

[33](ID 58, 14, 22, 29, 3, 52, 55).
[34](ID 48, 58, 35).
[35](ID 1, 14, 51, 59, 49, 50).

where the strength of the co-occurrence is visualized by the thickness of the edges in the network.

The strongest co-occurrence can be found between *Strategic* and *Anticipatory Competence* (jointly addressed in 24 courses), *Interpersonal* and *Strategic Competence* (addressed in 22 courses), and *Interpersonal* and *Anticipatory Competence* (addressed in 20 courses). The least connections can be found between *Normative* and *Shaping Competence* (addressed in 7 courses). The strongest interlinked competence is *Strategic Competence* with 93 mentions, followed by *Anticipatory Competence* with 85 mentions.

Anticipatory and Strategic Competence

Both are necessary for generating ideas for innovative products.[36] A prominent method used in both contexts is design thinking. Design thinking facilitates creative problem-solving and the development of customer-centric products and services.[37] In addition, service design thinking involves both competences to identify and design service offerings that meet customer demands and provide a sustainable competitive advantage.[38] Technology management also involves managing technological changes and anticipating future trends, which requires a foresightful and strategic operation of organizations.[39] Managing innovation involves both *Anticipatory* and *Strategic Competence* to drive and align innovation initiatives with organizational goals and build resilience.[40] Moreover, both competences are also necessary for managing human resources in the context of digital transformation and organizational change.[41]

Interpersonal and Strategic Competence

These two competences relate to various areas of organizational functioning, emphasizing the importance of effective communication, collaboration, leadership, and relationship-building skills for achieving strategic goals while fostering positive interpersonal dynamics. Effective change communication is crucial for both competences as it involves understanding and addressing the emotional and psychological aspects of individuals and teams during organizational transitions in strategic change processes, while also ensuring that change and innovation projects are effectively communicated and implemented.[42]

Digital transformation processes and teamwork require strong interpersonal skills to build effective relationships, foster open communication, and resolve conflicts, while also strategically managing resources, coordinating tasks, and

---

[36](ID 1, 9, 16, 45, 48, 68).
[37](ID 1, 20).
[38](ID 13, 20, 36, 37, 38).
[39](ID 9, 36, 37, 39, 62, 65).
[40](ID 39, 72).
[41](ID 11, 39, 70, 72).
[42](ID 9, 11, 12, 14, 18, 45, 52, 61, 72).

leveraging digital tools to achieve shared goals.[43] *Interpersonal Competence* is essential in innovation management as it involves fostering a culture of creativity, encouraging collaboration, and effectively communicating and engaging with employees to generate and implement innovative ideas.[44]

Strategic Competence is required to align innovation efforts with organizational goals, assess market opportunities, and develop effective strategies for successful innovation implementation.[45] Leadership and team development demand both *Interpersonal* and *Strategic Competence*. Effective leadership requires strong interpersonal skills to inspire, motivate, and empower team members, while *Strategic Competence* is needed to set goals, allocate resources, and guide teams toward achieving organizational objectives.[46] Communication and relationship-building are fundamental to both interpersonal and strategic competence. Effective communication skills enable individuals to establish strong connections, resolve conflicts, and build trust, which are crucial for successful collaboration and achieving strategic objectives within organizations.[47]

Interpersonal and Anticipatory Competence

These competences overlap and are simultaneously necessary in communication, change management, future-oriented thinking, and personal development. Effective communication and collaboration are crucial skills in today's global teams, as the ability to collaborate seamlessly across geographical boundaries and cultural differences is essential for achieving successful outcomes.[48] Courses emphasize the significance of open and hierarchy-free communication within teams. It is argued that transparent and inclusive communication supports teamwork and facilitates the exchange of ideas and knowledge.[49]

Additionally, course descriptions highlight the importance of effective communication skills to navigate the complexities of the digital world and build strong interpersonal relationships in virtual environments.[50] And they stress the significance of effective change communication in successful change management initiatives.[51]

Effective communication is vital in mitigating resistance, managing expectations, and ensuring a smooth transition during organizational change processes.[52] Both competences are essential for organizations to proactively analyze market trends, technological advancements, and emerging customer needs to gain a

---

[43](ID 11, 12, 18, 45, 46, 50, 61, 67, 72).
[44](ID 12, 14, 16, 18, 55, 56, 72).
[45](ID 5, 11, 45, 50, 67).
[46](ID 10, 12, 29, 45, 46, 54).
[47](ID 12, 14, 18).
[48](ID 14).
[49](ID 18, 45, 46).
[50](ID 41, 51, 69).
[51](ID 55).
[52](ID 28, 33, 41, 69).

competitive edge. Interpersonal skills are indispensable for understanding customers through thorough personal interaction and communication. The need for collaborative and diverse teams leverages collective expertise and perspectives to generate groundbreaking ideas.[53] By clearly communicating organizational goals, companies set clear learning goals for individual growth and organizational success. Leaders need to adapt their leadership styles to foster collaboration in changing environments.[54]

In conclusion, the sustainability competences examined in the sample are interconnected, with *Anticipatory* and *Strategic Competence* essential for generating innovative ideas. At the same time, *Interpersonal* and *Strategic Competence* are crucial for effective communication, collaboration, leadership, and relationship-building within changing organizations. *Interpersonal* and *Anticipatory Competences* are important in various areas of professional development. These competences overlap in areas such as change communication, digital transformation, innovation management, and leadership development, highlighting the interdependence between interpersonal skills and strategic thinking in achieving organizational goals and fostering sustainable practices.

Discussion and Conclusion

The purpose of this study was to gain a better understanding of how sustainability competences are integrated into innovation-related further education. We analyze course descriptions but add mission statements of the education providers for context. Our research findings provide evidence for incorporating sustainability competences into adult education. Without clearly referring to sustainability, fragments of the competence facets are found throughout the sample. The most frequently occurring competence is *Strategic Competence*, and the least frequent one is *Normative Competence*. *Shaping Competence* is a meta-competence as it incorporates aspects of all other competences.

Our results show that although *Normative Competence* is perceived to be easy to learn (Anderson & Krathwohl, 2001; Bloom et al., 1956; Brundiers et al., 2021), despite they are not well integrated into innovation-related further education. Only 17 courses teach *Normative Competence*. This pattern is in line with the previous finding of Lans et al. (2014): *Normative Competence* "is not central" (p. 43) to entrepreneurship-related education. As our sample focuses on underlying sustainability competence within general innovation-related courses; this finding is in line with Lans et al. (2014). However, this competence is crucial for sustainability because instead of doing things right, participants learn to "do the right thing" (Lans et al., 2014, p. 43). In their Delphi study, Brundiers et al. (2021) found *Normative Competence* to be an underlying and integrated competence. Applying "normative sustainability orientation" (Brundiers et al., 2021, p. 24) to other competences in other disciplines supports an underlying value system for

---

[53](ID 13, 23, 33,36, 37, 38, 65).
[54](ID 11, 28, 41, 51, 70).

sustainability transition processes with inclusivity, biodiversity conservation, and circular economy. Moreover, by integrating normative sustainability competences into non-sustainability focused education, a stronger focus on sustainable behavior and sustainability mindset would be supported. Therefore, further education should focus on applying other competences with sustainability norms and values in mind so that they also unconsciously apply *Normative Competence* (Brundiers et al., 2021; Trad, 2019).

Shaping Competence is identified as a meta-competence, representing a superior skill that involves the deliberate development of specific competences and their adept application in diverse situational contexts. This ability is also referred to as "Implementation Competence" (Redman & Wiek, 2021, p. 6), which encompasses the effective and efficient implementation of sustainability strategies (action plans to shape a sustainable outcome), including their execution, adaptation, transfer, and expansion (de Haan, 2006; Pérez Salgado et al., 2018). Furthermore, fragments of the other key competences are integral to addressing and resolving sustainability problems (de Haan, 2006). Redman and Wiek (2021) go as far as naming this framework "professional competenc(i)es" (Redman & Wiek, 2021, p. 5), stressing its significance in the context of sustainability and professionalism. To propel sustainability transformations within further education, the integration of all these competences is essential, complemented by generic competences encompassing both content-dependent and independent skills, along with overarching abilities like creativity and critical thinking. Ultimately, the effective application of *Shaping Competence* (or implementation competence) serves as a unifying force, enabling the harmonious integration and utilization of a comprehensive set of sustainability competences (Redman & Wiek, 2021).

Considering the KBV of the firm, adult education aims to make tacit knowledge (of the teachers and trainers) more explicit and accessible to the participants. Combining different kinds of knowledge and different kinds of learning builds the basis for successful innovation (Cohen & Levinthal, 1990; Leiponen, 2005; Levin et al., 1985; Rothwell et al., 1974). Further education courses do not only offer a transfer of theoretical and conceptual knowledge; they also practice methods (such as Design Thinking or brainstorming methods), the use of templates (such as the Business Model Canvas), or routines (for teamwork and communication). Practice methods, templates, and routines are closely related to the knowledge integration methods identified by Grant (1996). Rules and directives are prevalent in bureaucratic settings: rules for sustainable innovation integration, digitalization, or project management. By systematically integrating knowledge, one source of knowledge (e.g., employee training) distributes expertise throughout the whole organization. This is also observed in most innovation-related trainings, but the integrated knowledge does not seem tacit after all. Otherwise, the observed rules and policies would not be enough to successfully transfer it (Grant, 1996). Moreover, due to organizational barriers, an individual's knowledge may not find its way through the organization's hierarchy. In these cases, establishing routines or group problem-solving mechanisms can help (Grant, 1996). Many courses already mention group activities and cooperation among participants as important elements of their training programs. Wruck and Jensen (1994) studied knowledge integration in organizations, especially in the group context, and found that the successful establishment of team quality management measures has greater benefits "than the costs of training and time spent on such efforts" (Wruck & Jensen, 1994, p. 264). This is especially true when specific knowledge is needed for sustainable business processes.

In addition, the educational programs teach by implementing situated learning approaches. Situated learning is defined as an authentic, real-world, and meaningful way of learning. Learners trigger learning mechanisms by applying subject matter knowledge to real-world challenges, and the learning extends beyond the confines of the classroom to practical application (Lave & Wenger, 1991; Stein, 1998). Situated learning involves an instructional approach in which students gain knowledge by engaging in activities rather than receiving information in isolated and structured formats from instructors. The content is closely tied to the tasks being performed and is not divorced from the complexities, uncertainties, and group dynamics typical of real-world work settings. Rather than focusing solely on content delivery, learning is driven by dilemmas and challenges that prompt learners to exercise their intellectual and practical skills and prepare them for real-life applications in their homes, communities, or workplaces (Lankard, 1995; Stein, 1998). By integrating competences into the situated learning approach, knowledge, skills, and attitudes are applied directly to real-world contexts.

Our inclusion of *Shaping Competence* is a novelty in the international literature on sustainability competences. The leading German concept can be found in snippets and fragments that incorporate UNESCO's perspective (UNESCO, 2017) on key competences for sustainable development, which is closely aligned with the competence framework we used throughout this research. *Shaping Competence* was introduced to incorporate Education for Sustainable Development (ESD) concepts into the German education system (United Nations (UN), 1992, Chapter 36.3). In a more general definition, *Shaping Competence* means "having the skills, competencies and knowledge to change economic, ecological and social behavior" (de Haan, 2010, p. 320). Following the introduction of the SDGs and their targets, *Shaping Competence* helps to achieve "cross-cutting sustainability competences [...] and equipping them with the knowledge and competencies they need, not only to understand what the SDGs are about but to engage as informed citizens in bringing about the necessary transformation" (UNESCO, 2017, p. 8). Education, particularly lifelong learning, plays a fundamental role as a crucial catalyst for sustainable development, serving as a pivotal force for transformative change (Bianchi, 2020; UN, 2002). While there is still only limited research on sustainability competences in continuing education, our work hopes to contribute to this less explored area. We adopted the competence definitions from the literature and used a German regional sample of further education offerings to map the competences in innovation-related training. What we found resonates well with the existing frameworks: Sustainability competences are being taught in adult education, perhaps not decelerated as such. We found evidence for all key competences in addition to *Shaping Competence*. However, only a few courses identify their content as sustainability-related, even when key competences for sustainability are addressed. Hence, participants are exposed to learning input that supports the development of competences relevant to sustainability transition, although the courses do not explicitly label sustainability as a core topic of the education program. Sustainability competences serve as an ancillary augmentation in this context. Nevertheless, aligning with the endeavors for sustainable development, the integration of the SDGs and sustainability competences is positioned not in a prominent foreground but rather in a supportive background role.

Our research represents a first attempt to identify sustainability competences in further education. There are at least three potential limitations to the findings of this study. A first limitation concerns our limited sample of only innovation-related further education in the federal state of Baden-Württemberg, Germany. A larger sample might provide further insight into the competence development in lifelong learning initiatives. As Baden-Württemberg is characterized by a strong economy with few world-famous sectors such as automotive or machine tools, the educational offerings are likely biased toward these industries. As we have also included online offerings from national providers, we believe that the regional bias has not affected our analysis. A second potential limitation is that although we have incorporated a large amount of literature into the development of our framework, we have not conducted a fully fledged systematic literature review of the identified competences. We might have missed competences in our deductive coding step. This would be detrimental to our research. However, as we have openly looked at the course descriptions, we have not encountered hints pointing toward competences we might have missed in our framework. A third limitation is the timeframe of this study. We used qualitative data from June to December 2022; a longer timeframe may shed light on the transition from "conventional" business competences to more sustainable business competences.

Notwithstanding these limitations, our findings yield significant implications. From a practical standpoint, continuous education providers should enhance their emphasis on sustainability competences. Our study unveiled that these competences are already present to some extent within further education but are often integrated unconsciously. By intentionally focusing on and integrating sustainability, previously unnoticed connections can emerge. Additional cohorts of participants might be interested in including sustainability competences more explicitly. Teaching and incorporating norms and values for sustainable business practices in further education can play a pivotal role in fostering sustainable decision-making among managers. Emphasizing *Shaping Competence* may prove instrumental in facilitating successful sustainability transitions.

Regarding future research, it is pertinent to expand upon the present findings by investigating additional further education courses. To achieve this, conducting an extensive systematic literature review encompassing scientific, political, and gray literature would serve as a valuable foundation. Furthermore, exploring the level of learning attained in further education can provide valuable insights into the proficiency of the sustainability competences being taught. When large-scale data on course offerings is available, text-mining and topic modeling might offer new insights into the distribution of competences taught across time and space.

Throughout the research on employee education and sustainability competences we have the impression that the field of management requires further exploration to achieve a deep comprehension of the seamless integration of sustainability competence. To attain this goal, sustainable management transition processes should be developed, encompassing not only the managerial level but also prioritizing the individual employee's involvement. A crucial aspect of forming changemakers for tomorrow involves investing in comprehensive employee education across all hierarchical levels, founded on a well-structured training cycle, as this can guarantee the adoption and implementation of sustainable business practices.

References

Adomßent, M., & Hoffmann, T. (2013, March). The concept of competencies in the context of Education for Sustainable Development (ESD). *ESD Expert*, 1–21. http://esd-expert.net/assets/130314-Concept-Paper-ESD-Competencies.pdf

Anderson, L. W., & Krathwohl, D. R. (2001). A taxonomy for learning, teaching, and assessing. In L. W. Anderson, D. R. Krathwohl, P. W. Airasian, K. A. Cruikshank, R. E. Mayer, P. R. Pintrich, J. Raths, & M. C. Wittrock (Eds.), *A revision of bloom's taxonomy of educational objectives*. Addison Wesley Longman, Inc.

Ayers, J. (2020). Competence literate but context lacking? Investigating the potential of study abroad programs to promote sustainability competence acquisition in students. *Sustainability*, *12*(13), 5389. https://doi.org/10.3390/su12135389

Bianchi, G. (2020). Sustainability competences. Publications Office of the European Union, EUR 30555 EN, 1–73. https://doi.org/10.2760/200956

Bianchi, G., Pisiotis, U., & Cabrera Giraldez, M. (2022). In M. Bacigalupo & Y. Punie (Eds.), *GreenComp – The European sustainability competence framework*. Publications Office of the European Union. https://doi.org/10.2760/13286

Blok, V., Gremmen, B., & Wesselink, R. (2016). Dealing with the wicked problem of sustainability: The role of individual virtuous competence. *Business & Professional Ethics Journal*, *34*(3), 297–327. https://doi.org/10.5840/bpej201621737

Bloom, B. S., Engelhardt, M. D., Furst, E. J., Hill, W. H., & Krathwohl, D. R. (1956). Taxonomy of educational objectives. In B. S. Bloom, M. D. Engelhardt, E. J. Furst, W. H. Hill, & D. R. Krathwohl (Eds.), *The classification of educational goals, handbook I: Cognitive domain*. David McKay Company Inc.

Borg, C., & Mayo, P. (2005). The EU Memorandum on lifelong learning. Old wine in new bottles? *Globalisation, Societies and Education*, *3*(2), 203–225. https://doi.org/10.1080/14767720500167082

Boyatzis, R. E. (1998). *Transforming qualitative information: Thematic analysis and code development*. SAGE Publications.

Braun, V., & Clarke, V. (2006). Using thematic analysis in psychology. *Qualitative Research in Psychology*, *3*(2), 77–101. https://doi.org/10.1191/1478088706qp063oa

Braun, V., & Clarke, V. (2019). Reflecting on reflexive thematic analysis. *Qualitative Research in Sport, Exercise and Health*, *11*(4), 589–597. https://doi.org/10.1080/2159676X.2019.1628806

Braun, V., Clarke, V., & Weate, P. (2016). Using thematic analysis in sport and exercise research. In B. Smith & A. C. Sparkes (Eds.), *Routledge handbook of qualitative research in sport and exercise* (pp. 191–205). Routledge. https://doi.org/10.4324/9781315762012-26

Brewer, P. D., & Brewer, K. L. (2010). Knowledge management, human resource management, and higher education: A theoretical model. *The Journal of Education for Business, 85*(6), 330–335. https://doi.org/10.1080/08832321003604938

Brundiers, K., Barth, M., Cebrián, G., Cohen, M., Diaz, L., Doucette-Remington, S., Dripps, W., Habron, G., Harré, N., Jarchow, M., Losch, K., Michel, J., Mochizuki, Y., Rieckmann, M., Parnell, R., Walker, P., & Zint, M. (2021). Key competencies in sustainability in higher education – Toward an agreed-upon reference framework. *Sustainability Science, 16*(1), 13–29. https://doi.org/10.1007/s11625-020-00838-2

Brundtland, G. H. (1987). Our common future – Call for action. *Environmental Conservation, 14*(4), 291–294. https://doi.org/10.1017/S0376892900016805

Carneiro, A. (2000). How does knowledge management influence innovation and competitiveness? *Journal of Knowledge Management, 4*(2), 87–98. https://doi.org/10.1108/13673270010372242

Carrillo-Hermosilla, J., Del Río, P., & Könnölä, T. (2010). Diversity of eco-innovations: Reflections from selected case studies. *Journal of Cleaner Production, 18*(10–11), 1073–1083. https://doi.org/10.1016/j.jclepro.2010.02.014

Clarke, V., & Braun, V. (2013). *Successful qualitative research: A practical guide for beginners.* SAGE Publications.

Cohen, W. M., & Levinthal, D. A. (1990). Absorptive capacity: A new perspective on learning and innovation. *Administrative Science Quarterly, 35*(1), 128–152. https://doi.org/10.2307/2393553

Coopey, J. (1995). The learning organization, power, politics and ideology. *Management Learning, 26*(2), 193–213. https://doi.org/10.1177/135050769502600204

Cörvers, R., Wiek, A., de Kraker, J., Lang, D. J., & Martens, P. (2016). Problem-based and project-based learning for sustainable development. In H. Heinrichs, P. Martens, G. Michelsen, & A. Wiek (Eds.), *Sustainability science* (pp. 349–358). Springer. https://doi.org/10.1007/978-94-017-7242-6_29

Crabtree, B., & Miller, W. (1999). Using codes and code manuals: A template for organizing style of interpretation. In B. Crabtree & W. Miller (Eds.), *Doing qualitative research* (2nd ed., pp. 163–178). Sage.

de Haan, G. (2006). The BLK '21' programme in Germany: A 'Gestaltungskompetenz'-based model for education for sustainable development. *Environmental Education Research, 12*(1), 19–32. https://doi.org/10.1080/13504620500526362

de Haan, G. (2008). Gestaltungskompetenz als Kompetenzkonzept der Bildung für nachhaltige Entwicklung [Shaping competence as a competence concept in education for sustainable development]. In I. Bormann & G. de Haan (Eds.), *Kompetenzen der Bildung für nachhaltige Entwicklung* (pp. 23–44). VS Verlag für Sozialwissenschaften. https://doi.org/10.1007/978-3-531-90832-8_4

de Haan, G. (2010). The development of ESD-related competencies in supportive institutional frameworks. *International Review of Education, 56*(2), 315–328. https://doi.org/10.1007/s11159-010-9157-9

DeSantis, L., & Ugarriza, D. N. (2000). The concept of theme as used in qualitative nursing research. *Western Journal of Nursing Research, 22*(3), 351–372. https://doi.org/10.1177/019394590002200308

Dimante, D., Benders, J., Atstaja, D., & Tamboveca, T. (2016). Development of business education for circular economy in Latvia. *New Challenges of Economic and Business Development – 2016 Society, Innovations and Collaborative Economy.* https://www.researchgate.net/publication/311607044

Dlouhá, J., Heras, R., Mulà, I., Salgado, F. P., & Henderson, L. (2019). Competences to address SDGs in higher education-a reflection on the equilibrium between systemic and personal approaches to achieve transformative action. *Sustainability*, *11*(13), 3664. https://doi.org/10.3390/su11133664

Drejer, A. (2000). Organisational learning and competence development. *The Learning Organization*, *7*(4), 206–220. https://doi.org/10.1108/09696470010342306

European Commission. (2016). *A new skills agenda for Europe* (COM/2016/0381 final). https://eur-lex.europa.eu/legal-content/EN/TXT/?uri=CELEX%3A52016DC0381

European Parliament Council of Europe. (2006). Action programme in the field of lifelong learning (2004–2006). *Official Journal of the European Union*, *327*, 45–68.

European Parliament European Council. (2008). *Recommendation of the European Parliament and of the Council of 23 April 2008 on the establishment of the European Qualification framework for lifelong learning* (2008/C 111); Issue December 2008).

Evans, T. L. (2019). Competencies and pedagogies for sustainability education: A roadmap for sustainability studies program development in colleges and universities. *Sustainability*, *11*(19), 5526. https://doi.org/10.3390/su11195526

Fereday, J., & Muir-Cochrane, E. (2006). Demonstrating rigor using thematic analysis: A hybrid approach of inductive and deductive coding and theme development. *International Journal of Qualitative Methods*, *5*(1), 80–92. https://doi.org/10.1177/160940690600500107

Giangrande, N., White, R. M., East, M., Jackson, R., Clarke, T., Coste, M. S., & Penha-Lopes, G. (2019). A competency framework to assess and activate education for sustainable development: Addressing the UN sustainable development goals 4.7 challenge. *Sustainability*, *11*(10). https://doi.org/10.3390/su11102832

Glasser, H., & Hirsh, J. (2016). Toward the development of robust learning for sustainability core competencies. *Sustainability*, *9*(3), 121–134. https://doi.org/10.1089/SUS.2016.29054.hg

Grant, R. M. (1996). Toward a knowledge-based theory of firm. *Strategic Management Journal*, *17*(S2), 109–122. https://doi.org/10.1002/smj.4250171110

Hall, J., & Vredenburg, H. (2003). The challenges of innovating for sustainable development. *MIT Sloan Management Review*, *45*(1), 61–68.

Hatch, N. W., & Dyer, J. H. (2004). Human capital and learning as a source of sustainable competitive advantage. *Strategic Management Journal*, *25*(12), 1155–1178. https://doi.org/10.1002/smj.421

Hero, L.-M., Lindfors, E., & Taatila, V. (2017). Individual innovation competence: A systematic review and future research agenda. *International Journal of Higher Education*, *6*(5), 103–121. https://doi.org/10.5430/ijhe.v6n5p103

Iddris, F. (2016). Innovation capability: A systematic review and research agenda. *Interdisciplinary Journal of Information, Knowledge, and Management*, *11*, 235–260.

IHK Akademie. (2022). *IHK Akademie*. https://akademie.muenchen.ihk.de/live-online/?gclid=CjwKCAjw1ICZBhAzEiwAFfvFhJNKKGilDpSdFQvV8wSxlr1vsE5SfFgwxy6jGgemPJZjIAsp1YLQ4RoC9p0QAvD_BwE

IHK DIGITAL GmbH. (2022). *Seminarsuche [Seminar Search]*. WIS – Das Weiterbildungs-Innovations-System. https://wis.ihk.de/nc/seminare/seminarsuche.html

Keinänen, M., Ursin, J., & Nissinen, K. (2018). How to measure students' innovation competences in higher education: Evaluation of an assessment tool in authentic learning environments. *Studies in Educational Evaluation*, *58*, 30–36. https://doi.org/10.1016/j.stueduc.2018.05.007

Kemp, R., & Pearson, P. (2007). Final report MEI project about measuring eco-innovation. *UM Merit, Maastricht, 10*(2), 1–120.

Ketata, I., Sofka, W., & Grimpe, C. (2015). The role of internal capabilities and firms' environment for sustainable innovation: Evidence for Germany. *R & D Management, 45*(1), 60–75. https://doi.org/10.1111/radm.12052

Klemp, G. (1980, January). Assessment of occupational competence. *Final report: I. Introduction and overview* (pp. 2–23). National Institute of Education.

Komarkova, I., Gagliardi, D., Conrads, J., & Collado, A. (2015). Entrepreneurship competence: An overview of existing concepts, policies and initiatives. In M. Bacigalupo, P. Kampylis, & Y. Punie (Eds.), *JRC science and policy reports.* https://doi.org/10.2791/067979

Lankard, B. A. (1995). New ways of learning in the workplace. *ERIC Clearinghouse on Adult, Career and Vocational Education, 161*, 1–8.

Lans, T., Blok, V., & Wesselink, R. (2014). Learning apart and together: Towards an integrated competence framework for sustainable entrepreneurship in higher education. *Journal of Cleaner Production, 62*, 37–47. https://doi.org/10.1016/j.jclepro.2013.03.036

Lave, J., & Wenger, E. (1991). *Situated learning.* Cambridge University Press. https://doi.org/10.1017/CBO9780511815355

Leiponen, A. (2005). Skills and innovation. *International Journal of Industrial Organization, 23*(5), 303–323. https://doi.org/10.1016/j.ijindorg.2005.03.005

Levin, R. C., Cohen, W. M., & Mowery, D. C. (1985). R&D appropriability, opportunity, and market structure: New evidence on some schumpeterian hypotheses. *The American Economic Review, 75*(2), 20–24. https://www.jstor.org/stable/1805564

Lozano, R., Bautista-Puig, N., & Barreiro-Gen, M. (2022). Developing a sustainability competences paradigm in higher education or a white elephant? *Sustainable Development, 30*(5), 870–883. https://doi.org/10.1002/sd.2286

Lozano, R., Merrill, M. Y., Sammalisto, K., Ceulemans, K., & Lozano, F. J. (2017). Connecting competences and pedagogical approaches for sustainable development in higher education: A literature review and framework proposal. *Sustainability, 9*(10), 1889. https://doi.org/10.3390/su9101889

Marsick, V. J., & Watkins, K. (1990). *Informal and incidental learning in the workplace.* Routledge. https://doi.org/10.4324/9781315715926

Martínez Valdivia, E., Pegalajar Palomino, M. del C., & Burgos-Garcia, A. (2023). Active methodologies and curricular sustainability in teacher training. *International Journal of Sustainability in Higher Education.* https://doi.org/10.1108/IJSHE-05-2022-0168

Mention, A. L. (2012). Intellectual capital, innovation and performance: A systematic review of the literature. *Business and Economic Research, 2*(1), 1–37. https://doi.org/10.5296/ber.v2i1.1937

Mitchelmore, S., & Rowley, J. (2010). Entrepreneurial competencies: A literature review and development agenda. *International Journal of Entrepreneurial Behaviour & Research, 16*(2), 92–111. https://doi.org/10.1108/13552551011026995

Nowell, L. S., Norris, J. M., White, D. E., & Moules, N. J. (2017). Thematic analysis: Striving to meet the trustworthiness criteria. *International Journal of Qualitative Methods, 16*(1), 1–13. https://doi.org/10.1177/1609406917733847

OECD. (2005). *Definition und Auswahl von Schlüsselkompetenzen [Definition and selection of key competencies]*. https://www.oecd.org/pisa/35693281.pdf

Pacis, M., & VanWynsberghe, R. (2020). Key sustainability competencies for education for sustainability. *International Journal of Sustainability in Higher Education, 21*(3), 575–592. https://doi.org/10.1108/IJSHE-12-2018-0234

Pérez Salgado, F., Abbott, D., & Wilson, G. (2018). Dimensions of professional competences for interventions towards sustainability. *Sustainability Science, 13*(1), 163–177. https://doi.org/10.1007/s11625-017-0439-z

Pérez Salgado, F., De Kraker, J., Boon, J., & van der Klink, M. (2012). Competences for climate change education in a virtual mobility setting. *International Journal of Innovation and Sustainable Development, 6*(1), 53–65. https://doi.org/10.1504/IJISD.2012.046053

Quendler, E., & Lamb, M. (2016). Learning as a lifelong process – Meeting the challenges of the changing employability landscape: Competences, skills and knowledge for sustainable development. *International Journal of Continuing Engineering Education and Life Long Learning, 26*(3), 273–293. https://doi.org/10.1504/IJCEELL.2016.078447

Redman, A., & Wiek, A. (2021). Competencies for advancing transformations towards sustainability. *Frontiers in Education, 6*(November), 785163. https://doi.org/10.3389/feduc.2021.785163

Rieckmann, M. (2012). Future-oriented higher education: Which key competencies should be fostered through university teaching and learning? *Futures, 44*(2), 127–135. https://doi.org/10.1016/j.futures.2011.09.005

Rieckmann, M. (2018). Learning to transform the world: Key competencies in ESD. In A. Leicht, J. Heiss, & W. J. Byun (Eds.), *Issues and trends in education for sustainable development* (pp. 39–59). UNESCO Publishing.

Rittel, H. W. J., & Webber, M. M. (1973). Dilemmas in a general theory of planning. *Policy Sciences, 4*(2), 155–169. https://doi.org/10.1007/BF01405730

Rothwell, R., Freeman, C., Horlsey, A., Jervis, V. T. P., Robertson, A. B., & Townsend, J. (1974). SAPPHO updated – Project SAPPHO phase II. *Research Policy, 3*(3), 258–291. https://doi.org/10.1016/0048-7333(74)90010-9

Sanchez, A. V., Ruiz, M. P., Olalla, A. G., Mora, G. M., Paredes, J. A. M., Otero, J. M., San Ildefonso, M. I. M., & Eizaguirre, J. S. (2008). *Competence-based learning.* http://www.deusto-publicaciones.es/ud/openaccess/tuning/pdfs_tuning/tuning13.pdf

Senge, P. M. (1990). The leader's new work. *Sloan Management Review, 32*(1), 7–23.

Senge, P. M. (2006). *The fifth discipline: The art and practice of the learning organization* (Revised & reviewed). Doubleday.

Shephard, K., Rieckmann, M., & Barth, M. (2019). Seeking sustainability competence and capability in the ESD and HESD literature: An international philosophical hermeneutic analysis. *Environmental Education Research, 25*(4), 532–547. https://doi.org/10.1080/13504622.2018.1490947

Sinkula, J. M. (1994). Market information processing and organizational learning. *Journal of Marketing, 58*(1), 35–45. https://doi.org/10.2307/1252249

Smith, A., Courvisanos, J., Tuck, J., & McEachern, S. (2011). *Building innovation capacity: The role of human capital formation in enterprises – A review of the literature.* National Centre for Vocational Education Research (NCVER).

Stein, D. (1998). Situated learning in adult education. *ERIC Clearinghouse on Adult, Carreer, and Vocational Education, 195*, 640–649. http://files.eric.ed.gov/fulltext/ED418250.pdf

Stengele, D. (2022). *Weiterbildung in Baden-Württemberg [Further Education in Baden-Württtemberg]*. Ministerium Für Wirtschaft, Arbeit Und Tourismus Baden-Württemberg. https://www.fortbildung-bw.de/fuer-interessierte-2/kurs-finden/?typ=Kurs&akademisch=0&trainer=0&bildungsgutschein=0&migranten=0&digitizationBadge=0&umkreis=-1&sortby=beginn&sortorder=ASC

Trad, S. P. (2019). A framework for mapping sustainability within tertiary curriculum. *International Journal of Sustainability in Higher Education, 20*(2), 288–308. https://doi.org/10.1108/IJSHE-09-2018-0151

UNESCO. (2017). *Education for sustainable development goals: Learning objectives.* http://unesdoc.unesco.org/images/0024/002474/247444e.pdf

United Nations (UN). (1992). *Agenda 21: United Nations Conference on Environment & Development Rio de Janerio, Brazil, 3 to 14 June 1992.* https://sustainabledevelopment.un.org/content/documents/Agenda21.pdf

United Nations (UN). (2002). *Plan of implementation of the world summit on sustainable development ("Johannesburg plan of implementation"),* Pub. L. No. A/CONF.199/20.

Verloop, J. (2006). The Shell way to innovate. *International Journal of Technology Management, 34*, 243–259. https://doi.org/10.1504/IJTM.2006.009458

Volles, N. (2016). Lifelong learning in the EU: Changing conceptualisations, actors, and policies. *Studies in Higher Education, 41*(2), 343–363. https://doi.org/10.1080/03075079.2014.927852

Wiek, A., Bernstein, M. J., Foley, R. W., Cohen, M., Forrest, N., Kuzdas, C., Kay, B., & Keeler, L. W. (2016). Operationalising competencies in higher education for sustainable development. In M. Barth, G. Michelsen, M. Rieckmann, & I. Thomas (Eds.), *Handbook of higher education for sustainable development* (pp. 241–260). Routledge. https://doi.org/10.4324/9781315852249-20

Wiek, A., Withycombe, L., & Redman, C. L. (2011). Key competencies in sustainability: A reference framework for academic program development. *Sustainability Science, 6*, 203–218. https://doi.org/10.1007/s11625-011-0132-6

Wruck, K. H., & Jensen, M. C. (1994). Science, specific knowledge, and total quality management. *Journal of Accounting and Economics, 18*(3), 247–287. https://doi.org/10.1016/0165-4101(94)90023-X

Appendix

A1 – Six Step Approach to Thematic Analysis by Braun and Clarke (2006)

Phase one covers the familiarization with and immersion in the data set (Braun & Clarke, 2006; Braun et al., 2016; Nowell et al., 2017). The data set consists of information derived from two different databases. The data pertains to further education offerings and follows a specific structure, including course titles, descriptions, content outlines, teaching methods, target groups, and pricing details.

Phase two starts after reviewing all data. Initial codes are supposed to cover first impressions based on the data. Codes should highlight the content and meaning of a section in the text. Boyatzis (1998) advocates "good codes" (p. 1) are comprised of all the relevant qualitative information in the text sequence. Codes should be defined with clear and strict definitions as well as boundaries. Text is coded with as many codes as necessary to cover the underlying meaning (Braun & Clarke, 2006; Braun et al., 2016; Nowell et al., 2017). A codebook, also referred to as a coding frame, is used to define the codes and, when appropriate, how to commence the coding (Braun et al., 2016; Crabtree & Miller, 1999; Fereday & Muir-Cochrane, 2006). This chapter follows a deductive coding approach, meaning the sample is analyzed by codes derived from the theoretical framework described in Section "Theoretical Background".

Phase three develops overarching themes for the coded text parts (Clarke & Braun, 2013). Themes are described as "an abstract entity that brings meaning and identity to a recurrent experience and its variant manifestations. As such, a theme captures and unifies the nature or basis of the experience into a meaningful whole" (DeSantis & Ugarriza, 2000, p. 362). The six competences in *Anticipatory Competence, Interpersonal Competence, Normative Competence, Shaping Competence, Strategic Competence,* and *Systems-Thinking Competence* are classified as overarching themes. Additionally, knowledge dimensions, skills, and attitudes related to these competences are conceptualized as themes that differentiate the qualitative data (Braun et al., 2016; Clarke & Braun, 2013). Braun and Clarke (2006) claim that deductive analysis provides more detail but is less rich in describing all the data. The analyses of the further education programs are based on the competence framework and connections among competences. While evidence for all competences is found, the connections are discussed in more detail. A triad of core competence was identified in *Strategic, Anticipatory, and Interpersonal Competence.*

Phase four covers the review process of the themes. While renaming or creating other categories was not important for this thematic analysis, reviewing the coded text material and checking for accuracy are. Braun and Clarke (2006) suggest collapsing and overlapping themes or separating themes in individual text segments. As the coded themes are based on a theoretical framework, the themes will not be collapsed or separated. Referential adequacy is given by revisiting the raw data, as the text clues are matched to the developed themes to assure conclusions based on the data (Nowell et al., 2017).

Phases five and six comprise the definition and naming of the themes as well as reporting the process, respectively. An extensive report can be found in the results section of this chapter.

A2 – Codebook Overview

Competence	Descriptor
Anticipatory Competence (Adomßent & Hoffmann, 2013; Bianchi, 2020; Cörvers et al., 2016; Lozano et al., 2017; Wiek et al., 2011)	• Analyzing and developing comprehensive future scenarios, considering quantitative and qualitative information. • Addressing ambiguity, uncertainty, and risk in future planning. • Continuously refining and challenging one's future thinking in relation to the existing status quo. • Recognizing and examining implicit assumptions about society's functioning and their influence on the status quo. • Engaging in critical reflection on how these assumptions might impact future thinking.
Interpersonal Competence (Adomßent & Hoffmann, 2013; Ayers, 2020; Bianchi, 2020; Cörvers et al., 2016; Lozano et al., 2017; Martínez Valdivia et al., 2023; Shephard et al., 2019; Wiek et al., 2011)	• Motivating and collaborating with others through social and leadership skills and empathy. • Effectively persuading stakeholders with these interpersonal abilities. • Engaging and motivating diverse stakeholders by understanding and adapting to their communication styles. • Being self-aware of emotions, desires, thoughts, behaviors, and personality. • Utilizing emotional intelligence and social and emotional learning to regulate and improve oneself.
Normative Competence (Bianchi, 2020; Brundiers et al., 2021; Cörvers et al., 2016; Dlouhá et al., 2019; Evans, 2019; Lozano et al., 2017)	• Defining, applying, and negotiating sustainability values, principles, and goals. • Acquiring and processing normative knowledge related to ethics, justice, and equity. • Distinguishing between intrinsic and extrinsic values in the social and natural world.

(Continued)

Competence	Descriptor
	• Recognizing and addressing normalized oppressive structures. • Clarifying and understanding personal values. • Evaluating the alignment of stated values with sustainability values.
Shaping Competence (Adomßent & Hoffmann, 2013; de Haan, 2006, 2008; Dlouhá et al., 2019; OECD, 2005)	• Shaping competence is a component of sustainability competences. • It involves applying knowledge to analyze and anticipate sustainable and unsustainable development. • Informed decisions are made at individual, communal, and political levels to promote sustainable development processes.
Strategic Competence (Bianchi, 2020; Cörvers et al., 2016; Dlouhá et al., 2019; Pérez Salgado et al., 2012, 2018; Wiek et al., 2011)	• Developing and implementing sustainability interventions (intervention competence). • Understanding historical influences, barriers, feasibility, and effectiveness of interventions. • Considering consequences for stakeholders. • Recognizing historical origins and embedded resilience of unsustainability. • Identifying barriers to change. • Creating innovative experimental plans to test sustainability strategies.
Systems-Thinking Competence (Adomßent & Hoffmann, 2013; Bianchi, 2020; Cörvers et al., 2016; Lozano et al., 2017; Senge, 2006; Wiek et al., 2011)	• Dealing with complexity in organizational and systemic contexts. • Commitment to learning from past experiences. • Ability to change perspectives when necessary. • Analyzing complex systems across domains and scales. • Understanding system structure, dynamics, and sustainability features. • Utilizing acquired systemic knowledge and methodologies for analysis.

A3 – Table 2.1. Description of the Sample.

ID	Title (Translated)	Location of Organizer	Private/ Public	Duration in Days (8 hours = 1 day)	Online/ Offline	Competences Taught
1	Agile Leadership Training with SCRUM Certification	Berlin	Private	20	Online	SyC
2	Agile Innovation and Leadership Management	Villingen-Schwenningen	Public	1	Offline	InC, ShC
3	Agile Project and Innovation Management with SCRUM Certification	Berlin	Private	41	Online	AnC, NoC, ShC, StC, SyC
4	AI Manager (IHK)	Osnabrück	Public	9	Online	AnC, NoC, ShC
5	Business Development	Wiesbaden	Private	2	Online	AnC, NoC, IC, ShC, StC
6	Business Model Innovation	Erlangen	Private	1	Online	AnC, NoC, ShC, StC
7	Business Model Innovation with Lean Start-up	Fischbachtal	Private	1	Online	NoC, StC
8	CERTIFICATE COURSE – Artificial Intelligence	Reutlingen	Public	6	Offline	NoC, StC
9	Certificate Course Innovation and Technology Management	Ostfildern	Private	9	Offline	AnC, InC, StC, ShC, SyC
10	Certificate Course Innovation Management and New Business Development	Aalen	Public	2	Offline	ShC, StC, SyC

11	Certificate Course Modern Personnel Management for Non-HR Professionals	Ostfildern	Private	5	Offline	AnC, InC, StC, SyC
12	Certificate Course: The Construction and Development Manager – Medium-Sized Companies	Ostfildern	Private	3	Offline	AnC, InC, StC
13	Certified Service Design Thinker – Online	Cologne	Private	3	Online	AC, ShC, StC
14	Change and Innovation Management	Karlsruhe	Private	17	Offline	InC, NoC, ShC, StC, SyC
15	Change Management	Münster	Private	2	Online	AnC, InC, NoC, SyC
16	Creative Leadership	Ostfildern	Private	1	Offline	AnC, InC, NoC, StC
17	Creativity Methods for Marketing	Wiesbaden	Private	2	Online	AnC, InC, NoC
18	Creativity Techniques and Innovation	Münster	Private	2	Online	InC, StC
19	Creativity Techniques for Professionals and Managers	Ludwigslust	Private	5	Online	ShC
20	Design Thinking	Hamburg	Private	2	Online	AnC, ShC, StC, SyC
21	Design Thinking	Karlsruhe	Private	5	Offline	NoC
22	Design Thinking & Co.	Dortmund	Private	2	Online	ShC, StC
23	Design Thinking Basecamp – Online	Cologne	Private	2	Online	AnC, ShC
24	Design Thinking: Innovating with User-Centered Approach	Bielefeld	Public	1	Online	StC

(Continued)

(Continued)

ID	Title (Translated)	Location of Organizer	Private/ Public	Duration in Days (8 hours = 1 day)	Online/ Offline	Competences Taught
25	Design Thinking	Dortmund	Private	2	Online	AnC, ShC
26	Developing Innovative and Future-Proof Business Strategies	Dortmund	Private	2	Online	AnC, StC
27	Digital Innovation and Product Manager (IHK)	Weingarten	Public	11	Offline	InC, SyC
28	Digital Innovation and Product Manager (IHK)	Bielefeld	Public	9	Online	AnC, SyC
29	Digital Innovation and Product Manager (IHK) – IHK Certificate Course eLearning	Siegen	Public	9	Online	InC, StC, ShC
30	Digital Innovation and Product Manager (IHK) – Online	Münster	Public	9	Online	StC, SyC
31	Digital Innovation and Product Manager (IHK) – Online	Gera	Public	9	Online	AnC, SyC
32	Digital Innovation Management (Instructor-led Full-Time in-person or Telelearning)	Dortmund	Private	20	Online	NoC, StC,
33	Digital Transformation Design	Fischbachtal	Private	2	Online	AnC, InC, SyC
34	Digitalization Manager IHK (m/f/d)	Pforzheim	Public	9	Offline	NoC, ShC, StC
35	Digitization of Business Fields	Offenburg	Public	5	Offline	InC, NoC, ShC
36	Disrupt Yourself – Disruptive Innovation – Advanced	Seelze	Private	1	Online	AnC, ShC

37	Disrupt Yourself – Disruptive Innovation – Expert	Seelze	Private	5	Online	AnC, ShC, StC
38	Disrupt Yourself – Disruptive Innovation – Professional	Seelze	Private	1,5	Online	AnC, ShC, StC
39	Future and Innovation Management Seminar	Hundsangen	Private	1	Online	AnC, NoC, StC
40	Hack your Leadership Culture	Regensburg	Private	1,5	Online	NoC, StC
41	Innovation and Digital Leadership	Nuremberg	Public	2	Online	AnC, InC, ShC
42	Innovation and Change Management with ITIL ® and PRINCE2® – Technology	Königstein im Taunus	Private	125	Online	AnC, InC, NoC, SyC
43	Innovation and Patent Management	Nuremberg	Public	2	Online	ShC, StC
44	Innovation Culture as a Success Factor	Potsdam	Private	2	Online	InC, ShC
45	Innovation Management	Potsdam	Private	2	Online	AnC, InC, ShC, StC, SyC
46	Innovation Management (IM)	Willroth	Private	2	Online	StC
47	Innovation Manager (IHK)	Darmstadt	Public	66	Online	NoC
48	Innovation Manager IHK	Hameln	Public	14	Online	AnC, ShC, StC, SyC
49	IPMA®Level C – Certified Project Manager (ICB4)	Filderstadt	Private	6	Offline	InC, NoC, ShC, StC
50	IPMA®Level D – Certified Project Management Associate (ICB4)	Filderstadt	Private	6	Offline	InC, NoC, ShC, StC, SyC
51	Learning Coach 2.0 in Apprenticeships	Mannheim	Public	4	Offline	AnC, InC, NoC, ShC, SyC

(Continued)

(*Continued*)

ID	Title (Translated)	Location of Organizer	Private/ Public	Duration in Days (8 hours = 1 day)	Online/ Offline	Competences Taught
52	Managerial Effectiveness for Energy 4.0	Berlin	Private	21	Online	InC, NoC, ShC, StC
53	Methods of AI	Aalen	Public	20	Offline	AnC, ShC
54	New Digital Innovation and Product Manager (IHK)	Magdeburg	Public	12	Online	InC, StC, SyC
55	Online Training Leading Change	Berlin	Private	2	Online	AnC, InC, NoC, ShC, StC, SyC
56	Process-Oriented Innovation Management	Ostfildern	Private	3	Offline	InC, StC
57	Radical Customer Focus – Agility as the Key to Digitization	Bielefeld	Public	1	Online	AnC
58	Real-Time Innovation Card Set	Essen	Public	1	Online	AnC, ShC, StC
59	SCRUM – Agile Project Management in Development Projects	Bielefeld	Public	5	Online	ShC, StC
60	Seminar China – Access to the Market for Medical Devices	Ostfildern	Private	0,5	Offline	ShC
61	Seminar Engineers in the Future of Technical Sales	Ostfildern	Private	2	Offline	InC, StC
62	Seminar Improving Disposition and Production Control	Ostfildern	Private	2	Offline	AnC, StC
63	Seminar Innovation and Creativity in Design and Development	Ostfildern	Private	2	Offline	AnC, InC, SyC

64	Seminar Process-Oriented Innovation Management	Ostfildern	Private	1	Offline	AnC, InC, NoC, StC, SyC
65	Strategic Technology and Innovation Management	Ulm	Public	125	Offline	AnC, ShC, StC
66	Success with AI	Nuremberg	Public	1	Online	AnC, NoC
67	Sustainability Manager	Buxtehude	Private	2	Online	AnC, InC, NoC, StC
68	Systematic Implementation of Innovation Hunger in Sales	Heikendorf	Private	1	Online	AnC, InC, ShC, StC, SyC
69	University Certificate in Digitization	Nuremberg	Public	250	Online	AnC, InC, ShC
70	Work 4.0 – Changes in Business Administration and Management	Buxtehude	Private	5	Online	AnC, InC, StC, SyC
71	Work 4.0 – Competences for Digitization in the Commercial Sector	Buxtehude	Private	5	Online	InC, StC
72	Work 4.0 – Working in New Forms of Work	Buxtehude	Private	5	Online	AnC, InC, StC

Abbreviations: AnC = Anticipatory Competence; InC = Interpersonal Competence; NoC = Normative Competence; ShC = Shaping Competence; StC = Strategic Competence; SyC = Systems-Thinking Competence.

A4 – Table 2.2. Emerging Themes Based on the Sample.

Themes	Absolute Number	Relative Number
Agile Working	7	9.72%
Artificial Intelligence	4	5.56%
Digitalization	9	12.50%
Design Thinking	8	11.11%
Innovation (management)	33	45.83%
Project Management	6	8.33%
Sustainability and Change	5	6.94%
Total	72	100%

Chapter 3

Integrating Sustainability Into Business School Curriculum: Understanding the Impact

Lois Fearon

Royal Roads University, Canada

Abstract

The importance of developing and implementing sustainable business practices has never been greater. Business schools are increasingly tasked with
preparing students to contribute to this imperative and although progress is
being made, the impact of integrating sustainability into business school
curriculum has remained uncertain as studies exploring the impact have been
lacking. The purpose of this multi-case study was to examine the impact of
integration efforts in two distinct undergraduate business programs at Royal
Roads University. The research focused on how students' understanding of
sustainability and their associated attitudes and behaviors changed as they
progressed throughout their programs. In addition to considering the impact
of a sustainability-infused curriculum, other factors affecting sustainability
orientations were also explored. The study was unique in both its comparative nature and in its investigation of the various contextual factors shaping
sustainability orientations. Data were collected through semi-structured
interviews and through document analysis. Findings suggest a combination of approaches to integration is most effective in impacting sustainability
perspectives. While sustainability was generally understood in a multidimensional manner, there was a noticeable environmental bias and a tendency to view it within the business framework. A need for stronger and
more comprehensive conceptualizations was identified. Recommendations
include: (a) embed sustainability in a comprehensive manner across the
curriculum, (b) move beyond a disciplinary conceptualization of sustainability and introduce stronger sustainability discourse, (c) utilize powerful
experiential and place-based pedagogies, (d) pay attention to context and

Innovation in Responsible Management Education, 63–92
doi:10.1108/978-1-83549-464-620241005

ensure both the formal and the informal curriculum mutually reinforce a pro-sustainability agenda.

Keywords: Education for sustainability; impact of integrating sustainability into curriculum; business school; impact; higher education; sustainability orientations; contextual factors contributing to sustainability orientations

Introduction

Impacts of the climate emergency, the global pandemic, rising inflation, and an economic crisis that serves to exacerbate pre-existing inequities are reverberating around the world. With daily, weekly, and monthly global heat records continuing to be set, climate scientists agree that in terms of climate change, we are in uncharted territory. The anthropogenic activities that are at the root of the issue only continue to exacerbate it (Guardian Staff and Agencies, 2023). The health of the earth's systems and our very species has perhaps never been as vulnerable.

Businesses worldwide face a strong call to enhance climate action and more aggressively pursue Sustainable Development Goals (SDGs) (Gupta et al., 2019; UN Global Compact, 2021). Given this call and the urgency of the situation, one might expect business schools to be leading the way in terms of integrating education for sustainable development into curriculum (Hughes et al., 2018; Von Der Heidt & Lamberton, 2011). Unfortunately, it appears that this has not been the case. In particular, business schools have been faulted for not only failing to keep up with corporate interests in sustainability (Breyer, 2019) but also for perpetuating unsustainable ways of thinking through advancing destructive, profit driven, capitalistic ideologies (Brueckner et al., 2018; Ghoshal, 2005; Hughes et al., 2018; Jun & Moon, 2021; Mburayi & Wall, 2018; Russo et al., 2023). Although many business schools have responded and sustainability is increasingly being integrated into curriculum, opinions vary regarding how best to approach integration efforts (Kanashiro et al., 2020; Rusinko, 2010). Moreover, research exploring the impact of existing efforts is sparse (Cullen, 2017; Hay & Eagle, 2020; Rusinko, 2010). Relatively, little is known about how education for sustainability impacts the way business students think about the topic or the decisions they may make as a result (Cullen, 2017). Without a more fulsome understanding of how and if integration efforts impact students' attitudes toward sustainability, it is difficult to determine how best to prepare students to help. The lack of insight serves to impede progress in this important area.

This research addresses the gap that exists in terms of understanding how integrating sustainability into business school curriculum impacts the development of a sustainability mindset that is accompanied by behavior reflective of sustainable ways of living and conducting business. In addition, insights regarding the association between impact, integration efforts, the learning context, and pedagogies are explored. These insights will aid in the development of future sustainability initiatives within management education. The research will be of interest to business school leaders, instructors, special interest groups such as the Principles for Responsible Management Education Task Force, and industry professionals seeking to ensure that business school graduates are able and motivated to lead the way in terms of making sustainable business a reality and a norm.

The original research was submitted in 2020 as a Doctoral Thesis to the Graduate Program in Educational Research at the University of Calgary, Calgary, Alberta, Canada. In addition, the research was discussed, in part, by the author, in an article in Vol. 16, No. 1 (2023) of the *Social Innovations Journal*, an open access publication.

Education for Sustainable Development: Evolution of Efforts

The integration of education for sustainable development into academic curriculum is a relatively recent phenomenon, with the 1987 *Brundtland Report* frequently cited as the seminal document that not only provided the most commonly accepted definition of the term but also set the stage for further work in this area (Kagawa, 2007; Kopnina & Meijers, 2014). The *Brundtland Report*, produced by the UNs' World Commission on Environment and Development and positioned as a "global agenda for change," recognizes sustainable development as development "that meets the needs of the present without compromising the ability of future generations to meet their own needs" (World Commission on Environment and Development, 1987, I, 3.27). Throughout the report, environmental, economic, and social well-being are highlighted as the three pillars of sustainability. With an overall goal of charting the way to a sustainable future, numerous recommendations relevant to each domain are made, a number of which relate to the integration of sustainable development into education.

Since the *Brundtland Report*, a proliferation of projects, organizations, and partnerships specific to education for sustainable development have been detailed. Notably, the UN's Decade of Education for Sustainable Development, which ran between 2005 and 2014, focused on integrating sustainable development into all aspects and levels of education. In addition, in 2017, the postsecondary sector launched the SDG Accord (The Accord) as a collective response aimed at advancing the sector's role in the embedment of sustainability into all education, research, leadership, operations, and engagement activities (The SDG Accord, n.d.). By 2019, there were over 1,000 signatories to the accord spanning 85 countries and 42 international and national networks (Filho et al., 2019). Within the business school arena, the inclusion of sustainability is now considered a prerequisite for receiving accreditation from major international bodies such the Association to Advance Collegiate Business Schools (AACSB) and the European Foundation for Management Development's European Quality Improvement System (EQUIS) (Kanashiro et al., 2020). In addition, thousands of business schools currently participate in sustainability focused initiatives such as the

United Nation's Principle for Responsible Management Education (PRME), the Aspen Institute, and Net Impact (Singh & Segatto, 2020).

Committing to sustainable development through signing agreements, developing partnerships, or aligning with associated organizations are undoubtedly important first steps in advancing the sustainability agenda through education. Being a signatory to an agreement or a member of an organization devoted to the cause does not necessarily, however, mean that the principles of sustainable development are being meaningfully embedded into the institutional fabric and integrated into teaching practices. A 2019 international review assessing the status of the field noted that although there have been significant improvements, many universities are falling behind in terms of pursuing SDGs (Filho et al., 2019). Moreover, various scholars suggest that within education in general, nowhere has the challenge to embed sustainability into curriculum been more significant than within business education (Barber et al., 2014; Mburayi & Wall, 2018; Von Der Heidt & Lamberton, 2011). For higher education in general and for business schools specifically, evidence that integration efforts reflect current sustainability concerns is scant (Jun & Moon, 2021).

Barriers to Integration

A number of barriers have been identified as impeding action. One identified barrier relates to a lack of consensus regarding factors that contribute to sustainability learning (Singh & Segatto, 2020). The lack of agreement on what the relevant conceptualization of sustainability might be or what the appropriate educational frameworks for teaching are adds to the challenge (Kagawa, 2007; Painter-Morland et al., 2016; Rusinko, 2010; Singh & Segatto, 2020). Further, opinions vary with respect to whether the topic of sustainability should be integrated into existing offerings or taught in courses and/or programs focused specifically on sustainability (Painter-Morland et al., 2016). A lack of support from top management and a lack of training regarding how to integrate have also been noted (Filho et al., 2019; Singh & Segatto, 2020). Moreover, in spite of the fact that the prevailing profit maximization model has been considered inconsistent with the essence of sustainability thinking, it has long been a theoretical underpinning of traditional business school curriculum. Given this underpinning, faculty wishing to explore alternative conceptualizations of business success find it difficult to do so (Barber et al., 2014; Mburayi & Wall, 2018).

Integration Approaches and Assessment of Impact

In spite of these barriers, sustainability is increasingly being integrated into curriculum. Approaches to integration range from simply including sustainability-focused content within existing courses to adding specialized elective courses, developing cross-disciplinary sustainability-focused offerings, specialization options, or programs (Rusinko, 2010). In reviewing approaches, scholars have found that sustainability has primarily been integrated using narrow approaches which leave large numbers of students unexposed to the concept (Mburayi & Wall, 2018; Painter-Morland et al., 2016). To truly influence change in the sustainability attitudes and behaviors of students, most argue that a holistic approach extending beyond integrating the concept into curriculum is required (Blasco, 2012; Gramatakos & Lavau, 2019; Høgdal et al., 2019; Painter-Morland et al., 2016; Winter & Cotton, 2012). The PRME Steering Committee (n.d.-a), for example, contends that commitment from leadership, faculty, and staff; long-term planning; resource commitment; implementation over specific time frames; assessment of impact; reporting and communication; and strategic imperatives all must be supportive. In spite of support for holistic approaches, the relative impact that either holistic or piecemeal efforts have on sustainability mindsets or behaviors has been under-researched (Collado et al., 2022; Hay & Eagle, 2020; Koljatic & Silva, 2015; Zsóka & Ásványi, 2023) or, according to at least one review, completely absent (Schmitt-Figueiro & Raufflet, 2015).

Efforts to assess impact of integration efforts and approaches seem to be increasing, but studies indicate that short-term outcomes of single-subject content (Hay & Eagle, 2020) dominate. Cordano et al. (2003), for example, measured the impact of a specific course on students' attitudes toward environmental sustainability; Sharma and Kelly (2014) measured students' perception of the integration of sustainability into their curricula as well as their perceived understanding of the topic; Hay and Eagle (2020) compared attitudes toward and understanding of sustainability issues prior to and after student engagement in sustainability-related curriculum; and Brunstein et al. (2020) considered the shifts of sustainability mindsets as a result of incorporating sustainability into the finance discipline. A study done by Badea et al. (2020) did take a more holistic approach, looking at student perceptions of how their university education impacted their sustainability orientation and behaviors, taking into consideration campus sustainability initiatives, teaching staff involvement, and curricula.

Beyond the business school context, studies assessing the impact of integrating sustainability into curriculum have considered how students' conceptualize sustainability pre- and postrelated coursework (Zeegers & Clark, 2014); the impact of curriculum on sustainability orientations (Qu et al., 2020); how the nature of coursework taken impacts conceptualizations (Fisher & McAdams, 2015); how various educational experiences impact students' confidence in their ability to incorporate sustainability into their practices, how motivated they are to do so, and how confident they are that they can (McCormick et al., 2015); the impact of active learning, project- and service-based experiences (Birdman et al., 2021; Ngo & Chase, 2021); the impact of the hidden curriculum (Høgdal et al., 2019); nature and place (Gramatakos & Lavau, 2019; Orr, 1992; Selby, 2017; Selby & Kagawa, 2018); campus sustainability initiatives (Hopkinson et al., 2008); using the campus as a living lab to integrate sustainability learning (Pretorius et al., 2019; Zen, 2017); extra-curricular learning (Gramatakos & Lavau, 2019; Hopkinson et al., 2008); pedagogical approaches conducive to the adoption of a sustainability orientation (Dziubaniuk & Nyholm, 2021; Molderez & Fonseca, 2018; Pretorius et al., 2019); and the impact of sustainability orientations of students upon program entry (Kinzer, 2021; Lambrechts et al., 2018; Sidiropoulos, 2018; Sundermann & Fischer, 2019).

Consideration of this body of literature reveals that a multitude of factors combine to potentially influence changes in the sustainability orientations of students as they progress throughout their university experience. Understanding the impact of and the role that integrating sustainability into curriculum plays in these changes is important. While research in this area is emerging, business school–specific research is limited. In addition, research that looks at impact within the context of a broader framework and considers factors beyond integrating the concept into curriculum appears to be completely lacking. Considering the ever-increasing urgency of the sustainability crisis, it is clear that research providing additional insight in this important area is both timely and warranted.

Methodology

The research described in this chapter took the form of a qualitative multiple case study (Merriam, 1998; Yin, 2014). The phenomena investigated was how sustainability-related attitudes and the propensity to take sustainability into consideration when making decisions changed as business students progressed through their program of study. The contexts investigated were two distinct undergraduate business programs at Royal Roads University (RRU), a publicly funded postsecondary institution in Canada. The programs included the Bachelor of Commerce (BCom) in Entrepreneurial Management and the Bachelor of Business Administration (BBA) in Sustainability. The programs were intentionally selected as case studies because, in spite of sharing characteristics common across all RRU programs, the manner in which sustainability was integrated in the BCom was different than in the BBA and as such, one might expect the impact of integration efforts to vary. As Yin (2014) noted, in multi-case studies, choosing deliberately contrasting cases makes sense when contrasting results are predicted.

Students and faculty in each of the programs were introduced to the research and invited to participate through email invitations and, in a couple of cases, through classroom visits. Eight BBA students, 10 BCom students, and 11 faculty members participated in the study with 20 in person and nine phone interviews being held between September of 2018 and January 2019. Prior to commencing the interviews, ethical reviews were completed and approved, confidentiality was discussed with participants, and consent forms were signed. Participants could agree or disagree to being quoted and could choose to use their own names or a pseudonym. A semi-structured format was followed which included both structured and unstructured questions. Student interviews were between 60 and 90 minutes, and faculty interviews were approximately 60 minutes in length. Student interviews were designed to gauge how students defined sustainability, how multidimensional they believed it to be, how their understanding of it changed as they progressed throughout their program of study, how motivated they were to engage in behaviors conducive to promoting a sustainable way of being (both in a professional and in a personal context), and what influenced their understanding of the concept and the development of their sustainability mindset. Faculty were also questioned about their understanding of and perspective on sustainability and on how important they believed integrating sustainability into curriculum is, how they may have attempted to do so or why they have not, how they feel about their ability to do so, what their impression is regarding the propensity of students to engage in sustainability-related behaviors, what they believe influences the sustainability mindset of students, and what they believe the impact of integrating sustainability into curriculum is. To increase trustworthiness of findings and enhance the breadth and depth of the study, interview data were triangulated with document analysis and field notes.

A variety of documents, including all BBA and BCom course outlines, were analyzed for the purpose of increasing understanding of the role that sustainability played within the program and individual courses. Notes were made of how often sustainability or associated terminology was included as a course or program learning outcome and how often the term was referenced in content overviews, readings, and assignment instructions. Field notes were used to capture the researcher's observations throughout the study, most specifically, throughout the data collection and the transcribing process. Field notes included reflections on the researcher's personal reactions and potential biases to data being collected and analyzed.

Interview transcripts and data relevant to the specific programs were stored as individual cases within NVivo and within password-protected files. First cycle coding (Saldaña, 2013) was theory generated (Marshall & Rossman, 2016, p. 216) and holistic. As the cyclical process of coding evolved, ideas emerged that had not originally been considered in the review of the literature. In response to these new ideas, additional literature was consulted, which subsequently influenced latter stages of the coding process. Pattern codes were used to further explore themes, relationship, and constructs that assisted in answering the research question (Saldaña, 2013, p. 212). Inductive and comparative analysis strategies were both used during the coding and data analysis process. Data collection and analysis was done on an individual case and on a cross-case basis. Miles and Huberman's (1994) technique of studying patterns and themes on an individual case basis and then comparing the patterns and themes across the cases was implemented. Data and emerging themes were explored in detail, utilizing an approach similar to Glaser and Strauss's (1967) constant comparison method of analysis.

A number of strategies, as recommended by Merriam (1998), Marshall and Rossman (2016), were used to enhance the trustworthiness of findings. (1) Interviews, document analysis, and notes from two different cases combined to provide data that were triangulated. (2) Interview participants were provided with interview transcripts and asked to verify or correct responses and provide additional input as appropriate, serving, as Marshall and Rossman (2016) describe, as member checking. (3) The researcher worked closely with her doctoral supervisor throughout the data collection and analysis process, with the resulting conversations and feedback enhancing the clarity of data interpretation and logic flow. This communication reinforced the trustworthiness of findings by serving as a form of "peer examination: asking colleagues to comment on findings as they emerge" (Merriam, 1998, Chapter 10, section 2, para. 6). (4) At the outset of the study, the researcher was clear on her position within the cases, the basis for the selection of cases, the context of the cases, and assumptions being made. (5) Audit trails, descriptions of how the data were collected, stored, categorized, and analyzed, were maintained. (6) Data collection continued until it was clear that patterns were being repeated and theoretical sufficiency or data saturation had occurred. (7) The researcher remained sensitive to the possibility of ethical dilemmas and to maintaining high ethical standards, following all relevant ethics policies in the process. (8) In consideration of the fact that the researcher is a faculty member within the school being studied and may have had power and influence over students, care was taken to ensure that students did not inadvertently feel obligated to participate. (9) When collecting and analyzing data, vigilance to the fact that the researcher's own biases may have interfered with the process was maintained as an attempt to minimize any negative implications of potential biases.

The methodological framework set the stage for the subsequent exploration and analysis of the case findings which are presented in the following section.

Case Presentation and Analysis

The BBA and BCom programs shared a common learning and teaching model rooted in a social constructivist framework (Hamilton et al., 2013). Both of the programs and all courses within the programs were outcome, cohort, and team-based. Each program maintained unique features and targeted distinct market segments. The BBA program was designed with a specific focus on sustainability, and the concept was embedded in numerous courses. As a degree completion program, domestic students joined the BBA in year three, after completing the first two years of their undergraduate education elsewhere. International students completed years one and two through an RRU pathway specifically tailored for international students and then joined the BBA in their third year. Throughout the 20-month, full-time, on-campus delivery, students progressed through a set curriculum of 21 courses with no elective options. Students enrolled in the BBA program were on average 24 years old and had relatively little work experience. Approximately, 24% came from Canada, and 76% came from elsewhere. On average, cohorts were reported to be 65% male and 35% female.

The focus of the BCom was on entrepreneurial management, but there was also a commitment to "responsible and sustainable business practices" (Royal Roads University, n.d., para. 2). Sustainability issues were introduced in a "Business and Society" course and more specifically addressed in a course called "Environment and Corporate Social Responsibility." There were two delivery modes. In the full-time, on-campus delivery, students completed years three and four of their undergraduate studies within 12 months of accelerated learning. The blended delivery, designed for students who want to continue full-time employment, offered the same content over a 24-month period during which students engaged in a combination of online and residency courses (Royal Roads University, 2014). The curricula were the same across both options with no elective courses available. Students enrolled in the BCom program were on average 31 years old and had at least 2 years of work experience. In most BCom cohorts, well over 90% of the students came from Canada, and approximately 60% were male.

The document analysis revealed that sustainability appeared to be meaningfully embedded in at least 16 of the 21 courses in the BBA program and in five of the 21 courses in the BCom. Faculty participants, including five who taught in the BBA, three who taught in the BCom, and three who taught in both programs expressed strong support for the inclusion of sustainability in business curriculum. Numerous examples were provided of how they had incorporated it into courses they taught. Pedagogical approaches were reported to be, for the most part, similar across the BBA and BCom with the inclusion of live case studies, experiential learning, and the development of critical thinking skills being common threads. The intentional fostering of empathy for nature through direct exposure was noted as a pedagogical approach by two BBA but not by any BCom faculty. While a few faculty from each program specifically noted an environmental bias, with one exception, all faculty recognized sustainability as being multidimensional and having a long-term temporal focus. Findings from the document analysis and faculty interviews supported and triangulated findings from the student interviews that revealed the impact that integration efforts actually had.

Eight BBA students participated in interviews, four who had recently completed their program, two who were in their fourth year, and two who were in their third. Five of the eight BBA participants identified as female, two as male, and one as nonbinary. The age of participants ranged from 20 to 30 with the average age being 24.25. Three participants were from Canada, one was from Mainland China, one from Hong Kong, one from India, one from Chile, and one from the United States.

Ten BCom students participated in the study, seven who had just completed or were nearing the completion of their degree and three were midway through. Three of the seven who had completed or nearly completed were in the on-campus version of the program, while four had completed the blended version. All of the students who were midway through were enrolled in the blended delivery option. Seven of the 10 identified as female and three identified as male. The age of participants ranged from 24 to 52 with the average age being 35. Nine of the 10 participants were from Canada, and the one individual who was not originally from Canada had been in the country for 35 years and was a Canadian citizen.

Changes in Conceptualization of Sustainability

A major theme that emerged from the student interviews was that the manner in which students conceptualized and understood sustainability and their attitudes toward it, and their sustainability-related behaviors, changed over the course of their programs, but the nature of the change was moderated by the conceptualization and attitudes they had upon program entry and by coursework taken.

An overwhelming majority of BBA participants described how it was only throughout the program that they began to understand, in any meaningful way, what sustainability encompassed and that it was multidimensional, including, in addition to an environmental, a social, and economic domain. Comments such as "My mindset or my outlook completely changed by coming to Royal Roads.... I actually never thought about sustainability before taking a course at Royal Roads.... Well, just the environmental concept of it" were typical.

In addition to identifying sustainability as being multidimensional and associating it with environmental, social, and economic concerns, BBA students overwhelmingly rooted their definitions in concern for the future and about living and conducting business in a manner reflecting that concern. References to "future generations," the "longevity of the world," and "living and doing business in manners that do not have consequences for others down the road" reflected this orientation.

Only one BBA participant did not feel that their conceptualization of sustainability had become more multidimensional throughout the program. This participant had come into the program having been exposed to the concept in previous nonbusiness-related studies and already having an understanding of its multidimensionality. The student expressed pleasure in discovering the focus on the "triple bottom line" of people, planet, and profit throughout the program was consistent with conceptualizations introduced in previous studies.

Like BBA students, many BCom students also spoke, either implicitly or explicitly, of having, throughout their program, come to understand sustainability to be a tridimensional concept. References to the triple bottom were common, however, so was an emphasis on the environmental dimension. Comments like "giving back to the earth," minimizing an organization's "carbon footprint," and "tying environmental goals to business goals" represented the environmental orientation. That participants, regardless of coursework taken, unanimously understood sustainability to be closely linked to the environmental domain is a finding that is consistent with other studies (Eagle et al., 2015; Fisher & McAdams, 2015; Kagawa, 2007; Qu et al., 2020; Zeegers & Clark, 2014).

In contrast to BBA students, whose conceptualizations of sustainability seemed firmly rooted in a concern for the future, only one BCom student linked the initial definition they provided to this aspect of the concept. The finding suggests greater exposure to the temporal dimension of sustainability throughout the BBA as compared to the BCom program. As revealed in the document analysis, in the BCom, exposure to sustainability was gained through a limited number of business-focused courses. In the BBA, however, in addition to having sustainability specifically addressed in all business courses, students also studied topics such as ecology and environmental economics. The introduction to disciplinary perspectives extending beyond the business arena likely contributed to the broader and longer term perspective that BBA students appeared to have gained.

In terms of reporting changes in how they conceptualized and understood sustainability throughout the program, BCom as opposed to BBA participants fell into two distinct categories. All participants who were nearing or at program completion and who had therefore taken a sustainability focused course noted that for the most part, they had started with a narrow view of sustainability, but through the program, they had begun to appreciate different dimensions of the concept and also the connection to the business paradigm. In contrast, BCom participants who were only midway through their program and had not taken a sustainability course noted a heightened awareness of some aspects of the environmental pillar but not the social or economic.

That both BBA and BCom participants who had taken sustainability-focused coursework spoke of having developed a more comprehensive perspective as a result of their studies is not surprising and suggests that integrating sustainability into curriculum can broaden students' conceptualization of the term and enhance their sustainability knowledge, a finding that is consistent with research done by others (Briens et al., 2023; Fisher & McAdams, 2015; Qu et al., 2020; Zeegers & Clark, 2014).

Schmitt-Figueiro and Raufflet (2015) noted that various disciplines hold distinct interpretations of what falls under the sustainability umbrella. The triple bottom line perspective on sustainability is typical within the business arena, so it is not surprising that students conceptualized sustainability in a manner consistent with the discipline being studied. That they did so is also consistent with the research done by others such as Biasutti and Frate (2017) and Fisher and McAdams (2015) who, for example, found the nature of coursework taken impacts the manner in which sustainability is conceptualized.

An individual's conceptualization or understanding of sustainability is but one of several factors shaping behavior. For sustainability to influence decision-making, knowledge must be paired with pro-sustainability attitudes. To gain a comprehensive understanding of the impact of integrating sustainability into curriculum, it is therefore important to not only examine students' conceptualizations of sustainability but also their attitudes toward it. This will be the focus of the following section.

Changes in Attitudes

In addition to changes in how they conceptualized sustainability, the majority of students reported that their attitudes toward it had become more positive. For BBA students, there appeared to be little or no connection between the strength or nature of the changes and the length of time the students had been in the program, but for BCom students there was. BCom students who were close to completing their programs and had therefore taken a sustainability-focused course spoke of attitudinal shifts, whereas those who were midway through their programs and had not taken such a course, for the most part, did not. The manner in which sustainability is integrated into the BBA versus the BCom program likely contributed to the differences between the groups. Sustainability was meaningfully embedded across the entire curriculum in the BBA, whereas in the BCom, it was introduced only as a component of a few of the first courses taken but not integrated intensely until toward the end of the program when students took an

Environmental, Corporate, and Social Responsibility course that focused primarily on the topic. BCom students who had not taken the sustainability-focused course were the only ones in the study who did not feel their attitudes toward sustainability had changed or had not changed much. One such student indicated that she thought sustainability had become more important to her over the course of her program, but she was hesitant to link this change directly to her experience in the program. Another such student spoke of shifts that were limited to attitudes around recycling, and another was clear that no attitudinal shifts had occurred.

Although research on how students' sustainability attitudes change over the course of their education appears to be limited, there are studies that offer some basis of comparison. Cordano et al. (2003), Fisher and McAdams (2015), Hay and Eagle (2020), and Zsóka and Ásványi (2023), for example, all found that education specific to sustainability affects attitudinal positions in a positive manner. Findings from both the BBA and BCom cases support these conclusions. Moreover, research done by Sutton and Gyuris (2015) found that in the absence of sustainability-related coursework, the differences between the sustainability attitudes of first- and third-year students were "small and patchy" (p. 30). Similarly, the BCom students who were midway through their programs and had not taken a sustainability-focused course experienced what may be considered "small and patchy" attitudinal changes.

In considering the nature of attitudinal changes, it is interesting to note that both BBA and BCom students who came into the program with strong pro-sustainability attitudes spoke not necessarily of having developed much stronger sustainability orientations but rather of having developed an additional appreciation for the business perspective and particularly for the triple bottom line approach to sustainability. While developing stronger attitudes toward the importance of balancing environmental, social, and economic concerns within the business context could be considered positive, as noted previously, concerns that this approach represents a shallow form of sustainability suggests caution should be exercised in doing so.

Many sustainability advocates contend that the purpose of integrating sustainability into curriculum is to contribute to the development of individuals who can lead the kind of systemic changes necessary to build a sustainable future. Critical to this, many believe, is the ability to challenge the status quo and dominant paradigms (Lengyel et al., 2019; Piasentin & Roberts, 2018; Tilbury, 2009). Although the attitudinal changes experienced by BBA and BCom students could certainly be considered positive, some of the attitudes expressed prompt queries regarding whether the integration of sustainability into either program has contributed in this manner. For example, when participants were asked about prioritizing the protection of the environment versus economic development and growth, the ethics of growth and the capitalist system upon which growth is based was questioned by only a few, with the essence of capitalism being questioned in a serious manner by only one. Moreover, when asked whether or not they felt that radical change is necessary to combat climate change, the majority of BComs as well as a number of BBAs did not think it was. Given this is contradictory to the consensus of experts who increasingly agree that it is (UN, n.d.), this again raises questions about whether attitudinal changes, although positive, are sufficient to redress the unsustainability of current economic systems. Concerns regarding whether or not integration was serving to reinforce complicity in a broken system versus contributing to paradigmatic shifts necessary to reimagine that system remain. Similar concerns were evident when participants shared what they were doing in the interest of sustainability, and/or how they have changed their behaviors to align with their attitudes toward it. This will be the focus of the following section.

Changes in Sustainability-Related Behavior

Participants from both the BBA and the BCom program noted that throughout their studies, taking action in the interest of sustainability had become more important to them. There were many similarities between the groups in terms of what they themselves reported doing and what they thought individuals and businesses could do. Behaviors related to what could be considered conscious consumerism were the most commonly reported behaviors among BBA students and the second most commonly reported behaviors among BComs. Seven of the eight BBAs and half of the BComs noted they had become more intentional around purchase decisions and were doing things such as buying organic, ethically and locally made, eco-friendly products. In addition to giving more consideration to the social and environmental impacts of the products they were purchasing, half of the BBA participants and nearly half of the BComs (4/10) spoke of being more attuned to how much they were buying and to trying to buy less as the nature of consumerism itself was considered to be contributing to sustainability issues.

The most prevalent behavioral change mentioned by BComs was related to waste management with nine of the 10 BCom participants sharing efforts they were making to compost, recycle, and minimize waste. An overwhelming majority of the BBAs (6/8) also noted an increase in waste management efforts with this being the second most frequently mentioned sustainability behavior among this group. Making more sustainable transportation choices (cycling, walking, car-pooling) was mentioned by seven of the 10 BComs and half of the BBAs, and attempting to influence the sustainability thinking and behavior of others by taking a leadership role on related issues was mentioned by half of the BBAs and three BComs. Making a concerted effort to conserve energy was also noted by a number of BBAs and by one BCom, although the BCom mentioned it as something others could do rather than as something they were doing themselves. A number of BComs also mentioned that becoming more educated about related issues was something others could do but, interestingly, not as something they themselves were doing.

Behavioral changes being taken in the interest of sustainability that were noted by individual BBA students included spending time in nature and taking significant political action including participating in protests. Individual BComs noted making general efforts to be a better person and volunteering for related causes.

The major themes that arose when both BBA and BCom students spoke of what businesses could do in the interest of sustainability were related to embedding it into both the operations and culture of the organization. Including it as part of the vision, mission, and financial reporting structure; improving waste management; ensuring a sustainable supply chain; educating employees and consumers; incentivizing employees to make sustainable choices; providing work at home options; constructing green buildings; giving back to the community; and paying fair wages were all mentioned.

Turning to the literature to compare findings, it becomes evident that much of the literature supports the positive impact that integrating sustainability was found, in this study, to have on associated behavior. Research by Agu et al. (2022) and Zsóka and Ásványi (2023), found, for example, that students who had taken sustainability-related courses, like the BBA and BCom students in this study, were more likely to take it into consideration when making purchase decisions. Similarly, research by Zsóka and Ásványi (2023), Collado et al. (2022), and Cole et al. (2019) found a positive impact on waste management practices as did this research. Eagle et al. (2015), Kagawa (2007), and Rodríguez-Barreiroa et al. (2013), on the other hand, found that the integration of sustainability had a relatively low impact on conscious consumerism, a finding that appears contradictory to those from other studies.

Research done by Saleem et al. (2023) and Wang et al. (2022) may be used to help illuminate the mixed results. Saleem et al. found that the teaching approach significantly influenced knowledge, attitudes, and behavior. Holistic, pluralistic, and active learning approaches were found to have more pronounced effects than traditional lecture-based learning. Similarly, Wang et al. as well as Martínez Casanovas et al. (2022) found that real-world projects, case studies, and problem-based learning all contributed to positive change. Moreover, Briens et al. (2023) found that the number of courses taken was linked to the impact of integration efforts, with a minimum of three sustainability-infused courses being associated with the achievement of more significant learning and behavioral outcomes. It could be that in studies that found the integration of sustainability had little impact on behavior, the method or level of integration the students had been exposed to was not effectively conducive to motivating behavioral change.

In reflecting upon the behavioral changes that both BBA and BCom participants noted, it is worthwhile to point out that the sustainability actions that students purported to engage in and advocate for were, for the most part, related to the environmental domain. Moreover, most of the behaviors would be considered "light green" or reformist as opposed to "dark green" or radical in nature (Kagawa, 2007). Choosing more sustainable products and transportation options, being more cognizant of waste management practices, and conserving energy, for example, would all be considered what has been referred to as "feel good" or light green sustainability. A "feel good" sustainability stance, considered to be indicative of a "weaker or shallower" sustainability perspective, is characterized by actions which, although positive, do not address the underlying or root causes of the issue (Wals & Heymann, 2004).

While questioning what they buy would be considered a light green or a shallower sustainability response, questioning consumption itself, as many participants in this study did, would be considered a darker green or stronger stance (Selby & Kagawa, 2018). Stronger sustainability stances have been characterized as encompassing dematerialization and challenging both the status quo and the underlying economic systems upon which it relies (Loiseau et al., 2016). As such, the finding that many participants were buying less because of concerns that consumerism itself was contributing to sustainability challenges seems to point to the adoption of at least some aspects of a stronger sustainability positioning.

Although relatively little research on the impact of integrating sustainability appears to comment on the adoption of strong versus weak sustainability stances, the research itself seems to point to the adoption of weak stances as being more prevalent. Zsóka and Ásványi (2023), Eagle et al. (2015), and Kagawa (2007), for example, found that students reported taking actions that required minor lifestyle changes, characterized by things such as turning off lights and purchasing environmentally friendly products.

It is interesting to note that findings from the literature review revealed that few studies appear to have asked questions that would lend themselves to discovering or probing about deeper sustainability stances. For example, Haski-Leventhal and Manefield's (2018) survey of students attending Principles for Responsible Management Education (PRME) signatory schools asked about engagement in an array of sustainability-related behaviors, the majority of which would be considered light green or reformatory in nature. Research done by Al-Nuaimi and Al-Ghamdi (2022), Heeren et al. (2016), Rodríguez-Barreiro et al. (2013), and Zsóka et al. (2013) was similar in nature, in that they all asked only about specific light green sustainability actions. Similarly, Avelar and Farina's (2022) recently developed scale to measure student's self-reported sustainability behaviors appears to include nothing that would shed light on the propensity to go beyond reformatory responses. The scale, for example, includes questions on whether students give thought to companies' records in terms of achieving sustainable development goals, if they talk to classmates about environment issues, and if they take sustainability into consideration when making purchase decisions. There are no questions that would provide insight on the likelihood of students to take actions in support of deeper or dark green sustainability such as dematerializing or advocating for alternative economic systems. In sum, studies asking about deeper, more radical sustainability actions are scant, so it is difficult to compare the BBA and BCom's propensity in this regard to that of others.

It is noteworthy that the few comments that did reflect a more radical sustainability stance came primarily from BBA as opposed to BCom participants. Individual BBA participants, for example, referred to a need to "move away from the Western style of living," "have a complete change of thinking and goals," and "take radical political action to influence change." Although, as previously mentioned, a number of BCom students commented on efforts they were taking to shop and consume less, this was the extent of comments from this group reflective of stronger sustainability actions. Given the sustainability focus of the BBA, this difference is perhaps not surprising as it is likely that within the BBA, there would be more opportunities to introduce a stronger sustainability narrative and to extend discussions beyond conventional to more radical or transformational paradigms.

Comments from the BBA and BComs regarding what businesses could do in the interest of sustainability were, like the majority of comments regarding what individuals could do, primarily reflective of a reformist rather than a radical paradigm. Actions suggested such as enhancing the sustainability of internal operations and supply chains, offering consumers more sustainable options, and paying fair wages collectively have the potential to reduce the degradation of the environment and improve social conditions for some. These would, however, be considered "shallower pathways", i.e., pathways that contribute to green growth but also to the perpetuation of economic system and power structures that are part of the problem (Luederitz et al., 2017).

In spite of the finding that changes in sustainability orientation among BBA and BCom students were predominantly reformist in nature, the fact that an overwhelming majority spoke of having developed much more positive orientations over the course of their programs is encouraging. This speaks well to the potential of integrating sustainability into curriculum. Recognizing, however, that the curriculum may have been but one influencing factor, participants were also asked about other factors that contributed to their sustainability thinking and to the shifts experienced. Related findings will be discussed next.

Influences on Changes in Sustainability Related Knowledge, Attitudes, and Behaviors

Institutional and Community Commitment

A number of interlinking variables, both within and outside of the formal curricula, were identified as having influenced sustainability orientations. Every BBA participant and seven of 10 BComs mentioned the attitude and practices of the RRU and local community with several BBAs highlighting this first. Participants from both programs spoke of the significance of community recycling efforts and campus initiatives such as the collection of rainwater for use in washrooms and the use of compostable utensils. The impact of being surrounded by likeminded individuals who valued sustainability was notable. As summed up by one participant, "just living here" had an impact on sustainability orientations.

Hopkinson et al. (2008) described the culture reflected through sustainability initiatives as being the "campus curriculum" (p. 436). Winter and Cotton (2012) similarly referred to the "hidden curriculum" as "the implicit messages a university sends about sustainability through the institutional environment and values" (p. 753). Both argued that messages being transmitted through the organizational culture have the potential to significantly alter sustainability orientations. Comments from BBA and BCom participants about the significant impact these things had on their sustainability orientations definitely support this stance. The findings also support work done by Turner et al. (2022) and Erskine and Johnson (2012). Both researchers found that institutional sustainability practices had a significant impact on sustainability learning with Turner et al.'s finding that students felt they had learned more about sustainability through "campus initiatives" than through formal coursework.

While, collectively, BBA and BCom students provided a number of examples of campus sustainability initiatives related to the environmental domain, it is worthwhile to note that none related to the social or economic domain were mentioned. Winter and Cotton (2012) found a similar environmental bias in campus initiatives identified by students. The students in their study, however, unlike the vast majority of the BBA and BCom participants, questioned their university's commitment to sustainability and thought they should be doing much more. Similarly, students in Høgdal et al.'s (2019), research on responsible management education, felt the messages regarding sustainability being sent through the institution's hidden curriculum contradicted and devalued those of the formal curriculum. The finding that BBA and BComs were adamant that the attitudes and practices of the university community had been supportive of the sustainability message being communicated in the curriculum obviously differs from the findings of Winter and Cotton and Høgdal et al.

Place

In addition to the attitudes and practices of the university and local community, the physical beauty of the campus environment and its connection to nature was unanimously mentioned by BBA students as having been influential. BBAs spoke enthusiastically about how the old growth forests upon which the campus sits and the beauty of the surrounding mountains and ocean served to have an over-whelmingly positive effect on sustainability orientations. Referring to campus wildlife, to the creeks, to the trails, and even to specific trees was common among this group. In contrast, although the campus environment was mentioned as being influential by three BCom students, they spoke much less adamantly and provided less detail about the connection. Various factors likely played a role in terms of both the difference in the type and number of comments made in this regard.

BBA participants were all enrolled in a full-time on-campus program. BCom participants, on the other hand, were a mix of students enrolled in a full-time, on-campus program and a part-time blended program. The part-time program's blended delivery was inclusive of online courses and three relatively short residency periods. While only one of the seven BCom students enrolled in the blended delivery mentioned the impact of the campus's natural environment, all of the full-time on-campus BCom students, like all of the full-time on-campus BBA students, did. Considering the much longer time spent on campus by the fulltime students, it makes sense that they would be more influenced by the campus environment. This does not, however, explain the difference between the groups in terms of kind of comments about the natural environment made but other factors may.

As previously mentioned, an effort was made in the BBA program to expose students to nature throughout the curriculum. Coursework included classes held in the forest and in creek beds. During these classes, students were provided with opportunities to reflect on things such as the economic value of cutting down old growth trees versus the ecological impact of doing so as well as on the impact that business activities might have on various life-forms in and surrounding the creek beds. Such exposure to place-based learning may very well have contributed to the connection to the ecological environment that seemed to have developed among BBAs which in turn contributed to the association made between the natural environment and changes in their sustainability orientations.

The impact that place-based learning and specifically place in nature can have on sustainability orientations has, in fact, been supported throughout the literature (Gramatakos & Lavau, 2019; Orr, 1992; Selby & Kagawa, 2018). As Selby (2017) argued "we only stir ourselves to protect what we have come to love, and thus cultivating a sense of oneness with nature is vital if we are to have any chance of transforming the global environmental condition" (p. 9).

Integration Approach

In addition to the BBAs unanimity regarding the influence of the campus's natural environment and the attitude and practices of the community, there was also unanimity among this group that coursework had been impactful. Although different courses were discussed by different participants, most emphasized that it was having sustainability woven through all of the courses and seeing it from different perspectives that had made a significant difference. Many were explicit in noting that they did not think the impact would have been as great had this not been the case. This finding adds support to many who argue for mainstreaming sustainability across the curriculum and positioning it as a holistic paradigm relevant across disciplines and contexts (Blasco, 2012; Hueske & Aggestam Pontoppidan, 2020; Michel, 2020; Sterling, 2004).

In contrast to the BBAs who thought the totality of coursework had influenced their sustainability orientations, BComs highlighted a limited number of courses that had. All but one of the BComs who were nearing program completion and had therefor taken the Environmental, Social, and Corporate Responsibility (ESCR) course highlighted the significant impact it had had in altering their sustainability perspectives. They were, however, careful to point out that it was not this course alone. A Business in Society course, which they undertook at the beginning of the program, had introduced the concept and initiated a critical thinking process that fostered an appreciation for sustainability. Additionally, a Foundational Business Skills course, taken in the first term, included a practical case focused on recycling, which they noted, further set the stage for a sustainability orientation.

While the combined effect of various curriculum components appeared instrumental in promoting a mindset receptive to the content covered in ECSR, it was the ECSR course that students spoke of as having had the most effect. The fact that all of the students who had taken ECSR thought their sustainability orientations had changed significantly throughout the program but those who had not taken the course did not report similar changes speaks again to the impact it had. The focus of sustainability in the ECSR course, complemented by the introduction and peripheral coverage of related content in a few other courses, seemed to contribute significantly to positive changes in sustainability orientations. Overall, case findings point to the importance of a well-rounded approach to sustainability education, inclusive of at least one focused course but complemented by the integration of sustainability content in other courses throughout the program.

The finding that both BCom and BBA students attributed changes in sustainability orientations to coverage in a number of courses supports researchers such as Briens et al. (2023), Blasco (2012), Hueske and Aggestam Pontoppidan (2020), Michel (2020), and Sterling (2004), all of whom advocate that coverage of sustainability across the curriculum is important and most effective. The finding that BCom students who had not taken the sustainability-focused course but had taken other courses with sustainability content included seems to speak to the importance of at least one focused course. This finding also seems to support research by Briens et al. (2023) which revealed that a minimum of three sustainability-related courses was required to impact sustainability orientations.

Combined, the BBA and BCom case findings support scholars who advocates for coverage of sustainability across the curriculum. Findings also, however, suggest that while coverage in every course appears unnecessary, the incorporation of at least one sustainability focused course is. Additional research would be necessary to further confirm.

Faculty Support

As students in both programs spoke about their coursework, most of the BBAs and six of 10 BComs also spoke about the faculty's passion, enthusiasm, credibility, and facilitation skills. While numerous sources have identified faculty support as an important component in terms of integrating sustainability into curriculum (Avelar & Farina, 2022; Koljatic & Silva, 2015), the impact of faculty attitudes and quality of teaching is sparse (Koljatic & Silva, 2015). These factors have been considered by some, such as Blasco (2012), to be part of the hidden curriculum. As Blasco points out, if there are inconsistencies between "subtext communicated among school actors" (p. 366) and the formal curriculum, students are not likely to apply what they learn or take it to heart. Based on BBA and BCom case findings, it appears that the subtle messages communicated by faculty supported the formal curriculum and in doing so helped participants take what they were learning about sustainability to heart.

Pedagogical Approach

In discussing their course work, BBA and BCom participants also highlighted pedagogical approaches they thought were particularly impactful on sustainability orientations. Participants from both programs noted experiential learning through live cases. As participants described the cases, it became evident that they had involved using the campus in a manner that has been referred to throughout the literature (Pretorius et al., 2019; Zen, 2017) as well as by a faculty member in the study, as a living lab. Working on campus recycling plans with the sustainability office and on commuter challenges where they calculated carbon costs of various transportation options and developed plans to reduce cars on campus were some examples. The findings of the study are consistent with findings from the literature that have shown that using the campus in this manner contributes positively to sustainability learning (Martínez Casanovas et al., 2022; Pretorius et al., 2019; Zen, 2017).

Class discussions of real-world cases and hearing from faculty about their own real-world experiences were also mentioned as having had a positive impact. Case studies had helped to position sustainability as a legitimate business issue and enhance students' appreciation of the organizational impact of various interrelated issues. This finding supports the many advocates of case study learning who position it as an effective approach to sustainability education (Erskine & Johnson, 2012; Martínez Casanovas et al., 2022; Molderez & Fonseca, 2018; Zeegers & Clark, 2014).

A significant number of BBA students also mentioned internship experiences as well as an exercise where they calculated the carbon footprint of various behavioral choices and the class activities they had done in the forest that were previously discussed as all having contributed to their sustainability perspectives. These findings again supported research done by others who also found active learning and pedagogical approaches integrating real-world learning conducive to impactful sustainability learning (Bertossi & Marangon, 2022; Martínez Casanovas et al., 2022; Molderez & Fonseca, 2018; Pretorius et al., 2019; Zen, 2017).

Cocurricular Opportunities

Apart from factors related to the formal and informal or hidden curriculum, half of the BBAs and a few of the BComs mentioned extra or cocurricular activities such as a design thinking challenge that had also supported their sustainability thinking. When they spoke of these activities, they did not, however, speak of them as being particularly impactful but rather as having reinforced what they were learning through the curriculum. On the surface, this appears somewhat contradictory to research done by others. For example, Gramatakos and Lavau (2019) argue that such experiences play a more important role than previously recognized. Moreover, Caldana et al. (2023) found that students engaging in extracurricular activities showed higher levels of a number of sustainability-related competencies than students not engaging in such activities. In consideration of the findings of others that support the value that such activities can have on sustainability learning (Caldana et al.; Hopkinson et al., 2008), it seems there may be opportunities for a more intentional integration of extracurricular activities in the BBA and BCom programs.

Student's Sustainability Orientation Upon Program Entry

Apart from the factors explicitly mentioned by BBA and BCom participants as having influenced the manner in which their sustainability perspectives changed throughout their programs, their orientation toward the concept at program entry also appeared to have had an impact. Participants who felt they had started the program with fairly strong orientations toward the concept did not feel their orientations had changed significantly. They did, however, share that they had developed a more comprehensive understanding of the topic and the interrelatedness of different dimensions. More specifically, they had gained a greater appreciation for the economic pillar and the role that sustainability plays within the business context. They spoke of their preprogram perspectives being influenced by family, community, media, exposure to news, and time spent in nature.

The students who came into the programs being ambivalent to sustainability attributed their initial ambivalence to indifference among their families, communities, educational institutions, and work environments. All of these students felt that the impact of experiences they had throughout the program served to transform their sustainability perspectives. The transformational nature of the changes they spoke of contrasted significantly with the moderate changes spoken of by students who started the program already having pro-sustainability orientations.

The finding that students in this study were diverse in terms of their orientations toward sustainability at the start of their programs is consistent with those of other scholars who have found that individual sustainability perspectives vary in business school populations specifically (Lambrechts et al., 2018; Ng & Burke, 2010; Sharma & Kelly, 2014) as well as in postsecondary populations in general (Sidiropoulos, 2018; Sundermann & Fischer, 2019). The finding that the student's sustainability orientation at program outset (part of their personal context) seemed to have moderated the impact that integrating sustainability had, is moreover, also consistent with findings from others (Sidiropoulos, 2018).

Researchers have argued that because of the diversity of sustainability perspectives among student populations, a combination of pedagogical approaches is appropriate to effectively address and appeal to this diversity (Lambrechts et al., 2018; Sidiropoulos, 2018). Although it was not apparent in this study if different pedagogies impacted individual students in different ways, it was apparent that a variety of pedagogies had been used in each program. It was also apparent that the cumulative impact was positive. This was the case regardless of the orientation toward sustainability at the program outset, a finding that lends support to scholars who advocate for using a variety of teaching approaches.

Discovering that integrating sustainability into curriculum in these cases helped students to broaden their understanding of the concept, develop more positive attitudes toward it, and strengthen related behavior is encouraging and speaks to the benefits of education for sustainability. Moreover, the finding that other variables also influenced shifts in sustainability orientations underscores the significance of considering context and adopting a holistic approach. However, evidence that the sustainability orientations embraced may have been grounded in shallow or weak conceptualizations raises questions regarding the conceptualizations that underpinned integration efforts and suggests opportunities to integrate stronger forms of sustainability so as to contribute to even greater paradigm shifts. Reflecting on the examined cases, the findings obtained, and on the intricate dynamics of maximizing the impact of sustainability integration in business education, the following conclusions and recommendations are proposed.

Conclusions and Recommendations

This study sought to examine how integrating sustainability into two distinct business programs impacted students' sustainability orientations. The cases were purposefully selected as each program had a unique approach to integration, and as such, the impact of alternative approaches could be compared. In addition to exploring the impact of integrating sustainability into curricula, the study also explored other factors affecting sustainability orientations. It is unique both in its comparative nature and in the exploration of the diverse contextual factors influencing sustainability orientations.

A number of interrelated variables combined to affect sustainability orientations. To maximize the impact of integrating sustainability into curriculum, none of those variables should be overlooked. A holistic and integrated approach is called for. Four key recommendations flow from the findings.

Recommendations for Practitioners

- *Greater Integration for Maximum Impact*: To respond effectively to the global call for change, business schools should aim for comprehensive sustainability integration across various curricular courses. A dedicated sustainability-specific course in the early stages of business programs can set the stage for developing a deeper understanding of the concepts' interrelatedness to conventional management topics. Careful consideration of the underlying conceptualization of sustainability in all integration efforts is crucial.
- *Move Beyond a Disciplinary Conceptualization*: Introduce students to varied sustainability perspectives and encourage challenges to the predominant business paradigm. Incorporating critical theory and exploring diverse perspectives, including Indigenous and nonhuman viewpoints, would help, for example, foster deeper sustainability dialogue.
- *Powerful Pedagogies*: Utilize pedagogies that facilitate meaningful engagement with real-world sustainability issues, such as experiential, problem, and case-based learning. Adopt approaches that promote a connection to place and to the ecological world such as using the campus as a living laboratory.
- *Attention to Context and Institutional Commitment*: Create a supportive institutional culture that reinforces sustainability principles both in formal curricula and hidden curriculums. Incorporate a positive sustainability agenda within the institution and transparently demonstrate efforts in social, economic, and environmental sustainability. Provide opportunities for students to actively participate in and contribute to these initiatives as part of the formal and informal curricula.

Implications for Future Research

To build on the findings of this study, future research should explore sustainability integration beyond a single institution, encompassing diverse programs and universities. Comparative studies examining the holistic impact of the entire university experience on sustainability orientations would be beneficial. Longitudinal research tracking alumni over time can also provide insights into long-term effects. Further investigation into approaches that prepare students as transformative change agents within the business domain and the impact of introducing stronger sustainability perspectives is also necessary.

Conclusions

The study highlights that greater integration of sustainability can contribute to greater impact on sustainability orientations. However, it also underscores that sustainability orientations remained rooted in dominant paradigms. Considering the ever-increasing urgency to deal with the sustainability crisis, one must question if, by perpetuating this paradigm, business schools are contributing to sustaining the unsustainable. The need to transcend traditional disciplinary conceptualizations of sustainability and embrace alternative viewpoints seems evident. Pedagogical approaches that encourage deeper and more radical perspectives contribute to this process. The campus community's role in fostering sustainability values and supporting holistic learning is also crucial. Ultimately, the study advocates for a comprehensive approach that challenges existing business paradigms and fosters a collective responsibility toward sustainability.

References

Agu, A. G., Etuk, S. G., & Madichie, N. O. (2022). Exploring the role of sustainability-oriented marketing education in promoting consciousness for sustainable consumption. *Sustainability*, *14*(13), 8077. https://doi.org/10.3390/su14138077

Al-Nuaimi, S. R., & Al-Ghamdi, S. G. (2022). Assessment of knowledge, attitude and practice towards sustainability aspects among higher education students in Qatar. *Sustainability*, *14*(20), 13149. https://doi.org/10.3390/su142013149

Avelar, A. B. A., & Farina, M. C. (2022). The relationship between the incorporation of sustainability in higher education and the student's behavior: Self-reported sustainable behavior scale. *International Journal of Sustainability in Higher Education*, *23*(7), 1749–1767. https://doi.org/10.1108/IJSHE-07-2021-0260

Badea, L., Şerban-Oprescu, G. L., Dedu, S., & Piroşcă, G. I. (2020). The impact of education for sustainable development on Romanian economics and business students' behavior. *Sustainability*, *12*(19), 8169. https://doi.org/10.3390/su12198169

Barber, F., Wilson, F., Venkatachalam, V., Cleaves, S., & Garnham, J. (2014). Integrating sustainability into business curricula: University of New Hampshire case study. *International Journal of Sustainability in Higher Education*, *15*(4), 431–449. https://doi.org/10.1108/IJSHE-01-2103-0008

Bertossi, A., & Marangon, F. (2022). A literature review on the strategies implemented by higher education institutions from 2010 to 2020 to foster pro-environmental behavior of students. *International Journal of Sustainability in Higher Education, 23*(3), 522–547. https://doi.org/10.1108/IJSHE-11-2020-0459

Biasutti, M., & Frate, S. (2017). A validity and reliability study of the attitudes toward sustainable development scale. *Environmental Education Research, 23*(2), 214–230. https://doi.org/10.1080/13504622.2016.114666

Birdman, J., Redman, A., & Lang, D. J. (2021). Pushing the boundaries: Experience-based learning in early phases of graduate sustainability curricula. *International Journal of Sustainability in Higher Education, 22*(2), 237–253. https://doi.org/10.1108/IJSHE-08-2019-0242

Blasco, M. (2012). Aligning the hidden curriculum of management education with PRME: An inquiry-based framework. *Journal of Management Education, 36*(3), 364–388. https://doi.org/10.1177/1052562911420213

Breyer, Y. (2019). *Aligning business education with industry expectations on employability and sustainability, final report, 2019.* Australian Government, Department of Education and Training. https://ltr.edu.au/resources/SD15-5133_Breyer_FinalReport_2019.pdf

Briens, E. C. M., Chiu, Y., Braun, D., Verma, P., Fiegel, G., Pompeii, B., & Singh, K. (2023). Assessing sustainability knowledge for undergraduate students in different academic programs and settings. *International Journal of Sustainability in Higher Education, 24*(1), 69–95. https://doi.org/10.1108/IJSHE-10-2021-0455

Brueckner, M., Spencer, R., & Paull, M. (2018). Teaching for tomorrow: Preparing responsible citizens. In M. Brueckner, R. Spencer, & M. Paull (Eds.), *Disciplining the undisciplined? CSR, sustainability, ethics and governance* (pp. 1–18). Springer. https://doi:10.1007/978-3-319-71449-3

Brunstein, J., Brunnquell, C., & Jacob Perera, L. C. (2020). Sustainability in finance teaching: Evaluating levels of reflection and transformative learning. *Social Responsibility Journal, 16*(2), 179–197. https://doi.org/10.1108/SRJ-07-2018-0164g

Caldana, A. C. F., Eustachio, J. H. P. P., Lespinasse Sampaio, B., Gianotto, M. L., Talarico, A. C., & Batalhão, A. C. D. S. (2023). A hybrid approach to sustainable development competencies: The role of formal, informal and non-formal learning experiences. *International Journal of Sustainability in Higher Education, 24*(2), 235–258. https://doi.org/10.1108/IJSHE-10-2020-0420

Cole, L. B., Quinn, J., Ktruk, A., & Johson, B. (2019). Promoting green building literacy through online laboratory experiences. *International Journal of Sustainability in Higher Education, 20*(2), 264–287. https://doi.org/10.1108/IJSHE-09-2018-0149

Collado, S., Moreno, J. D., & Martín-Albo, J. (2022). Innovation for environmental sustainability: Longitudinal effects of an education for sustainable development intervention on university students' pro-environmentalism. *International Journal of Sustainability in Higher Education, 23*(6), 1277–1293. https://doi.org/10.1108/IJSHE-07-2021-0315

Cordano, M., Ellis, K., & Scherer, R. (2003). Natural capitalists: Increasing business students' environmental sensitivity. *Journal of Management Education, 27*(2), 144–157. https://doi.org/10.1177/1052562903251417

Cullen, J. (2017). Educating business students about sustainability: A bibliometric review of current trends and research needs. *Journal of Business Ethics, 145*, 429–439. https://doi.org/10.1007/s10551-015-2838-3

Dziubaniuk, O., & Nyholm, M. (2021). Constructivist approach in teaching sustainability and business ethics: A case study. *International Journal of Sustainability in Higher Education, 22*(1), 177–197. https://doi.org/10.1108/IJSHE-02-2020-0081

Eagle, L., Low, D., Case, P., & Vandommele, L. (2015). Attitudes of undergraduate business students toward sustainability issues. *International Journal of Sustainability in Higher Education, 16*(5), 650–668. https://doi.org/10.1108/IJSHE-04-2014-0054

Erskine, L., & Johnson, S. (2012). Effective learning approaches for sustainability: A student perspective. *The Journal of Education for Business, 87*, 198–205. https://doi.org/10.1080/08832323.2011.590162

Filho, W., Shiel, C., Paço, A., Mifsud, M., Ávila, L., Brandli, L., Molhhan-Hill, P., Pace, P., Azeiteiro, U., Vargas, V., & Caeiro, S. (2019). Sustainable development goals and sustainability teaching at universities: Falling behind or getting ahead of the pack? *Journal of Cleaner Production, 232*, 285–294. https://doi.org/10.1016/j.jclepro.2019.05.309

Fisher, B., & McAdams, E. (2015). Gaps in sustainability education: The impact of higher education coursework on perceptions of sustainability. *International Journal of Sustainability in Higher Education, 16*(4), 407–423. https://doi.org/10.1108/IJSHE-08-2013-0106

Ghoshal, S. (2005). Bad management theories are destroying good management practices. *The Academy of Management Learning and Education, 4*, 75–91.

Glaser, B., & Strauss, A. (1967). *The discovery of grounded theory*. Aldine.

Gramatakos, A. L., & Lavau, S. (2019). Informal learning for sustainability in higher education institutions. *International Journal of Sustainability in Higher Education, 20*(2), 378–392. https://doi.org/10.1108/IJSHE-10-2018-0177

Guardian Staff and Agency. (2023, July 7). UN says climate change 'out of control' after likley hottest week on record. *The Guardian*; online edition. https://www.theguardian.com/environment/2023/jul/07/un-climate-change-hottest-week-world

Gupta, A., Raghunath, A., Gula, L., Rheinbay, L., & Hart, M. (2019, September). *The United Nations Global compact-accenture CEO study on sustainability 2019. The decade to deliver. A call to business action*. https://www.accenture.com/_acnmedia/pdf-109/accenture-ungc-ceo-study.pdf

Hamilton, D., Marquez, P., & Gupta, N. (2013). *The RRU learning and teaching model*. http://media.royalroads.ca/media/marketing/viewbooks/2013/learning-model/index.html#p=4

Haski-Leventhal, D., & Manefield, S. (2018). *The state of CSR and RME in business schools: The students' voice, fourth biennial survey*. https://www.unprme.org/resource-docs/PRMESurvey2018FINAL.pdf

Hay, R., & Eagle, L. (2020). Impact of integrated sustainability content into undergraduate business education. *International Journal of Sustainability in Higher Education, 21*(1), 131–143. https://doi:10.1108/IJSHE-05-2019-0174

Heeren, A. J., Singh, A. S., Zwickle, A., Koontz, T. M., Slagle, K. M., & McCreery, A. C. (2016). Is sustainability knowledge half the battle? An examination of sustainability knowledge, attitudes, norms, and efficacy to understand sustainable behaviours. *International Journal of Sustainability in Higher Education, 17*(5), 613–632. https://doi.org/10.1108/IJSHE-02-2015-0014

Høgdal, C., Rasche, A., Schoeneborn, D., & Scotti, L. (2019, June). Exploring student perceptions of the hidden curriculum in responsible management education. *Journal of Business Ethics*, 1–21. https://doi.org/10.1007/s10551-019-04221-9

Hopkinson, P., Hughes, P., & Layer, G. (2008). Sustainable graduates: Linking formal, informal and campus curricula to embed education for sustainable development in the student learning experience. *Environmental Education Research*, *14*(4), 435–454. https://doi.org/10.1080/13504620802283100

Hueske, A. K., & Aggestam Pontoppidan, C. (2020). GEROCO: A model for integrating sustainability in management education at HEIs. In E. Sengupta, P. Blessinger, & C. Mahoney (Eds.), *Leadership and strategies: International perspectives on civil society and social responsibility in higher education. Innovations in higher education teaching and learning* (Vol. 24, pp. 93–109). Emerald Publishing Limited. https://doi.org/10.1108/S2055-364120200000024009 (pp. 1–18).

Hughes, U. M., Upadhyaya, S., & Houston, R. (2018). Educating future corporate managers for a sustainable world: Recommendations for a paradigm shift in business education. *On the Horizon, 26*(3), 194–205. https://doi.org/10.1108/OTH-01-2018-0007

Jun, H., & Moon, S. (2021). An analysis of sustainability integration in business school curricula: Evidence from Korea. *Sustainability, 13*, 2779. https://doi.org/10.3390/su13052779

Kagawa, F. (2007). Dissonance in students' perceptions of sustainable development and sustainability: Implications for curriculum change. *International Journal of Sustainability in Higher Education, 8*(3), 317–338. https://doi.org/10.1108/14676370710817174

Kanashiro, P., Iizuka, E. S., Sousa, C., & Dias, S. E. F. R. R. (2020). Sustainability in management education: a biggs' 3p model application. *International Journal of Sustainability in Higher Education, 21*(4), 671–684. https://doi.org/10.1108/IJSHE-05-2019-0176

Kinzer, K. (2021). Integrating professional sustainability literacy into the master of public administration curriculum. *International Journal of Sustainability in Higher Education, V22*(5), 982–1001. https://doi.org/10.1108/IJSHE-07-2020-0266

Koljatic, M., & Silva, M. (2015). Do business schools influence students' awareness of social issues? Evidence from two of Chile's leading MBA programs. *Journal of Business Ethics, 131*(3), 595–604. https://doi.org/10.1007/s10551-014-2295-4

Kopnina, H., & Meijers, F. (2014). Education for sustainable development (ESD). *International Journal of Sustainability in Higher Education, 15*(2), 188–207. https://doi.org/10.1108/IJSHE-07-2012-0059

Lambrechts, W., Ghijsen, P., Jacques, A., Walravens, H., Van Liedekerke, L., & Van Petegem, P. (2018). Sustainability segmentation of business students: Toward self-regulated development of critical and interpretational competences in a post-truth era. *Journal of Cleaner Production, 202*, 561–570.

Lengyel, A., Szoke, S., Kovacs, S., David, L., Bacsne- Baba, E., & Muller, A. (2019). Assessing the essential pre-conditions of an authentic sustainability curriculum. *International Journal of Sustainability in Higher Education, 20*(2), 309–340. https://doi.org/10.1108/IJSHE-09-2018-0150

Loiseau, E., Saikku, L., Antikainen, R., Droste, N., Hansjürgens, B., Pitkänen, K., Leskinen, P., Kuikman, P., & Thomsen, M. (2016). Green economy and related concepts: An overview. *Journal of Cleaner Production, 139*, 361–371. https://doi. org/10.1016/j.jclepro.2016.08.024

Luederitz, L., Abson, D. J., Audet, R., & Lang, D. (2017). Many pathways toward sustainability: Not conflict but co-learning between transition narratives. *Sustainability Science, 12*(3), 393–407. https://doi.org/10.1007/s11625-016-0414-0

Marshall, C., & Rossman, G. (2016). *Designing qualitative research* (6th ed.). Jossey-Bass.

Martínez Casanovas, M., Ruíz-Munzón, N., & Buil-Fabregá, M. (2022). Higher education: The best practices for fostering competences for sustainable development through the use of active learning methodologies. *International Journal of Sustainability in Higher Education, 23*(3), 703–727. https://doi.org/10.1108/IJSHE-03-2021-0082

Mburayi, M., & Wall, T. (2018). Sustainability in the professional accounting and finance curriculum: An exploration. *Higher Education, Skills and Work-Based Learning, 8*(3), 291–311. https://doi.org/10.1108/HESWBL-03-2018-0036

McCormick, M., Bielefeldt, A., Swan, C., & Paterson, K. (2015). Assessing students' motivation to engage in sustainable engineering. *International Journal of Sustainability in Higher Education, 16*(2), 136–154. https://doi.org/10.1108/IJSHE-06-2013-0054

Merriam, S. (1998). *Qualitative research and case study applications in education.* Jossey-Bass.

Michel, J. O. (2020). *An assessment of teaching and learning about sustainability across the higher education curriculum* (Publication No. 13805642). [Doctoral dissertation, Columbia University]. ProQuest Dissertations and Theses Global database.

Miles, M. B., & Huberman, A. M. (1994). *Qualitative data analysis: An expanded sourcebook* (2nd ed.). Sage Publications.

Molderez, I., & Fonseca, E. (2018). The efficacy of real-world experiences and service learning for fostering competences for sustainable development in higher education. *Journal of Cleaner Production, 172*, 4397–4410. https://doi.org/10.1016/j.jclepro.2017.04.062

Ng, E., & Burke, R. (2010). Predictor of business students' attitudes toward sustainable business practices. *Journal of Business Ethics, 95*(4), 603–615. https://doi.org/10.1007/s10551-010-0442-0

Ngo, T. T., & Chase, B. (2021). Students' attitude toward sustainability and humanitarian engineering education using project-based and international field learning pedagogies. *International Journal of Sustainability in Higher Education, 22*(2), 254–273. https://doi.org/10.1108/IJSHE-06-2020-0214

Orr, D. (1992). *Ecological literacy: Education and transition to a postmodern world.* State University of New York Press.

Painter-Morland, M., Sabet, E., Molthan-Hill, P., Goworek, H., & de Leeuw, S. (2016). Beyond the curriculum, integrating sustainity into business schools. *Journal of Business Ethics, 139*(4), 737–754. https://doi.org/10.1007/s10551-015-2896-6

Piasentin, F., & Roberts, L. (2018). What elements in a sustainability course contribute to paradigm change and action competence? A study at Lincoln University, New Zealand. *Environmental Education Research, 24*(5), 694–715. https://doi.org/10.1080/13504622.2017.1321735

Pretorius, R., Anderson, R., Khotoo, A., & Pienaar, R. (2019). Creating a context for campus sustainability through teaching and learning: The case of open, distance and e-learning. *International Journal of Sustainability in Higher Education, 20*(3), 530–547. https://doi.org/10.1108/IJSHE-02-2019-0066

PRME Steering Committee. (n.d.-a). *Our 2030 vision: Six principles.* http://www.unprme.org/about-prme/the-six-principles.php

Qu, Z., Huang, W., & Zhou, Z. (2020). Applying sustainability into engineering curriculum under the background of "new engineering education" (nee). *International Journal of Sustainability in Higher Education, 21*(6), 1169–1187. https://doi.org/10.1108/IJSHE-11-2019-0342

Rodríguez-Barreiroa, L. M., Fernández-Manzanal, R., Serrac, L. M., Carrasquer, J., Murillo, M. B., Moralese, M. J., Calvo, J. M., & delValle, J. (2013). Approach to a causal model between attitudes and environmental behaviour: A graduate case study. *Journal of Cleaner Production, 48*, 116–125. https://doi.org/10.1016/j.jclepro.2012.09.029

Royal Roads University. (2014). *School of Business five year perspective.* Unpublished manuscript, Faculty of Management, Royal Roads University.

Royal Roads University. (n.d.). *Bachelor of Commerce in entrepreneurial management, program description.* http://www.royalroads.ca/prospective-students/bachelor-commerce-entrepreneurial-management/program-description

Rusinko, C. (2010). Integrating sustainability in management and business education: A matrix approach. *The Academy of Management Learning and Education, 9*(3), 507–519. https://doi.org/10.5465/AMLE.2010.53791831

Russo, F. Wheeldon, A. L., Shrestha, A. & Saratchandra, M. (2023). Responsible management education in business schools – High on principles but low on action: A systematic literature review. *International Journal of Management in Education, 21*(3), 1472–8117. https://doi.org/10.1016/j.ijme.2023.100843

Saldaña, J. (2013). *The coding manual for qualitative researchers* (2nd ed.). Sage Publications.

Saleem, A., Aslam, S., Sang, G., Dare, P. S., & Zhang, T. (2023). Education for sustainable development and sustainability consciousness: Evidence from Malaysian universities. *International Journal of Sustainability in Higher Education, 24*(1), 193–211. https://doi.org/10.1108/IJSHE-05-2021-0198

Schmitt-Figueiro, P., & Raufflet, E. (2015). Sustainability in higher education: A systematic review with focus on management education. *Journal of Cleaner Production, 106*(1), 22–33. https://doi.org/10.1016/j.jclepro.2015.04.118

SDG Accord. (n.d.). *The university and college sectors collective response to the global goals.* https://www.sdgaccord.org/

Selby, D. (2017). Education for sustainable development, nature and vernacular learning. *Center for Educational Policy Studies Journal, 7*(1), 9–27.

Selby, D., & Kagawa, F. (2018). Teetering on the brink: Subversive and restorative learning in times of climate turmoil and disaster. *Journal of Transformative Education, 16*(4), 302–322. https://doi.org/10.1177/1541344618782441

Sharma, U., & Kelly, M. (2014). Students' perceptions of education for sustainable development in the accounting and business curriculum at a business school in New Zealand. *Meditari Accountancy Research, 22*(2), 130–148. https://doi.org/10.1108/MEDAR-12-2012-0042

Sidiropoulos, E. (2018). The personal context of student learning for sustainability: Results of a multi-university research study. *Journal of Cleaner Production, 181,* 537–554. https://doi.org/10.1016/j.jclepro.2018.01.083

Singh, A. S., & Segatto, A. P. (2020). Challenges for education for sustainability in business courses: A multicase study in Brazilian higher education institutions. *International Journal of Sustainability in Higher Education, 21*(2), 264–280. https://doi.org/10.1108/IJSHE-07-2019-0238

Sterling, S. (2004). Higher education, sustainability, and the role of systemic learning. In *Higher education and the challenge of sustainability* (pp. 49–70). Springer.

Sundermann, S., & Fischer, D. (2019). How does sustainability become professionally relevant? Exploring the role of sustainability conceptions in first year students. *Sustainability, 11*(19), 5155. https://doi.org/10.3390/su11195155

Sutton, S. G., & Gyuris, E. (2015). Optimizing the environmental attitudes inventory: Establishing a baseline of change in student's attitudes. *International Journal of Sustainability in Higher Education, 16*(1), 16–33. https://doi.org/10.1108/IJSHE-03-2013-0027

Tilbury, D. (2009). Learning-based change for sustainability: Perspectives and pathways. In A. E. J. Wals (Ed.), *Social learning: Towards a sustainable world* (pp. 117–131). Wageningen Academic Publishers.

Turner, L. M., Hegde, S., Karunasagar, I., & Turner, R. (2022). How university students are taught about sustainability, and how they want to be taught: The importance of the hidden curriculum. *International Journal of Sustainability in Higher Education, 23*(7), 1560–1579. https://doi.org/10.1108/IJSHE-03-2021-0105

United Nations Global Compact. (2021). *Heads of States join CEOS and UN Chiefs in calling for accelerated corporate action in sustainability to recover better from COVID-19.* https://unglobalcompact.org/news/4711-06-16-2021

United Nations. (n.d.). Shaping our future together. *Climate Change.* https://www.un.org/en/sections/issues-depth/climate-change/index.html

Von Der Heidt, T., & Lamberton, G. (2011). Sustainability in the undergraduate and post graduate business curriculum of a regional university: A critical perspective. *Journal of Management and Organization, 17*(5), 670–690.

Wals, A., & Heymann, F. (2004). Learning on the edge: Exploring the change potential of conflict in social learning for sustainable living. In A. Wenden (Ed.), *Education for a culture of social and ecological Peace* (pp. 123–144). State University of New York Press.

Wang, Y., Sommier, M., & Vasques, A. (2022). Sustainability education at higher education institutions: Pedagogies and students' competences. *International Journal of Sustainability in Higher Education, 23*(8), 174–193. https://doi.org/10.1108/IJSHE-11-2021-0465

Winter, J., & Cotton, D. (2012). Making the hidden curriculum visible: Sustainability literacy in higher education. *Environmental Education Research, 18*(6), 783–796. https://doi.org/10.1080/13504622.2012.670207

World Commission on Environment and Development. (1987). *Our common future.* https://sustainabledevelopment.un.org/content/documents/5987our-common-future.pdf

Yin, R. K. (2014). *Case study research: Design and methods* (5th ed.). Sage Publications.

Zeegers, Y., & Clark, I. F. (2014). Students' perceptions of education for sustainable development. *International Journal of Sustainability in Higher Education, 15*(2), 242–253. https://doi.org/10.1108/IJSHE-09-2012-0079

Zen, I. (2017). Exploring the living learning laboratory: An approach to strengthen campus sustainability initiatives by using sustainability science approach. *International Journal of Sustainability in Higher Education, 18*(6), 939–955. https://doi.org/10.1108/IJSHE-09-2015-0154

Zsóka, Á., & Ásványi, K. (2023). Transforming students' behaviour preferences: Achievable changes by a sustainability course. *International Journal of Sustainability in Higher Education, 24*(1), 141–159. https://doi.org/10.1108/IJSHE-01-2022-0018

Zsóka, Á., Szerényi, Z. M., Széchy, A., & Kocsis, T. (2013). Greening due to environmental education? Environmental knowledge, attitudes, consumer behavior and everyday pro-environmental activities of Hungarian high school and university students. *Journal of Cleaner Production, 48*, 126–138. https://doi.org/10.1016/j.jclepro.2012.11.030

Chapter 4

Responsible Research and Innovation: Buzzword or a Tool for Universities to Address Grand Societal Challenges? Learnings From a Swiss Case Example

Alexandra Grammenou

ZHAW School of Management and Law, Switzerland

Abstract

This chapter focuses on Responsible Research and Innovation (RRI) as a new approach for academic institutions, such as universities and Universities of Applied Sciences (UASs) as organizations based on empirical evidence. A University of Applied Sciences in Switzerland was selected as a case. An analysis of the organization's most representative documents, extensive interviews with employees having expertise in the different RRI keys (public engagement, gender equality/diversity, science education, open access, ethics) and Anticipation, Inclusiveness, Reflexivity, Responsiveness (AIRR) dimensions, as well as a focus group produced interesting insights regarding the discourse and institutionalization of the RRI approach in the organization. Furthermore, the drivers, barriers, best practices, and monitoring of each of the RRI keys and AIRR dimensions were further described. The findings suggest that RRI could be a helpful policy framework at a time that universities are going through a systemic change.

Keywords: Responsible research and innovation; RRI; organizations; universities; universities of applied sciences; governance; practice; policy

Introduction

In a world that is facing massive environmental and societal issues accurately called Grand Societal Challenges (GSCs) from climate change to disruptive

Innovation in Responsible Management Education, 93–114

Copyright © 2024 Alexandra Grammenou

Published under exclusive licence by Emerald Publishing Limited

doi:10.1108/978-1-83549-464-620241006

immigration and inequality, from global pandemics to most recently war and a global energy crisis (Ferraro et al., 2015; Voegtlin et al., 2022), universities, which for the purpose of this chapter we use as an umbrella term, where Universities of Applied Sciences (UASs) are also included, are struggling to evolve, and reinvent themselves as organizations contributing to sustainable development through academic research. The same time they seem to be losing trust from society, receiving heavy criticism for failing to offer the skills that students need for successfully coping with these challenges in their future positions (Longmore et al., 2018), for being at the Ivory Tower producing research with no value for society (Vogt & Weber, 2020) or for their competitive role focusing on serving governments, the market economy, and "audit society" (Engwall, 2020) rather than interests and needs of society itself. Changes toward transformative learning and education that will equip learners with important competencies and a mindset for contributing to sustainable innovation are required (Rieckmann, 2018).

In this context, international organizations like UNESCO and the European Commission (EC) have been rethinking the role of universities in the past years and have been calling them to collaborate with their partners, come closer to society, and focus more on research and innovation. At the recent report of UNESCO (2021) universities are asked to contribute to the renewal of education through research and innovation by coming in dialogue with those already involved such as teachers and schools, families, and students and their communities at large. The EC has gone a step further developing two frameworks on Responsible Innovation (RI) and Responsible Research and Innovation (RRI) emerging from the EC's Seventh Framework Programme and continuously evolving in the EC policy context since 2011 through (EU, 2013; Horizon, 2020; Owen et al., 2012; Stilgoe et al., 2013). At a time of great distrust against public institutions and democracy in Europe, RRI was introduced as a survival tool for preserving the practice of "Science with and for Society" (SwafS) (Owen et al., 2021b). Building on the statement by Geoghegan-Quinn (2012) and the definition by von Schomberg (2013), RRI was defined in the Rome Declaration, 2014 as:

> ... the on-going process of aligning research and innovation to the values, needs and expectations of society ... [RRI] requires that all stakeholders including civil society are responsive to each other and take shared responsibility for the processes and outcomes of research and innovation.

Scholars argue that RI can be a very effective means to address GSCs (Owen et al., 2012; Stilgoe et al., 2013; Voegtlin & Scherer, 2017) in the sense that as a framework it allows to detect potential harmful consequences and positive contributions of innovations to societal challenges through governance and evaluation (Voegtlin et al., 2022). However, in the context of universities, scholars remain doubtful about the effectiveness of RI or RRI to drive the change that is needed to address societal challenges. Owen et al. (2021a) investigated the organizational institutionalization of RI in Engineering and Physical Sciences Research Council (EPSRC) in the United Kingdom, particularly in universities.

One of their main findings was that RI although policy driven by societal challenges, it is more likely to receive resistance in the institutionalization, if it is not corresponding with the primary policy priority of UK universities, which is to drive economic growth through innovation. For others RRI remains a buzzword, as it lacks the norms, the structure, and political governance that are needed to drive responsible research (Vogt & Weber, 2020).

As the literature on RI and RRI and their effect on organizations particularly in different contexts is still rather limited (Owen et al., 2021a; Voegtlin et al., 2022), the novelty of this chapter is to draw insights in the effectiveness of the RRI as new policy framework to address GSCs through its embeddedness in university governance at a Swiss context. Since universities in Europe have vastly been studied in the context of Germany, France, and the United Kingdom (Krücken, 2020), but to the best of knowledge not as much in Switzerland, a further contribution would be added to the literature. Taking a Swiss university as case example, is particularly interesting, considering that Switzerland is among the most innovative countries in the world, ranking 1st in the Global Innovation Index 2022 among 132 economies (WIPO, 2022).

For this chapter, a case study and qualitative methods were used. Firstly, there was a collection and analysis of the university's most representative documents; secondly extensive expert interview in the organization were conducted. Lastly, a focus group with a different group of experts produced interesting insights regarding the discourse and level of RRI embeddedness in the organization. Furthermore, the drivers and barriers of the different aspects of RRI to address different challenges were further analyzed. The findings offer a contribution with regards to best practices of RRI applied in a university at a Swiss context that can serve as an inspiration for other universities, globally, in their efforts to address GSCs through research and innovation and gain back trust by coming closer to society. The chapter of the main findings is based in an individual internal review report contributed by this author, as part of the RRI-LEADERS project funded by EC Horizon 2020 as found in Hajdinjak et al. (2022).

Universities and Grand Societal Challenges

GSCs are rightfully being characterized as complex (constituted from a great number of elements and interrelationships), uncertain (the prediction of their development is problematic), and value-laden (their interpretation and meaning varies depending on the value system of involved actors) (Ferraro et al., 2015). Universities have a significant role to play on addressing these challenges, as they are transforming to an organizational actor characterized by accountability, goal-orientation, strong organizational structures, and managerial agency (Krücken & Meier, 2006). In their strategies, the missions are changing from merely teaching and research to a third one of the "entrepreneurial" university (Etzkowitz, 2017), supporting social innovations and innovations in technology. As organizational actors, they are expected to actively participate in the development of solutions that do not just mitigate the effects of the GSCs, but mostly their causes (Voegtlin et al., 2022), by transferring knowledge to society and promoting equal opportunity, internationalization, and sustainability (Engwall, 2020; Krücken, 2020; Stehr, 1994). The idea of the university as a multiversity, (Kerr, 1963) focusing mainly on economic growth, competitiveness, and industrial innovation (Sigurdson, 2013) is therefore in need of reconsideration, pushing universities toward transformation.

At a time when universities, in some countries, seem to have distanced themselves from the needs of society, as an impressively declining number of student enrolments shows (Anderson, 2022; McKinsey & Company, 2020), transformation is crucial as means to reinvent themselves and reduce the gap.

An adoption of a holistic view on the university and a strong emphasis on adapting responsibility and respect freedom through dialogue between science and society, support the transformation process of these organizations (Vogt & Weber, 2020). The societal embeddedness of the university's knowledge production is a great step in this process, while stronger democratic engagement is highly demanded in a "Mode 2" society that is characterized by major changes in economic, political, and sociocultural level (Scott, 2020). In this Great Transformation, sustainability, and sustainable development are becoming core values of the strategy, while special focus is laid on transferring and producing "robust knowledge", meaning knowledge that is generated outside the laboratory, has been validated by experts and has been generated through society's participation (Mittelstrass, 2020).

Responsible Research and Innovation and University Governance

When looking back at 10 years of various EC funded research projects, where the RRI concept was applied, one can observe that RRI was translated into five very specific keys: public engagement, ethics, open access, science education, and gender equality, as keys to succeed in building a community beyond academics, including business and policymakers (Owen et al., 2021b). Furthermore, the Anticipation, Inclusion, Reflexivity and Responsiveness (AIRR) dimensions emerged, as a way for scientists to address challenging questions regarding the path to innovation and implications with governance (Stilgoe et al., 2013). While Vogt and Weber (2020) argue that RRI is lacking the norms and the structure for the political governance of responsible research at university level, Owen et al. (2021a) suggest that RRI is apparently an emerging policy in universities at the initial phase of institutionalization. Furthermore, the development of the RRI keys and AIRR dimensions adds clear norms and structure to RRI as a policy framework.

The Quadruple Helix Approach

RRI also fosters a quadruple helix approach (Carayannis & Campbell, 2009) rather than a triple helix one (Etzkowitz, 2008), where the relationships between the university, businesses, the public authorities, and the civil society are strengthened. Recent studies particularly suggest that when RRI similarly to RI is integrated in the governance structure of organizations, like businesses, it can facilitate the way they address the GSCs, as it allows reflexive governance and open dialogue between the stakeholders of the organization (Voegtlin et al., 2022), making RRI a promising tool for universities.

Research Design and Methodology

This chapter seeks to answer the following research question: "Is RRI well embedded in the UAS's governance to enable the organization to efficiently address the GSCs?" One of Switzerland's major UASs, where academic research is very prevalent, was selected as a case to answer the question. A qualitative study of three stages was executed to answer the question of RRI embeddedness at university level. The study was part of the RRI-LEADERS research project funded by the European Union's Horizon 2020 research and innovation program. At a first stage, a content analysis of 10 of the UAS's most representative policies and strategies of approximately 250 pages was executed. The documents were analyzed through the lens of the RRI keys and AIRR dimensions. The first step was the exploration of the five RRI keys according to the MoRRI indicators (MoRRI Consortium, 2018) in the main documents, which were perceived as following:

(1) **Public Engagement** focuses on the societal alignment of a university's mission and purpose, concretely interpreted through its research activities and the level of positive impact those have on society. In that sense, the university as an organization has a "social licence to operate" since the outcomes from new research and new technologies are serving the needs and expectations of society.

(2) **Gender Equality** and its promotion is an important aspect of a university's role. However, as the term is too narrow it would be more appropriate to speak today of diversity. The university sets as a profound priority to establish a research environment where all members of society independently of their gender, sex, cultural background, age, or disability are included equally in all teams and decision-making bodies.

(3) **Science Education** is about disseminating research results through the reinvention of the education process, through new educational programs that will enable citizens and organizations to better understand the challenges they will face in the future.

(4) **Open Access** or as is more widely accepted today Open Science means the fast and easy accessibility to research results and scientific work. A university's support of open science can enable more efficient partnerships between academic staff and the same time a more constructive dialogue with the civil society.

(5) **Ethics** addresses all issues related to research integrity that need to be taken into account to guarantee the highest quality of scientific results. Widely accepted ethical values, norms, and standards must be respected to ensure that future technological developments will be accepted by the civil society.

As a second step the AIRR dimensions (Stilgoe et al., 2013) were applied to enable a deeper analysis of the documents:

- **Anticipation** is about the systematic consideration of all possible scenarios and the ability to establish a strategic foresight as an organization.
- **Inclusiveness** means the involvement of all actors of society in a constructive dialogue, especially ensuring the participation of marginalized groups and actors that have less power. This can be achieved through the organization of focus groups or citizen panels.
- **Reflexivity** addresses the responsibility of an institution to hold a mirror at its governance, namely at its activities and its commitments. It is also connected with the need for the development of reflexive capacity among scientists under the same institution.
- **Responsiveness** is the ability of innovation to respond to the needs of the society, as they are described under the "grand challenges".

The documents allowed the identification of the UAS's experts related to RRI, mapping those to be invited for the interviews at the second stage.

At a second stage, semi-structured expert interviews were conducted to monitor the discourse of RRI at the UAS and to assess its relevance and importance for the organization and the participants' work. The drivers, barriers, best practices, and monitoring mechanisms, for each of the RRI keys and AIRR dimensions closely related to the participants teaching and research work were asked. Eight experts from all hierarchy levels (senior, middle, and junior management) of the university participated. A general description of the goals of the current study, as well as a form of confidentiality was sent prior to the interview with the list of set questions. The interviews were held in English and in German, recorded using MS Teams, transcribed and translated when necessary. At a third stage, a focus group was organized with eight different group of experts than those of the interviews representing all hierarchy levels (senior, middle, and junior management). During the focus group, the participants were asked to evaluate each of the RRI keys and AIRR dimensions based on their relevance to their own research and teaching work, as well as their relevance to the UAS as a whole. The main goal was to check the level of convergence or disagreement between the results in the interviews and the focus group.

Main Findings

The document analysis revealed that RRI has not been perceived as an official concept or policy framework for the university under study. However, many policies were found to represent the specific RRI keys like the Diversity Policy, Gender Policy, Open Educational Resources (OER) Policy, Open Access Policy, and Research & Development Policy (Table 4.1). Surprisingly, a Code of Ethics or

Table 4.1. List of Most Important Documents and Their Connection to RRI.

Document	RRI Keys	Public Engagement	Gender Equality/ Diversity	Open Access	Science Education	Ethics
University Strategy 2015–2025	X	X		X		
Diversity Policy			X			
Gender Policy			X			
Regulation against Discrimination, Sexual Harassment, and Bullying			X			
Open Access Policy				X		
Open Educational Resources Policy				X		
Research and Development Policy				X	X	X
Sustainability Strategy			X			X
Quality Strategy 2015–2025			X	X		X
Annual Report 2020	X		X	X		

Source: Own Source.

Code of Conduct has been missing. Moreover, most of the RRI keys and AIRR dimensions were mentioned in the University Strategy 2015–2025, the Quality Strategy 2015–2025, and the Annual Report 2020 (Table 4.2). Important data were gathered based on the documents and a map was created with regards to the departments, units, programs, committees that are mainly responsible for implementing and monitoring RRI in the organization.

Table 4.2. List of Documents and Their Connection to the AIRR Dimensions.

Document	AIRR Dimensions	Anticipation	Inclusiveness	Reflexivity	Responsiveness
University Strategy 2015–2025			X	X	
Diversity Policy		X		X	X
Gender Policy		X		X	X
Regulation against Discrimination, Sexual Harassment, and Bullying		X	X		X
Open Access Policy		X			X
Open Educational Resources Policy		X	X	X	X
Research and Development Policy				X	X
Sustainability Strategy		X	X	X	X
Quality Strategy 2015–2025		X		X	X
Annual Report 2020		X		X	X

Source: Own Source.

Level of RRI Embeddedness Based on Expert Interviews

The interviews shed light on the discourse of RRI in the organization in the last decade and particularly since 2015, when the university's development strategies, like the Sustainability Strategy and University Strategy 2015–2025, were conceived and launched. During that exact same year, two other key events drove significant change. At global level, the introduction of the Sustainable Development Goals (SDGs) initiated a move toward more societal engagement for all countries. At the national level, the new Coordination (HEPC) Act brought new priorities for all Swiss universities. In addition, some respondents underlined that RRI aligns with the accreditation requirements for academic institutions. For most respondents it was clear that the RRI keys and AIRR dimensions are already reflected in the main actions and commitments of the university and are part of its foundational principles. They gave examples from their work in teaching or/and research that were related to one or more of the

RRI keys. Some participants emphasized that all RRI topics have been acknowledged and prioritized, as significant themes in strategy, not only by the President's Office, but also by the Strategic Units, the Committees, and all eight departments. Nevertheless, some departments seem to be more advanced in comparison to others, while barriers that prevent further implementation were named. When looking closer to the level of embeddedness through each of the RRI keys and AIRR dimensions, the following main results gave a clear picture about the current situation in the university.

Public Engagement

For the respondents this key goes hand in hand with the reason of existence of every academic institution in Switzerland and therefore has always been embedded in the university. Since its founding days, the university has constantly strived to engage publicly by adjusting existing and developing new strategies and by supporting students and businesses through a variety of good practices. The creation of the university's was a further step in this direction, as well as developing, a strategic program about sustainability under the President's Office.

The university's culture as defined in its mission statement has clearly served as a significant driver for societal engagement. Addressing societal needs and achieving positive societal impact is a mean to differentiate its position in the academic world regionally and internationally by becoming a well-recognized and respected institution. There are also a lot of motives coming from Europe, where open science/open innovation initiatives were promoted creating a wave that strengthened the university's societal engagement even further. There are many initiatives that strengthen the dialogue of the university with the society like a free of charge magazine that is published four times annually and provides information about research projects, studies, and new continuous learning programs. An internal funding program dedicated to the promotion of sustainable project ideas from students and researchers was launched in 2020. Special funding is given annually to an impact entrepreneurship program that supports innovative start-ups through safaris, hackathons, and incubation programs, whereas there are a lot more initiatives organized by the Sustainability Office like think tanks, workshops, lunch seminars, research networks, etc.

Limited time and financial resources from third parties were underlined as the main reasons for not having public engagement higher on the list of priorities, but also lack of information of the higher management units resulting in a top-down passiveness. Moreover, no official monitoring mechanism of the level of the university's societal engagement was reported and the first sustainability report will not be published before the end of 2023.

Gender Equality/Diversity

Gender equality and diversity have been part of the founding principles of the university back in 2007 according to the respondents. At that time, the focus was more on gender equality, while in recent years there has been shift toward inclusion of more aspects of diversity. Since 2007, the existence of the Diversity Committee has contributed immensely to inform and create awareness among the different departments and coordinate initiatives. A big success was the submission of the Gender Equality Management Plan to the Executive Board and the launching of a university wide campaign that creates awareness for gender and diversity issues. Since 2016 a report that monitors the gender equality numbers in the organization is published every two years. It includes a detailed evaluation and monitoring of the number of women working in the university according to hierarchy level, the amount of their salaries in comparison to men in equal positions and recommendations for further developments in this area. However, there are no KPIs available for monitoring and no goals for diversity topics, while there is no evaluation of the performance of the Diversity Unit.

The department of Social Work is exclusively focused on doing research in this field and there are cases of diversity experts from other departments like the department of Management and Law that have integrated the subject in the curricula creating a new module for the students that focuses on partnerships and projects with businesses to help them address real diversity management challenges.

A major driver for stronger embeddedness of this RRI key was the Swiss Federal Law, which has put political pressure to the President of the university to act, initiate, and implement a gender equality management plan. More action is expected in equality of wages and there are federal initiatives for a larger representation of women in administrative boards. There has also been a lot of societal pressure due to strikes of women in the recent years, for example that made the whole subject very relevant.

Nevertheless, for a more effective implementation more actions are needed, especially in terms of hiring more women in leadership positions and for establishing a diversity strategy. In terms of research, the department of Social Work is mainly responsible for doing research in this area.

Some respondents assumed that the university's Executive Board and the Council might have been guided by unconscious biases in their decisions and priorities. Reasons for this could be the relatively old average age of the members, lack of relevant education, and understanding of gender issues in research, as well as an unbalanced gender composition of these instances. As a result, the main strategic goals have concentrated for long time on environmental sustainability and tended to leave behind social sustainability issues, which resulted in a low focus on diversity. As one interviewee noted "political correctness is perceived differently by people, so it is sometimes challenging to come to agreement about the direction that needs to be followed". Ultimately, the low budget at disposal does not allow for further initiatives in this direction.

Open Science

The level of embeddedness of Open science is quite high with many initiatives run by the Strategic Affairs Office for R&D like the one on Open Research Data Management and by the University Library in the areas of open access to research publications, OER, and citizenship access. This case of a university is one of the first in Switzerland and among the few in Europe that has established an OER policy, as an interviewee explicitly stated. The creation of a digital platform for open access articles was a first step toward the implementation of an open science culture. Moreover, at the University Library a special OER competence team was established to support lecturers and students with information about how to produce material that can be accessed from all over the globe. Regarding data management, a special university service that supports the research staff through the data collection process, is responsible to make the data open and reusable for everyone. Another incentive for authors to publishing open access was initiated by the University Library and relates to a special fund that covers the cost of these articles. The University Library is also responsible to monitor the initiatives related to open science in the different departments.

However, the respondents agreed that there is still plenty of room for a deeper implementation. The high expenses asked by commercial journals limit the motivation for publishing open access. The old structures do not facilitate its embeddedness; for example, for some departments there are hardly journals to be found in their discipline that are open access. "The Swiss culture is considered a barrier since it is a culture of owning rather than sharing", according to the opinion of one of the respondents. In the recent years, there is a general understanding that Open Science has been pushed legally both at European and Swiss level. In Switzerland there is a national strategy that commands all research that is financed by public funds to be published in open access mode by 2024. Furthermore, the implementation of open science policies from universities is an important prerequisite to guarantee research grants from bodies like the Swiss National Science Foundation and the EC. For all these reasons, open science is expected to continue widely being implemented across the organization.

Science Education

Science education is the RRI key that is the most widely embedded in the organization, since the main purpose of the university is to focus on research and let the results flow into teaching to equip students with the updated knowledge they need to prevail as professionals in society. The lecturers have for long time served as a bridge that connects students both with science and the practice. The research that is taking place always has as a goal to have a positive impact in society because it is financed by the society, as it is a publicly funded university.

The main driver lies at the university's own mission statement and the fact that its competitive advantage as a UAS is to bring the businesses close to the students. The demands that society puts into universities in terms of responsible education are also constantly increasing because universities prepare the students to become multipliers of responsible action. In this context, there was a strong collaboration with the edX online platform and the allocation of funding to create and offer free online courses in a variety of sustainability topics. Other worth noting initiatives include the launching of seminar series for staff and the public in "Higher Education of the Future" together with international experts, the OER initiative from the University Library on sensitising and informing lectures and students about creating open educational material and teaching the use of creative commons, and the UN PRME initiative for integration of responsible management in the curricula and research projects of the different units of the department of Management and Law.

Every department of the university has its own quality management team that is responsible for the frequent evaluation of the performance in the fields of lecturing, R&D, continuous education, and services based on the Quality Management Strategy 2015–2025. The Sustainability Office is responsible to monitor how sustainability is embedded in the curricula of the different departments and in research projects. However, a clear barrier was spotted during the interviews regarding science education and its connection to the operational environment of higher education institutions, which is becoming more and more complex, and pushes for structural and systemic changes. The low financial resources and the conflicts of interests regarding how and on which topics these resources should be invested are not to be underestimated.

Ethics

The implementation process in ethics is still ongoing and according to an interviewee "Our university is halfway through it". The University's Research Integrity Policy published by the the the Swiss Academies of Arts and Sciences (SAAS) provides the general guidelines. Some departments like the department of Management and Law and the department of Health have developed their own departmental Codes of Ethics and Ethics Committees. However, as another respondent described "these Committees are mostly functioning like toothless tigers", meaning they do not have the power to change or improve the current lack of an ethical framework at university level.

The dialogue between departments and between lecturers and students regarding ethical assessment is not yet well established, while decisions are mainly left to be taken by the Executive Board. There are implications on how ethics should be taught and tested in the courses offered due to the ethical standards being perceived differently among different disciplines, while constantly changing and evolving. Profit making was also proposed to be a barrier for the further implementation of ethics at university level.

On one hand the drivers for ethics are legal, as the university under study, like all universities in Switzerland, must follow the federal and cantonal laws regarding research integrity. On the other hand, drivers are also political, such as the recent debate on whether the university shall discontinue research partnerships with Russian institutions, as they are perceived as unethical due to the Ukrainian war. Following ethical standards has always been part of the university's culture to show transparency and credibility to its various stakeholders and to guarantee a worldwide good reputation. Specifically, the development of ethical consciousness was a condition for the department of Management and Law to receive international accreditation and to integrate the UN PRME principles. The creation of a Research Data Base as a digital platform, where the public can have detailed information about the current and past research projects of all the departments, the researchers involved, the body of funding, and the publications was a step toward more transparency.

From the interviews it was clear that the departments are individually responsible for the approval of their own research proposals and making sure that the main research process will be carried out respecting the existing research integrity policies. A more official evaluation mechanism like those found in American Universities is currently lacking. It was underlined by some that an Ethics Committee with representatives from all departments is about to be launched and will focus explicitly on handling research integrity issues and creating an updated and uniformed Code of Ethics.

Anticipation

This dimension is quite well embedded especially when looking at all the strategic offices, programs, and initiatives that have been established in the last few years in the university. The work of the Sustainability Office, R&D Strategic Office, and the Higher Educational Development (HED) Unit were outlined in particular by participants. The fact that strategies should at least look to the next 5 years was taken very seriously, especially by the respondents in senior management positions. However, they were also comments that in terms of gender equality/ diversity, there is lack of strategical thinking and better planning for the future.

The financial resources determine in which areas the planning and the strategies should focus. The staff seems to be demotivated to participate in the development of strategies, preferring to focus mostly on their own tasks, due to lack of financial incentives or because of a rather old-fashioned mindset that does not realize the importance of change.

All academic institutions, especially in Switzerland, are expected to anticipate and plan effectively for the future, addressing issues that are crucial like digitalization, environmental impact, etc.

The structure of the university under study is a good example on why anticipation mechanisms work well, namely mainly due to the teams being divided in a very efficient way to promote strategic initiatives. The HED Unit runs the "Strategic Observatory", which works closely together with expert committees from all the departments in order to develop draft proposals for strategies that are then further submitted to the Executive Board for feedback.

The Strategic Offices are responsible for the evaluation of the implementation of their respective strategies. A risk inventory at university level is formed annually were potential risks and future trends are concretely assessed.

Inclusiveness

From a student perspective, this dimension is well embedded in the organization, as it is a very crucial aspect that allows them to focus exclusively on their studies without any disturbances. However, from an employee perspective, the inclusion of more women researchers and professors, as well as work–life balance, should be further improved.

Experience has shown that many employees are afraid to express freely about certain things regarding their working conditions, because they feel they will be discriminated. Change of culture in the organization to achieve more inclusion is considered challenging.

Internationalization is an important condition for guaranteeing accreditations, but it cannot be achieved without developing an inclusive environment in an organization for people coming from different cultural backgrounds. The new laws and gender equality strategies were also mentioned as well as initiatives like UN PRME in the department of Management and Law.

Since 2013, the Diversity Unit has assigned a representative for people with disabilities and since 2020 there is also a representative for the LGBTQ+ community, while both are focused on the promotion of more initiatives in these areas. A survey was carried out in the department of Management and Law, focusing on inclusive leadership to set light on the different perceptions of leaders. Furthermore, a campaign aimed at increasing awareness among employees about a zero-tolerance attitude against any act of discrimination, mobbing and bullying, while a university service offers special consulting services for students and employees free of charge.

For the moment there are general annual surveys evaluating the satisfaction of employees, where inclusiveness is only indirectly addressed through some of the questions. The department of Social Work with its Institute of Diversity and Social Integration is carrying further evaluation through research projects on that matter.

Reflexivity

This a significant dimension in the university in terms of the organization running frequent self-evaluations to achieve higher quality of services provided. Most evaluations are carried out by the students and focus on lecturers, nevertheless there are surveys directed to the employees, too. The university as a whole and the departments in particular have been awarded with multiple accreditations that require continuous self-evaluations, as well as evaluations from third parties.

The Quality Strategy 2015–2025 comes together with several hundreds of indicators creating an "illness" toward working hard on being overly perfect. The frequency and the importance that is given to these evaluations can be counterproductive for the employees. The students are overloaded with too many evaluations and these evaluations are not always representative of the performance of the lecturers.

Reflexivity is pushed by the Council, by the university's mission statement, and the accreditations. It is about the main ambition to stand out from other academic institutions and always becoming better.

Since 2020, the university is institutionally accredited according to the HEPC Act based on a self- and third-party evaluation that lasted two years. The work of the Quality Committee at the university is consisting of all the quality manager representatives from all departments is another example. A staff satisfaction survey is run once a year in collaboration with an external consultant that gives insights into the perception of the employees about the organization.

Each department has its own mechanisms for quality assurance and implementation of the strategies. In the case of the department of Management and Law there are also reviews, as part of the renewal of the accreditations like AACSB, an organization that sets its own special criteria for evaluation.

Responsiveness

Mixed views on the level of embeddedness in the organization were reported regarding the dimension of responsiveness. Some mentioned that the strategies and policies are not as fast and not as well implemented as they could and should be, especially when referring to gender equality. Some participants were convinced that the university has managed to sufficiently respond to the big challenges of the time, for example, the COVID-19 pandemic.

When financial resources are limited and the expectations of the stakeholders are divided, like in the case of the implementation of the Sustainability Strategy, it is difficult to decide how to respond. Taking own responsibility to implement things has been a challenge. There is lack of being proactive and taking own initiative from the side of the leaders. Although a risk assessment exists, a precise action plan in case of a pandemic event or a nuclear war were never clearly defined.

The reviews that are taking place due to the accreditations are a very important driver that pushes for the actual implementation of the university's strategies.

The very fast response on the pandemic situation based on dialogue with the students and the employees to address their varied needs can be considered a good practice. Frequent Executive Board meetings also bring important contributions, as solutions are given fast due to the long, but efficient discussions among the deans of the departments.

The annual report of the university is a well written document, where the degree of responsiveness of the whole organization is generally monitored. The Sustainability Office is also monitoring the research projects and other initiatives from the departments in terms of the degree of implementation of the Sustainability Strategy and other green inititiaves.

Level of RRI Embeddedness Based on the Focus Group

The focus group brought the discussion on RRI more forward and gave the chance for different perspectives to be heard, especially with regards to the anticipatory, inclusive, reflexive, and responsive governance of the university. The profound priority of the university's higher management to anticipatory governance was highlighted, while inclusiveness and responsiveness were perceived not as well embedded in the structures, as it would have been expected. At the anticipatory level, it was stretched that readaptation of strategies, thinking of the rapid changes in society, is not happening fast enough. Interestingly, many participants agreed that the public engagement of the university is limited to exchanges with businesses rather than with policymakers and the civil society, while they felt that it is one of the RRI keys that is not reflected in their research and teaching.

Drivers

The main drivers for all RRI keys and AIRR dimensions were agreed that could be found in the university's strategic documents and policies, but also in Swiss Law. Science education is naturally a crucial domain, prioritized and supported by all management levels, as the university strives to provide its students with excellence in quality education. The frequent quality controls certainly serve as a good incentive for the members of staff to work harder toward this goal. With regards to department of Management and Law, it was precisely mentioned that the accreditation of AACSB and its formal reward system and initiatives like UN PRME have been playing a significant role that pushes lecturers and researchers to continuously achieve more in research. In terms of ethics, on one hand the high demand from society on universities and on the other hand the students asking clear definitions on how research should be done, has strengthened the organization's focus on that matter. There is a discourse at university level on what kind of research should or should not be done and why. The principles that need to be followed by the departments encourage the integration of modules in the curricula like that of responsible leadership. For open access or open science, the University Library is providing financial support to researchers, as an incentive to encourage them to publish openly, which is considered effective to a certain extent. It has also been considered as a very important strategic goal and part of the public engagement of the university to offer more open access publications since scientific journals have become more expensive and universities can not afford the access to those as before. Public engagement was named to be one of the university's most significant strategic goals, as transformation and the response to societal needs has been part of the mission statement since a long time and therefore integrated into important decisions of the management. Gender equality and diversity in general have also been forwarded as a societal need that must be efficiently addressed by public institutions like a UAS; therefore fighting "unconscious bias" has been a key driver for the organization. Examples such as dealing with integration issues from incoming students of different cultural backgrounds, the subject of work–life balance among the employees, and how senior managers react to those matters were noted as motives.

Barriers

The barriers that were mentioned regarding the implementation of RRI were the same related to all keys and dimensions and they can mainly be summarized into lack of funds and lack of time. With regards to science education there was a debate about the UASs being at a state of academization that serves as a barrier due to the research conditions not being clear like in academic universities. The university's Individual Performance Agreement (IPA) system was criticized to prevent the realization of further research projects in RRI topics due to the way resources are allocated. It was highlighted that a major number of the university's lecturers feels overloaded with their duties of teaching, acquiring research projects, doing research, and publishing. For example, one participant expressed disappointment that when a research project is over, the funding for publications is not always guaranteed. The different perception of ethics among the disciplines in the departments has prevented the creation of an Ethics Committee. Other barriers for open access rise from accreditation bodies, which give a very inclusive list of scientific journals available for publications, excluding, for example, German speaking journals. The concentration on reflexivity was thought to be too high and the fact that self-evaluations are taking place annually was considered counterproductive. The old-fashioned mindset by many employees and students about diversity and inclusiveness not only in the organization, but in society in general was also underlined, as well as the fact that discrimination and "unconscious bias" are still very evident and hard to be overcome. Finally, most participants agreed that there is a gap between anticipation and responsiveness, while implementation of the current strategies is not happening at a satisfactory level.

Good Practices

Over the course of the past year, the R&D Unit has established a working group that is focused on developing an Ethics Committee for the university with representatives from all the departments. Students are planned to be involved and give their opinion. An external expert, who is one of the authors of the Research Integrity guidelines by the SAAS is also included in the process. In the next session of this working group, hopefully the Committee will be put into action. As for science education, the Sustainability Office is running a working group on integrating sustainable topics further into the curricula of all departments across the university. Emphasis was given by the participants to the fact that the university is among the few in Switzerland with an OER policy, having special funds and a dedicated team for it, while the President is the Head for Open Innovation for Swiss Universities. The fact that more than 70% of the university's partnerships are with private businesses was mentioned as best practice for public engagement but there was no example of partnerships with civil society organizations. Another perfect example is the collaboration with municipalities like the city of Winterthur to turn it into a Smart City. Towards strengthening diversity, the awareness campaign for diversity and equality has been a success, whereas there is a lot of demand to participate in the peer groups that are organized. The offer of consultation by external experts for employees and students for diversity issues has also worked well. The initiation of research in social gerontology has been highlighted as good example.

The Strategic Observatory initiative by the HED Unit was mentioned as a very effective instrument for strengthening anticipation providing the opportunity to exchange with experts in the university and to identify the important strategic future topics in environment and society.

Monitoring and Evaluation

The evaluation for each of the RRI keys and AIRR dimensions takes place by each of the departments separately and it does not happen at a university level. Accreditation bodies, like AACSB, use their own special indicators to evaluate anticipation and responsiveness at the department of Management and Law. The University Library monitors the open access level by arranging meetings with each of the departments, where it informs their representatives about their performance in terms of the percentage of publishing open access using different metrics. Some departments have more funds for open access in comparison to others, which of course influences the rate accordingly. The gender equality plan and the related report were mentioned as a good practice where standardization was achieved by monitoring the numbers of female students and employees per department, the salaries, and their position in hierarchy level. However, no evaluation mechanisms for ethics, public engagement, or inclusiveness were reported.

Discussion

The results from the document analysis, the interviews, and the focus group revealed overall interesting insights on the position of the RRI-AIRR approach in the university, which may be assessed as strong. All the keys and dimensions have been found to be very relevant and strongly linked to the work of all the respondents, some to a higher and some to a lesser extent, although most of them admitted that they were not exactly aware of the RRI-AIRR concept before the current study took place.

A closer look at the documents has shown that even though the RRI terminology is missing, at least one policy could be connected to each of the RRI keys, which is serving as a roadmap for the whole organization. Regarding the AIRR dimensions, there is a lot of content particularly in the university's strategic documents. It is remarkable that inclusiveness is among the AIRR dimensions that are not as well integrated as it would have been expected and is even missing entirely from the documents. On the other hand, in the interviews and the focus group, it was discovered that there is a gap between anticipation and responsiveness, meaning a lot of work has been done on developing strategies and planning for the future, but there is a lack on the implementation of them. There was also common agreement that too much effort and time are invested in reflexivity, which serves as a barrier for more efficiency in responsiveness. Several good examples of best practices regarding all the RRI keys were explicitly mentioned. Science education is predominantly the key that has the most importance, as it is connected to the mission statement and the nature of the university as an institution. Especially in the field of open access/open science the university seems to be taking a pioneering role compared to other institutions in Switzerland and abroad. A gender equality plan is already in place for some time, while an Ethics Committee is currently being developed. More initiatives were mentioned with regards to public engagement and the collaboration with private businesses, but there is certainly space for improvement in strengthening the position of the university in this area.

Along the reviewing process, the precise actors that play a key role for the integration of the RRI keys and AIRR dimensions inside the organization were identified. On one hand there are the strategic initiatives related to entrepreneurship and the Strategic Initiative for Sustainability that enable public engagement. The Sustainability Committee was observed to have more of a responsive role, dedicated to the implementation of the Sustainability Strategy. The Strategic Affairs Office for R&D focuses on research integrity, ethics, and open science. The Strategic Office for Academic Affairs is directed toward science education. The HED Unit is also very important for developing and bringing strategies to the President's and Executive Board's attention focusing on anticipation. The Diversity Unit develops the policies on the topics of diversity/gender equality/discrimination and to a certain extent also performs monitoring tasks. It is considered very positive that one department is strongly focused on research in that field, the department of Social Work. The Diversity Committee with representatives from all eight departments is responsible for discussion and further adaptation of gender equality and inclusiveness. In open science the University Library with dedicated teams in open access and OER is the main actor; however, the proactive role of the university's President is also worth to mention. Finally, reflexivity is left to the Quality Committees of each of the departments and the Quality Committee at university level, who focus on self-evaluation and the renewal of accreditations.

Although it was generally understood that all the RRI keys and AIRR dimensions are quite well embedded in the organization, there were a lot of suggestions for further improvement. Increasing awareness of the importance of each of the keys among the Executive Board and the management at all levels was considered important. Better allocation of resources for more research on these topics could be very beneficial and it could further strengthen science education. For research integrity and ethics, the development of a Committee at university level is underway and will bring more standardization on the topic. A change of institutional culture with regards to gender equality and most of all diversity should be more encouraged and get better established, while evaluation mechanisms should be launched. The same holds true for cultivating a new mindset toward the usefulness of open science and publishing in open access, which is still missing. The AIRR dimensions should all be considered of equal significance for the organization and overconcentration on anticipation and reflexivity should be rather avoided. Inclusiveness and responsiveness should be more efficiently addressed in the policies and in practice.

Conclusion

This study has given important insights on how RRI is embedded in UASs in the Swiss national education system, a context that differs from similar studies (Owen et al., 2021a). The RRI keys and AIRR have provided a structured framework to evaluate the implementation of RRI in the organization. The findings from the expert interviews showed that RRI has been unofficially part of the university's policies and strategies mainly since 2015 and has been a driving force for transformation in all departments in the field of research. RRI is quite well embedded, and many good practices have been identified that support the RRI keys and AIRR dimensions. Given the insights and feedback from participants, it seems that the better RRI is embedded in the strategy of universities, the more it enables the university to find ways to address efficiently GSCs. Since the findings are based solely on one case study, it would be important to extend the research in more higher education institutions in Switzerland and in Europe and particularly business schools to compare the embeddedness of RRI in different national education systems.

References

Anderson, J. (2022). Harvard EdCast: Is the college enrollment decline really a crisis? The Harvard Graduate School of Education. https://www.gse.harvard.edu/news/ 22/03/harvard-edcast-college-enrollment-decline-really-crisis. Accessed on 4th January 2023.

Carayannis, E. G., & Campbell, D. F. (2009). "Mode 3" and "Quadruple Helix": Toward a 21st century fractal innovation ecosystem. *International Journal of Technology Management, 46*(3–4), 201–234.

Engwall, L. (Ed.). (2020). The governance and mission of universities. *Missions of universities* (pp. 1–19). Springer.

Etzkowitz, H. (2008). *The triple helix: University-industry-government innovation in action*. Routledge.

Etzkowitz, H. (2017). The entrepreneurial university. In *Encyclopedia of international higher education systems and institutions* (pp. 1–5).

European Commission, Directorate-General for Research and Innovation. (2013). *Options for strengthening responsible research and innovation: Report of the expert group on the state of Art in Europe on responsible research and innovation*. Publications Office. https://data.europa.eu/doi/10.2777/46253

Ferraro, F., Etzion, D., & Gehman, J. (2015). Tackling grand challenges pragmatically: Robust action revisited. *Organization Studies, 36*(3), 363–390.

Geoghegan-Quinn, M. (2012). Commissioner Geoghegan-Quinn Keynote Speech at the "Science in Dialogue". Conference, Odense, April 23–25.

Hajdinjak, M., Dimova, A., & Damianova, Z. (2022). D2.4 synthesis report on individual partner internal review reports. RRI-LEADERS- Grant Agreement No 101006439. https://www.rri-leaders.eu/wp-content/uploads/2022/09/D2.4-Internal-RRI-reviews-FINAL.pdf

Kerr, C. (1963). The idea of a multiversity. In C. Kerr (Ed.), *The uses of the university* (pp. 1–34). Harvard University Press.

Krücken, G. (2020). The European university as a multiversity. In *Missions of universities* (pp. 163–178). Springer.

Krücken, G., & Meier, F. (2006). Turning the university into an organizational actor. In *Globalization and organization: World society and organizational change* (pp. 241–257).

Longmore, A. L., Grant, G., & Golnaraghi, G. (2018). Closing the 21st-century knowledge gap: Reconceptualizing teaching and learning to transform business education. *Journal of Transformative Education, 16*(3), 197–219.

McKinsey * Company. (2020). Higher education enrolment: Inevitable decline or online opportunity? https://www.mckinsey.com/industries/public-and-social-sector/our-insights/higher-education-enrollment-inevitable-decline-or-online-opportunity. Accessed on 4th January 2023.

Mittelstrass, J. (2020). The idea and role of universities in society. In *Missions of universities* (pp. 21–30). Springer.

MoRRI Consortium. (2018). The evolution of responsible research and innovation in Europe: The MoRRI indicators report. Monitoring report (D4.3). https://morri.netlify.com/reports/2018-02-21-theevolution-of-responsible-research-and-innovation-in-europe-the-morri-indicators-report-d4-3. Accessed on 15th July 2020.

Owen, R., Macnaghten, P., & Stilgoe, J. (2012). Responsible research and innovation: From science in society to science for society, with society. *Science and Public Policy, 39*(6), 751–760.

Owen, R., Pansera, M., Macnaghten, P., & Randles, S. (2021a). Organisational institutionalisation of responsible innovation. *Research Policy, 50*(1), 104–132.

Owen, R., von Schomberg, R., & Macnaghten, P. (2021b). An unfinished journey? Reflections on a decade of responsible research and innovation. *Journal of Responsible Innovation, 8*(2), 217–233.

Rieckmann, M. (2018). Learning to transform the world: Key competencies in education for sustainable development. *Issues and Trends in Education for Sustainable Development, 39*, 39–59.

Rome Declaration. (2014). Rome declaration on responsible research and innovation in Europe. https://ec.europa.eu/research/swafs/pdf/rome_declaration_RRI_final_21_November.pdf

Scott, P. (2020). Universities in a 'Mode 2' society. In *Missions of universities* (pp. 95–113). Springer.

Sigurdson, K. T. (2013). Clark Kerr's multiversity and technology transfer in the modern American Research University. *The College Quarterly, 16*(2), n2.

Stehr, N. (1994). *Knowledge societies*. Sage.

Stilgoe, J., Owen, R., & Macnaghten, P. (2013). Developing a framework for responsible innovation. *Research Policy, 42*(3), 1568–1580.

United Nations Educational, Scientific and Cultural Organisation (UNESCO). (2021). Reimagining our futures together. A new social contract for education. https://unesdoc.unesco.org/ark:/48223/pf0000379707

Voegtlin, C., & Scherer, A. G. (2017). Responsible innovation and the innovation of responsibility: Governing sustainable development in a globalized world. *Journal of Business Ethics, 143*, 227–243.

Voegtlin, C., Scherer, A. G., Stahl, G. K., & Hawn, O. (2022). Grand societal challenges and responsible innovation. *Journal of Management Studies, 59*(1), 1–28.

Vogt, M., & Weber, C. (2020). The role of universities in a sustainable society. Why value-free research is neither possible nor desirable. *Sustainability, 12*(7), 2811.

von Schomberg, R. (2013). A vision of responsible research and innovation. In *Responsible innovation: Managing the responsible emergence of science and innovation in society* (pp. 51–74). Wiley.

World Intellectual Property Organisation (WIPO). (2022). *Global Innovation Index 2022: What is the future of innovation-driven growth?* WIPO. https://doi.org/10.34667/tind.46596

Part 2

Innovations in Teaching and Learning Methods

Chapter 5

Futures Thinking: Fostering Creativity for a Sustainable World

Antje Bierwisch[a] *and Marina Schmitz*[b]

[a]MCI | The Entrepreneurial School, Austria
[b]IEDC-Bled School of Management, Slovenia

Abstract

In an era of polycrisis, we argue that responsible leaders need to unlearn common thinking patterns imprinted by old (management) paradigms in order to find new solutions to the grand challenges of our time. To be able to overcome the "crisis of the imagination" and spur narratives about more sustainable futures, leaders need to update and restructure their skill sets and invest in developing anticipatory and futures (thinking) skills, as well as futures literacy as a competence. To achieve this on the student level, we also need to rethink business and management education at the university level by challenging the ways we teach, i.e., teaching pedagogics, as well as the content and story we want to tell about the future of management. Thus, with this chapter, we aim to rethink pedagogical methods and tools by introducing educators to potential pathways for equipping students with adequate skills to be able to "use-the-future". As the process of unlearning is difficult, we argue that we need to venture out of the business discipline and push the barriers of the business and management curriculum so as to be able to further unleash creativity and imagination. To achieve this aim, we propose the integration of methods and approaches from art-related disciplines, such as theater, visual arts, or design, into the business curriculum.

Keywords: Futures thinking; futures literacy; education for sustainable development; creativity; teaching pedagogy; management education revisited

Innovation in Responsible Management Education, 117–139
Copyright © 2024 Antje Bierwisch and Marina Schmitz
Published under exclusive licence by Emerald Publishing Limited
doi:10.1108/978-1-83549-464-620241008

Futures Thinking and Art in Management Education: An Introduction

"The future" is not a distant final destination, but a creative process that we all have the agency to participate in. As educators, our role is to equip students with the skills to navigate and shape this process. This requires us to rethink our pedagogical methods and tools, venturing beyond the traditional business discipline to unleash creativity and imagination. Futures Studies is an academic discipline that frequently relies on the utilization of creativity and the capacity to navigate unexplored domains of human experience (Miller et al., 2022).

However, unlearning or "decolonizing" said imagination is a difficult process (Björkén-Nyberg & Hoveskog, 2023). It involves challenging established norms and pushing the boundaries of the business and management curriculum, reintroducing creativity and imagination (Bol & Wolf, 2023) so that we can act upon the grand challenges of our time and become more resilient (Häggström & Schmidt, 2021; Inayatullah, 2020) as we invite more perspectives (Mangnus et al., 2021). We argue that, to achieve this, it is necessary to equip students with the skills to "use-the-future", as futures literacy must be learned, sustained, and reclaimed and thus requires a continuous, anticipative, and iterative approach (Kazemier et al., 2021), to not only help students but also provide potential for impact-oriented business schools (Spanjol et al., 2023). Such work involves establishing connections and promoting transformative outcomes via our scholarly endeavors – especially driving efforts to integrate it into the curriculum (Kononiuk et al., 2021).

Art-related disciplines such as theater, visual arts, and design offer unique methods and approaches that can be integrated into the business curriculum. These disciplines foster creativity, encourage out-of-the-box thinking, and provide new perspectives on problem-solving (Harris & Carter, 2021). However, despite their advantages, efforts to integrate the arts into management education have been slow, albeit showing a steady interest, as a recent bibliometric study by Safaa et al. (2023) showed. Therefore, it is probably not surprising that we are still seeing application examples and edited volumes on these topics continuing to emerge for the discipline of management education (Byrnes, 2022; Ferreira, 2018; Purg & Sutherland, 2017) but also for education in general (Gibson & Ewing, 2020; Hunter, 2018; Irimiás et al., 2022), providing insights into the transformation of curricula and use of pedagogics/ androgogics. Topics on leadership and ethics in particular have reemphasized the benefits and significant overlaps of the two (Freeman et al., 2022; Harrison & Akinc, 2000). Not only can the educational space benefit from a stronger intertwinement of them but also practitioners are looking into this matter much more (Mortensen et al., 2021; Schiuma; Schiuma, 2012).

Throughout history, art has consistently played a crucial role in both personal and collective forms of communication, serving as a means to connect disparate individuals and convey ideas that may be difficult to explain through verbal language (Nahm, 1947). Art, whether in the form of representation or abstraction, has the capacity to facilitate individuals' comprehension of the intricacy of future thoughts and to illuminate that which is concealed from view (Noddings & Brooks, 2017). Poetry and art serve as a means of conveying alternate and influential viewpoints (North, 2018), so offering fresh perspectives on potential future scenarios. Additionally, they facilitate dialogs concerning the desired and apprehended trajectories of our future (Noddings & Brooks, 2017). However, despite these observations, the profoundly innovative processes involved in visual arts, music, dance, and theater are sometimes regarded as an add-on to the curriculum rather than the core of it (Saunders, 2021), despite an increasing effort to bring the two disciplines together (Safaa et al., 2023).

Therefore, the aim of this chapter is threefold: First, we want to outline the potential of intertwining arts and management education, which is based on our belief that universities should be places for fostering imagination and creativity. Second, we want to provide and highlight examples of methods and tools that could be applied to bring arts to the field of futures studies. Third, we will flag up common pitfalls and best practices to guide interested educators who want to employ these methods and tools in their classrooms.

Overview of the Futures Literacy Laboratory (FLL) Approach

Futures literacy laboratories (FLLs) are one method for increasing futures thinking competence in the classroom. The application variety of this methodology is huge (Bergheim et al., 2018), also covering educational topics (Raleigh et al., 2018) and pressing challenges such as climate change (Hamid et al., 2022). The primary objective of FLLs is to emphasize and prioritize forward-looking assumptions, stimulate introspection and creativity, and motivate individuals to pose novel inquiries regarding diverse futures, thereby empowering them to effectively utilize future-oriented thinking and enhance their proficiency in understanding and shaping their own futures by rethinking the present (UNESCO, 2023). To guarantee the latter, i.e., empowering individuals to "embrace the future," it is essential to motivate participants in FLLs to openly discuss and contemplate their worldviews (i.e., their anticipatory assumptions) in order to get a deep understanding of how these beliefs influence the futures they may see.

In brief, the four phases of an FLL can be described as follows (please see Table 5.1 for further details and an applied example) (UNESCO, 2023):

(1) Phase 1: Reveal – This is the entry point to thinking about futures. It involves revealing participants' expected/probable and preferred/desirable futures and their underlying assumptions.
(2) Phase 2: Reframe – In this phase, a reframed alternative future is explored based on the identified underlying assumptions about the expected and preferred futures. This involves the introduction of disruption and provocation so as to invent new images of the future.
(3) Phase 3: New Questions – Participants ask new questions about the present, considering different images of the future.
(4) Phase 4: Next Steps – In the final phase, new questions and learnings are connected to what is to be done in the present, so as to "use the future".

Table 5.1. Futures Literacy Labs: Combining Futures Thinking and Management Education.

FLL Phase	What Is Important When Structuring the Phase?	Aim	Potential Methods/Tools	Possible Questions/Assignments[a]
Phase 1: Reveal	• Make diverse images of the future visible • Consensus is not necessary • No right or wrong – nobody knows the future • Use words that appeal to predictive thinking (e.g., "what do you expect/ what would you bet your money on?") • Stimulate participants' wishful and imaginative thinking through meditation/mind journeys	• Exploring probable and desirable futures • Connecting to participants and topic • Activating imagination and seeing barriers • Visualizing futures and their different anticipatory assumptions	• Visualizing futures with drawings/pictures • Journey of the mind • Trend and risk reports; megatrend maps • Systems mapping (iceberg model, causal loops, connected circles) • Stakeholder mapping • Futures wheel	Probable Futures (40 mins) *Individual writing:* Record on text cards what you expect to happen in 2035 regarding management in organizations. Formulate in the present tense. *Joint discussion:* Share the elements in the group one by one. Sort, deepen, and add to them. *Selection:* Agree on five cards that should be taken to the common "harvest" for a probable future of management in organizations. Choose a presenter to explain your shared probable future. *Present in the plenary:* Share your results with the other groups.

				Desirable Futures (30 mins) [Educator shares mind journey/meditation, 15 mins] *Share and create a collage/mashup:* Tell each other about the images you have seen on the journey to your desirable futures. Using drawings/pictures, emojis, or bullet points, create a collage that depicts your group's desirable futures on text cards. *Present in the plenary:* Share your results with the other groups.
Phase 2: Reframe	• Different from futures shared in Phase 1 • Avoid usage of dystopias as emotional triggers • Balance between demanding too much *vs* too little	• Experimenting with challenging, new, and thought-provoking futures • Strengthening imagination • Breaking out of old and familiar thinking • Broadening horizon	• Improvisation methods • LEGO® Serious Play® • Gamification (Thing from the Future, Sarkar Game, Future Game 2050) • Roleplay • Scenario methods	Alternative Futures (50–90 mins) *New assumption: In 2040, people have a great perceptiveness toward themselves, the environment, and the global economy. The absence of*

(Continued)

Table 5.1. (*Continued*)

FLL Phase	What Is Important When Structuring the Phase?	Aim	Potential Methods/Tools	Possible Questions/Assignments[a]
		• Practicing dealing with the unfamiliar • Creativity catalyst • Enabling the emergence of new assumptions	• Causal Layered Analysis • Walt Disney Method • Science fiction stories	*money and competitiveness characterize the economy itself.* "In 2040, Toni wakes up in the morning and starts a new working day. After a fresh coffee, he/she checks the agenda for the current day …" *Improvise a story* of this alternative future by considering the new setting/assumption above. Together in your group, you will improvise a story about Toni's working day in this alternative future of management in organizations in 2040. In each group, one person will start with the suggested sentence, then the next

person will continue with a sentence or a few words. Go in turns and build the story together.
Be spontaneous and quick. Say the first thing that comes to mind. Do not write anything down. Have fun!
What does management look like in this alternative future?
Record your group ideas on text cards/post-its.
Formulate bullet points or sentences and draw pictures.
Please do not discuss whether this future is likely or desirable, but fill it with details. There is no right or wrong!
Present in the plenary:
Share your results with the other groups.

(Continued)

Table 5.1. (*Continued*)

FLL Phase	What Is Important When Structuring the Phase?	Aim	Potential Methods/Tools	Possible Questions/ Assignments[a]
Phase 3: Rethink	• Facilitators should ensure a slow transition inputs from Phases 1–2 back into the room (e.g., via pinboards) • Bring all collective	Comparing futures and finding new, emerging questions, use this openness to see new things	• Reflective journaling • Open discussions	Powerful new questions (50–90 mins) Take two text cards, walk through our collection of futures, and *write your questions down.* Please indicate your name in the lower right corner. • What questions come up? What is still open? • What do you find exciting? • What would you most like to deal with right now? • *Share your questions in the plenary* – no explanation necessary. • Are there connections between questions? Assign your own question to similar ones on the pinboard.

| Phase 4: Act | • Participants choose or prioritize, after the creativity, openness, and diversity of Phase 2
• Discuss implementation challenges of new ideas (e.g., hierarchies, silos) | Realizing and implementing futures by producing tangible and presentable results: "What came out?/What was the result?" | • Backcasting/ roadmapping
• Mind-mapping and clustering of ideas
• Task lists and working groups
• Networking
• Research questions
• Scenario technique
• Future personas
• Prototyping | Ideas for action (50–90 mins)
Working with powerful questions: Individually choose a cluster of questions.
• What is this cluster about?
• What connects the individual questions?
• Do new ideas for action emerge?

Use respective tools (e.g., backcasting, prototyping) to realize your vision. |

Source: Reprinted with permission from Schmitz and Cordova (2023).

[a]These instructions were part of a Futures Literacy Laboratory conducted in September 2022, on the topic "Futures of Management in Organizations."

Futures Thinking, Art, and Creativity in the Classroom: Status Quo

Future competencies are in high demand in the educational field for tackling the grand challenges of today (Gáspár et al., 2021; Rieckmann, 2012; UNESCO, 2021). Futures thinking is one way of "using the future", embracing uncertainty, and being able to deal with complexity. It has been labeled among the essential competencies students are required to accomplish in the larger context of sustainability (Brundiers et al., 2021). Additionally, responsible futures have emerged that aim to shed light on the boundaries of where corporations' (but also an individual's) responsibility ends, i.e., whether they might consider the full-time span of their (business) activities' effects (Fuller et al., 2024), which is aligned with the idea of sustainable development and impact.

As an associated concept, drawing on responsibility, futures consciousness refers to an individual's capacity to comprehend, predict, and make arrangements for future events and circumstances (Lalot et al., 2021). Within this ecosystem of future-related competencies and skills, "futures literacy" especially (Miller, 2015; Miller & Sandford, 2019), or anticipatory competence and systems thinking, can be fostered through the arts and sustainability, these forming a powerful combination for imagining positive and inclusive futures for all (Cremers, 2022; Molderez & Ceulemans, 2018).

The call for fostering imagination, creativity, and innovation in education has increased over the last years (Krzeski, 2017) – especially in connection with the field of sustainability as we need new educational approaches to deal with climate-related anxiety and other emotions (Ponzelar, 2022). Cultivating imagination may also trigger a behavioral shift that could empower students to realize their agency and move from cognitive to emotional and behavioral learning outcomes. Such a process can be enhanced through a reconnection of management education with other disciplines that provide multifaceted perspectives, e.g., fostering sociological imagination to make sense of organizational phenomena (Facer, 2022) or reintroducing learning in settings of discursive plurality by questioning certain phenomena from a power or historical perspective (Clegg & Ross-Smith, 2003). The process of using imagination as a core component of futures thinking could enable students to find their own narratives to construct their personal futures (Sools, 2020). Also, by entering this process of fostering futures thinking competence in higher education curricula, evolutionary learning ecosystems can be created that make education future-fit and empower students to find, tell, and navigate their own stories (Spencer-Keyse et al., 2020).

As appealing as the concept is, there are certain challenges and barriers in place (Mortensen et al., 2021; Poli, 2021). Thus, guidelines and compendia are required that explain the concept from a very practical perspective (Bergheim, 2021; Sippl et al., 2023; World Business Council for Sustainable Development [WBCSD], 2017). Numerous tools and approaches employed in this discipline are specifically designed to facilitate the exploration and realization of individual and communal imaginations, which are essential for the development of alternative futures.

The Power of Art-Related Disciplines in Rethinking (Sustainable) Futures

Universities should be places for fostering imagination and creativity (Facer, 2022) – however, we need to assess the fact that oftentimes they are not. By integrating the arts into management education, we can create an environment that encourages innovative thinking and problem-solving. This can add a fresh perspective and innovative methods to traditional business education, fostering said creativity and imagination, which are crucial for the leaders of tomorrow. Thus, the combination of arts and futures, and their integration into management education, holds immense potential. First, art-related disciplines foster creativity and imagination, skills that are increasingly being recognized as essential in the business world for imagining alternative futures. Second, they encourage the embracing of complexity and out-of-the-box thinking, which are essential for uncovering new questions, and thereby rethinking present and future and developing a holistic understanding of the world, appreciating the interconnectedness of different systems, and understanding the broader impact of business decisions. Third, art-related disciplines can empower students to enact the change they want to see by first exploring uncertain terrain, by allowing plurality and variety, even in settings characterized by controversial discussions. Lastly, integrating futures and the arts into management education can make learning more engaging and enjoyable. It can break the monotony of traditional lectures and assignments, increasing student engagement and improving learning outcomes.

To be more specific, the following examples illustrate how arts and futures can be combined to foster creativity in management education settings. Whereas examples within the section on visual arts and music can be integrated during Phases 1 and 2 of the FLL, the more embodied experiences of theater and dance lend themselves very well to Phases 3 and 4.

Visual Arts and Storytelling

Visual arts can be used to encourage visual thinking among students. Techniques such as mind-mapping or sketching can help students visualize complex business strategies or processes, leading to innovative ideas and solutions. For example, they could create a mind map to outline a business strategy, or a sketch to illustrate a complex process.

Working with trends in the form of megatrends maps such as "Mega Trends and Technologies 2017-2050" by Watson (2023) can help, as a starting point to broaden the horizon and as a way to build scenarios in 2x2 matrixes. These four scenarios can be populated with different pictures that describe the envisioned scenario at hand (Zuehlke et al., 2020).

Foresight and forecasting-related tools provide a structured approach to exploring futures and help students understand trends, identify opportunities, and make informed decisions. The foresight instrument scenario technique (e.g., Gausemeier et al., 1998) is a crucial tool in management education at universities, as it equips students with the ability to anticipate and strategically navigate complex future landscapes, fostering a proactive and innovative mindset that is essential for effective leadership in an ever-evolving business world. Through the development and integration of scenario pictures with stories, it offers a comprehensive approach that vividly expresses the relevant factors and their potential developments in future scenarios.

Scenario stories, as a form of storytelling, offer a narrative framework that allows students to delve into hypothetical futures, enhancing their strategic-thinking and decision-making skills (Ramírez & Selin, 2014). These stories, rich in detail and context, enable learners to grasp complex business dynamics and potential outcomes in a more relatable and engaging manner. The scenario pictures serve as a visual tool, providing a tangible representation of these future possibilities. These visual elements not only facilitate a better comprehension of abstract concepts, but also stimulate creative thinking, encouraging students to visualize and prepare for various future scenarios (Eppler & Platts, 2009). This blend of strategic foresight and artistic expression not only enhances cognitive skills but also fosters emotional engagement. Together, these art-related elements – narrative storytelling and visual representation – significantly enrich the learning experience in management education, fostering a deeper understanding and a more holistic approach to strategic planning and foresight.

Originally from the field of design, the approach of design thinking has found its way into business problem-solving. It involves empathizing with users, defining problems, ideating solutions, prototyping, and testing. This iterative process encourages creative thinking and innovation. It involves providing students with a real-world problem, guiding them through the design-thinking process, and encouraging them to come up with innovative solutions (Johansson-Sköldberg et al., 2013) to foster visioning. These elements can be paired with prototyping, e.g., using card decks outlining different future persona (The Future Game 2050, 2023). These imagined worlds can then be built using, e.g., LEGO® bricks in LEGO® Serious Play® prototyping attempts, providing tangible ways for students to explore these visions.

Music

Music can be used to explore patterns and rhythms which are also present in business cycles. Understanding these patterns can lead to creative problem-solving strategies that can be discussed in collaborative exchanges between scientists and musicians. Educators can start exploring ways to incorporate music into their lessons so as to find pathways for advocating for sustainability (European Music Policy Exchange [EMPE], 2023; Litchfield, 2023) and social change (Rabinowitch, 2020). The protest song of Indian rap singer, Sofia Ashraf, against Unilever (Rahman, 2015) or those of Indigenous Brazilian musicians against ecocide and ethnocide (Miranda, 2020) can serve as just two examples rich enough to portray and enable learning about sustainable futures expressed through art.

Theater

In management education, theater can be used to simulate real-life business scenarios. This method allows students to step into the shoes of different stakeholders, understand their perspectives, and come up with creative solutions. For instance, a student playing the role of a CEO in a crisis management scenario would need to think creatively to navigate the company through the crisis. Educators could also simulate a board meeting or a negotiation scenario and assign different roles to students. This would require them to think from different perspectives and come up with creative solutions.

Drawing inspiration from (socio) drama (Ødegaard, 2023) and improvisation in theater studies (Schwenke et al., 2021), role play can be a powerful tool in management education – especially from a sustainability angle. Role play can encourage students to envision alternative futures and explore different societal roles. Further, it can help students better understand different perspectives, enhancing their ability to lead diverse teams and negotiate effectively, as well as develop empathy (Johnson, 2020). The genre of solarpunk – the word stemming from "solar" energy as a renewable resource, and "punk", symbolizing nonconformity and rebellion against established norms – as a subgenre of science fiction, provides powerful narratives for this kind of storytelling. It explores a future in which we successfully address major ecological or social contemporary challenges like climate change, pollution, and social inequality (X. R. Wordsmiths, 2023).

Dance

Bringing futures narratives and storytelling to life can be done not only through theater but also through dance. Although its application potential to business and management education might not be straightforward, educators have made various attempts to uncover learnings for organizations and their leaders (Biehl, 2017; Springborg & Sutherland, 2016). For example, educators could share case studies in the form of stories or encourage students to present their projects as stories through dance. As venturing into the field of dance might be quite challenging for educators in the field of management, exploring co-creation might be one starting point (Springborg, 2017).

Integrating Art-Related Practices and Pedagogies Into the Management Curriculum

As integrating arts into management education can be a powerful statement, there are only a few examples of schools that have considered this integration. Table 5.2 includes selected examples of arts integration across different HEIs and their business programs.

Finally, we want to discuss common pitfalls to avoid when integrating these methods into curricula, as well as some best practices to ensure a successful implementation.

Table 5.2. Overview of Selected Art-Related Practices Worldwide.

School	Continent	Description
George Mason University's School of Business	North America	This school has applied the liberal education approach to the study of business. They use a combination of high-impact practices, such as first-year seminars, common intellectual experiences, learning communities, collaborative assignments, undergraduate research, community-based learning, internships, capstone courses and projects, and diversity and global learning (Magro et al., 2022).
NYU's Stern School of Business	North America	Students at NYU's Stern School of Business can take up to half their courses in the College of Arts and Sciences (Roman-Cohen, 2021).
Escola de Administração de Empresas de São Paulo da Fundação Getulio Vargas (FGV-EAESP	South America	This school integrates art into a required sustainability course, where students create and exhibit their own paintings and sculptures to express and discuss sustainability issues.
Goa Institute of Management	Asia	This school uses theater and music as pedagogical tools in organizational behavior and general management courses. Students prepare skits based on workplace experiences and use music to illustrate social movements.
IEDC Bled School of Management	Europe	This school requires all business students to take the course Art and Leadership, where they interact with prominent artists and learn how art can be a source of reflection, inspiration,

Table 5.2. *(Continued)*

School	Continent	Description
		and motivation for management.
Grenoble Ecole de Management	Europe	This school offers an online course called Art and Management, where students collaborate with artists and use the arts to develop experiential marketing projects.
Stockholm School of Economics (SSE)	Europe	This school has an Art Initiative that embeds the arts into the academic environment and makes art central to the school's overall mission. The school organizes exhibitions, workshops, talks, and book clubs related to art and sustainability.
University of Navarra	Europe	This school collaborates with the Museum of the University of Navarra to organize Lead Creative, a platform that brings together professionals, experts, faculty, and students to promote creative leadership and innovation.
IAE Lyon School of Management	Europe	This school offers free workshops delivered by professional artists to help students develop their creativity. The workshops include photography, design, dance, and theater.
University of Southampton	Europe	This school organizes Green Stories, a series of writing competitions that encourage experts, professional writers, and students to use short stories to imagine how sustainable

(Continued)

Table 5.2. *(Continued)*

School	Continent	Description
		business models could work in practice.
Ivey Business School	North America	This school has an extensive collection of Canadian art displayed throughout the buildings. The school believes that art can inspire creativity, curiosity, and awe in students.
Aalto University	Europe	The Creative Sustainability Program brings students from various fields together to work on multidisciplinary teams that create novel sustainable solutions for human, urban, industrial, and business environments (Aalto University, 2023).
University of New South Wales	Australia	This university offers a Bachelor of Arts and Business, a unique interdisciplinary collaboration between UNSW Business School and the university's departments of arts, design, and architecture (UNSW Sydney, 2022).
Özyeğin University	Eurasia	Here, students put together an exhibition of artworks from the school's collection, in which the works selected represented different Sustainable Development Goals (Pala, 2021).

Source: Own depiction based on Weybrecht (2022).

Common Pitfalls and Practical Recommendations

Integrating art-related disciplines into management education can be a rewarding endeavor, but it also comes with its own set of challenges. Based on Weybrecht (2022), here are some common pitfalls that educators should be aware of:

- Resistance to change: Students and faculty may resist the integration of arts into the management curriculum as doing so deviates from traditional teaching methods. It is important to communicate the benefits clearly and provide support during the transition.
- Lack of expertise: Not all educators may feel comfortable or have the necessary skills to teach art-related disciplines. Professional development or collaboration with arts faculty can help overcome this challenge.
- Time constraints: Incorporating new methods and activities can be time-consuming. Educators need to plan carefully to ensure that they can cover all necessary material.
- Assessment challenges: Assessing creativity and imagination can be subjective and challenging compared to traditional exams and assignments. Developing clear assessment criteria and assessment formats is crucial.
- Overemphasis on creativity: While creativity is important, it is also essential not to neglect other important business skills such as critical thinking, analytical skills, and practical business knowledge.
- Lack of resources: Depending on the methods used, integrating arts into the curriculum might require additional resources like art supplies, space for performances, equipment, etc.

To avoid some of the pitfalls outlined above, it is important to experiment, perhaps by integrating arts-related activities into a few lessons or a single course, and then gradually expanding as you gain more experience and confidence. Two resources provide some general ideas on how to incorporate art into lessons to enhance student engagement and creativity (Foster, 2013), as well as discussing benefits and pathways for implementation into the core curriculum (Davis, 2013). The goal is not to turn management students into artists but rather to use arts as a tool to foster creativity, enhance understanding, and make learning more engaging. To achieve this, educators may want to consider the following practices to ensure a successful integration:

- Start small: Begin by integrating arts-related activities into a few lessons or a single course. This allows you to gauge student response and make necessary adjustments before expanding to other areas of the curriculum. This can also help to overcome a lack of resources and time constraints.
- Collaborate: Collaborate with arts faculty or professionals in your institution or community. They can provide valuable insights and guidance on how to effectively incorporate the arts into your teaching. Connect with fellow peers who follow the "sharing is caring" principle so as to accelerate learning, overcome the lack of expertise, and ensure you diversify your network.
- Provide context: Always provide context for why you are using art-related activities and how they relate to the learning objectives. This helps students understand the relevance and value of these activities and reduces resistance.
- Encourage participation: Create a safe and supportive environment that encourages students to participate, take risks, and express their creativity.

- Reflect and debrief: After each activity, take time to reflect and debrief. Discuss what students learned, what they found challenging, and how they can apply these learnings in a business context.
- Continuous learning: As an educator, be open to learning and trying new things. Attend workshops, read relevant literature, and continuously seek ways to improve your teaching practice.
- Assess creatively: Develop clear criteria for assessing creativity and provide constructive feedback. This could include peer assessment, self-assessment, or project-based assessments. Come up with alternative ways on how to mirror creative learning formats with matching assessment formats, such as reflective journals, video design, or podcasts.

Conclusion

As educators, we have a responsibility to prepare our students for the future. By integrating art-related disciplines into our curriculum, we can equip them with the skills they need to navigate this uncertain landscape, such as futures thinking, which sparks imagination and creativity. Creativity is a crucial skill for the future of work, according to the World Economic Forum that lists creativity as one of the top 10 skills of 2025 (World Economic Forum, 2020). It is not only about generating new ideas but also about seeing the world through different lenses and rethinking what is possible or desirable – a common aim that arts and futures-related methods share.

Currently, business schools are using various methods to integrate arts and futures into their courses: Some offer dedicated courses on art or futures and management, some embed both topics into their overall missions and environments, some collaborate with artists/museums or futurists, and some organize extracurricular activities and competitions. Integrating futures and arts into the management curriculum can be a transformative experience for both educators and students – it is worth trying it and finding out which implementation pathway works best for you.

References

Aalto University. (2023). *Creative sustainability: Re-thinking design, business and chemical engineering.* https://www.aalto.fi/en/creative-sustainability

Bergheim, S. (2021). *Futures–open to variety: A manual for the wise use of the later-than-now.* ZgF Publishers.

Bergheim, S., Rhisiart, M., Cagnin, C., Garrido Luzardo, L., Nosarzewski, K., Koch, P. M., Kamara, K., Gouguet, J.-J., Karuri-Sebina, G., Miller, R., Bellettini Cedeño, O., Arellano, A., Marasco, M. G., Rudkin, J., Akomolafe, B., Eyakuze, A., Matotay, E., Coulibaly Leroy, S., Djidingar, N., ... Cruz, S. (2018). The futures literacy laboratory-novelty (FLL-N) case studies. In R. Miller (Ed.), *Transforming the future: Anticipation in the 21st century* (pp. 110–229). UNESCO Publishing; Routledge Taylor & Francis Group.

Biehl, B. (2017). *Dance and organization: Integrating dance theory and methods into the study of management. Routledge studies in management, organizations and society.* Taylor and Francis.

Björkén-Nyberg, C., & Hoveskog, M. (2023). Decolonizing the imagination: Designing a futures literacy workshop. In E. Brooks, J. Sjöberg, A. K. Møller, & E. Edstrand (Eds.), *Design, learning, and innovation. DLI 2022. Lecture notes of the institute for computer sciences, social informatics and telecommunications engineering* (pp. 168–181). Springer. https://doi.org/10.1007/978-3-031-31392-9_13

Bol, E., & Wolf, M. de (2023). Developing futures literacy in the classroom. *Futures, 146,* 103082. https://doi.org/10.1016/j.futures.2022.103082

Brundiers, K., Barth, M., Cebrián, G., Cohen, M., Diaz, L., Doucette-Remington, S., Dripps, W., Habron, G., Harré, N., Jarchow, M., Losch, K., Michel, J., Mochizuki, Y., Rieckmann, M., Parnell, R., Walker, P., & Zint, M. (2021). Key competencies in sustainability in higher education – Toward an agreed-upon reference framework. *Sustainability Science, 16*(1), 13–29. https://doi.org/10.1007/s11625-020-00838-2

Byrnes, W. J. (2022). *Management and the arts* (6th ed.). Taylor & Francis Group.

Clegg, S. R., & Ross-Smith, A. (2003). Revising the boundaries: Management education and learning in a postpositivist world. *The Academy of Management Learning and Education, 2*(1), 85–98. https://doi.org/10.5465/amle.2003.9324049

Cremers, P. H. M. (2022). Futures literacy, arts, and sustainability: A powerful match? In N. Deutzkens, K. van Poeck, M. Deleye, J. Læssøe, J. Lönngren, H. Lotz-Sisitka, J. Lysgaard, J. Öhman, L. Östman, E. Vandenplas, & A. Wals (Eds.), *Challenges for environmental and sustainability education research in times of climate crisis: 15th invitational seminar on environmental & sustainability education research* (pp. 43–46). Ghent University. https://uwe-repository.worktribe.com/OutputFile/10019788#page=50

Davis, M. (2013, April 17). *Arts integration: Resource roundup.* George Lucas Educational Foundation. https://www.edutopia.org/arts-integration-resources

Eppler, M. J., & Platts, K. W. (2009). Visual strategizing: The systematic use of visualization in the strategic-planning process. *Long Range Planning, 42*(1), 42–74. https://www.sciencedirect.com/science/article/pii/s0024630108001180

European Music Policy Exchange. (2023). *Welcome to the European music cities policy guide.* https://www.europeanmusicpolicyexchange.eu/home

Facer, K. (2022). Imagination and the future university. *Critical Times, 5*(1), 202–216. https://doi.org/10.1215/26410478-9536559

Ferreira, F. A. (2018). Mapping the field of arts-based management: Bibliographic coupling and co-citation analyses. *Journal of Business Research, 85,* 348–357. https://doi.org/10.1016/j.jbusres.2017.03.026

Foster, R. (2013, March 22). 50 ways to integrate art into any lesson. *Open Colleges.* https://www.opencolleges.edu.au/blogs/articles/50-ways-to-integrate-art-into-any-lesson

Freeman, R. E., Dunham, L., Fairchild, G., & Parmar, B. L. (2022). Leveraging the creative arts in business ethics teaching. In M. Dion, R. E. Freeman, & S. D. Dmytriyev (Eds.), *Humanizing business: What humanities can say to business* (pp. 355–370). Springer. https://doi.org/10.1007/978-3-030-72204-3_26

Fuller, T., Marchais-Roubelat, A., Roubelat, F., Heraclide, N., & Ward, A. K. (2024). Responsible futures. In *The handbook of futures studies.* Edward Elgar Publishing. https://philpapers.org/rec/fulrfe

Gáspár, J., Hideg, E., & Köves, A. (2021). Future in the present: Participatory futures research methods in economic higher education – The development of future competencies. *Journal of Futures Studies, 26*(2), 1–18.

Gausemeier, J., Fink, A., & Schlake, O. (1998). Scenario management. *Technological Forecasting and Social Change, 59*(2), 111–130. https://doi.org/10.1016/S0040-1625(97)00166-2

Gibson, R., & Ewing, R. (2020). *Transforming the curriculum through the arts* (2nd ed.). Springer International Publishing; Imprint Palgrave Macmillan. https://doi.org/10.1007/978-3-030-52797-6

Häggström, M., & Schmidt, C. (2021). Futures literacy – To belong, participate and act. *Futures, 132*, 102813. https://doi.org/10.1016/j.futures.2021.102813

Hamid, S., Anwer, S., & Khatani, S. A. (2022). IMAGINE – Designing futures literacy labs for sustaining climate change. *Journal of Futures Studies.* https://jfsdigital.org/imagine-designing-futures-literacy-labs-for-sustaining-climate-change/

Harris, A., & Carter, M. R. (2021). Applied creativity and the arts. *Curriculum Perspectives, 41*(1), 107–112. https://doi.org/10.1007/s41297-020-00127-z

Harrison, J. K., & Akinc, H. (2000). Lessons in leadership from the arts and literature: A liberal arts approach to management education through fifth discipline learning. *Journal of Management Education, 24*(3), 391–413. https://doi.org/10.1177/105256290002400309

Hunter, M. A. (2018). *Education, arts and sustainability: Emerging practice for a changing world. SpringerLink Bücher.* Springer. https://doi.org/10.1007/978-981-10-7710-4

Inayatullah, S. (2020). Scenarios for teaching and training: From being "Kodaked" to futures literacy and futures-proofing. *CSPS Strategy and Policy Journal, 8*, 31–48. http://www.csps.org.bn/wp-content/uploads/2021/05/csps-volume-8.pdf#page=39

Irimiás, A. R., Mitev, A. Z., & Volo, S. (2022). Digital arts-based collaborative learning in management education. *International Journal of Management in Education, 20*(3), 100727. https://doi.org/10.1016/j.ijme.2022.100727

Johansson-Sköldberg, U., Woodilla, J., & Çetinkaya, M. (2013). Design thinking: Past, present and possible futures. *Creativity and Innovation Management, 22*(2), 121–146. https://doi.org/10.1111/caim.12023

Johnson, I. (2020). "Solarpunk" & the pedagogical value of utopia. *Journal of Sustainability Education, 23.*

Kazemier, E. M., Damhof, L., Gulmans, J., & Cremers, P. H. (2021). Mastering futures literacy in higher education: An evaluation of learning outcomes and instructional design of a faculty development program. *Futures, 132*, 102814. https://doi.org/10.1016/j.futures.2021.102814

Kononiuk, A., Sacio-Szymańska, A., Ollenburg, S., Trivelli, L., & Trivelli, L. (2021). Teaching foresight and futures literacy and its integration into university curriculum. *Foresight and STI Governance, 15*(3 (eng)), 105–121.

Krzeski, J. (2017). Overcoming a crisis of imagination: The university and its futures. *Cadernos CIMEAC, 7*(2), 204–212. https://doi.org/10.18554/cimeac.v7i2.2479

Lalot, F., Ahvenharju, S., & Minkkinen, M. (2021). *Aware of the future? Psychological test adaptation and development.* Advance Online Publication. Article 2698-1866/a000014. https://doi.org/10.1027/2698-1866/a000014

Litchfield, A. (2023, June 27). How music can support sustainability work. *Network for Business Sustainability (NBS)*. https://nbs.net/how-music-can-support-sustainability-work

Magro, A., Gring-Pemble, L. M., & Bishop, C. R. (2022). Integrating liberal education, business, and high-impact practices – The case of George Mason University's School of Business. *Journal of International Education in Business, 15*(1), 32–51. https://doi.org/10.1108/JIEB-03-2021-0041

Mangnus, A. C., Oomen, J., Vervoort, J. M., & Hajer, M. A. (2021). Futures literacy and the diversity of the future. *Futures, 132*, 102793. https://doi.org/10.1016/j.futures.2021.102793

Miller, R. (2015). Learning, the future, and complexity. An essay on the emergence of futures literacy. *European Journal of Education, 50*(4), 513–523. https://doi.org/10.1111/ejed.12157

Miller, R., Feukeu, K. E., & Raleigh, N. B. (2022). *Futures studies, anticipation, and futures literacy: An invitation to co-create a living framework.*

Miller, R., & Sandford, R. (2019). Futures literacy: The capacity to diversify conscious human anticipation. In R. Poli (Ed.), *Springer ebook collection. Handbook of anticipation: Theoretical and applied aspects of the use of future in decision making* (pp. 73–91). Springer. https://doi.org/10.1007/978-3-319-91554-8_77

Miranda, B. (2020, October 26). "The way I am is an outrage": The indigenous Brazilian musicians taking back a burning country. *The Guardian*. https://www.theguardian.com/music/2020/oct/26/brazil-music-indigenous-tribes-environment-bolsonaro

Molderez, I., & Ceulemans, K. (2018). The power of art to foster systems thinking, one of the key competencies of education for sustainable development. *Journal of Cleaner Production, 186*, 758–770. https://doi.org/10.1016/j.jclepro.2018.03.120

Mortensen, J. K., Larsen, N., & Kruse, M. (2021). Barriers to developing futures literacy in organisations. *Futures, 132*, 102799. https://doi.org/10.1016/j.futures.2021.102799

Nahm, M. C. (1947). The functions of art and fine art in communication. *The Journal of Aesthetics and Art Criticism, 5*(4), 273–280. https://doi.org/10.2307/426134

Noddings, N., & Brooks, L. (2017). *Teaching controversial issues: The case for critical thinking and moral commitment in the classroom.* Teachers College Press.

North, K. (2018, October 2). Poetry has a power to inspire change like no other art form. *The Conversation*. https://theconversation.com/poetry-has-a-power-to-inspire-change-like-no-other-art-form-99722

Ødegaard, M. (2023). Using drama in science education and for sustainability issues. In D. McGregor & D. Anderson (Eds.), *Learning science through drama: Exploring international perspectives* (pp. 69–86). Springer. https://doi.org/10.1007/978-3-031-17350-9_5

Pala, O. (2021, October 25). *CoArt CoAct – Sustainability through art*. Global Business School Network. https://gbsn.org/coart-coact-sustainability-through-art/

Poli, R. (2021). The challenges of futures literacy. *Futures, 132*, 102800. https://doi.org/10.1016/j.futures.2021.102800

Ponzelar, C. (2022). Care in times of climate crisis. In N. Deutzkens, K. van Poeck, M. Deleye, J. Læssøe, J. Lönngren, H. Lotz-Sisitka, J. Lysgaard, J. Öhman, L. Östman, E. Vandenplas, & A. and Wals (Eds.), *Challenges for environmental and sustainability education research in times of climate crisis: 15th invitational seminar on environmental & sustainability education research* (pp. 56–58). Ghent University.

Purg, D., & Sutherland, I. (2017). Why art in management education? Questioning meaning. *Academy of Management Review, 42*(2), 382–396. https://doi.org/10.5465/amr.2016.0047

Rabinowitch, T.-C. (2020). The potential of music to effect social change. *Music & Science, 3.* https://doi.org/10.1177/2059204320939772

Rahman, M. (2015, August 7). Indian rapper "overwhelmed" by success of protest song against Unilever. *The Guardian.* https://www.theguardian.com/world/2015/aug/07/indian-rapper-sofia-ashraf-success-protest-song-unilever

Raleigh, N. A. B., Pouru, L., Leino-Richert, E., Parkkinen, M., & Wilenius, M. (2018). *Futures literacy lab for education: Imagining complex futures of human settlements at Finland futures academy summer school 2017.* https://www.utupub.fi/bitstream/handle/10024/147415/ffrc_ebook_3-2018.pdf

Ramírez, R., & Selin, C. (2014). Plausibility and probability in scenario planning. *Foresight, 16*(1), 54–74. https://doi.org/10.1108/FS-08-2012-0061

Rieckmann, M. (2012). Future-oriented higher education: Which key competencies should be fostered through university teaching and learning? *Futures, 44*(2), 127–135. https://doi.org/10.1016/j.futures.2011.09.005

Roman-Cohen, T. (2021, May 4). Why liberal arts majors thrive in business. *Mba. Com.* https://www.mba.com/business-school-and-careers/career-possibilities/why-liberal-arts-majors-thrive-in-business

Safaa, L., Khazi, A., Perkumienė, D., & Labanauskas, V. (2023). Arts-based management between actions and conjunctions: Lessons from a systematic bibliometric analysis. *Administrative Sciences, 13*(9), 200. https://doi.org/10.3390/admsci13090200

Saunders, J. N. (2021). The power of the arts in learning and the curriculum: A review of research literature. *Curriculum Perspectives, 41*(1), 93–100. https://doi.org/10.1007/s41297-021-00138-4

Schiuma, G. Mapping arts-based initiatives: Assessing the organisational value of the arts. http://www.arts4business.org/content/resources/reports/Mapping-Arts-Based-Initiatives.pdf

Schiuma, G. (2012). *The value of arts for business* (1st paperback ed.). Cambridge University Press. https://doi.org/10.1017/CBO9780511852015

Schmitz, M. A., & Cordova, M. (2023). A new approach for teaching and learning sustainability: Futures studies meet international business. *AIB Insights.* https://doi.org/10.46697/001c.84254

Schwenke, D., Dshemuchadse, M., Rasehorn, L., Klarhölter, D., & Scherbaum, S. (2021). Improv to improve: The impact of improvisational theater on creativity, acceptance, and psychological well-being. *Journal of Creativity in Mental Health, 16*(1), 31–48. https://doi.org/10.1080/15401383.2020.1754987

Sippl, C., Brandhofer, G., & Rauscher, E. (Eds.). (2023). *Pädagogik für Niederösterreich: Band 13. Futures literacy: Zukunft lernen und lehren.* StudienVerlag. https://doi.org/10.53349/oa.2022.a2.170

Sools, A. (2020). Back from the future: A narrative approach to study the imagination of personal futures. *International Journal of Social Research Methodology, 23*(4), 451–465. https://doi.org/10.1080/13645579.2020.1719617

Spanjol, J., Rosa, A., Schirrmeister, E., Dahl, P., Domnik, D., Lindner, M., La Cruz, M. de, & Kuhlmann, J.-F. (2023). The potential of futures literacy for impact-oriented business schools. *Futures, 146,* 103084. https://doi.org/10.1016/j.futures.2022.103084

Spencer-Keyse, J., Luksha, P., & Cubista, J. (2020). *Learning ecosystems. An emerging praxis for the future of education.* https://learningecosystems2020.globaledufutures. org/

Springborg, C. (2017). Teaching co-creation in higher education through dance exercises. In T. Chemi & L. Krogh (Eds.), *Creative education. Co-creation in higher education: Students and educators preparing creatively and collaboratively to the challenge of the future* (pp. 49–65). SensePublishers. https://doi.org/10.1007/978-94-6351-119-3_4

Springborg, C., & Sutherland, I. (2016). Teaching MBAs aesthetic agency through dance. *Organizational Aesthetics, 5*(1), 94–113.

The Future Game 2050. (2023). *Scenona cards – Future journey.* https://www. thefuturegame2050.com/scenonacards

UNESCO. (2021). *Futures literacy: An essential competency for the 21st century.* https://en.unesco.org/themes/futures-literacy

UNESCO. (2023). *Futures literacy & foresight: Using futures to prepare, plan, and innovate.* https://unesdoc.unesco.org/ark:/48223/pf0000386511

UNSW Sydney. (2022). *Handbook – Arts and business.* https://www.handbook.unsw. edu.au/undergraduate/programs/2022/3444?year=2022

Watson, R. (2023). *What's next – Thinking tools.* https://nowandnext.com/thinking-tools/

Weybrecht, G. (2022, November 15). Teaching business through an artful lens. *AACSB.* https://www.aacsb.edu/insights/articles/2022/11/teaching-business-through-an-artful-lens

Wordsmiths, X. R. (2023). *XR Solarpunk storytelling showcase.* https://www. solarpunkstorytelling.com/

World Business Council for Sustainable Development. (2017). *A guide to futures thinking – World Business Council for Sustainable Development (WBCSD).* https:// www.wbcsd.org/Archive/Sustainable-Lifestyles/Resources/A-Guide-to-Futures-Thinking

World Economic Forum. (2020). *These are the top 10 job skills of tomorrow – And how long it takes to learn them.* https://www.weforum.org/agenda/2020/10/top-10-work-skills-of-tomorrow-how-long-it-takes-to-learn-them/

Zuehlke, H. M., Boehler, C., & Ermer, M. (2020). *Sustainarama – How sustainability will change the world in 2050.* Roland Berger GmbH.

Chapter 6

Critical Reflection on Food-Related Challenges: Co-Curricular Service Learning With Food Banks

Marcus Kreikebaum and Pratibha Singh

EBS Universität for Business and Law, Germany

Abstract

This contribution responds to the call of various researchers for a shift in Responsible Management Education (RME) to adopt a more human-centered and less organizational-centered approach. Service learning (SL) is introduced as a possibility to offer didactical opportunities for participants to connect real-world experiences to system thinking in various ways. We suggest an approach called a "Prism of Reflections" to pique participants' hermeneutical, technical, and emancipatory interests so they can delve deeply into local social and environmental issues and be able to connect them to broader global issues as encapsulated in the Sustainable Development Goals (SDGs). We exemplify our method by demonstrating how students reflect on their experiences working at food banks, and how they relate to concerns of sustainability, poverty, and access to food. Our research suggests that this approach offers a way to situate organizational thinking and instrumental reasoning in a larger framework that considers the aims of hermeneutics, technical and emancipatory discourses. Our findings demonstrate that there are conflicts and dissonances when connecting intersubjective real-world perceptions to emancipatory interests and technical knowledge, particularly when it comes to challenges in the realm of food.

Keywords: Service learning; Habermas; Prism of Reflection; Responsible Management Education; SDGs

Innovation in Responsible Management Education, 141–164
Copyright © 2024 Marcus Kreikebaum and Pratibha Singh
Published under exclusive licence by Emerald Publishing Limited
doi:10.1108/978-1-83549-464-620241009

Introduction

Since the UN's Sustainable Development Goals (SDGs) were established, more business schools have tried to incorporate the SDGs into their teaching and outreach initiatives. Simultaneously, the body of research that attempts to evaluate and analyze the efforts made by business schools in relation to Responsible Management Education (RME) is also expanding (Azmat et al., 2023; Beddewela et al., 2017; Haertle et al., 2017; Kioupi & Voulvoulis, 2019; Rasche et al., 2012).

The SDGs serve as a good entry point for establishing inclusive societies and driving transformative development. The SDG system provides a comprehensive normative framework to understand sustainability and encompasses a vision for transforming the global economies and political systems toward an inclusive and sustainable society. This demands an integrative approach that combines all SDGs from a systems perspective (Kioupi & Voulvoulis, 2019). To make use of the synergies between the 17 goals, researchers have pointed out that it is necessary, "to connect all sorts of important issues, structures and institutions in society, and disciplinary and methodological considerations" (EuropeNow, 2022).

However, since the SDGs do not automatically translate into a "fixed and predefined version of a sustainable state" (Kioupi & Voulvoulis, 2019, p. 6), scholars argue that the implementation and translation of the SDG's crucially depends on their localization. Localization implies engaging stakeholders (citizens, local leaders, and government bodies) in the cocreation of community spaces, values, relations, and priorities with regard to local issues of sustainability (Kioupi & Voulvoulis, 2019).

This corresponds to the advocacy for real-life applications and experiential learning to engage the students in critical and engaging discussions on issues, challenges, and opportunities to advance the implementation of the SDGs. Experiential approaches, like service learning (SL), are believed to be beneficial for delving deeply into the goals and problems associated with a particular SDG and analyzing how the experience and insights gained from the SL project might illuminate the difficulties in achieving its objectives (Lela Melon, EuropeNow, 2022).

Azmat et al. (2023) underline that some business schools still lack citizenship and value education, particularly with regards to RME, and that there persists a low level of understanding of the SDGs. Applying Habermas's theory to the issue of RME, we would agree that "SDG/PRME is not yet an integral part of the lifeworld of university stakeholders and it requires value education through communicative action to instill this change."

In the following contribution, we will attempt to exemplify how the pedagogy of SL can be used to link the lifeworld of communities, in this case the issue of food and food banks, to a system perspective.

SL provides students with the opportunity to gain experiences and to use the theories, methods, and techniques acquired in the class as a citizenship contribution for the public good. SL can be instrumental in adding vocational aspects to education and has the potential to create value for communities. Quantitative and qualitative studies that have been conducted in this field confirm that SL has positive effects on students' personal growth and their social behavior (Astin et al., 1999;

Giles & Eyler, 2013; Whiteley, 2014). By condensing different research studies, Celio et al. (2011) have listed five positive effects that might be seen in students once they complete the SL tasks, namely, "attitudes toward self, attitudes toward school and learning, civic engagement, social skills, and academic achievement" (Celio et al., 2011).

In a similar vein, Prentice and Robinson (2010) who researched the outcomes of SL cohorts of 9 years (2003–2012) conclude that "in the same way that a beam of light is refracted into a greater spectrum of colors through a prism, students who participate in service-learning may enter their academic and community-based experiences with limited goals but achieve a broad array of personal and professional benefits. Some of these benefits are planned by faculty; others are unintentional and sometimes life changing" (Robinson, 2014).

In the context of SL, food banks serve as "magnets for research" (De La Salle & Unwin, 2016). Students may learn to reflect on pragmatic issues along the lines of "food, hunger and poverty" (social other) as well as "think global – act locally" in political and economic contexts from a system perspective (Sullivan-Catlin, 2002).

This is in line with guideline for an education for sustainable development that aims at "developing competencies that empower individuals to reflect on their own actions, considering their current and future social, cultural, economic and environmental impacts, from a local and a global perspective. Individuals should also be empowered to act in complex situations in a sustainable manner, which may require them to strike out in new directions; and to participate in socio-political processes, moving their societies towards sustainable development" (Education for Sustainable Development Goals, 2017, p. 7). Authors such as Garcia et al. (2017) have underlined how education for sustainable development approach can be used as a lever to inculcate critical and interdisciplinary thinking, an integral aspect of the 17 SDGs (Garcia et al., 2017).

Hence, the aim of this study is to conduct a qualitative assessment based on the reflections of the students to demonstrate the broad range of perspective changes that students undergo with regard to their food consumption habits and attitudes toward people from different social contexts and to issues of global food production and consumption.

Through this chapter, we intend to demonstrate that the experiential SL at the food banks equips the students with a lens to situate food related problems in a larger context and how these different learning processes in this field can be understood within the theory of communicative action of Jürgen Habermas (1987). Substantial analysis of learning journals and essays reveals that the students develop a higher sense of purpose and empathy, enhance their knowledge about the community and food-related issues, and situate the issue of food security, consumption, access, poverty, hunger, etc., in a global context (Ross, 2011).

SL as a Communicative Action

In his theory, Habermas distinguishes between system and lifeworld. Both operate on different logics and have different interests and functions for social integration.

The concept of the lifeworld is taken from phenomenological sociology (Hohendahl, 1992) and refers to everyday situations where human beings interact. It can be described in terms of narrative presentations of historical events and social situations. It primarily uses a hermeneutic approach as it reconstructs the lifeworld from the point of view of the participating actors.

The lifeworld comprises the informal, unregulated, and unmarketized domains of social life (Patzer et al., 2018) and encompasses all assumptions, understandings, knowledge, and values of members of a society but also their conflicts and discussions on the shared norms and values. There is constant flux in which social integration plays a central role, both as a process of introducing new members to society as well as modifying the commonly shared norms and values. Changing what is common is only possible through communicating with each other. Therefore, Habermas sees the lifeworld as the locus of communicative action (Habermas, 1981) (Hohendahl, 1992; Patzer et al., 2018). However, there isn't just one lifeworld. The concept of lifeworld can be seen as a metaphor for subjective phenomenological interpretations of the world around us.

The technical interest of forecasting and controlling objectified processes through instrumental action is related to systems and systems thinking. This implies a reification of the phenomenological analysis of the lifeworld. "When the analysis moves to this level, we step out of the commonly acknowledged cultural tradition of our lifeworld and shift to a functional reading of the events, norms, and objects in which we normally participate as actors" (Hohendahl, 1992, p. 123).

Since social relations cannot be reduced to social interactions, the inside perspective of society has to be supplemented by external perspective offered in systems theory to conceptualize society as both a system and a lifeworld (Habermas, 1987) (Hohendahl, 1992).

But Habermas does not simply want to replace the hermeneutical interpretation of the lifeworld by the system perspective. He rather seeks to combine them to counter the fallacies or shortcomings of the phenomenological interpretation of the lifeworld and to legitimate certain aspects of systems theory. Habermas is however also well aware of the historical process of differentiation and detachment that have resulted in a rift between system and lifeworld when he writes: "The social system definitively explodes the horizon of the lifeworld, removes itself from the pre-understanding of communicative everyday praxis, and remains accessible only to the counter-intuitive knowledge of the social sciences that have developed since the eighteenth century" (Habermas, 1981, p. 258). Habermas therefore sees the dominance of technical interest under the pressure of economic growth and the organizational accomplishments of the state as a forced process of social modernization, that is "penetrating deeper and deeper into the previous forms of human existence" (Habermas, 1981, p. 7). Following from this, he calls for communicative rationality, which is meant to relink the specialized institution or expert opinion back to situations, actions, and issues of ordinary life, to undermine the strength of the economic and administrative logic that governs the process of modernization.

Transferring this aspect to SL at food banks, it will be interesting to examine how their local experiences and knowledge can be connected to expert theories in discussions and debates in this field.

This is in alignment to the critical debate on the implementation of the Principles of Responsible Management Education (PRME), which was introduced as a UN Global Compact Initiative in 2007 to support the work of business schools to leverage the SDGs to drive changes for RME.

About 800 business schools have already committed themselves to PRME, but the extent to which they "really walk the talk" remains an issue of discussion and debate. One of the main problems and barriers for RME that scholars agree on is the prioritization of an organization-centered worldview over a human-centered worldview and the primacy of economic and administrative logic over social justice and environmental issues in business schools (Beddewela et al., 2017).

Our program takes this into account as well as the call for localized strategies to implement the SDGs. The program stresses upon the advocacy for real-life applications and experiential learning to engage the students in critical and engaging discussions on issues and opportunities to advance the implementation of the SDGs. The idea here is to demonstrate that experiential approaches, like SL in food banks, can be beneficial for delving deeply into the goals and problems associated with a particular SDG and analyzing how the experience and insights gained from the SL project might illuminate the difficulties in achieving its objectives (Lela Melon, EuropeNow, 2022).

Prism of Perspectives on Service Experiences

Over the past few years, EBS has established strong links with community organizations to facilitate experiential learning for the students. Since 2012, the cocurricular SL program empowers the students to become more aware of societal challenges and conflicts around them through community service. As a result, students can experience and reflect on changes in their perspectives as well as learn skills for their personal and professional development through the broad range of programs offered at EBS. Eventually, students also gain an understanding of some of the complex social, political, and ecological issues underlying the SL projects (Kyle, 2020).

By processing their experiences in the context of an expanded knowledge base, the students enter what is referred to as a learning circle, oscillating between concrete lifeworld experiences and their explanations and interpretations from a system perspective. However, connecting real-world experiences to system thinking is neither an easy nor a straightforward procedure. It frequently results in an investigation of cultural boundaries, cognitive dissonances, difficult ethical dilemmas, and wicked problems that are not amenable to simple solutions.

To facilitate sensemaking of this dilemma and address the complexities, we designed a "Prism for Service-Learning Project Experiences" that examines the interactions, circumstances, and difficulties encountered in the projects from many viewpoints related to various social, emancipatory, and technological objectives.

Four perspectives (cultural, social, virtues, and cognitive) focus on the practical and hermeneutical interest of the participants and are related to their views from the inside of their projects and activities with the nongovernmental organizations (NGOs) and their clients. These perspectives invite students to reflect on their intersubjective understanding associated with life in the context of their SL project. As the practical interest is associated with the knowledge developed by the human disciplines such as history or the social sciences, we also invite students to reflect their experiences from a cultural, social, and humanistic perspective (Habermas, 1981; Patzer et al., 2018).

Four more perspectives (political, operational, strategic, and utilitarian) involve a flip to a system perspective. They are designed to provoke and stimulate the technical interest of the students on the economic and political system and its effects on the lifeworld in which they operate. The logic that drives interpretations of these perspectives is that of prediction and control of objectified processes, i.e., instrumental action or instrumental reasoning.

Two perspectives are concerned with the emancipatory interest that Habermas associates with the knowledge generated by what he calls critical sciences. What is emancipatory about this interest is its aim to liberate oneself from the seemingly "normal" or "natural" but constructed and therefore ideological constraints of worldviews and value systems. Individually, this interest might show itself in terms of constructing or developing an identity that is not totally shaped by the current social patterns, expectations, and roles (Deakin Crick & Joldersma, 2007). Socially, the critical interest might well be embodied in the norms and legitimations a society accepts or calls into question. In our prism, the questions on the cognitive as well as the personal perspective appeal to the emancipatory interests of the participants. They invite them to reflect on what it means to get "out of the bubble," a metaphor by which they describe the default state of mind as a business student, and how to keep this kind of thinking and behavior alive after the program.

To accommodate a broad range of reflections, the prism is interdisciplinary in nature. Different perspectives on service and project experiences are brought into connection with approaches and findings from various streams such as social sciences, psychology, philosophy, politics, and economics. By presenting a comprehensive and circular model (Fig. 6.1) for reflection on SL experiences, it encourages the ongoing iterative dialogical practice in the reflection of volunteer experiences as a more circular than linear process. All people involved in the project can be included in these questions. Special attention should be paid to interactions between the participants, partners, and clients in answering the questions. Since each SL project has different conditions and objectives, the questions can be adapted in each case to the specific conditions of the project as well as the individual and situational framework.

The prism has been developed through iterative dialogs with colleagues, partners, clients, and students in a cocurricular SL program for undergraduate students at EBS Business School from 2012 until 2023. They are then instructed to

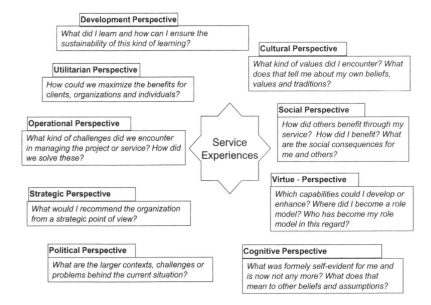

Fig. 6.1.   Prism for Reflecting Service Experiences (Authors' Own Compilation).

form teams of 4–6 people and choose a service. It is essential to get the students ready for their service activities because they will be entering a social milieu and lifeworld that are extremely different from their own. We discuss with each team how to help, complete duties, or address issues as their service objectives with the appropriate NGO partner. The next step is for teams and students to determine their own learning objectives, which must be recorded and improved upon throughout the process. They regularly reflect on their service experiences in a learning journal, share their key takeaways with their partner in a final meeting, and contextualize their project considering their academic work in an essay.

Students learn how to react and act responsibly regarding diversity and inclusion when they deal with people of lesser privileges in these relatively new and uncertain settings. About 25 national and international partner organizations comprise the SL partner network, where students can complete assignments, volunteer, and learn. The majority of these organizations are welfare organizations, such as food banks, elder care facilities, refugee camps, or facilities for the homeless, migrants, or individuals with special needs. Students gain knowledge by planning, carrying out, and assessing the programs of international NGOs and welfare organizations with the intention of making a social impact. By doing this, they acquire the skills necessary to put their theoretical models into reality, improve upon them, and apply what they learn to their academic work and future employment.

One of the tools we use to stimulate reflections is that we ask the students to tell us stories from their lifeworld experiences (Describe) and ask them then to explore (Examine) and interpret their lessons learned from these stories and how they could implement these in their further actions (Articulate Learnings). The application of the DEAL Model, that has been proposed by Robert Bringle et al. (Lyon et al., 2022) allows students to relate their serving experiences to develop an understanding of their own calling, which is an important aspect of RME.

However, discovering one's "calling" is neither an instantaneous nor an easy process. According to research, narrative arcs are built by connecting episodic learning events and real-world experiences over a long period of time. It is believed that writing is a "coherent self-narrative that depicts career as a series of unfolding events that make sense sequentially" (Ibarra & Barbulescu, 2010). Thus, episodical self-narratives, such as the stories that students tell about their experiences, may act as strong transitional links between the discovery and development of a potential called identity (Bloom et al., 2021).

We offer an extensive mileu of options for students to engage in SL. However, for the purpose of this chapter, we focus on students who have served at the food banks to decipher the relationship between SL and food waste plus responsible consumption. In our examination of the student stories, we looked specifically at the motives of the students for engaging in food banks and how they describe themselves in the process of becoming socially embedded. Furthermore, we consider the kind of role models the students may have developed through their encounters with mentors, role models, clients, and coworkers and how this has impacted their learning. We also examine their cognitive reactions and how the potential conflicts between their inner calling and their exterior professional selves are manifested in this field as business administration students often do not volunteer at food banks.

We encourage students to volunteer at food banks in their hometowns or while studying abroad, but we also provide them the opportunity to do so while on campus. At EBS Business School, we currently collaborate with more than 30 food banks in Hong Kong, Canada, England, Germany, and the United Kingdom.

Reflecting on food "can make it possible for citizens, practitioners, policy-makers and academics to understand the connections between the social, economic and ecological aspects of sustainability" (Knezevic et al., 2017, p. 14), and we encourage students to find localized ways to support our partners and their volunteers to tackle the acute issues they face and to contribute to transform the current food system into a more sustainable one. We will show how organizations and clients benefit through these SL activities in several ways.

In the following, we like to demonstrate the scope of linkages between "learning" and "serving" that can be established through critical reflection (Celio et al., 2011) in cultural, social, and cognitive as well as in economic–political, professional, and personal dimensions as a way to understand our "daily bread" as a "complex interaction of economic, social, environmental, and political systems" (Sachs, 2015, p. 11).

Findings

Methodology

We analyzed our findings by using a grounded constructivist theoretical approach. According to Roy Suddaby, grounded theory should not be an excuse to ignore the literature, and by no means a presentation of raw data be used for theory testing by doing content analysis or word counts following a routine application of formulated techniques to data. In order to advance a field grounded theory should rather be considered as a neither perfect nor easy method to enter an "interplay between induction and deduction as in all sciences" (Strauss & Corbin, 1998, p. 137; Suddaby, 2006).

We also demand this from our students by having them take a deep dive into social practices while encouraging them to read as much as possible on issues related to their services [and the corresponding SDGs to initiate an iterative learning process that] oscillate[s] between global, systemic and local lifeworld perspectives.

Our data collection consists of close readings and evaluations of about 180 learning journals, essays, and presentations of our students during and after their services from 2012 to 2022. We also interviewed our NGO partners constantly and invited them to participate by addressing their needs to the students' teams and reflecting on the students' efforts together. Through focused coding and memo writing, we have been sampling annually three to four cohorts of student's teams of about 6 students per team serving at three to four food banks per year. From semester to semester, we developed and constantly refined the emerging categories or perspectives on service experiences. Through this long-range process of theoretical sampling, we hope to build up some precision, density, and complexity into our theoretical statements.

However, we are aware that our categories are much more constructed through our interpretations of the data than of the data itself. We did not enter the field without having our own interpretative frames, biographies, and interests, and the categories have undergone some changes since the early stages of the research. Our theoretical analysis should therefore provide more of an interpretative rendering of a fluent field of social practice than an objective report of the reality of food banks.

Social Dimensions

SL inevitably has social consequences for all participants because regardless of the scope, duration, or outcome, SL is always done by individuals with individuals (Butin, 2005). Therefore, participants in this dimension focus on the direct effects of their SL activities on their own behavior and the behavior of others, ranging from detailed interpretation of insightful situations and encounters to the consequences of their own habits and values in a wider context.

A food bank's lifeworld is far removed from a business school. Food banks are typically managed by individuals from extremely diverse socioeconomic and professional backgrounds who get together to fight food waste and support the free distribution of food to those in need.

Students occasionally express their surprise at the differences in attitudes between them as business students and the volunteers when they enter such open and communicative workplaces where people volunteer regardless of their social status, age, or tradition.

> When I first came to the Tafel, I recognized immediately that everyone was working on the tasks with joy. They were motivated to do a great job and offer delicious food for the people who need it the most. The workers all seemed happy and what interested me the most was: If we only have so little time in our lives, how do people manage to work somewhere for free?

Especially, business students often enter this service with an organization-focused mindset that disqualifies any kind of activity that does not maximize their own interest. Before they understand the motives of the volunteers, they experience this as a cognitive dissonance that often leads them to change their normative assumption that humans only strive to maximize self-interests with minimal efforts.

In their stories, students describe food banks as spaces where people who do not conform to the social norm not only receive food but also acceptance and encouragement, where meetings and discussions are possible for which there is usually no other public space. Food banks in the sense qualify as a case of a communicative action as a response to the economic and political system and its effects on individuals and society. This would also explain the strong humanizing effect on students serving at food banks.

Deconstructing societal preconceptions is the most frequent theme we discover in students' reflections on this viewpoint. The moment students connect with marginalized persons in food banks, their societal assumptions and biases are challenged. They begin to consider their basic human values as well as the privileges and social prestige that may come with them, as well as the potential blindness and ignorance that may be associated with these.

Cultural Dimensions of Serving at Food Banks

Cultural shifts of perspectives take place in the SL because people from different cultural backgrounds and origins meet during the activities. Food banks are places where people that have different ways of life and sets of values and behaviors meet. These differences can be the cause and reason for conflicts between groups representing different perspectives, interests, and power relationships (Littlejohn & Foss, 2011) but also an invitation to mutual learning and enrichment.

Food banks provide a platform for cross-cultural interaction, making them useful for facilitating dialogs that dispel stereotypes and break down barriers between cultures. Students frequently claim that they join this program with a great deal of cultural prejudice, especially toward migrants who frequently use food banks as consumers. The students' perspectives shift as a result of interaction and hearing their stories. Through those interactions, students start to question their preconceptions and their own cultural customs and ideas.

Students, for example, refer to their former belief, that it is only a matter of discipline and intelligence, if people become successful or not. As soon as they start to communicate with volunteers and clients, they deconstruct this commonly held belief as a modern myth. These anecdotes from students frequently describe how they come across elderly folks who have worked hard all their lives but do not receive enough pension to acquire fresh food. They talk about encountering persons who had successful careers before falling ill and losing everything or immigrant families that struggle to fit into society. All of this leads to the awareness that the reasons of poverty are far more intricate than initially believed.

(Virtue Ethics) New Role Models

The focus of virtue-ethical reflection is on those traits of others encountered in SL, that respond or resonate with the values and character of oneself. According to Aristotle, virtues are not innate but acquired character traits that enable a person to lead a good life. Virtues can be divided into intellectual virtues – "wisdom" being the best known – and moral virtues, which include a long list of possible character traits, such as goodness, courage, friendship, mercy, faithfulness, modesty, patience, etc. Since these traits are not innate, we acquire them only through repeated practice and especially through reflective behavior in our interactions with others and through role modeling (Crane & Matten, 2016). For Aristotle, every ethical virtue is a condition intermediate (a "golden mean" as it is popularly known) between two other states, one involving excess and the other deficiency, which involves the training of appropriate emotional responses and not purely intellectual skills (Kraut, n.d.).

Students who volunteer at food banks sometimes express their admiration for the dedication of the senior volunteers who are still performing duties that are sometimes physically taxing. They acknowledge their gratitude and respect for people who they would have overlooked before. But it can also be the clients who may teach them important lessons regarding virtuous behavior. Here is a story of M. who served during the corona epidemic by delivering food packages to clients. He writes:

> Our very last stopover led us to a woman beyond her nineties, living on her on in an apartment. She was a preciously amicable lady, who was pretty vital for a person her age. As soon as she said something that appeared important to her, she hit the carpet with her walking stick. After having handed over the box, we engaged in some small talk. Before leaving, she gifted me some chocolate sweets and wished me all the best. So far, so good. It was only later that day that I learned this kind lady's story. Her family had

consisted of Kazakh Jews living in Germany, and she was the only one who survived the Holocaust. This really touched me, because after all she had gone through, she didn't have anyone to interact with, she was all on her own, crammed into 40 sqm. (Statement from a service-learning student)

Deriving from the above statement, the student starts to reflect on this event; he realizes that he has been given a lesson in empathy and dignity. He was initially perplexed by the elderly woman's gift of candy, given despite the fact that they were the ones providing her with the food she could not afford, and that she was a lonely person with few physical possessions. But then, he realized that by the way this lady approached him as a stranger with curiosity, care, and openness, he had been given a very important "lesson of a kind in sharing – be it sharing possessions, time, or affection." (M.) By giving something back, the old lady disrupted the normativity of the welfare situation, that is defined by clear boundaries between the giver (donor) and the receiver (beneficiary). Giving something back allowed her to maintain her human dignity and her reputation as a virtue by allowing her to strike a balance between taking and giving. The elderly woman also started a chain of reciprocal gifts by giving a gift, which requires response.

Sadly, this episode is rather an exceptional one with regard to some descriptions of students of behaviors and emotional situations of clients at food banks. Students often describe that some clients seem uneasy with the situation and do not want to engage with others because they feel ashamed of their situation.

Numerous users of food banks endure consequences of stigmatization, which can result in persistent harm to self-confidence and image, according to research on the psychological repercussions of food bank users. When individuals feel ashamed of their current living conditions, they find it difficult to speak up and express, for instance, their culinary preferences. They are afraid to speak up, so they keep quiet and, in the end, only express their gratitude for the food they can get (Pineau et al., 2021).

Students who dig deeper into this issue might conclude that countries where a social welfare system should be successfully implemented show the most considerable lack of support for those in need, not necessarily from a financial perspective but rather from a social component. Stigmas, shame, and a sense and feeling of powerlessness occlude any other positive emotions of food bank clients. Instead of psychological support to reenter society, these people are demoted and dehumanized as second-class citizens (Strong, 2022). In their conclusions, students stress the importance of maintaining an environment of open and honest communication at eye level among all participants in food banks to combat stigmatization, but they also point out that there are deeper underlying systemic problems that must be addressed.

Phenomenological Dimension

We normally share the assumption that to form a new habit or to act differently, you first have to gain knowledge and form an idea in your mind and then act accordingly through bodily actions. This is often a difficult and long process that takes a lot of attention, discipline, and effort. In our program, we approach knowledge from another direction. We asked students first to act differently and then think about their actions. It is in the experience that enables them to jump to the right conclusions, not vice versa. This seems and feels a bit counterintuitive because we usually try to change our doings based on what is already known. Now there is this unknown other through whom we experience a shift in our mindset and perspective.

Phenomenology focuses on the individual's conscious experience of a phenomenon – an object, event, or experience. Interpretation is seen as an active process of assigning meaning to an experience. To interpret is to move back and forth between experiencing an event or a situation and attributing meaning, e.g., from the particular to the general and back. The process of oscillating between experience and meaning is called a hermeneutic circle (Cf. Littlejohn & Foss, 2019, p. 100).

By placing us in circumstances where we interact with people from various social origins, SL initiatives open the door for the hermeneutic circle to be used in a very concrete way. We frequently discover that prior presumptions or customary views are no longer true when we start to understand these events. In contrast to philosophy, where this occurs on an abstract, intellectual level, in SL, the nonself-evident is found through practical endeavors for the benefit of others (service). Since SL can be viewed as a type of hermeneutic activity, it is clear from this vantage point that it calls into question what was previously taken for granted or considered to be normal.

When students serve at food banks, they usually experience a visceral learning by handling the food waste and turning it back into edible food. This includes all senses as they touch, feel, see, and smell the food in order to decide what is edible as well as cleaning or washing and preparing it to be handed out again. In addition, they perceive the food market and its logistic chain from an end-to-front perspective. Whereas customers only perceive food as marketized products, the students and volunteers are able to witness a process of de-reification. Food which cannot be sold anymore has lost its value as a commodity. Picking up this potential food waste is a way to give it its original value. By doing so, people may alter their relation to food in general by treating it with more respect and awareness.

In their stories, our students often tell us about changes in their individual consuming behavior based on this cognitive insight. They begin to rethink their own methods of food consumption since they deal with food in different ways than usual. In particular, this applies to goods that have passed their expiration date. The students no longer see a need to discard these items in their own homes because the food bank gathers and distributes items whose minimum legal date of expiration has passed. Additionally, students claim that they now shop much more carefully and have a different perspective on what they eat. Here, we show strong evidence that SL at food banks significantly influences participants' decisions to consume food in a more sustainable way.

Our results are consistent with specific outcomes of ethnographic research that examines opportunities for political and ethical learning by contrasting various methods of handling and educating about food. Food can be seen as fuel and as "an instigator and tool for learning about ecological impacts, wellbeing, food journeys, health, and pleasure" (Spring et al., 2019). They conclude that the redistribution of wasted food has to potential to challenge its stigmatizing potential and address serious material issues of food insecurity in the community. Handling wasted food can also lead to more vibrant sympathies between people and food. However, the authors also point out that a more systemic transformation would be required as these practices would be rooted in environmentally damaging and unequally distributed foodscapes (Spring et al., 2019).

This is in line with the stories students narrate, when they reflect their service on a political perspective. In these stories, they express deep concerns on the negative effects of the commodification of food and the industrialization of the food sector from a social but also ecological perspective and look for alternative solutions for their personal consumption as well as on the community level.

Political Dimension

SL projects call for taking a position in the political discourse, e.g., by reflecting on experiences in dealing with mostly marginalized groups or individuals in the context of broader social and political developments (Butin, 2005). Taking a political perspective is usually achieved by linking the voices of the people whom we serve and whose interests are hardly heard in the public discourse, to issues of power, policies, and regulatory practices. Central to this perspective are questions about the economic power relations and regulatory policies and practices in relation to the production and distribution of food regarding the SDGs.

In their analyses, participants mostly identify SDGs 2 (Zero Hunger) and 12 (Sustainable Consumption and Production) as those goals to which food banks respond directly. Regarding social issues, they also refer to SDGs 1 (No Poverty) and 10 (Reduced inequality) as an aim of food banks.

Participants frequently critically evaluate the role of food banks in the political context of public welfare during their tasks at food banks. Though they have a strong sense of solidarity and connection to the food bank movement, they also express their worries that the "outsourcing" and privatization of social welfare may have detrimental effects on policymakers as it absolves them of their obligations to look out for those who are less fortunate. They criticize policymakers for failing to support food banks and for not altering their stance on the expanding population of people who are forced to use food banks because their incomes are insufficient to purchase food.

A second strain of analysis links the lifeworld experiences to the economic system. Students claim that the economic issue to which food banks respond is rooted in the structural shortcomings of the global food industry as they relate their personal experiences to their knowledge of the food market and the ensuing ever-growing worldwide inequities between producers and consumers. Markets are forced to supply an increasing number of products in response to growing demand, and these products must regularly be disposed of whenever they lose their appeal. Then, usually wrapped in plastic, these are dropped in enormous numbers.

Students also identify individual overconsumption as a big factor that contributes to the problem. Overconsumption does not only lead to more waste and CO_2 emissions but also to severe health problems and expenses related to obesity in developed countries. Health-related problems play a major role, especially among those who cannot afford a healthy diet. As the free food market industry is only interested in revenues, there are only a few regulations for products who are not healthy because they contain too much sugar, salt, and fat.

Altogether, students often form the opinion that food banks are organizations that can only address the symptoms of poverty and global inequality rather than its root causes, which are ingrained in the political and economic systems, in both types of analysis. This prompts them to adopt two positions: They do express their support for the food bank movement because they have connected, bonded, and engaged with the individuals and their shared goal. However, they also express their dissatisfaction with its very existence and continued unease over the trends and outcomes of the economy and politics, which they see as the cause of the problems that food banks try to solve.

In both cases, the lifeworld and the system do not align and even oppose each other. From a welfare system point of view, organizations such as food banks should not be needed and exist at all. From a lifeworld perspective, the failings of the current food industries and the political policies on these issues are both responsible for the rise of food banks as citizens respond to these failures through communicative action. The wicked problems that these failures produce cannot be easily resolved. Since they are systemically embedded in our economic and political systems, they must also be tackled in systemic ways. This is one of the important political lessons of SL at food banks that students express.

When students realize this complexity, they start to argue for a shift in the discourse from the charitable food bank model to community food security. The concept of community food security comprises a combination of local activities, advocacy, and change around social and food system policies. This can lead the community, for example, to look for alternative solutions to ensure communal food security such as community gardening, farmers markets, food preparation workshops, and collective cooking events (Dodd & Nelson, 2020) and to measures such as individual systemic coaching programs to support the clients in handling other problems they face, for example, with regard to education, health, and housing (Martin et al., 2013).

Strategic Dimension

The strategic dimension implies considerations on how the organization could improve in moving forward to reach its long-range goals or what must be further done to fulfill its mission. In this dimension, we ask students to look at strategies or actions that could help the organization to advance and what kind of strategic alliances at the institutional level might be helpful for this. Leaders of food banks often remain enmeshed in the day-to-day operations. As such, they benefit from the "out of the box" solutions that emerge as an outcome of SL projects. Strategic solutions should take the whole lifeworld and circumstances of people into account. In the case food banks, we already discussed from a political perspective that "food pantries provide a steady flow of fish, but they often do not teach their clients how to fish" (Van Newkirk Hoffman & Martin, 2014, p. 9). Questions like: "Can we bring more human dignity to the process of donating food rather than simply using one-way giving?" or "Can we increase our personal involvement with those in crisis to assist them with other resources such as housing, day care, or other support?" or "How can we help the poor to thrive?" (Lupton, 2011, 2015) could therefore be a good starting point for strategic considerations.

In their responses to this dimension, students often propose the creation of strategic partnerships with educational institutions such as schools, universities, employment centers but also with health and housing services. To ensure and enhance its services, students also suggest building partnerships with commercial and noncommercial food institutions who are interested to take on social responsibility and are committed to ensure local food security on a long-term sustainable basis.

Students' recommendations include providing food bank volunteers and clients with free training opportunities in systems coaching, health and nutrition, mindfulness, and financial literacy through workshops and cooking classes.

In their contributions on this dimension, students frequently refer to innovative approaches of food banks, which aim to transform the charity-based model to a person-centered system of assistance, coaching, and support. Innovative approaches of food banks such as "Freshplace" serve them as the best practice examples how local partnerships between universities, food banks, and endowments can mutually improve on food security and increased self-sufficiency on people in the community by addressing the underlying causes of poverty. Interventions include a client-choice pantry, monthly meetings with a project manager to receive motivational interviewing, and targeted referrals to community services (Martin et al., 2013; Van Newkirk Hoffman & Martin, 2014).

Operational Dimension

In this dimension, participants interact with the partner organization and discuss what kind of additional measures could improve or enhance the service to clients, volunteers, and the institution. This usually starts with an assessment of current organizational challenges and needs.

Regarding food banks, students report on various operative and managerial challenges such as meeting the rising and pressing needs, since there are more and more clients, whereas the collected food is decreasing due to saving measures of the markets. Another problem they identify is that most volunteers are rather old, and there is little growth on younger volunteers. Management teams of food banks may also face challenges of digitalization. Since many food banks struggle with similar issues, students can also provide scalable solutions such as digital tools, handbooks on campaigns, or educational material for attracting younger volunteers. Due to their existing abilities and competencies, students can assist in overcoming many of these obstacles. By applying their expertise – whether it is in accounting, marketing, logistics, or finances – to the food banks, they are able to enhance operations. The story of A. is exemplary in this regard. After having served a couple times directly in the food bank, she offered to extend her support with the regard to management and improving operations. A. explains:

> As a business student, I am familiar with many aspects involved in a successful operation: accounting, finance, marketing, strategy, organizational behavior, and leadership (....) While we learn related theories and approaches in school, the only real way to develop and improve one's problem-solving skills is through experience. As an organization, the food bank is constantly working to solve problems faced by many members of the community and as a volunteer, it is my responsibility to work with my team to resolve the day-to-day challenges faced in practice. (A.)

Transferability is important for such programs because it boosts the reciprocal impacts and improves the quality of outcomes for participants and partners. Amy's involvement resulted in her nomination to the Board of Directors and therefore an even stronger commitment in the sense of what is known as professional identity building. She concludes her reflection on the development of her competencies:

> Through this experience, I have learned how to handle stressful, sometimes high-pressure situations by demonstrating poise, flexibility, and the ability to think quickly. In my short time on the board, I have already been exposed to some of the greater challenges faced by the organization, relating to regulation, fundraising, partnerships, capacity, and usage. These challenges have already begun to build my creative thinking, proactiveness, persuasion skills, analytical skills, and resilience. (A.)

This example shows that the knowledge produced by business schools can be transferred very well beyond academic boundaries through community outreach such as SL to enhance community services. This finding is confirmed by several studies. "Hunger Free Texas" is, for example, a SL program run by the University of Texas, that includes hundreds of students from different disciplines to work remotely with food pantries to conduct need assessments and provide support to respond to those needs. Responses to question on the project's impact on professional skills showed that over 85% of the participants indicated that they had either developed new skills or improved existing skills throughout this project

(Natarajarathinam et al., 2023). Another study by Tobias Schönherr on a similar SL program with the focus on logistics and supply chain management confirmed that students can significantly gain an increase in skills and knowledge by experimenting and engaging in real-world situations.

The operational perspective should therefore be an important component of any SL project. Focusing only on operational issues might however narrow the perspective to an organizational worldview and technical interests and runs the risk to minimize the stimulation of further interests of the students to fully comprehend and explore the complexities of the issue at hand.

Utilitarian Dimension

Social innovations refer to society as the central actor for the realization of sustainable solutions. This relates to new social practices of living and working together. It is about concrete changes in social practices and consumption habits (Howaldt et al., 2016). Therefore, ways of scaling up or scaling out SL effects to promote social innovations in individuals, organizations, and communities should be at the forefront of benefit-ethical considerations of SL projects.

Students, for example, transfer the motto of the food banks "Waste less – share more" to other realms of the everyday life, such as clothes and other goods and look for large scale solutions. They also develop ideas how SL at food banks could be integrated in schools so that children could become ambassadors for a more sustainable consuming behavior in their families.

Any more in-depth utilitarian analysis of the relationship between food banks and hunger refers to the wider context of the problem. Therefore, it should fully consider questions of social justice as well as ecological sustainability, health, and democracy.

Reflections on this perspective lead students to promote the development of better community food system resilience and more just food systems. They argue for opening up food banks to schools and other groups, such as local farming initiatives and other organizations. They discuss how to establish networks of academics, community partners, and practitioners to create more equitable and sustainable food systems (Knezevic et al., 2017).

In this context, students refer to SDG 11 (Sustainable Cities and Communities) and SDGs 13–15 (Action on Climate Change, Life under Water and on Land) as important aims to pursue. They also mention SDG 17 (Partnerships to achieve the Goals) as critical for a successful development of community food system resilience and just food systems.

Community food system scholars look at food systems as composed of many biological, material, and social elements in complex sets of relationships that evolve as "the food from the fields, forests and oceans travel to our plates and back into the soil" (Knezevic et al., 2017, p. 7). The focus of this scholarship is on links between people, nature, government, and in sharp contrast to an economic perspective whose instrumental logic is criticized for its segmentizing and stratifying tendencies that are considered as damaging because they pull people apart from the sources of their food and from one another. This research echoes the appeal of Habermas for raising public awareness of the industrial and political colonization of the food system as a first step in communicative action by criticizing the segmenting and stratifying tendencies of the economic and political subsystem. Food systems academics conduct inter-disciplinary, community-based participatory action research in "alternative food initiatives" and "communities of food practice" to examine the connections between people, ecosystems, and food (Knezevic et al., 2017).

In their search for more just and sustainable food systems which pertains to the utilitarian dimension in local foodscapes, scholars are exploring elements and paths of transformative food politics, which can be defined as a kind of dialectic between "what is and what ought to be with a focus on the processes of transformation" (Levkoe, p. 185 in: Knezevic et al., 2017). To this extent, Levkoe (2011) identifies three interrelated elements in this field: transition to collective subjectivity, a comprehensive food systems approach, and a politics of reflexive localization.

Collective subjectivity can be traced back to a "claim of the commons" and refers to a shift from individualized market mechanisms as the mode for change to collaborative mobilization around collective needs. The idea of a comprehensive food systems can be seen as the quest for "integration of social justice, ecological sustainability, health and democracy throughout all aspects of a food system – from production to processing to distribution to consumption to waste manage-ment" (p. 186).

The final element are processes of reflective localization, which refer to the abilities of local initiatives to move beyond their experiences by using networks to connect across localities and to negotiate food politics on a broader range. According to Charles Levkoe, there are two ways that local food initiatives engage in reflexive localization. They can either try to scale up their services or activities or scale out their place-based initiative and attempt to build multi-scale strategic collaborations, which may lead to larger communities of food practice and to connected local efforts to broader social and political processes (Levkoe, 2011, p. 197; Knezevic et al., 2017).

When examining the utilitarian aspect of an SL project, both approaches are worthwhile to examine, not just from the perspective of a local food bank but also for other localized initiatives around the SDG's challenges.

Personal Dimension

Participants are expected to summarize their experiences and link them to their future aspirations in this emancipative component. This provides them the ability to consider the SL initiative as a chapter in their philanthropic life experience. It provides students with the chance to develop a self-narrative that is in line with their values and might cause them to feel a calling for a future career. Here is a student voice:

I am glad that I participated in a Service-Learning project. I can only recommend this experience to anyone considering such service. The lessons I drew from this service are probably much more comprehensive than any lesson I have learned during my studies. This is not least due to the fact that I did not only learn something about serving society, but about my own character. Certainly, I will continue my learning journey, staying curious about strangers, unknown situations and my own personality. I am convinced that both my social environment and I myself will benefit largely from this continuous curiosity. (B.)

Self-narratives like the one above are common in our students' essays. Numerous students express their gratitude for taking part in our immersive "learning shock therapy" program and their desire to continue learning "outside the box," "bubble," or "mental cockpit."

What students describe as a distinguishing feature between this course and all other course is that this course teaches them not what but how to think differently. We do this, for example, by asking them to relate the text "This is water" by David Foster Wallace to their SL experience. Wallace talks about the automatic, unconscious belief in all of us, that we are the center of the world and that our needs, wishes, and feelings should be prioritized by the world around us. He calls this mode of thinking the "default set of worship" and illustrates his thesis with an example of the mindset of supermarket customer (sic) who is totally annoyed by their fellow shoppers and the personnel because he is in his own mental cockpit and just wants to get out of that place.

A shift in perspective can only take place when one becomes aware of being in his own mindset and decides to replace this default mode of thinking by attention, awareness, and empathic care about other people. In his story, the author flips the perspective by looking at fellow shoppers and the personnel as human beings with problems and challenges just like him. Shifting the perspective is what Wallace calls "real freedom," but he admits that this kind of freedom involves discipline, effort, "and being able truly to care for others and to sacrifice for them, over and over again, in myriad petty little unsexy ways, every day" (Wallace, 2021, p. 8).

It is difficult to leave our social comfort zones, yet doing so has a big impact on our ability to think freely, flip perspectives, and not be constrained by our mental cockpit. This type of emancipative learning in SL projects, which is also a crucial element of lifelong learning, demands the immersive component (Deakin Crick & Joldersma, 2007; Deeley, 2010).

Conclusion

In this chapter, we tried to demonstrate how SL with food banks can give students opportunities to explore different interests by diving deep into topics related to food production, distribution, and consumption as well as the corresponding SDGs with their heads (cognitive), hands (visceral learning), and hearts (social). For this, we suggested a method to stimulate and integrate hermeneutical, emancipatory, and technical interests to find localized solutions that address issues of food security and social justice related to food.

Such efforts have been however extremely rare so far. Many business schools still lack citizenship and value education, particularly with regards to RME, and that there persists a low level of understanding of the SDGs and PRME. Applying Habermas's theory to the issue of RME, we agree that "SDG/PRME is not yet an integral part of the lifeworld of university stakeholders and it requires value education through communicative action to instill this change" (Azmat et al., 2023).

Giving students opportunities to engage in civil society initiatives can help to achieve this requirement. Participation in civil society initiatives allows students to maintain and enhance their social integrity and responsiveness which is much needed in today's business world. Exposing future decision makers to real-world settings helps them to develop the knowledge, understanding, skills, dispositions, values, and attitudes required for communicative integrity (Deakin Crick & Joldersma, 2007).

Thus, linking the SDGs to real-world experiences can encourage students to explore their interests and gain an understanding of how systems impact the lifeworld and how communities can deal with these impacts through cooperative action to encourage local change. Especially when dealing with issues such as poverty, hunger, and global inequalities, business students should be exposed to local situations and immersed in welfare situations so that they can explore the consequences of today's economic systems and its impacts on the social other and the local environment as part of their education on the SDGs.

Our findings suggest that SL with food banks encourages critical thinking and triggers a transformation of perspectives and habits. Food banks offer a space where people from different backgrounds and walks of life come together and have tremendous potential to foster social cohesion and integration as well as to reduce individual consumption and waste management. The SL experience apprizes the students of the prevalent issues in community, systemic issues and solutions, organizational challenges, etc. It is a vital contribution to inculcate values for responsible citizenship (Sullivan-Catlin, 2002).

Given that these fundamental transformations that are a "must" to survive as a species, we as educators must also change our roles to lead learners and communities how to work better collectively in order to change and to adjust to our role in the living world.

References

Astin, A., Sachs, L., & Avalos, J. (1999). Long-term effects of volunteerism during the undergraduate years. *The Review of Higher Education, 22*(2), 17.

Azmat, F., Jain, A., & Sridharan, B. (2023). Responsible management education in business schools: Are we there yet? *Journal of Business Research, 157*, 113518. https://doi.org/10.1016/j.jbusres.2022.113518

Beddewela, E., Warin, C., Hesselden, F., & Coslet, A. (2017). Embedding responsible management education – Staff, student and institutional perspectives. *International Journal of Management in Education, 15*(2), 263–279. https://doi.org/10.1016/j.ijme.2017.03.013

Bloom, M., Colbert, A. E., & Nielsen, J. D. (2021). Stories of calling: How called professionals construct narrative identities. *Administrative Science Quarterly, 66*(2), 298–338. https://doi.org/10.1177/0001839220949502

Butin, D. W. (Ed.). (2005). *Service-learning in higher education: Critical issues and directions.* Palgrave Macmillan.

Celio, C. I., Durlak, J., & Dymnicki, A. (2011). A meta-analysis of the impact of service-learning on students. *Journal of Experiential Education, 34*(2), 164–181. https://doi.org/10.5193/JEE34.2.164

Crane, A., & Matten, D. (2016). *Business ethics: Managing corporate citizenship and sustainability in the age of globalization* (4th ed.). Oxford University Press.

De la Salle, J., & Unwin, J. (2016). *Social innovation in food banks an environmental scan of social innovation in Canadian and US Food Banks* [PDF]. http://www. feedopportunity.com/wp-content/uploads/2016/11/Social-Innovation-Scan-of-Food-Banks.pdf

Deakin Crick, R., & Joldersma, C. W. (2007). Habermas, lifelong learning and citizenship education. *Studies in Philosophy and Education, 26*(2), 77–95. https://doi. org/10.1007/s11217-006-9015-1

Deeley, S. J. (2010). Service-learning: Thinking outside the box. *Active Learning in Higher Education, 11*(1), 43–53. https://doi.org/10.1177/1469787409355870

Dodd, W., & Nelson, E. (2020). Shifting discourse and practice on food banks: Insights from a community–university partnership. *Voluntas: International Journal of Voluntary and Nonprofit Organizations, 31*(5), 881–893. https://doi.org/10.1007/ s11266-018-0012-0

Education for sustainable development goals: Learning objectives. (2017). UNESCO.

EuropeNow. (2022). *Teaching the sustainable development goals: Challenges and opportunities: An interview with László Pintér, Lydia Cole, and Lela Mélon. Europe Now, Campus interview.* https://www.europenowjournal.org/2022/05/17/teaching-the-sustainable-development-goals-challenges-and-opportunities-an-interview-with-laszlo-pinter-lydia-cole-and-lela-melon/

Garcia, J., Da Silva, S. A., Carvalho, A. S., & De Andrade Guerra, J. B. S. O. (2017). Education for sustainable development and its role in the promotion of the sustainable development goals. In J. P. Davim (Ed.), *Curricula for sustainability in higher education* (pp. 1–18). Springer International Publishing. https://doi.org/10. 1007/978-3-319-56505-7_1

Giles, D. E., Jr., & Eyler, J. (2013). The endless quest for scholarly respectability in service-learning research. *Michigan Journal of Community Service Learning, 20*(1), 53+.

Habermas, J. (1981). *Theorie des kommunikativen Handelns. Bd. 1: Handlungsrationalität und gesellschaftliche Rationalisierung; Bd. 2: Zur Kritik der funktionalistischen Vernunft.* Suhrkamp.

Habermas, J. (1987). *Eine Art Schadensabwicklung. Kleine Politische Schriften VI.* Suhrkamp Verlag.

Haertle, J., Parkes, C., Murray, A., & Hayes, R. (2017). PRME: Building a global movement on responsible management education. *International Journal of Management in Education, 15*(2), 66–72. https://doi.org/10.1016/j.ijme.2017.05.002

Hohendahl, P. (1992). Dialectic of enlightenment revisited: Habermas's critique of the Frankfurt School. In *Reappraisals. Shifting alignments in postwar critical theory.* Cornell University Press. https://www.jstor.org/stable/j.ctt1g69xjd.8

Howaldt, J., Domanski, D., & Kaletka, C. (2016). Social innovation: Towards a new innovation paradigm. *RAM. Revista de Administração Mackenzie, 17*(6), 20–44. https://doi.org/10.1590/1678-69712016/administracao.v17n6p20-44

Ibarra, H., & Barbulescu, R. (2010). Identity as narrative: Prevalence, effectiveness, and consequences of narrative identity work in macro work role transitions. *Academy of Management Review, 35*(1), 135–154. https://doi.org/10.5465/AMR.2010.45577925

Kioupi, V., & Voulvoulis, N. (2019). Education for sustainable development: A systemic framework for connecting the SDGs to educational outcomes. *Sustainability, 11*(21), 6104. https://doi.org/10.3390/su11216104

Knezevic, I., Blay-Palmer, A., Levkoe, C. Z., Mount, P., & Nelson, E. (Eds.). (2017). *Nourishing communities: From fractured food systems to transformative pathways.* Springer International Publishing. https://doi.org/10.1007/978-3-319-57000-6

Kraut, R. (n.d.). Aristotle's ethics. In *The stanford encyclopedia of philosophy* (Fall 2022 Edition). https://plato.stanford.edu/archives/fall2022/entries/aristotle-ethics/

Kyle, W. C. (2020). Expanding our views of science education to address sustainable development, empowerment, and social transformation. *Disciplinary and Interdisciplinary Science Education Research, 2*(1), 2. https://doi.org/10.1186/s43031-019-0018-5

Levkoe, C. Z. (2011). Towards a transformative food politics. *Local Environment, 16*(7), 687–705. https://doi.org/10.1080/13549839.2011.592182

Littlejohn, S. W., & Foss, K. A. (2011). *Theories of human communication* (10th ed.). Waveland Press.

Littlejohn, S. W., & Foss, K. A. (2019). *Theories of human communication* (11th ed.). Waveland press.

Lupton, R. D. (2011). *Toxic charity: How churches and charities hurt those they help (and how to reverse it)* (1st ed.). HarperOne.

Lupton, R. D. (2015). *Charity detox: What charity would look like if we cared about results* (1st ed.). HarperOne, an Imprint of HarperCollinsPublishers.

Lyon, M. L., Sikes, K. L., Clayton, P. H., & Bringle, R. G. (2022). Designing transformative service-learning: Mindfulness and healing-centered engagement. In B. L. Bromer & C. M. Crawford (Eds.), *Advances in educational technologies and instructional design* (pp. 1–21). IGI Global. https://doi.org/10.4018/978-1-6684-4240-1.ch002

Martin, K. S., Wu, R., Wolff, M., Colantonio, A. G., & Grady, J. (2013). A novel food pantry program. *American Journal of Preventive Medicine, 45*(5), 569–575. https://doi.org/10.1016/j.amepre.2013.06.012

Natarajarathinam, M., Qiu, S., & Lu, W. (2023). Designing and assessing a multi-disciplinary service-learning course in supply chain management. *INFORMS Transactions on Education, 23*(3), 196–209. https://doi.org/10.1287/ited.2022.0280

Patzer, M., Voegtlin, C., & Scherer, A. G. (2018). The normative justification of integrative stakeholder engagement: A Habermasian view on responsible leadership. *Business Ethics Quarterly, 28*(3), 325–354. https://doi.org/10.1017/beq.2017.33

Pineau, C., Williams, P. L., Brady, J., Waddington, M., & Frank, L. (2021). Exploring experiences of food insecurity, stigma, social exclusion, and shame among women in high-income countries: A narrative review. *Canadian Food Studies/La Revue Canadienne Des Études Sur l'alimentation, 8*(3). https://doi.org/10.15353/cfs-rcea.v8i3.473

Prentice, M., & Robinson, G. (2010). "Improving Student Learning Outcomes with Service Learning". *Higher Education*, 148. https://digitalcommons

Rasche, A., Gilbert, U., & Ingo, S. (2012). Cross-disciplinary ethics education in MBA programs: Rhetoric or reality? *The Academy of Management Learning and Education, 2013*, 40. https://ssrn.com/abstract=2129671

Robinson, W. I. (2014). *Global capitalism and the crisis of humanity*. Cambridge University Press. https://books.google.de/books?id=9KkdBAAAQBAJ

Ross, N. J. (2011). Hunger at home: A higher education service learning course of appraisal and action in community food security. *Journal of Nutrition Education and Behavior, 43*(1), 71–72. https://doi.org/10.1016/j.jneb.2010.06.002

Sachs, J. (2015). *The age of sustainable development*. Columbia University Press.

Spring, C., Adams, M., & Hardman, M. (2019). Sites of learning: Exploring political ecologies and visceral pedagogies of surplus food redistribution in the UK. *Policy Futures in Education, 17*(7), 844–861. https://doi.org/10.1177/1478210318819249

Strauss, A., & Corbin, J. (1998). *Basics of qualitative research: Techniques and procedures for developing grounded theory* (2nd ed.). Sage Publications.

Strong, S. (2022). Facing hunger, framing food banks, imaging austerity. *Social & Cultural Geography, 23*(9), 1333–1350. https://doi.org/10.1080/14649365.2021.1921247

Suddaby, R. (2006). From the editors: What grounded theory is not. *Academy of Management Journal, 49*(4), 633–642.

Sullivan-Catlin, H. (2002). *Food, hunger, and poverty: A thematic approach to integrating service learning - Teaching sociology* (pp. 39–52). American Sociological Association. https://www.jstor.org/stable/3211519

Van Newkirk Hoffman, C., & Martin, K. (2014). *Freshplace manual: A resource guide for an innovative food pantry model*. Chrysalis Center, Inc., Foodshare, Junior League of Hartford, and the University of Saint Joseph.

Wallace, D. F. (2021). *Das hier ist Wasser: Gedanken zu einer Lebensführung der Anteilnahme vorgebracht bei einem wichtigen Anlass = This is water* (U. Blumenbach, Trans.) (*26. Auflage, zweisprachige Ausgabe*). Kiepenheuer & Witsch.

Whiteley, M. A. (2014). A draft conceptual framework of relevant theories to inform future rigorous research on student service-learning outcomes. *Michigan Journal of Community Service Learning, 20*(2), 22.

Chapter 7

Integrating Sustainability in Teaching Business Strategy: Sharing Experiences of Adaptation and Delivery of an Action and Experiential Learning Type Sustainability Module

Avvari V. Mohan

Monash University Malaysia, Malaysia

Abstract

There has been considerable discussion about the poor outcomes of irresponsible management, which are often discussed as being the result of "shortcomings" of contemporary capitalism: runaway self-interest, quarterly focus, elite orientation, volume orientation, and one-pattern capitalism (Kim, 2022). In order to address such shortcomings in business education, particularly with strategy-related modules that were taught with a focus on creating "shareholder value," the Sustainable Decisions and Organisations (SDO) module was designed by academics as the capstone module for the master of business administration (MBA) program and delivered with the aim of developing capabilities of students to be leaders and future generators of sustainable value for business and society at large. The students participating in the module are shown how a "stakeholder" approach to developing business strategy can lead to more sustainability-oriented value creation. The module addresses how companies can contribute to "sustainability" by aligning their economic/ financial, societal, and ecological impacts with limited resources through strategy. This contribution discusses the implementation of this module and demonstrates how students are provided learning opportunities around how sustainability-related issues can be embedded into a business organization's strategy to enhance the organization's performance while addressing risks by working with stakeholders to create value and thus be able to contribute to relevant UN Sustainable Development Goals (SDGs).

Innovation in Responsible Management Education, 165–184

Copyright © 2024 Avvari V. Mohan

Published under exclusive licence by Emerald Publishing Limited

doi:10.1108/978-1-83549-464-620241010

Keywords: Integrating sustainability into strategy; responsible business strategy; stakeholders and strategy; design and delivery of sustainability strategy; innovation for sustainability; leadership for sustainability

In the recent past, there has been discussion about the poor outcomes of irresponsible management, which are often the result of "shortcomings" of contemporary capitalism: runaway self-interest, quarterly focus, elite orientation, volume orientation, and one-pattern capitalism (Kim, 2022). In order to address these shortcomings, particularly with business strategy–related modules that were taught with a focus on creating "shareholder value," the Sustainable Decisions and Organisations (SDO) module was designed by academics at the Nottingham University Business School (NUBS) in collaboration with senior executives from industry and other stakeholders. The aim of the SDO module was to develop capabilities of students to be future generators of sustainable value for business and society at large, thus making for a more inclusive and sustainable global economy. The SDO module was designed in such a way that any updates in research and practice related to sustainability can be accommodated continuously, without needing to adjust the delivery and governance matters. This chapter is based on the author's experience as a convenor on the adapted SDO module that was delivered in the Malaysia campus of NUBS.

This chapter starts with a background discussion based on gleanings from literature on the teaching methods for sustainability in business and about action learning and experiential learning approaches as appropriate methods for teaching sustainability in business. An overview of the SDO module is provided, describing how it takes an action learning type approach and also how sustainability/environmental, social, and governance (ESG) principles, stakeholder considerations and the UN SDGs are incorporated into the module.[1] This chapter concludes with a reflective summary of the module by the author.

Background Discussion About Action Learning and Experiential for Teaching Sustainability in Business Education

Business schools are seen as having an important and critical role in educating future leaders to focus beyond only financial value creation (shareholder value) but to also see themselves as solving "wicked problems and help in achieving the UN SDGs" (Dziubaniuk & Nyholm, 2021). Sterling (2004) outlined three ways of teaching sustainability: (1) educating about sustainability by adding modules in degree/training programs, (2) education for sustainability that focuses on the transformation of the entire institution by adopting sustainable approaches, and (3) capacity building, which focuses on the development of the students or participants in study programs by developing their skills for sustainability.

Dziubaniuk and Nyholm (2021), based on their review of literature, argue that business schools require a more transformative approach to sustainability education

---

[1]Environmental, social, and governance issues.

to address, among others, the need of facilitating a shift in thinking from a seller–customer view to a more holistic stakeholder approach, improving critical self-reflection skills that can enable individuals/managers to reflect on their actions and decision-making processes.

In a recent article titled "Sustainability Is Essential in Business Education," Sewchurran (2022) discusses that despite sustainability being a hot topic in business and management education, business schools are struggling to integrate and expand sustainability-related content within the curricula. Sewchurran (2022) goes on to state that for the most part, business schools are "taking on" pedagogical approaches to meet new world challenges, which usually involves implementing existing frameworks into the program. Sewchurran argues that treating sustainability as a straightforward transfer of knowledge to current and future managers alone is not enough. There is a need to find ways to encourage students or executives in the MBA programs to gain genuine self-insight into how they are contributing to solving the world's sustainability challenges. "Integrative Thinking" is seen as key for sustainability education in business schools. Integrative thinking, in addition to bringing together the various functional aspects of business, also involves the integrating social and environmental agendas into business practice. An action learning approach is seen as the way to address these requirements, i.e., combining integrative problem-solving approaches as a group while also providing space for individual reflection for self-insight.

Action learning offers advantages like being more engaging for participants, allows for the integration of teaching with application to current challenges or issues in the work place, and is flexible as it also lends itself to both virtual working and self-facilitation (Brook & Pedler, 2020). Based on their literature review, Brook and Pedler (2020) discuss the evolving attitudes toward action learning and experiential learning in management education. They argue experiential learning emphasizes ideally situating learners in real-world scenarios where they can apply theoretical knowledge. This approach is often seen as beneficial for developing practical skills and critical thinking but could overemphasize individual experience which can lead to a decontextualized understanding of management, lacking in broader social and organizational perspectives.

To summarize the above discussion, there is a need for having a holistic problem-solving approach, i.e., an integrative approach, a need for individual reflection and learning around what the individual values are and how one can bring these to decision-making for learning about sustainability in business. The action learning approach, which is a process "that involves a small group working on real problems, taking action, and learning as individuals, as a team, and as an organization" (World Institute for Action Learning, 2022), is seen as an appropriate pedagogical approach for teaching sustainability in business. Action learning, developed in the early 1980s by Revans (Pedler, 2016), has been well received by the business/corporate world and has been seen as an effective approach for organizations to develop creative, flexible, and successful strategies for pressing problems. Action learning is an approach to problem-solving involving taking action and reflecting upon the results. Action learning as a pedagogical approach is seen as helping improve the problem-solving process as well as simplifying the solutions developed by a team. In addition to action learning, adding a flavor of experiential learning where the learner engages in an activity, observes the results, and draws conclusions is also seen as helpful for addressing the challenging of teaching sustainability in business.

Thus, the SDO module was designed to be delivered using an action learning approach incorporating some elements of experiential learning.

Overview of the SDO Module

The SDO module is the capstone module for the MBA program and was designed to be delivered as an action learning type module with some experiential learning (Cho, 2013). The module aims to enable participating students who are executives to develop business and management skills in general and while being able to have an integrated view of their learning across their program of study. And most importantly, the module is seen as a safe space in which participants can experiment with concepts of financial, social, and environmental sustainability as they relate to business strategy. In the UK campus, the SDO module takes on a simulation approach with a fictitious case study from a particular industry. Each year, given the dynamics of the industry, the key issues or problems change and thus offer students to engage with current problems and topical cases. In the Malaysia campus, the case scenario approach of real-life company was developed, using a different company each year. This allowed for some experiential learning also. The use of a real-life case allowed for bringing in executives from the selected case company to share the problems or issues they face and sometimes even permitted site visits. Thus, the module in Malaysia was delivered with an action learning approach along with some experiential learning. The following passages explain how this is done in the SDO module.

The SDO module is delivered as a block module over 7 days (including full days on the weekend and evenings on the weekdays). The module takes the form of a series of lecture/presentations by the module convenor and guest speakers from industry and civic society and group work during the first 2 days. This is followed by a project style work in the form of a role-play by the groups of the participating executives. The groups work, among other interrelated tasks, on developing a sustainability strategy for a real-life company chosen as the case each year (this choice of the case company can be different each year). The focus is on the role of different business stakeholders in achieving economic, social, and environmental sustainability. The module expects the participants to examine the contradicting and contradictory objectives, values, and decision-making processes when having to embed social and environmental agendas into business strategy and operations. Students or participants are provided inputs and learning experiences around working with relevant stakeholders in order for the sustainability-related issues to be embedded into a business strategy to enhance the organization's performance while simultaneously addressing risks. While doing so, they also come to an understanding of how this approach to strategy can help in contributing to relevant UN SDGs.

The SDO Module as an Action Learning Type Module

This section describes how the SDO modules apply the process of action learning and some experiential learning embedded into this. Action learning took the form of groups of students from diverse backgrounds who worked collaboratively to solve business problems using sustainability principles. The experiential learning aspect involved these groups being engaged in a role-play on a project guided by the convenor. This allowed them to gain new insights, perspectives, and attitudes as they worked with groups' members and applied their learning. The SDO module follows in principle Kolb's experiential learning style theory (McLeod, 2024) with activities and tasks designed and delivered in ways that offer each learner a chance to engage as much as possible in the manner that could suit them best. The module aims to provide for the participating students a concrete experience of working on a real-life situation with safe experimentation – as in the Kolb's four-stage learning cycle as in the Fig. 7.1 below:

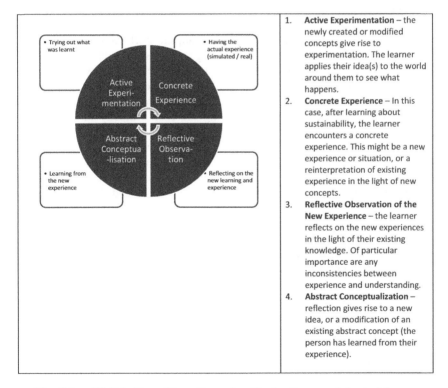

1. **Active Experimentation** – the newly created or modified concepts give rise to experimentation. The learner applies their idea(s) to the world around them to see what happens.
2. **Concrete Experience** – In this case, after learning about sustainability, the learner encounters a concrete experience. This might be a new experience or situation, or a reinterpretation of existing experience in the light of new concepts.
3. **Reflective Observation of the New Experience** – the learner reflects on the new experiences in the light of their existing knowledge. Of particular importance are any inconsistencies between experience and understanding.
4. **Abstract Conceptualization** – reflection gives rise to a new idea, or a modification of an existing abstract concept (the person has learned from their experience).

Fig. 7.1.   Kolb's Four-Stage Learning Cycle. *Source:* Adapted from - Kolb, DA (1984). *Experiential learning: Experience as the source of learning and development* (Vol. 1). Englewood Cliffs, NJ: Prentice-Hall.

The argument here is that effective learning is seen when a learner goes through a cycle of four stages. Other active learning/experiential learning approaches provide different steps, and while there are varying "steps" in different action learning approaches, the key elements are (i) identifying and addressing problem/s / challenge/s (ii) forming and working in groups to solve these problems (iii) questioning and reflecting on the solutions (iv) taking action (v) revisiting/reviewing and learning and (vi) implementing the change. Given that the SDO module is run as an intensive block module, i.e., delivered over a week by groups of executives who are the students participating in the MBA program, the final step, i.e., implementing the change, is the only element that is more or less simulated.

Explained below are the components of the action learning cycle in the SDO module.

* *The Problem or Challenge:* Each year, the module convenor identifies a (preferably listed) company in the country (in this case Malaysia or Singapore) that is facing a major problem. There were times when a company is chosen not so much because of a problem but because they were facing a stagnation in terms of market growth. A case scenario is developed.
* *The Groups:* The module convenor forms groups to work on the problem. Each group is formed to be diverse, comprising members from different organizations with expertise in different areas (finance, marketing, quality, etc.). Care is taken to also ensure diversity of gender and seniority. These groups do a role-play as the C-suite management team of the case company who will work on solving the problem/challenge facing the case company throughout the week.
* *Questioning and Reflecting:* Once the briefings/lecture sessions are completed, the group work starts with members guided to ask questions and challenge the assumptions behind the problem. They reflect on the problem and brainstorm potential solutions. This phase is characterized by open-ended questioning and reflective listening.
* *Taking Action:* The team then decides on a course of action. This is not a mere conceptual exercise – the groups even conduct some market research (using secondary and sometimes even primary data) to develop the solution, in this case the strategy, embedding sustainability principles.
* *Reviewing and Learning:* After the brainstorming session, the groups conduct an external environment analysis, a stakeholder analysis, and review their initial assumptions and start working on developing a holistic and integrated strategy for the case company.
* *Reflection:* In addition to the group work, there is also an individual assessment component providing the space for individual reflection that will be explained later.

In addition to the above, the module also has other aspects like leadership development, communications to board members, and also a small component of crisis communications involving media.

Group and Individual Tasks/Assessment Around Sustainability Strategy

The core of the module is designed around two activities that are also form the basis for the assessment.

The Group Activities and Assessment

- *Group Work on Sustainability Strategy Report Development and Presentation:* Each group over the week has to develop a strategy document (embedding sustainability/ESG elements into it) and submit it on the 6th day. This strategy has to be presented in a "board Meeting" by the end of the week. The board meeting has a panel consisting of real members of boards of companies who role-play as the board members of the company chosen as the case for the module. These board members are selected on the basis of their backgrounds in embedding social and environmental agendas. Care is taken to also have diversity of board members (gender, race, and industry related). At times, we have had the board member from the case company also participating (A sample of the case scenario provided is in Appendix A).

Board Presentation – while the board Meeting is chaired by the "Chair" of the Board (with the module convenor overseeing the meeting), each group playing the role of the management will need to manage the board meeting, particularly in terms of how to make the presentation and how to respond to questioning. This includes making decisions about how to deploy different group members. Each group's Board meeting is scheduled to last 20 minutes. The Board provides general feedback to all groups.

- *Responding to an Intervention/Crisis – Media Statement and Press Conference:* The group also has to respond to an intervention/crisis that is introduced, and they have to manage a (mock) "media conference" by the end of the week.

Even the best-prepared companies face unexpected events and issues. The way in which companies manage these will be crucial to whether they are just events and issues or whether they turn into crises which damage the company, under-mining corporate strategy and reputation. This component of the module is designed to provide an experience of dealing with the unexpected.

So while the main focus of the module is on how sustainability/ESG issues can help in value creation and not just addressing risks, the participants are also provided an experience around "Crisis" and crisis communications in terms of dealing with the media, the learning focus being to understand the role of media as an important stakeholder.

Press Conference

On day 5 of the module (one day before the group strategy document is to be submitted), the "Intervention" in the form of a crisis is introduced in the form of a press release (Appendix B has a sample) which is given out to the CEOs of each group. This intervention is adapted from a real-life crisis event from the business world. Once the crisis is revealed, the groups, i.e., the management teams need to develop a "Media Response" in the form of a media statement while also continuing to work on the strategy document.

On the final day, once the groups complete their presentation to the board, they face a panel of members of media (each year journalists or media professionals are invited to be a part of the panel). The groups have to role-play as the management team who "have called" the media conference to present their response to the interventions. Each group has to manage the media conference, present their response, and respond to media questioning. This includes making decisions about how to deploy different group members. The media conference is scheduled to last 15–20 minutes, and it is left to the groups to decide how they want to use that time.

The Individual Task: A Reflective Essay

After the group project is completed with the submission and presentation of the strategy document and mock media conference, the participants are given 2 weeks to develop a reflective essay based on the group activities.

Individual reflection is a rare but vital learning opportunity and enables individual endeavor and excellence to shine. Critical reflection is an ability senior management wants to see in potential leaders. This essay aims to build this ability and provides the following benefits: (i) from a content point of view, the individual student gets a chance to write their views/experiences of the group work on strategy and intervention and (ii) it is also designed to alleviate any risk of group performance going wrong. As the groups are formed by the module convenor, there are chances of challenging group dynamics, conflicts, etc. This individual reflection with a significant weightage provides some alleviation of such a risk.

Individual Reflection

Reflective learning helps to develop critical thinking, self-awareness, and analytical skills and is important to both staff and students. It involves involvement by an individual in a reflective process. This can help to inform about what worked or didn't work, what might need to be done differently, or how individuals may need to develop their behavior or practice.[2] There are no right or wrong answers to this assignment. Marks are awarded on the basis of the seriousness with which the key instructions are addressed and engaged with. Students are asked to critically reflect on the selected strategy and presentation to the board, the experiences in the response to the crisis and media presentation, the

---

[2]http://www.heacademy.ac.uk/hlst/resources/a-zdirectory/reflectivelearning

group's processes, and their individual roles in the group. The students are asked to identify what they take away from these experiences and what they would have done differently.

In summary, the SDO module involves groups of participating executives solving the problems as a team for a real company, in real time, and learning while doing so. The dual outcomes are solving the problem and learning from the experience; hence, the emphasis is as much on the problem-solving outcome as it is on the learning outcome.

Integrating Stakeholder Views and the UN SDGs in Strategy

As mentioned before, the group work in the module is to reflect realities of organizations and shared effort with the activities (development of strategy and operations) built around the real-life case company assigned. The groups in addition to scanning the general/industry environment analysis for risks and opportunities are guided to also conduct an analysis of stakeholders that can impact or are impacted by the company. But more importantly, the stakeholder analysis involves not only identifying possible risks but also opportunities while addressing the needs of the stakeholders through the business strategy.

The students participating in the module are shown how a "stakeholder" approach (Freeman, 2010) to developing business strategy can lead to more sustainability-oriented value creation not just for the company/organization but also for the society and environment. In addition, frameworks for analyzing and managing stakeholders like the "Salience Model" by Mitchell et al. (1997) are introduced to help the groups in their work.

Aligning the Stakeholders Expectations and UN SDGs to Business Priorities: Introducing the "Materiality Analysis"

The students/executives participating in the SDO module are introduced to the concept of materiality analysis, which is a process that helps managers to identify the most important social and environmental areas to focus on by looking at which aspects are of most concern to stakeholders, and how they impact the business.[3] The materiality approach is based on the Global Reporting Initiative (GRI) standards.[4] This materiality analysis helps to align sustainability strategy with stakeholder expectations. In the newer versions of the module, the alignment with the UN SDGs is also asked for.

It is this aspect of the module that allows for adaptation of the module based on the different local contexts as the business environment scanning and stakeholder analyses are done based on the locations where the SDO module is delivered.

---

[3]https://www.globalreporting.org/media/jrbntbyv/griwhitepaper-publications.pdf
[4]The *Global Reporting Initiative* (known as *GRI*) is an international independent standards organization on Sustainability Reporting.

Role of Module Convenors as Facilitators and Mentors

Given this background to the module design based on action learning with some experiential learning approaches, it is important to note the role of the module convenors for SDO. In addition to developing the key readings, videos, and case illustrations, SDO convenors have the following duties:

* Delivering the briefings/lecture sessions on the group work and assessments.
* Identifying the companies that are apt for developing the case scenario for the group strategy development work.
* Identifying real-life crisis situations and adapting one for the crisis intervention.
* Identifying members of boards for the board panel and media experts for the (mock) media conference. This involves considerable communications with the group for them to develop an understanding of the module aims, the assessments, and the role the board and media have to play.
* Identifying companies who have experienced the transformation of their organizations based on sustainability and organizing guest speaker sessions or site visits to these organizations.
* Arrange for a "crisis communications" session – this is the session where an intervention is provided to the students to address as a crisis.
* Organizing the Board meeting and the media conference on the last day.

The most important role of the module conveners is to act as a mentor or consultant to the different groups doing the role-play as the management teams for the case company. Throughout the week, the convenor has to be available to the groups for their queries and also sometimes to manage the group dynamics.

Summary of How the Module Is Delivered Over the Week

Days/Sessions 1 and 2

The module starts with an overview of what is to come for the week, introducing the case company assigned, forming of groups along with the group activities around the case company and explanation of the assessments.

The class members are organized into groups by the module convenor. These groups address the group assignment: development of the strategy document, a response to the intervention/crisis that is introduced, managing a (mock) media conference, and presenting the strategy in a "Board Meeting." These groups are allocated prior to the start of the class, and each group needs to have a CEO selected within the groups by group members. When class members are allocated to their groups, the groups then need to decide and agree on job roles/descriptions/responsibilities and then allocate these to group members. Each member is then required to sign a contract.

The groups who role-play as the new management team are presented with key challenges to address in the form of a memo from the "Chairman" of the board of the company assigned. The memo asks the groups to consider the issue of sustainability and where it should sit strategically. It is emphasized to the students that the issue of utmost importance for them is to demonstrate how the financial performance and market value of the company will be enhanced. However, of equal importance is the issue of sustainability and how the organization might capture the value from social and environmental opportunities.

In the session, there is a discussion around what sustainability is and how businesses/companies are integrating sustainability into their core business strategy. Students are made aware that there is no easy answer to this question (Dyllick & Muff, 2016). Sustainability and some of the models for sustainability could be a contested topic with many definitions (Crane et al., 2014). Business organizations have varying and often divergent perspectives and undertake a broad range of disparate activities under the banner of sustainability.

In the next session, the concept of stakeholder analysis and how to apply it specifically to the question how to prioritize stakeholder requirements into strategies for sustainability is presented (Mitchell et al., 1997). Frameworks for stakeholder analysis and engagement are introduced. Finally, a briefing on materiality assessment (GRI) as a tool for companies to start off their sustainability journey is provided. While the usage of this tool is not mandatory, it helps the students to understand the sustainability aspects in terms of ESG components that are important to the organization and its stakeholders.

After the stakeholder analysis, business models for sustainability like the stewardship model (Hart & Milstein, 2003), creating shared value (Porter & Kramer, 2011), circular economy business models (Stead & Stead, 2009), etc., are introduced, along with case studies of top global and local businesses/companies that are building their core strategies around sustainability issues. There could be models that the group would like to refer to for areas for innovation and value creation and apply to "their company." The class discussion involves relooking at the concept of strategy and then moving into different frameworks for understanding stakeholders. These are discussed and contrasted, highlighting the importance of understanding and managing stakeholder expectations in strategy formation for sustainability. In addition, the UN SDGs are introduced, and students consider how they can inform or provide a guide to identify the area of interest for the companies to develop their strategy.

During the first 2 days, senior executives (CEOs or sustainability directors) of companies that have initiated sustainability-embedded strategy and operations in their organizations are invited to make presentations and discuss with the students the challenges involved and outcomes of their initiatives.

When possible, a site visit to companies that have interesting sustainability initiatives is also arranged for the groups to get an idea around the practical aspects of developing and implementing a stakeholder and sustainability strategy in organizations.

These sessions during the first 2 days are like prepping days. From the end of day 2 onward, the groups are allocated their breakout rooms to start working on the case organization.

Days/Sessions 3–6 of the Module

The groups, i.e., the management teams, start their work. CEOs coordinate with their team members and start to prioritize the sustainability agenda to promote sustainability more aggressively across their respective organizations in a variety of ways. The challenge for them as the management team is to make sense of varying perspectives around sustainability and decide how and to what degree they should integrate sustainability into the company's core strategy and value proposition (Dyllick & Muff, 2016).

There is a formal starting off on the group work, where each group, i.e., the management teams do an assessment of the company case and start off their preparation of the strategy formulation. This involves some brainstorming and confirmation/agreements about individual roles of each member within the group, integration and timelines, and agreeing on decision-making processes. Students start getting familiar with the case organization and the case-related materials and draft the plan for the next few days.

The teams are then guided to assess the company case more closely and begin to think about the sort of future of the company their strategy could be directed at. They start thinking about the risks/opportunities through a business environment scanning, the current market positioning, resource analysis using tools like value chain, etc. The relevant role-playing group members start to understand the business environment, the market/s and who the customers are, and the other key stakeholders (suppliers, government agencies, community, etc.) and begin to identify what the sustainability issues to consider are.

Aligning Stakeholders Expectations, UN SDGs and Business Priorities: Materiality Analysis

The groups start to realize that there are countless sustainability/environmental and social issues that could be addressed. In order for them to distil the relevant ones, they are introduced to the materiality analysis from the GRI standards organization.[5] Through materiality analyses, the groups learn to align sustainability strategy with stakeholder expectations and now also with the UN SDGs.

The external business environment is analyzed using framework like PESTLE and sometimes Porter's five forces model to help them understand industry forces and for the analysis of the strengths of the company. The value chain analysis is done along with understanding the market positioning. At this time, the groups, i.e., the management teams are guided to be focusing on the following questions: "What sort of strategy do we wish to pursue and why? Think: Mission, Vision, Values, and Objectives. How do these elements underpin each other? How are they going to achieve the proposed strategy?" The groups are asked to think of the process of change and assess the potential implications of this change process (staff layoffs, increased costs, changes in supply chain, etc.).

---

[5]https://www2.deloitte.com/content/dam/Deloitte/nl/Documents/risk/deloitte-nl-risk-double-materiality.pdf

The CEOs in the groups guide their teams to start thinking about the research to inform the strategy being proposed (i.e., the departmental/functional strategies to be in the appendices). This step could include financial analysis, market analysis, human resources (HR) analysis, and nonmarket analysis. Here, students start thinking about the different functions, i.e., marketing, operations, research and development (R&D), HR, etc., and the resources they will require to support the sustainability strategy that they have formulated for the business. The groups also focus on the question how they are going to achieve the proposed strategy. Here, they assess the process of change and the potential implications of this change process (staff layoffs, increased costs, change in supply chain, etc.). All this can vary for different groups based on the strategic direction (new or amended visions/missions and objectives).

As the penultimate day approaches – the groups start thinking about how to integrate the different departmental/functional strategies so that they will support or fit with the overall strategy and do a final test of the strategy developed with "what if" scenarios. This is the strategy that they have to submit as a report and present to a panel of board members. On the penultimate day, there is also an "Intervention" in the form of a real-life crisis related to sustainability that the management teams have to address, and they have to develop a media statement and face real media in a media conference format. The groups are provided a briefing on "crisis communications" by professionals from the media organizations or corporate communications experts to prepare them for this task.

Final Day: Communicating a Cohesive Vision and Action for Business Sustainability

The final day of the module requires students to make two key presentations to the media conference and to the Board. The primary objective of the Board presentation is to communicate the sustainability strategy succinctly and convincingly to the board of the company (represented by a panel of real-life board members). The memo from the Chairman (mentioned in the beginning) gives hints on what the Board expects the teams to cover. It is absolutely critical that the groups take note of the financial plan to be provided for a 5-year period (from the time of the module) to ensure that all investments, assumptions, and projections are fully integrated and include a value for the business that demonstrates a competitive return on investment. They have to do all this while also ensuring social and environmental agendas relevant to the company's stakeholders are addressed.

The media presentation is far less predictable and will focus on the press release/media statement that the group prepares on the penultimate day in response to the "surprise" intervention. There is an individual reflection component to the assessment, which is a vital learning opportunity as its ability something senior management wants to see in the potential leaders.

Summary and Reflections

One of the strengths of the design of the module is its ability to incorporate or update the quickly changing issues in the landscape of sustainability. Some key points or strengths of the module include:

- Being flexible and allowing for updates without having to get "clearances." There is no "content curriculum" or "topics" to be covered dictated a priori – this is very important as it allows for updates of the content and as in some regulatory environments (like Malaysia or Singapore) this helps avoid the need for clearances from authorities.
- Local institutional context – a culture of harmony in local businesses and differences in stakeholder expectations: The module not only incorporates "ESGs" but also issues related to the institutional context of where the module is delivered including different local key stakeholder and their views.[6] Here, the stakeholder analysis is not just to identify risks but to see how value creation can be done – in contexts like Malaysia or Singapore, the role of stakeholders like trade unions or civic society organization is very different from that of other locations, especially in the United Kingdom. There could be less "activist" approaches and more advocacy approaches in civic society in the region. There is also a strong risk-averse culture among the businesses which has implications for identifying critical crisis in real business world (there are fewer big corporate crisis in this part of the world).
- Engagement of the student in the class – the group (role-play)-based project style module allows for all the class members to be involved.

  - The use of real-life (local) cases as the basis for the assignment provided for experiential learning as this not only helps them to relate better with the local business environment but also allows them to learn by researching the issues that were current in relation to the real company chosen as the case for the assignment. All this creates strong engagement within the group members. The local students are resourceful in getting information of the local context, and the foreign students have the opportunity to learn about local businesses and the environment.
  - One of the challenges of role-play-oriented group work in Southeast Asian context is that there may not be heated debates in the group discussions due to the business/social culture of harmony.[7] This has implications for group discussions being more accepting of what more dominant persons may propose and also for the role of the convenor as it becomes critical to mentor

---

[6]Organizational culture profile of Malaysian high-tech industries accessed from https://www.emerald.com/insight/content/doi/10.1108/APJBA-08-2013-0088/full/html (on 30th Dec.'23).
[7]Organizational culture profile of Malaysian high-tech industries accessed from https://www.emerald.com/insight/content/doi/10.1108/APJBA-08-2013-0088/full/html (on 30th Dec.'23).

and coach the groups by challenging them as a team to providing bold solutions and encourage quieter individual members in the group to speak up/debate with their team members for the best solution. The team leaders (CEOs in their role-play) also are mentored to coordinate to get the best ideas from group members during the first 2 days and then move to execution in the later days.

• Leadership development – The class members learn business leadership away from the traditional capitalism approach. Here, as part of the role-play, the CEOs and the supporting senior managers are challenged to think and execute a strategy that incorporates both environmental + social + governance (ESG/ sustainability) agendas that help improve business performance. This decision-making for incorporating of ESG/sustainability agendas cannot be generic – these agendas have to be conceptualized as solutions to the problems/ issues and contextualized to the local company chosen as the case. The group tasks and assessment push them to understand societal issues and incorporate stakeholders' interests and to work collaboratively. They also learn to communicate the "business case," i.e., the viability of their strategy to convince the company board and get buy in or be able to manage media as a stakeholder.

The module has been able to keep with the developments in the environment in both academic content and practice aspect. The content related to sustainability issues from conceptual frameworks to emerging standards for sustainability and what the local regulatory requirements are, for example, climate taxonomies of ASEAN counties, etc., can all be incorporated into the learning and applications. The global standards for sustainability be they GRI or the climate-related ones like the Task Force on Climate-related Financial Disclosures (TCFD) and many more emerging ones can be incorporated into the group assignments.

When the module was started more than two decades ago, the issue of incorporating UN SDGs was not there – now the module has been able to address how the UN SDGs have been incorporated as one of the outcomes of the strategy developed. The module also introduces some frameworks from sustainability reporting. More importantly, the action learning approach of identifying of the business problem in tandem with the social and environmental externalities is done as a group effort. The role-playing and real-life case being provided as the basis allows for some experiential learning flavor. This is also followed by an individual reflection on the group dynamics and also individual views of how the participant could do better are incorporated into the module.

There are some challenges. One of them is that the SDO module as a capstone or standalone unit can have a disconnect with the way the functional modules that lead up to SDO are taught, i.e., modules such as marketing, economics, operations management, etc., may still be taught without full consideration of the social and environmental externalities. This is now being addressed as there are two critical issues that are being reviewed in all modules (i) sustainability and (ii) digital technologies. The other challenges of the module are always around two issues (i) prereadings that students do not at all complete when coming to the session and (ii) the time factor, given that the module is run in a block format, i.e., over 1 week intensively.

Overall, the module has been well received over the past decade based on the feedback documents and also in discussions with alumni. This is a core module, and some of the participants struggle at the beginning, particularly those participants who come from purely technical backgrounds. In addition to the briefings sessions that include lectures, guiding sessions around the content made available on the online platform help guide the participants. The module convenor acting as mentors/consultants helps to guide the development of the group activities in a more customized way, which helps the individuals and each group to get comfortable with the content and task.

The SDO module is a component of the MBA program designed to foster sustainable and responsible management decision making among the participants. This module, developed by the Nottingham University Business School, uses an action learning approach to encourage students to develop sustainable business strategies. The module's core is centered around real-world cases, allowing students to actively engage with sustainability issues. It includes various activities like group strategy development, board meetings, and media conferences, emphasizing stakeholder analysis, materiality analysis, and alignment with UN SDGs. The module's success lies in its adaptability, relevance, and hands-on approach to teaching sustainability, preparing students to address contemporary sustainability challenges in business.

Acknowledgment

I would like to place on record my thanks to Professors Jeremy Moon, Prof Wendy Chapple who first designed and delivered the Sustainable Decisions and Organisations (SDO) Module while they were at the Nottingham University Business School (NUBS), University of Nottingham. In addition to some industry experts, Mr Thomas Thomas (Honorary Professor at NUBS) was one of the key contributors in the development of this module. I had the privilege doing the convenor of SDO in Malaysia about a decade ago when I did some adaptations, including incorporating some experiential learning flavor.

References

Brook, C., & Pedler, M. (2020). Action learning in management education: A state of the field review in higher education. *International Journal of Management in Education, 18*(3), 100415.

Cho, Y. (2013). What is action learning? Components, types, processes, issues, and research agendas. *Learning and Performance Quarterly, 1*(4), 1–11. https:// creativecommons.org/licenses/by-nc/4.0/

Crane, A., Palazzo, G., Spence, L. J., & Matten, D. (2014). Contesting the value of "creating shared value". *California Management Review, 56*(2), 130–153. https:// doi.org/10.1525/cmr.2014.56.2.130

Dyllick, T., & Muff, K. (2016). Clarifying the meaning of sustainable business: Introducing a typology from business-as-usual to true business sustainability. *Organization & Environment, 29*(2), 156–174. https://doi.org/10.1177/10860 26615575176

Dziubaniuk, O., & Nyholm, M. (2021). Constructivist approach in teaching sustainability and business ethics: A case study. *International Journal of Sustainability in Higher Education, 22*(1), 177–197. https://doi.org/10.1108/IJSHE-02-2020-0081

Freeman, R. (2010). *Strategic management: A stakeholder approach.* Cambridge University Press. https://doi.org/10.1017/CBO9781139192675

Hart, S., & Milstein, M. (2003). Creating sustainable value. *The Academy of Management Executive, 17*(2), 56–69. https://doi.org/10.5465/ame.2003.10025194

Kim, R. C. (2022). Rethinking corporate social responsibility under contemporary capitalism: Five ways to reinvent CSR. *Business Ethics, the Environment and Responsibility, 31*(2), 346–362. https://doi.org/10.1111/beer.12414

McLeod, S. A. (2024). Kolb – Learning styles. www.simplypsychology.org/learning-kolb.html

Mitchell, R. K., Agle, B. R., & Wood, D. J. (1997). Toward a theory of stakeholder identification and salience: Defining the principle of who and what really counts. *Academy of Management Review, 22*(4), 853–886. https://doi.org/10.2307/259247

Pedler, M. (2016). Reginald Revans: The pioneer of action learning. In D. Szabla, W. Pasmore, M. Barnes, & A. Gipson (Eds.), *The Palgrave Handbook of organizational change thinkers.* Palgrave Macmillan. https://doi.org/10.1007/978-3-319-49820-1_20-1

Porter, M. E., & Kramer, M. R. (2011). Creating shared value. *Harvard Business Review, 89*(1/2), 62–77.

Sewchurran, K. (2022, May 10). Sustainability is essential in business education. *AACSB Insights.* https://www.aacsb.edu/insights/articles/2022/05/sustainability-is-essential-in-business-education

Stead, J. G., & Stead, W. E. (2009). *Management for a small planet* (3rd ed.). Routledge. https://doi.org/10.4324/9781315702698

Sterling, S. (2004). Higher education, sustainability and the role of systemic learning. In P. Corcoran & A. Wals (Eds.), *Higher education and the challenge of sustainability: Contestation, critique, practice, and promise* (pp. 49–70). Kluwer Academic.

World Institute for Action Learning: What is action learning? (2022). https://wial.org/action-learning/. Accessed on August, 2023.

Appendices

Appendix A: Sample of Case Scenario for the Group Work

– for developing the sustainability strategy and presentation to the Board.

    The chairperson of FZ Holdings (real name not being used here), Malaysia, has written to you, the management team, to review and come up with a refreshed sustainability strategy document to present to the board of directors.

(Continued)

(*Continued*)

While there are many sustainability initiatives the organization has started and communicated in its sustainability report, they would like to develop further such initiatives and make FZ Group the leader in overall sustainability in a more holistic way. While the group has shown a rise in terms of top line figures and many other performance metrics, there is a need to relook at the strategy in general and also to take into consideration the disruptions/long-term impacts due to the COVID-19 pandemic.

It is important to note that competition is growing from local and overseas brands, and there are several emerging local artisan businesses that are competing away market for some of our flagship products. Moving forward in the postpandemic era, it is hoped that a refreshed sustainability-oriented strategy can leverage new opportunities and sustain the overall good performance of the organization.

(Several documents and website links to support the case scenario are provided on the online platform.)

What You Are Expected to Do

Given these challenges (and of course stock exchange/regulatory requirements), the board of FZ Holdings has decided to relook at its strategy and is considering how to develop further sustainability aspects and make it the pillar of the company's overall strategy. Your team is to prepare an initial 5-year plan in the form of a strategy document (incorporating the sustainability issues).

In addition, the management team will need to respond to an "intervention" in the form of a statement for media release. You will also be required to explain and justify your initial strategy and the subsequent response in two "live events" both on [insert date] day:

(1) a Board presentation (supported by a Board presentation document that you will also prepare).
(2) a media conference (supported by a media statement that you will also prepare).

Appendix B: Sample of the Crisis Given as the Intervention

– for the group work on media statement and media conference.

Media Release: [Insert Date] Date

AWAKE, a New NGO in Malaysia (and Singapore) Calls for a Boycott of FZ's Products From DATE

AWAKE, an association for women rights with global presence has called for boycott of all FZs products. They will be starting a massive social media campaign with Y-Gov (a global public opinion and data organization) starting on [insert date] to highlight FZs "callous attitude" toward workplace harassment. This is the first campaign of this nature directly against a Singapore/ Malaysia business organization.

This decision to call for the boycott of FZ follows allegations of sexual harassment by senior management members from three women executives, who are threatening to file a class action legal suit if company does not act on culture of sexual harassment. Two of the board members of the organization had requested their secretaries and a woman translator, to join them in a karaoke evening with China clients, ostensibly to translate and record minutes of discussions. The three women said they felt most outraged when they were discouraged repeatedly from going to her HR department to raise the issue of workplace sexism.

One of the women (the translator) happens to be the sister of the leader of AWAKE, the NGO leading the protest. This led them to go to AWAKE and lodge their complaint. The spokesperson for AWAKE said that this campaign was extremely important as the regulations in Singapore are not strong enough to deter such cases. Although Singapore launched the Tripartite Advisory on Managing Workplace Harassment (in 2015) – it advises but does not require employers to develop a harassment prevention policy. According to Lim, "the problem with regulation in Malaysia and the Advisory is that they do not create legal obligations on companies to address workplace harassment. Thus, most local companies do not have the specific anti-workplace harassment policies and are not equipped to deal with harassment cases if they arise." Even when a survivor of workplace harassment files a police report, employers are still not required to address the harassment itself. Justice Lim, the spokesperson for AWAKE, feels that if every one of us as consumers plays our part, it will send a strong signal to the companies. Hence, AWAKE has decided to organize this boycott campaign.

When contacted by the media, FZ claimed that they are currently "investigating" the matter.

What has enraged the group is that when FZ's PR was contacted, they refused to meet/or comment about this. "FZ" is trying to avoid us and think they can get away. "They don't think we're serious about holding them

(Continued)

(*Continued*)

accountable for what's happened. But we've got a surprise for them," said Justice Lim, the spokesperson who is also representing AWAKE's campaign. She said in addition to hurting the sentiment of the people we do not want this situation affecting the image of Malaysia or Singapore.

What Can You Do?

- JOIN the campaign online at www.awake.org.my from Monday 15th to spread the message via fb, twitter, Instagram.[a]
- Take the poll on Y-gov.com – which will be released as a report to the press.[b]
- MEDIA – PLEASE CONTACT JUSTICE LIM from AWAKE

WE CAN!

End All Violence Against Women

This has happened before, and we do not want this to repeat ......

[a]URLs have been changed for assignment purposes.
[b]URLs have been changed for assignment purposes.

Chapter 8

Framing Tomorrow With Play and Purpose: Global Goals Design Jam

Helga Mayr[a] and Christian Baumgartner[b]

[a]University College of Teacher Education Tyrol, Austria
[b]FHGR University of Applied Sciences of the Grisons in Chur, Switzerland

Abstract

Amid multiple crises and increasing volatility, sustainable development is a pressing concern. Higher Education for Sustainable Development, especially Responsible Management Education (RME), drives transformative change by fostering new perspectives on work, decision-making and leadership. Conferences serve as pivotal sustainability discussion platforms, yet many remain traditional and lack interactive student engagement. This hinders active involvement and collaborative problem-solving. The Global Goals Design Jam, a dynamic, nontraditional format explored in this study offers an alternative approach. By blending design thinking and playful learning and constructivist learning methods, the Global Goals Design Jam offers a space for collaborative and creative Sustainable Development Goals (SDGs) solutions. At the ninth Responsible Management Education Research Conference (RMERC) in September 2022, students from various universities took part in a Global Goals Design Jam. The current prestudy postulates that participation in a Global Goals Design Jam is primarily associated with positive attributes related to emotions and a sense of coherence. The potential for empowering learners to navigate real-world complexities and contribute to sustainability is highlighted, establishing formats like the Global Goals Design Jam as a valuable addition to educational conferences with a sustainability focus. The results also highlight potentials and limitations of the format and provide insights into further research requirements.

Keywords: Responsible management; Sustainable Development Goals; design thinking; playful learning; sense of coherence; emotions

Innovation in Responsible Management Education, 185–217
Copyright © 2024 Helga Mayr and Christian Baumgartner
Published under exclusive licence by Emerald Publishing Limited
doi:10.1108/978-1-83549-464-620241011

Introduction

The world is characterized by numerous crises (Brand, 2009, 2016), that threaten the natural livelihoods of countless people, and societal imbalances that jeopardize the social fabric. The world is characterized by rapid and unpredictable developments that are tried to be captured by using different attributes, summarized under acronyms like VUCA: volatility, ambiguity, complexity, and uncertainty (Bennett & Lemoine, 2014; Hadar et al., 2020; Heller, 2019); TUNA: turbulent, uncertain, novel, and ambiguous; BANI: brittle, anxious, nonlinear, and incomprehensible; or RUPT: rapid, unpredictable, paradoxical, and tangled (Glaeser, 2022; Ray, 2023).

The need to embark on a sustainable development path is more urgent and evident than ever. Responsible management that is rooted in ethics, responsibility, and sustainability (Abdelgaffar, 2021) embodies a holistic approach that transcends immediate gains and focuses on long-term conservation of natural resources and social equity. It is a strategic orientation that not only guides current decisions but also contributes to the creation of a resilient, ethical, and sustainable business ecosystem.

Great hopes are placed in (higher) education for sustainable development (ESD) in general and in education for responsible management (RME) in particular. ESD/RME should enable people to think critically, make responsible decisions, and participate in shaping a sustainable future (Heinrichs & Michelsen, 2014; Michelsen, 2014; Stoltenberg & Burandt, 2014). The increase in relevant academic programs, inter-university collaborations, and many events on this important topic are indicators that this need is being recognized (Cornuel & Hommel, 2015; Painter-Morland, 2015). However, a gap persists between recognition on the one side and holistic integration in RME programs on the other (Abdelgaffar, 2021; Cornuel & Hommel, 2015). To bridge this gap, ESD/RME needs to be integrated system-wide and holistically throughout the institution, permeating all facets of the organization: From pedagogy and academic research to operational practices, organizational ethos, and active community engagement, sustainability must be woven into the fabric of the educational institution. This holistic approach is then consistently reflected in events such as conferences, which serve as platforms for knowledge transfer and collaboration. To be coherent, consistent, and credible, they must be aligned with the institution's commitment to sustainability.

The awareness of responsible management and the United Nations Principles for Responsible Management Education (UN PRME), to be credible and authentic, should therefore be reflected in the design of international conferences and events in general and of the Responsible Management Education Research Conference (RMERC) specifically. Conferences may provide an opportunity to share and deepen experiences and best practices in responsible management and RME. These conferences showcase the latest developments, research, and innovative approaches to strengthen the link between academic teaching and real-world business challenges. The exchange can build a bridge to further close the gap between theoretical understanding and practical implementation. Years of observation by the authors show that academic conferences often follow traditional formats, characterized by passive lectures and workshops, often lacking real interaction and not being in line with the underlying concept. Interactive sessions that facilitate deeper exploration of challenges, identification of specific problems, and collaborative generation of ideas for feasible solutions are still rare.

However, a departure away from this practice was observed at the RMERC hosted by MCI | The Entrepreneurial School ® in September 2022. Eleven students from various degree programs took part in a Global Goals Design Jam (Mayr et al., 2023) during the conference. This educational format, based on design thinking, appeared to stimulate engagement, involvement, and problem-solving among participants. The generated solutions have the potential to form the foundation for future endeavors. Starting from the overarching challenge of "How might we make our living world the most innovative sustainable living world in the world?" participants navigated a design thinking journey. This journey involved delving into developments and challenges related to selected Sustainable Development Goals (SDGs) through discussions with experts, identifying specific problems (design challenges), and co-creatively developing ideas for solutions and realizing them in the form of prototypes.

The Global Goals Design Jam at the RMERC serves as a model for a novel style of conference, blending playfulness, entertainment, and productivity, while simultaneously encouraging motivation (Mayr & Vollmer, 2024). This method of addressing important issues was tested with students at the RMERC and can be considered a prototype for alternative conference formats. The small accompanying preliminary study aimed to determine the level of coherence (meaningfulness, comprehensibility and manageability) perceived during the jam activities as well as the associated emotions. Positive emotions such as joy and negative emotions such as anger or boredom and situational interest as well as (perceived) situational competence may affect students' interest, motivation, and further involvement.

Based on a design-based research approach (Anderson & Shattuck, 2012; Barab & Squire, 2004), the data attained from the group of participants and experts offer preliminary insights into evaluating the format and serve as a foundation for determining whether further research in this direction is warranted. The preliminary evaluation results could offer the conference organizers valuable feedback on the event and recommendations for its future development in the best interests of the participants, particularly the students.

The purpose of this event was to give students the opportunity to interact with chosen SDGs, to co-creatively develop specific solutions while getting to know and reflecting on the design thinking approach. This should strengthen their confidence toward being able to contribute to the implementation of the 2030 Agenda (United Nations, 2015) and to reaching selected SDGs. This aligns with the ESD for 2030 roadmap (UNESCO, 2019, 2020), a framework "adopted with the aim of increasing the contribution of education to building a more just and sustainable world" (UNESCO, 2020, n.d.).

This chapter is guided by the overall research goal of evaluating the suitability of interactive ESD/RME formats that follow a design thinking approach. In this specific case, the preliminary study focuses on the following research questions:

(1) How did participants and experts perceive the Global Goals Design Jam? What were their opinions about it?

- What emotions did they experience during the Global Goals Design Jam?
- To what extent did the participants perceive the activities during the Global Goals Design Jam as coherent, and how does this perception correspond to exerts' external perception?

(2) What insights did participants gain from the Global Goals Design Jam, and to what extent do they consider them useful for their personal or professional development?

(3) Where do participants and experts identify the potentials and constraints of the Global Goals Design Jam format, and what recommendations do they propose to enhance or tailor it?

Based on past experience, observations, and informal discussions with participants and experts, the following propositions are outlined. In the first instance, they are tested for confirmation and may consequently serve as a foundation for deriving hypotheses in the frame of a subsequent research project.

P1. Both participants and experts share a similar perception of the Global Goals Design Jam, although participants may place more emphasis on the event's experiential and collaborative aspects while experts evaluate it from a broader viewpoint, considering its impact on innovation and sustainable development. They both highlight the event's playful, creative, and collaborative nature, as well as its focus on problem-solving.

P2. Participants in the Global Goals Design Jam and experts perceive the activities as rather coherent. Of the three constructs of the sense of coherence, namely understandability, manageability, and meaningfulness, meaningfulness is rated the highest due to the thematic framing of sustainability, and manageability is rated weakest due to its novelty for the participants.

P3. Participants gain insights into creative problem-solving and interdisciplinary collaboration as well as a deeper understanding of the SDGs. They perceive this experience as highly valuable for their personal growth and professional development. This may be an indicator for a positive correlation between participation in the Global Goals Design Jam and skill enhancement.

P4. Both participants and experts recognize that the Global Goals Design Jam format has the potential to foster innovative thinking and collaborative working, leading to creative solutions for complex global challenges. However, there are limitations such as time constraints that may lead to superficiality in outcomes, the necessity for more diversity in representation, and the potential challenges in translating concepts into practical outcomes.

Participants and experts will propose ways to enhance the event, including lengthening its duration, providing more structured guidance, and improving the integration of real-world implementation strategies.

Theoretical Background

Responsible Management Education in the Context of Education for Sustainable Development

The Global Goals Design Jam was part of the RMERC preopening program. RMERC is the annual RMERC organized by the members of the PRME DACH Chapter, the PRME Anti-Poverty Working Group, and the University of the Applied Sciences of the Grisons in Switzerland. Its mission is to integrate ESD into management training in the form of RME.

PRME focuses on management education within the context of sustainable development and the integration of sustainable development into management training following the principles Purpose, Values, Method, Research, Partnership, and Dialogue (UN Global Compact, 2007). Educators in management-related degree programs are encouraged to empower current and future leaders to create value in terms of sustainability for business and society (Principle 1 – Purpose). Education institutions that offer management-related degree programs "are called on to incorporate into academic activities and curricula values of global responsibility (Principle 2 – Values)" (Haertle et al., 2017, p. 66). Principle 3 (Method) refers to the frameworks, materials, methods, processes, and teaching-learning environments that facilitate effective learning experiences related to responsible leadership, while Principle 4 (Research) addresses engagement in "conceptual and empirical research that advances our understanding about the role, dynamics, and impact of business in creating of sustainable social, environmental and economic value" (UN Global Compact, 2007, p. 4). Principles 5 (Partnership) and 6 (Dialogue) call for active engagement in partnerships and the promotion of open dialogue among educators, business, government bodies, civil society, and stakeholders to explore and understand critical global issues related to social responsibility and sustainability.

With reference to various sources, Kolb et al. (2017) outline the key areas that need to be transformed, including reorienting curricula, focusing on developing relevant competencies among students (and faculty), raising public awareness of sustainable development, conducting relevant research, or implementing sustainability in one's own institution. This requirement reflects a holistic understanding of education for sustainability in terms of a whole-institution approach (Kohl et al., 2022; Kolb et al., 2017; Leal Filho et al., 2017) enabling the development of key sustainability competencies (de Haan, 2008; Rieckmann, 2018; Vare et al., 2018; Wiek et al., 2011).[1] Achieving this requires a series of shifts between from incoherence

---

[1] Competencies are "the cognitive abilities and skills available in or learnable by individuals to solve specific problems, and the associated motivational, volitional, and social dispositions and skills to use the problem solutions successfully and responsibly in variable situations" (Weinert, 2001, p. 27).

(and fragmentation) to coherence (and integration), loss of connectedness to connectedness, or from an unsustainable to a sustainable society (Kolb et al., 2017), among others. These considerations highlight the importance of integrating a transformative ESD (Rodríguez Aboytes & Barth, 2020; Singer-Brodowski, 2016; Vare et al., 2018) into management education practices.

The broader goal of ESD, including its specific application to management education in form of RME, is to empower individuals to contribute to both current and future sustainable development efforts (Stoltenberg & Burandt, 2014). This concept received global political recognition as early as 1992 during the Earth Summit with Agenda 21 (United Nations, 1992) and has been reaffirmed in subsequent conferences (United Nations, 2002, 2015). Various United Nations Educational, Scientific, and Cultural Organization (UNESCO) programs, such as the ESD Decade (2005–2014), the Global Action Programme (2015–2019), and the ongoing ESD for 2030 program (2020–2030), have supported this approach (UNESCO, 2013, 2019, 2020). The framework entitled "Education for Sustainable Development: Toward achieving the SDGs" (ESD for 2030) emphasizes the alignment of the education system with the 2030 Agenda and the 17 SDGs. It calls for the structural and holistic integration of ESD into educational institutions, with the aim of fostering the capacity of individuals to make a positive impact on the world. Notably, three out of the five priority action areas (PAAs) outlined by UNESCO (UNESCO, 2019, 2020) directly relate to responsible higher (management) education: "empowering young people to participate in transforming the world" (PAA2), "building capacity among educators" (PAA3), and "transforming learning environments accordingly" (PAA4).

According to a critical-emancipatory understanding (Arnold & Pachner, 2011; Barth, 2011; Dubs, 1995), ESD is education that enables people to help shape a sustainable world (Vare & Scott, 2007; Wals, 2011). It is part of the social process of learning, exploring, and designing (Stoltenberg & Burandt, 2014) that constitutes sustainable development. Universities in particular play an important role in the context of ESD, as they offer students the opportunity to (further) develop and strengthen relevant competencies (de Haan, 2008; Rieckmann, 2018; Wiek et al., 2011), on the one hand, and to experience themselves as self-effective actors in sustainable development, on the other. In recent years, various concepts of competence have been developed which, despite the differences, have much in common in terms of what is considered to be important in relation to sustainable development, such as critical and systems thinking competence, anticipatory, normative and strategic competence, collaboration or integrated problem-solving competence (Ahel & Lingenau, 2021; de Haan, 2008; Rieckmann, 2018; Wiek et al., 2011) as well as creativity (Dede, 2010; Ohio Department of Education, 2016), and the ability to (co)create (new) value (OECD, 2019). In addition, sustainability competencies largely align with concepts such as 21st century competencies/skills (Brewer, 2018; Dede, 2010; Fadel, 2008; Ohio Department of Education, 2016) or the Organization for Economic Cooperation and Development (OECD) Learning Compass (OECD, 2019), as well as with key characteristics of design thinking (Micheli et al., 2018).

Educational institutions are challenged to provide appropriate learning environments and opportunities that prepare students to confidently navigate an uncertain future (International Commission on the Futures of Education, 2021) and help shape it in the spirit of sustainable development (Scheer et al., 2012), as well as provide opportunities to engage with the SDGs and contribute to their achievement (Ahel & Lingenau, 2021).

Activity Emotions, the Sense of Coherence, and Motivation

Positive activity emotions and motivational outcomes (Itzek-Greulich & Vollmer, 2017; Schmidt, 2019; Schneider et al., 2021) as well as the perceived sense of coherence (Antonovsky, 1993; Bauer et al., 2015; Eriksson, 2017) play an important role in learning and taking action. Activity emotions, which encompass feelings like anger or joy experienced during learning activities, play influential roles. Positive emotions, like enjoyment, excitement, and interest, can enhance learning by increasing engagement and motivation (Itzek-Greulich & Vollmer, 2017; Pekrun et al., 2011; Randler et al., 2011). In the context of ESD, positive activity emotions can promote a deeper connection and emotional engagement with sustainability-related subjects (Schneider et al., 2021; Zelenski & Desrochers, 2021). Motivation is essential for learning and acting (Hamann et al., 2016; Heckhausen & Heckhausen, 2018; Hunecke, 2022; Itzek-Greulich & Vollmer, 2017; Ryan & Deci, 2000). Participating in activities which promote autonomy, relevance, and a sense of competence enables learners to link their objectives and values with sustainable behavior. Consequently, motivation for sustainable development can be enhanced. The perceived sense of coherence, as derived from salutogenesis theory, pertains to an individual's conviction about the meaningfulness, comprehensibility, and designability or manageability (Antonovsky, 1993; Eriksson, 2017) of their experiences.

Comprehensibility refers to the degree to which individuals perceive their internal and external experiences as understandable, structured, and/or predictable and clear (Antonovsky, 1993; Geyer, 1997; Jenny et al., 2017). It encompasses a perceptive grasp of causality and the ability to discern patterns and connections, allowing for predictability and coherence in one's personal experiences. In the context of ESD, a strong sense of coherence supports the learner's development of critical and systems thinking perspective that renders the interconnectedness of environmental, social, and economic dimensions tangible (Bennett & Lemoine, 2014; Hadar et al., 2020; Heller, 2019). This includes understanding interdependencies between various stakeholders and the systemic nature of sustainability challenges. Having a sense of comprehensibility enables individuals to grasp the complexity of sustainability issues, make informed decisions, and act in favor of positive change.

Manageability/designability pertains to the conviction that individuals possess the skills, strategies, and resources to manage the challenges and demands they face with proficiency and effectiveness. It encompasses the sense of control, of self-efficacy, and the belief that one can influence and navigate their surroundings to achieve the desired outcomes (Antonovsky, 1993; Geyer, 1997; Jenny et al., 2017). In the context of sustainable development, manageability is perceiving oneself as capable of contributing to positive change. This involves recognizing one's agency and understanding that individual actions, combined with collective effort, can have a significant impact. It contributes to an individual's confidence, motivation, and effectiveness in facing sustainability challenges. The concept encompasses the capacity to adjust to changing circumstances, embrace sustainable habits and behaviors, and utilize resources and networks to drive sustainability initiatives. By regarding situations as manageable and by enhancing the ability to influence them, individuals can take proactive and innovative steps toward encouraging sustainable practices and contribute to sustainable development.

Meaningfulness is associated with the extent to which a person perceives its experiences, actions, and goals as personally significant, purposeful, and aligned with its values and beliefs (Antonovsky, 1993; Geyer, 1997; Jenny et al., 2017). In terms of sustainable development, meaningfulness plays a fundamental role in facilitating individual commitment and involvement. When people find personal significance in sustainability issues, they are more likely to engage and inspire others to join in sustainable actions. Additionally, this meaningfulness extends to the wider societal and global context, as it involves acknowledging the interconnectedness of environmental, social, and economic systems and comprehending how individual actions can contribute to positive change at various scales. When individuals perceive their contribution to have meaning and connection to a larger purpose, they may become motivated to take part in shaping a sustainable future.

Incorporating activities that encourage positive activity emotions, promote intrinsic motivation, and facilitate the establishment of a perceived sense of coherence could potentially enhance the efficacy of ESD and RME (Dunlop & Rushton, 2022; Martiskainen & Sovacool, 2021; Schneider et al., 2021; van der Linden, 2015). This aligns with the principles of positive psychology (Blickhan & Eid, 2018; Macharis & Kerret, 2019; Seligman, 2012) which empower learners to shape a future worth living, shifting away from feeling helpless toward major global challenges (Dunlop & Rushton, 2022). Educators have the potential to create engaging and transformative learning experiences, inspiring individuals to become active participants in sustainable development efforts.

Playful Learning

We understand learning in the sense of constructivism as an active and constructive yet unpredictable process, where outcomes are contingent on learners' preconceptions, perceptions, and perspectives (Dewey, 1913; Duffy & Jonassen, 1992; Keller, 2017). Constructivist learning settings entail a comprehensive approach that creates an immersive environment for learners to engage actively with real-world challenges aligned with their interests (Keller, 2017; Scheer et al., 2012). Providing an opportunity that is driven by interest and therefore motivating enables learners to confront real-world challenges head-on and thus gain empowerment.

The question is of how learning processes, both generally and specifically in the context of RME, can be adequately initiated and supported to promote the development and enhancement of 21st-century skills/competencies (Brewer, 2018; Dede, 2010; Fadel, 2008; Ohio Department of Education, 2016). By addressing this question, educators can create corresponding learner-centered spaces that promote active engagement, participation, and motivation as well as creativity, critical thinking, collaboration, and problem-solving. Play supports cognitive development and facilitates learning (Plass et al., 2014; Rice, 2009), promotes imagination and creativity as well as spontaneous learning (Rice, 2009). Playful learning refers to an approach that integrates elements of play into the learning process.

While a clear definition of play remains absent (Rice, 2009), certain characteristics are used to describe adult play including its experiential nature and intrinsic rather than extrinsic motivation. Additionally, greater emphasis is placed on the process rather than the outcome, and some level of active engagement is required (Hendriks, 1999; Whitton, 2018, p. 2) in playful learning. "Learning through play requires the process or experience to be fun, which can increase student engagement" (Rice, 2009, p. 96). Therefore, playful learning techniques can become a crucial element in future-oriented learning environments (Axelsson & Kocher, 2022; Kangas, 2010a, 2010b) that aim to create a stimulating and dynamic space, as mentioned earlier, facilitating the growth of competencies necessary to overcome 21st-century challenges. Play can serve as a dynamic method that fosters the construction of knowledge, as well as nurturing creativity and imagination (Rice, 2009). The inclusion of play in educational settings may help generating enjoyment and excitement as well as interest and therefore have a motivational effect and promote engagement (Rice, 2009). While playful learning approaches become increasingly prevalent in tertiary education, it is crucial to consider critical aspects. Notably, there has been criticism regarding the absence of "a coherent definition, evidenced pedagogic rationale or framework of implementation approaches" (Whitton, 2018, n.p.) for playful learning. Another challenge is the reservations about the perceived childishness of playful learning despite its underlying pedagogical principle. However, it is aligned to the needs of 21st-century learners and can positively impact higher education by engaging all learners in active and experiential learning, problem-solving and critical thinking, creativity, and innovation, collaboration, and communication.

One important aspect is that engaging in playful activities can foster the establishment of a secure (learning) environment (Nørgård et al., 2017; Stickdorn et al., 2018), particularly by using techniques such as surprise or humor. In a secure learning environment, mistakes are viewed positively (Harteis et al., 2006; Mayer, 2020; Oser et al., 1999). It is regarded as an important means of education that facilitates learners to completely engage in the (learning) activity, attain an understanding of the learning process, and cultivate innate motivation as a source of learning (Whitton, 2018). Furthermore, in the context of ESD, playful learning can assist in nurturing a positive outlook toward sustainability by providing a safe and inspiring space for students to investigate intricate matters, trial with solutions, and cooperate with their peers. Learners are enabled to approach sustainability challenges with objectivity and gain deeper understanding. Design thinking presents a potential, playful, and solution-oriented approach for addressing real-world challenges.

Design Thinking and the Design Jam

In recent years, the application of the design thinking approach has notably risen in higher education institutions (Beligatamulla et al., 2019; Guaman-Quintanilla et al., 2018; Matthews & Wrigley, 2017; McLaughlin et al., 2022). While there is no clear definition of design thinking (Micheli et al., 2018), which is sometimes referred to as a methodology, mindset, or approach, it can be identified by key characteristics such as creativity, a gestalt perspective, innovativeness, interdisciplinary collaboration to a thorough grasp of the problem context and identification of crucial insights, a concentration on problem-solving, communication abilities, abductive reasoning, tolerance of ambiguity, iteration and experimentation, tolerance of ambiguity and failure, and uniting analysis and intuition (Micheli et al., 2018).

Dosi et al. (2018) offer an insight into the components which create the design thinking mindset, including empathy, comfort with ambiguity and uncertainty, collaboration across multiple disciplines, a focus on the learning process, curiosity, creative confidence, a desire, and optimism for making an impact. Design thinking may promote a comprehensive perspective on issues and their context, employing an iterative and nonlinear approach consisting of alternating phases of problem recognition and solution, as well as conducting research and formulating key insights as a foundation for specific design challenges. These problems require collaborative development of solutions through a creative process resulting in prototypes (Mayr, 2023; Mayr et al., 2023). The prototypes undergo testing and refinement. Design thinking facilitates the exploration and experimentation of multiple iterations to devise the optimal solution (Clune & Lockrey, 2014). Design thinking offers an action-oriented approach that incites participants to promptly prototype and assess ideas to garner feedback and learn from real-world experiences. The approach prioritizes hands-on experimentation and learning by doing (Bowler, 2016), making it more of a "design doing" philosophy than "design thinking" (Kelly, 2016; Micheli et al., 2018; Stickdorn et al., 2018). Originally, design thinking placed the user at the center, developing solutions from their perspective. However, considering the global challenges humanity faces in the 21st century, it is time to shift the focus from user-centeredness to planet-centeredness (Poleac, 2022; Talgorn & Ullerup, 2023; Tironi et al., 2022).

A design jam is a brief and condensed design thinking format (Kagan et al., 2020; Mayr et al., 2023; Randler et al., 2011; Tang et al., 2020). Participants meet to collaboratively tackle design challenges using the principles and techniques of design thinking (Tang et al., 2020). The jam is a dynamic and interactive workshop that adheres to a structured process aligned with the design thinking stages, including empathizing, defining, ideating, prototyping, and testing (Meinel & von Thienen, 2016; Waidelich et al., 2018). However, the compressed individual phases of a design jam foster rapid ideation and prototyping and gaining valuable insights within a short period of time, despite not allowing for a comprehensive exploration or challenging existing concepts (Kagan et al., 2020). Design jams typically have a lively and playful atmosphere (Tang et al., 2020). Participants are urged to adopt a mentality of experimentation, taking risks, and being open-minded.

Design thinking, design jams, and playful learning bear similarities in that they prioritize creativity, innovation, and problem-solving. While there is a lack of a clear definition for each, all three advocate for dynamic and collaborative approaches to address (design) challenges. They urge participants to assume an attitude of experimentation, open-mindedness, and risk-taking, creating an environment that supports the creation of rapid ideas and prototypes. These approaches and formats offer opportunities for individuals to get involved with hands-on problem-solving, acquire valuable insights, and develop skills required for tackling complex real-world issues. Constructivist learning complements the principles of design thinking, design jam, and playful learning by offering a theoretical framework that highlights active engagement, learner agency, collaboration, and knowledge construction (Mayr, 2023; Pande & Bharathi, 2020; Scheer et al., 2012). Like design thinking, this approach inspires learners to embrace experimentation and open-mindedness. It also fosters the growth of problem-solving skills through genuine, real-life challenges (Pretorius et al., 2021; Stickdorn et al., 2018). When paired, these methods can generate profound and purposeful learning opportunities, encouraging learners to take the initiative and become innovative problem-solvers.

In the context of ESD, design thinking offers a methodical framework for students to evaluate sustainability problems, understand the perspectives of stakeholders, generate innovative ideas, and construct models of sustainable solutions. It cultivates critical thinking, a systems thinking approach, and the amalgamation of diverse perspectives. By utilizing design thinking principles, students can acquire a deep understanding of sustainability issues and cultivate a mindset of problem-solving that steers toward taking action (Andrews, 2015; Brown, 2016; Buhl et al., 2019).

The Global Goals Design Jam

The Global Goals Design Jam (Mayr et al., 2023) builds upon the shared principles of design thinking, design jams, playful learning, and constructivist learning offering participants a space to engage in collaborative problem-solving and opportunities to contribute to the achievement of the SDGs also known as the Global Goals. The aim of the Global Goals Design Jam is to facilitate learners in becoming active, co-creative problem-solvers equipped with the necessary skills to tackle the pressing challenges of our world in a meaningful and impactful way. As shown in Fig. 8.1, they follow a design thinking process, by moving from problem to solution space.

Preparations for the Global Goals Design Jam begin before the actual event. Participants receive the task of immersing themselves in the subject matter by engaging in conversations with individuals about the significant challenges of our era, potential advancements, opportunities, and associated risks. Moreover, they investigate why some transformations achieve success whereas others face obstacles. The event itself commences with a relaxed beginning, providing attendees with an opportunity to unwind upon arrival with refreshments, maybe a small snack, and ambient music as part of a concept to establish a secure environment.

After a formal welcome and provision of necessary organizational information, the research phase commences with a keynote speech which explores grand global challenges and potential solutions set forth in the 2030 Agenda and the SDGs. This lays the foundation for an interactive icebreaker activity aimed at fostering team spirit among participants. Using sociometric data such as shoe size or birth month, individuals order themselves sequentially. Culminating with a light-hearted inquiry about preferred foods, this exercise prompts participants with similar tastes to converge into groups. These groups then embark on a collaborative discussion, centered around the preassigned task.

After collecting brief inputs from the individual groups, they attend a World Café. In this phase, participants engage in discussions with experts regarding various SDGs and, in the context of RMERC 2022, also about the IDGs, which are inner development goals (IDG project initiators, 2021). Throughout the World Café phase, students attend 3–4 stations to obtain additional insights that stimulate them to draft their personal design challenge. This falls under today's overarching challenge: "How can we make the living environment of our

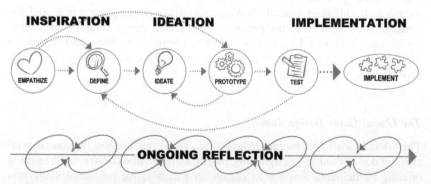

Fig. 8.1.   Design Thinking Process. *Source:* Helga Mayr; illustrated by Gerd Pircher.

university/company the most innovative and sustainable in the world?" Using the game-like technique "Benny Hill Sorting" aca "Thirty-five" (Stickdorn et al., 2018), individual design challenges are evaluated in pairs over several rounds. The participants then select the design challenge they want to work on as a team. After locating each other, the teams are provided with an additional chance to artic-ulate the team design challenge, which then serves as the foundation for the ensuing process of generating ideas.

Prior to the ideation phase, participants are instructed to engage in a playful exercise known as "Yes, but – Yes, and." This approach enables them to appreciate the significance of adopting an open mindset ("Yes, and") when generating ideas and a closed mindset ("Yes, but") when selecting or making decisions (Stickdorn et al., 2018). During the ideation phase, the participants are encouraged to generate as many ideas as possible. In the following concept development phase, an initial selection is made. Before conceptualization, but at the very latest, before prototyping, another playful technique known as "draw your counterpart" (Stickdorn et al., 2018) can be utilized. This entails drawing a counterpart without diverting one's gaze from her/his face. The resultant drawings often evoke laughter, demonstrating that everyone has visualization ability, and that the "shitty first draft" stands for the quality required. Concepts and pro-totypes do not need to be perfect, but they should be presented in a way that allows people to envision how the solution(s) will work.

The concept sketches undergo testing, and subsequent feedback is integrated into the next step of solution development – prototyping. Following a brief introduction, teams utilize materials such as LEGO, modeling clay, and similar resources to construct prototypes. These physical materials enable teams to translate their ideas into tangible representations, allowing for a more interactive and hands-on exploration of design possibilities. The application of materials provides a versatile and adaptable basis for prototyping – promoting experi-mentation, iteration, and the visualization of potential solutions. The prototypes also facilitate communication on the design challenge and the corresponding solution(s). The subsequent testing of the prototype, with ideally the target group and experts, constitutes the ensuing stage. During the RMERC's Global Goals Design Jam, experts provided critical yet constructive feedback to the teams to aid them in enhancing their solutions. Following a revision based on the feedback, the prototypes were presented to a wide audience during the RMERC's official opening event.

Methods

Participants and Data Collection

Data were collected through an online questionnaire on www.soscisurvey.de in 2023, 8 months after the Global Goals Design Jam at the RMERC had taken place. The survey was sent to all 11 participants, of whom four students (36.36%)

completed the survey and provided signed consent. Furthermore, one of the students agreed to participate in an in-depth interview. To obtain expert insights, we approached 52 people who had previously hosted an SDG station in the World Café and provided feedback on prototypes as test subjects were approached. These experienced experts were invited to complete a semi-structured questionnaire. Of those approached, 19 (36.54%) completed the questionnaire.

Instruments

A semi-standardized questionnaire consisting of quantitative and qualitative components was utilized in this study. To measure the perceived sense of coherence (Antonovsky, 1993) and activity emotions during the Global Goals Design Jam, reliable and validated short scales were employed, which have been previously developed, tested, and used in other studies. Open-ended questions were fashioned to generate qualitative data in accordance with the research questions. The survey was evaluated solely for its comprehensibility by one student and one expert. As it was conducted as a preliminary study, its assessment within the scope of this work is regarded as a pretest.

The study analyzed the sense of coherence of both participants and the experts using the Leipziger Kurzform Skala SOC-L9 (Bauer et al., 2015), a robust self-assessment tool consisting of only nine items. The semantic differential of this scale enables associative assessment through a (seven-point) bipolar scale marked by opposite adjectives (Schäfer, 1983; Schulten, 2017). Three pairs of adjectives represent each of the three dimensions of the sense of coherence: (1) meaningfulness (meaningless – meaningful, insignificant – significant, and not worthwhile – worthwhile), (2) manageability (unmanageable – manageable, uninfluenceable – influenceable, and uncontrollable – controllable), and (3) comprehensibility (unclear – clear, chaotic – structured, and unpredictable – predictable).

In relation to activity emotions, including joy, anger, and boredom, and motivational outcomes such as situational interest and situational competence, we utilized the measurement approach detailed by Itzek-Greulich and Vollmer (2017). To evaluate activity emotions, we employed the 5-level learning-related emotion scale developed by Pekrun et al. (2011). This scale encompasses the three activity emotions: anger (measured through three items, e.g. "I was stressed out"), joy (e.g. "I was happy"), and boredom (e.g. "I was so bored that I almost fell asleep"). To determine the motivational outcomes, we used a three-item scale devised by Willems (2011) to assess situational competence beliefs (e.g. "I was able to solve the different tasks") and situational interest, employing four items (e.g. "It was interesting"). The participants conducted this evaluation through self-assessment.

In addition to the scales, we asked open-ended questions to the participants and experts regarding the potentials and limitations of the format. Furthermore, an introductory question aimed at capturing personal associations, impressions, and memories was included in the questionnaire to determine respondents' and experts' recollections of the Global Goals Design Jam concept. Moreover, participants were asked about their learning process and to what extent they believe that what they have learned is useful.

Data Analysis Strategy

Quantitative data analysis was conducted using Statistical Package for the Social Sciences (SPSS) 28. Due to the low response rate, we could only calculate descriptive statistics (means [*M*] and standard deviation [SD]) for the Leipziger Kurzform Skala SOC-L9, used to evaluate the perceived sense of coherence, as well as for the learning-related emotional scale and scale for measuring the motivational outcomes during the Global Goals Design Jam and its related activities. We compared the answers of both participants and experts to those of the Leipziger Kurzform Skala SOC-L9. As adjectives determining the polarities alternated in meaning to prevent respondents from displaying a tendency to side (Table 8.1), the correlation was executed, and the assessment was modified based on the findings.

The analysis of qualitative data was conducted using MAXQDA Analytics Pro 2022 software and followed the qualitative content analysis approach suggested by Kuckartz (2014). The survey responses were compared to the in-depth interview responses.

Research Findings

Qualitative Analysis

In the survey, the open-ended queries illustrated in Table 8.1 were provided to the enrolled pupils. Because of the limited size of the sample, all responses are provided (Table 8.2).

The sole student who took part in the detailed interview found the event to be well-structured concerning both its content and the workshop's organization. She remembered positive emotions, mainly enjoyment and interest, throughout the workshop. Despite initially feeling nervous due to uncertainty about the proceedings and being unfamiliar with other participants, she soon felt comfortable. The student highlighted the playful approach and recollected specific techniques used. Overall, the participant thoroughly enjoyed the event and expressed a keen interest in participating again. Moving forward, she suggested exploring alternative areas of focus for individuals already acquainted with the SDGs.

Inductive categorization was used to group responses to the open-ended question according to common themes and recurring answers.

Table 8.1. Correlation of Sense of Coherence (SoC) – Attributes.

Correlations of SoC – Attributes	1	2	3	4	5	6	7	8	9
1 Manageable/not manageable	–								
2 Meaningless/meaningful	-0.528	–							
3 Structured/chaotic	0.535	-0.394	–						
4 Influenceable/uninfluenceable	0.110	0.062	0.333	–					
5 Insignificant/significant	0.026	0.259	0.104	-0.045	–				
6 Unclear/clear	-0.063	0.104	0.015	-0.329	0.272	–			
7 Controllable/noncontrollable	0.237	-0.090	0.319	0.224	-0.124	-0.505	–		
8 Not worthwhile/worthwhile	-0.452	0.457	-0.175	-0.321	0.536	0.172	-0.362	–	
9 Predictable/unpredictable	-0.081	0.112	0.366	0.448	-0.117	-0.202	0.534	-0.109	–

Table 8.2. Questions and Answers of Participants.

Question	Exemplary Answers
When recalling the Global Goals Design Jam, what stands out today?	"Our surprise at not using PowerPoint, but Lego for our presentation" (S1) and "the ability to generate numerous brilliant ideas in a short time," (S1 + S3) "Challenging and creative" (S2) "The event was very inspiring, new ideas, new people, energetic spirit & fun:" (S3) "It was designed in a playful and interactive manner, which I greatly appreciated. Essentially, it focused on familiarising oneself with the SDGs in an enjoyable way, and I thoroughly enjoyed the design brainstorming session in the afternoon, which generated many creative ideas." (S4)
Describe what you learned and what you attribute it to.	"I was familiar with Design Thinking from an university project week. However, the idea that it could be completed within a day was new to me. Additionally, I had previously studied the SDGs extensively, thus it was pleasant to observe their practical translation on a smaller scale." (S1) "How to come up with ideas that aren't perfect, but good enough, in the limited amount of time available." (S2) "Design thinking process, quickly coming up with topics, ideas. Quickly sorting out and moving on with the ideas which make sense and want to be developed further by all participants. Super intense, super exciting, will do again!" (S3) "I already knew the SDGs, but I was able to explore them in more depth that day. The group discussions helped to find my way around it, there was a playful exchange and brainstorming, which I liked very much." (S4)
How was or is what you learned useful to you (today/future)?	"Design thinking for idea generation and elaboration, along with practical implementation guidelines provided by the

(Continued)

Table 8.2. *(Continued)*

Question	Exemplary Answers
	SDGs, are two essential factors to consider." (S1) "Absolutely." (S2) "I haven't used the Design Thinking approach again, but I think the presenters were 1A prepared and led through the process in a structured way. I found it exciting to work on a topic within a few hours, work out and then present, super platform, I think great!" (S3) "I was able to retain some concepts that reappeared in my subsequent studies, particularly those related to the SDGs and their significance." (S4)
What do you think are the potentials of the format (Global Goals Design Jam)? Where do you see limitations? Why do you see it this way?	"I found the student exchange to be highly valuable. However, I was disappointed that most participants were from the SBD program, as we approach situations similarly and share a common understanding of values. While we all have varying technical/commercial backgrounds, it is still advisable to incorporate alternative perspectives." (S1) "Would be cool if the projects could be followed up. I find it a bit frustrating that after hours of brainstorming, the idea comes to nothing. Would be interesting to find sponsors for the ideas." (S3) "I could imagine that now that I have dealt with the SDGs in depth during my studies, I might not be able to learn as much as I used to. But on the other hand, I found the afternoon brainstorming on new ideas very exciting, and I can imagine that this would be just as enriching if I were to participate again." (S4)

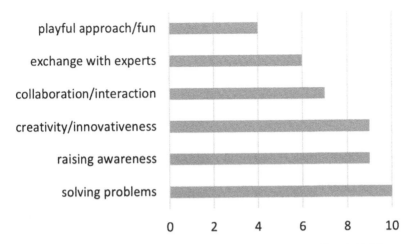

Fig. 8.2.   What Makes the Global Goals Design Jam Special? Most Frequent Answers of Experts.

Question 1: From your point of view, what makes the Jam special?

As demonstrated in Fig. 8.2, the most cited aspects were problem-solving (10 out of 19 participants), raising awareness of the topic (9/19) and creativity and innovation (9/19), followed by collaboration and interaction (7/19). Additionally, exchange with experts (6/19) and a playful approach and enjoyment (4/19) were mentioned.

The following quotes support the presentation of the aggregate data:

"For me, the Global Goals Design Jam is a dynamic tool that is fun to work with" and "leaves room for new and unconventional solutions to problems." (E1),

"A Global Goals Design Jam thrives on an interactive, dynamic setting that offers space for creativity, trial and error, etc., in which people work together on concrete project/implementation proposals. I also find it exciting that different groups of people/ages with correspondingly different (life) experiences come together." (E2),

"Co-creation, creative and innovative collaboration." (E4) and "Exciting, creative approach to solving a problem." (E10)

Question 2: What Potentials Do You See in the Global Goals Design Jam?

As displayed in Fig. 8.3, responses to the inquiry regarding the potential of the Global Goals Design Jam were relatively consistent. The highest number of responses fell under the category of "mastering challenges, developing solutions" (9/19), followed by "fostering interest and motivation" (6/19), collaboration (5/19),

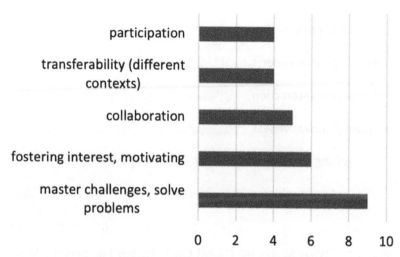

Fig. 8.3.   Potentials Experts See in the Global Goals Design Jam.

and the possibility of transferring the format to different contexts (4/19) – tied with the possibility of participation (4/19).

Again, the following citations supports the presentation of the most frequently mentioned potentials:

"The Global Goals Design Jam provides space for new and sometimes unconventional ideas and problem-solving approaches and is a great format to engage youth in achieving the SDGs." (E1)

"The greatest potential is probably that the pupils/students realize that it is possible to meet great challenges in small teams and with different ideas. Experiencing self-efficacy is important for confidence and motivation to grow gradually." (E2)

"Children and young people can see themselves as actors in sustainable development; the starting point for this are visible points of criticism, problems with the status quo in their immediate living environment." (E5)

"Strengthening of key competencies for sustainable development: problem solving competence, critical thinking, strategic planning competence, system competence – regarding some of these competencies the format could be further developed, e.g., phases of critical systemic examination of one's own solution idea (ecological, economic, social aspects; etc.)." (E8)

"Creative thinking and teamwork can be stimulated. The beauty of this is that there is no MUST. The participants don't have to work but can approach the jam creatively and with new tools." (E18)

Question 3: What Are the Limitations You See in the Global Goals Design Jam?

Regarding limitations, the desire for subsequent implementation of the ideas was the most frequently mentioned issue (11/19), which is associated with doubts about their sustainable impact (5/19) and the risk that challenges are superficial (3/19) if they are not executed properly. This is in line with the results of a recently published study (Mayr & Vollmer, 2024) which indicate that a 1-day event does not produce any discernible effects on attributes such as self-efficacy, intentions to act, or actions. Therefore, maintaining the commitment, e.g. by implementing projects appears crucial.

The following statements from experts are intended to illustrate this:

"Good project ideas emerge – but cannot be implemented further (for whatever reason)." (E2)

"Implementability of solutions difficult, results should be even more integrated into political decision-making processes. Organize Global Goals Design Jam also with the participation of decision makers. Promote pilot projects that can be implemented and tested." (E4)

"There is a need to pursue these issues further. Otherwise, the Global Goals Design Jam is ONLY an interesting event that gives you an idea of how it could work." (E5)

"Relatively short time span restricts in-depth examination of topics, only a teaser is possible at a time. More time is needed for in-depth study (possibly further treatment in class), and the interest of the students." (E12)

"If it takes place once, the effect will fizzle out. It would have to be possible to translate the results into everyday life." (E18)

During the experts' assessment, new questions emerged, as the following quotations illustrate:

"Sometimes the project ideas were very creative etc. and when testing/giving feedback it was sometimes not easy to assess: does this make sense (i.e., in the sense of contributing to Sustainable Development through this? How does it fit into the current local situation (what is there already)? etc.? You must be able to get involved in this creative and open thinking. You are always challenged to reflect a little by yourself: What does sustainability actually mean in the specific context against the background of the developed ideas (maybe this is also a potential?)." and "How much does a jam allow you to think outside of the box, to really come up with ideas that are "innovative" in terms of the SDGs?" (E2)

"Accessibility – which young people will benefit (social boundaries?) Again, aren't we working precisely with those who are already sensitive, interested, and motivated?" (E6)

Quantitative Analysis

Activity Emotions and Motivational Outcomes

Table 8.3 display the means (*M*) and standard deviations (SDs) of the activity emotions anger, boredom, and joy, as well as the situational outcomes, situational interest, and situational competence.

Results from the survey indicate that taking part in the Global Goals Design Jam correlates with increased positive emotions and enhanced motivation, as demonstrated on a scale ranging from 1 to 5.

Sense of Coherence

The responses to the sense of coherence queries demonstrate a positive tendency.

Fig. 8.4 illustrates that self-assessment and external evaluation produced comparable outcomes. Additionally, the lowest score was recorded for comprehensibility, which could be attributed to the unforeseen course of events.

Table 8.3. Means (*M*) and Standard Deviation (SD) of Activity Emotions and Motivational Outcomes.

Category	Item	M	SD
Anger	I was stressed out. I got angry. I was frustrated and annoyed.	1.17	0.33
Boredom	I was bored. I was so bored that I almost fell asleep. I was so bored that I stopped following.	1.00	0.00
Joy	I was happy. I had fun. I had so much fun, I was eager to participate.	4.42	0.57
Situational interest	I liked the topic(s). I want to know more about the topic(s). It was interesting. The lesson was exciting.	4.25	0.87
Situational competence	I followed easily. I was up to par with the demands. I was able to solve the different tasks.	4.75	0.50

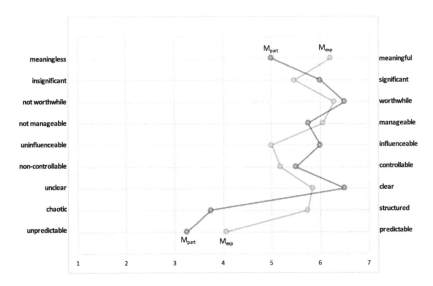

Fig. 8.4. Self-Assessment and Peer Assessment in Relation to the Perceived Sense of Coherence.

Table 8.4. Sense of Coherence – Aggregated Data (Category, Items, Means, and Standard Deviation).

Category	Item	M_{part}	M_{exp}	SD_{part}	SD_{exp}
Meaningfulness	Meaningless – meaningful Insignificant – significant Not worthwhile – worthwhile	5.83	5.98	1.04	0.81
Manageability	Nonmanageable – manageable Uninfluenceable – influenceable Noncontrollable – controllable	6.17	5.68	1.11	0.82
Comprehensibility	Unclear – clear Chaotic – structured unpredictable – predictable	4.50	5.29	1.04	1.07

The items were also aggregated in this section. Table 8.4 displays the category, associated items, mean values (M) for participants (M_{part}) and experts (M_{exp}), and respective standard deviations (SD: SD_{part} and SD_{exp}).

Discussion

The aim of this study is to explore the overall perceptions of both participants and experts in relation to the Global Goals Design Jam. The research delved into participants' perceptions of the event, specifically regarding sense of coherence, emotional engagement during related activities, and the resulting motivational outcomes. Additionally, this study aims to investigate the level of concurrence among self-evaluation and peer evaluation of the sense of coherence, along with the views of participants and experts on the potentials and constraints of the Global Goals Design Jam.

P1, regarding the perception of the Global Goals Design Jam by both participants and experts, can neither be confirmed nor refuted. This is primarily due to the small sample size and the research design which involved only one open-ended question within a questionnaire. Some responses suggest similar themes, such as the generation of innovative solutions or an approach with a playful tone.

Participants who were actively involved in the Global Goals Design Jam reported a significant sense of coherence. The dimensions manageability and meaningfulness scored higher than that of comprehensibility, which may be attributed to the unfamiliar procedure. There was a high degree of agreement between self-assessment and external assessment regarding the sense of coherence. Consequently, *P2* is confirmed, albeit with some reservations.

By *P3*, we assumed that students gained insights in creative problem-solving, interdisciplinary collaboration, and a deeper understanding of the SDGs. These insights were found to be highly valuable for their personal growth and professional development, indicating a positive correlation between their participation in the Global Goals Design Jam and skill enhancement. This proposition cannot be adequately answered due to the lack of data, although responses indicate a potential trend in this regard.

Finally, *P4* assumed that participants and experts in the Global Goals Design Jam format recognized the potential to encourage innovative thinking, problem-solving, and collaborative work, along with limitations like time constraints and the need to be able to work on selected complex problems over a longer period of time. Moreover, P4 assumed that participants and experts propose several improvements to the format, such as possibly extending the duration of the event, offering more structured guidance, and enhancing the incorporation of practical implementation strategies. The data available provide considerable support for *P4*, as the format was noted for its potential to facilitate problem-solving and innovation. Nonetheless, limitations to its employment were reported, particularly with regards to the necessity for prolonged engagement that allows for in-depth study, an aspect that is highly relevant given the complexity of the sustainability problems.

Little was suggested in terms of improvements. E8 and E14 mentioned the need for "more time," while E9 suggested professionalization of the involved experts and suggested that the experts should be more involved. Further suggestions can be inferred from comments on potential limitations.

Since this chapter is guided by the overall research objective of assessing the suitability of interactive ESD/RME formats that adhere to a design thinking approach, the outcomes support the more precise classification of potentials and limitations, ultimately facilitating the format's development in a way that is tailored to the desired target audience.

Limitations

However, this study has limitations. The reliability and value of the results are restricted due to the use of solely an online questionnaire and one in-depth interview, a small sample size, absence of a control group, and the voluntary participation of students in the Global Goals Design Jam out of personal interest. According to a recently published study (Mayr & Vollmer, 2024), participating in a 1-day Global Goals Design Jam neither significantly influences self-efficacy feelings nor action intentions or actions. Nonetheless, the Global Goals Design Jam has been favorably rated by college students and teachers alike as an intrinsic motivational learning opportunity that ignites situational interest (Mayr & Vollmer, 2024). The unsurprising results/findings indicate that while the Global Goals Design Jam may serve as a motivational starting point, it falls short of the demands for a comprehensive understanding of the complexities of sustainable development issues. Therefore, a more profound design thinking approach is required, perhaps by permitting a thorough exploration within the project's framework. Even if this evaluation may only be classified as a preliminary study, it provides crucial initial findings and valuable indications for further research.

Conclusion

There is a research gap regarding emotions and the sense of coherence in design thinking based educational formats in the context of SD. The current preliminary study reveals promising indications that require further investigation through comprehensive studies. A potential area for further research questions could explore the impact of the sense of coherence and of emotions on resilience (Rifkin, 2022), empowerment, and preparedness of individuals to address major global issues and support global restoration. One potential research direction involves salutogenic viewpoints/perspectives to design restorative environments (Axelsson & Kocher, 2022; Geyer, 1997; Jenny et al., 2017; Kangas, 2010a, 2010b).

Moreover, as stated previously, it is necessary to have alternate conference and teaching methods that allow for transdisciplinary, cooperative, and collaborative problem-solving. One student expressed that a blend between interactive and innovative formats is ideal, thus indicating that they should be given equal importance to traditional lectures or workshops at conferences. With this in mind, events like the Global Goals Design Jam can be viewed as a beneficial supplement to conferences.

While the Global Goals Design Jam presents a promising learning opportunity to engage students, a more comprehensive approach is necessary to effectively address sustainability issues. By integrating play-based learning and design thinking within the framework of ESD/RME, a dynamic and emotive learning experience can be fostered, inspiring dedication towards sustainability and the promotion of positive change.

9. Acknowledgments

We extend our gratitude to all attendees of the Global Goals Design Jams and the survey including college students and experts. We would also like to express our appreciation to the Vice Rectorate for Research of the University of Innsbruck and the Sinnbildungsstiftung (funding program Bildünger) for their generous funding of our project.

References

Abdelgaffar, H. A. (2021). A review of responsible management education: Practices, outcomes, and challenges. *The Journal of Management Development, 40*(9/10), 613–638. https://doi.org/10.1108/JMD-03-2020-0087

Ahel, O., & Lingenau, K. (2021). Digitale Ansätze zur Vermittlung der SDGS in der Hochschullehre im deutschsprachigen Raum. In W. Leal Filho (Ed.), *Digitalisierung und Nachhaltigkeit*. Springer Nature.

Anderson, T., & Shattuck, J. (2012). Design-based research: A decade of progress in education research? *Educational Researcher, 41*(1), 16–25. https://doi.org/10.3102/0013189X11428813

Andrews, D. (2015). The circular economy, design thinking and education for sustainability. *Local Economy, 30*(3), 305–315.

Antonovsky, A. (1993). The structure and properties of the SoC scale. *Social Science & Medicine, 36*(6), 725–733. https://doi.org/10.1016/0277-9536(93)90033-Z

Arnold, R., & Pachner, A. (2011). Konstruktivistische Lernkulturen für eine kompetenzorientierte Ausbildung künftiger Generationen. In T. Eckert, A. Von Hippel, M. Pietraß, & B. Schmidt-Hertha (Hrsg.), *Bildung der Generationen* (pp. 299–307). VS Verlag für Sozialwissenschaften. https://doi.org/10.1007/978-3-531-92837-1_24

Axelsson, C., & Kocher, M. (2022). Playful times—Exploring world … PHEW! In A. M. Loffredo, R. Wenrich, C. Axelsson, & W. Kröger (Hrsg.), *Changing time—Shaping world: Changemakers in arts & education* (Vol. 16, 1, pp. 129–138). Transcript Verlag. https://doi.org/10.14361/9783839461358

Barab, S., & Squire, K. (2004). Design-based research: Putting a stake in the ground. *The Journal of the Learning Sciences, 13*(1), 1–14. https://doi.org/10.1207/s15327809jls1301_1

Barth, M. (2011). Den konstruktiven Umgang mit den Herausforderungen unserer Zeit erlernen: Bildung für nachhaltige Entwicklung als erziehungswissenschaftliche Aufgabe. *SWS Rundschau*, 275–291.

Bauer, G. F., Vogt, K., Inauen, A., & Jenny, G. J. (2015). Work-SoC–Entwicklung und Validierung einer Skala zur Erfassung des arbeitsbezogenen Kohärenzgefühls. *Zeitschrift für Gesundheitspsychologie, 23*(1), 20–30. https://doi.org/10.1026/0943-8149/a000132

Beligatamulla, G., Rieger, J., Franz, J., & Strickfaden, M. (2019). Making pedagogic sense of design thinking in the higher education context. *Open Education Studies*, *1*(1), 91–105. https://doi.org/10.1515/edu-2019-0006

Bennett, N., & Lemoine, G. J. (2014). What a difference a word makes: Understanding threats to performance in a VUCA world. *Business Horizons*, *57*(3), 311–317. https://doi.org/10.1016/j.bushor.2014.01.001

Blickhan, D., & Eid, M. (2018). *Positive Psychologie – Ein Handbuch für die Praxis*. Junfermann Verlag.

Bowler, L. (2016). Experiences and design thinking in the education of librarians. *Creativity and Innovation*, *42*(5), 58–61.

Brand, U. (2009). Die Multiple Krise. In *Dynamik und Zusammenhang der Krisendimension, Anforderungen an politische Institutionen und Chancen progressiver Politik*. Heinrich-Böll-Stiftung.

Brand, U. (2016). "Transformation" as a new critical orthodoxy: The strategic use of the term "transformation" does not prevent multiple crises. *GAIA – Ecological Perspectives for Science and Society*, *25*(1), 23–27. https://doi.org/10.14512/gaia.25. 1.7

Brewer, A. M. (2018). *Encountering, experiencing and shaping careers: Thinking about careers in the 21st century*. Springer International Publishing. https://doi.org/10. 1007/978-3-319-96956-5

Brown, T. (2016). *Change by Design. Wie Design Thinking Organisationen verändert und zu mehr Innovationen führt*. München.

Buhl, A., Schmidt-Keilich, M., Muster, V., Blazejewski, S., Schrader, U., Harrach, C., Schäfer, M., & Süßbauer, E. (2019). Design thinking for sustainability: Why and how design thinking can foster sustainability-oriented innovation development. *Journal of Cleaner Production*, *231*, 1248–1257. https://doi.org/10.1016/j.jclepro. 2019.05. 259

Clune, S. J., & Lockrey, S. (2014). Developing environmental sustainability strategies, the Double Diamond method of LCA and design thinking: A case study from aged care. *Journal of Cleaner Production*, *85*, 67–82. https://doi.org/10.1016/j.jclepro. 2014.02.003

Cornuel, E., & Hommel, U. (2015). Moving beyond the rhetoric of responsible management education. *The Journal of Management Development*, *34*(1), 2–15. https://doi.org/10.1108/JMD-06-2014-0059

de Haan, G. (2008). Gestaltungskompetenz als Kompetenzkonzept der Bildung für nachhaltige Entwicklung. In I. Bormann & G. de Haan (Eds.), *Kompetenzen der Bildung für nachhaltige Entwicklung. Operationalisierung, Messung, Rahmenbedingungen, Befunde* (pp. 23–44). Verlag für Sozialwissenschaften.

Dede, C. (2010). Comparing frameworks for 21st century skills. In J. A. Bellanca & R. S. Brandt (Hrsg.), *21st century skills: Rethinking how students learn* (pp. 51–76). Solution Tree Press.

Dewey, J. (1913). *Interest and effort in education*. Houghton Mifflin Company.

Dosi, C., Rosati, F., & Vignoli, M. (2018). Measuring design thinking mindset. In *DS92: Proceedings of the DESIGN 2018 15th International Design Conference* (pp. 1991–2002). https://doi.org/10.21278/idc.2018.0493

Dubs, R. (1995). Konstruktivismus: Einige Überlegungen aus der Sicht der Unterrichtsgestaltung. *Zeitschrift für Padagogik*, *41*(6), 889–903. https://doi.org/10. 25656/01:10535

Duffy, T. M., & Jonassen, D. H. (1992). Constructivism: New implications for instructional technology. In T. M. Duffy & D. H. Jonassen (Eds.), *Constructivism and the technology of instruction. A conversation* (pp. 1–16). Routledge.

Dunlop, L., & Rushton, E. A. C. (2022). Education for environmental sustainability and the emotions: Implications for educational practice. *Sustainability*, *14*(8), 4441. https://doi.org/10.3390/su14084441

Eriksson, M. (2017). The SoC in the salutogenic model of health. In M. B. Mittelmark, S. Sagy, M. Eriksson, G. F. Bauer, J. M. Pelikan, B. Lindström, & G. A. Espnes (Eds.), *The handbook of salutogenesis*. Springer International Publishing. https://doi.org/10.1007/978-3-319-04600-6

Fadel, C. (2008). 21st century skills: How can you prepare students for the new Global Economy? In *Partnerships for 21st century skills*. https://www.oecd.org/site/educeri21st/40756908.pdf

Geyer, S. (1997). Some conceptual considerations on the SoC. *Social Science & Medicine*, *44*(12), 1771–1779. https://doi.org/10.1016/S0277-9536(96)00286-9

Glaeser, W. (2022). *VUCA, BANI, RUPT or TUNA*. VUCA-World. https://www.vuca-world.org/vuca-bani-rupt-tuna/

Guaman-Quintanilla, S., Chiluiza, K., Everaert, P., & Valcke, M. (2018). Design thinking in higher education: A scoping review. In *ICERI2018 Proceedings* (pp. 2954–2963). https://doi.org/10.21125/iceri.2018.1663

Hadar, L. L., Ergas, O., Alpert, B., & Ariav, T. (2020). Rethinking teacher education in a VUCA world: Student teachers' social-emotional competencies during the Covid-19 crisis. *European Journal of Teacher Education*, *43*(4), 573–586. https://doi.org/10.1080/02619768.2020.1807513

Haertle, J., Parkes, C., Murray, A., & Hayes, R. (2017). PRME: Building a global movement on responsible management education. *International Journal of Management in Education*, *15*(2), 66–72. https://doi.org/10.1016/j.ijme.2017.05.002

Hamann, K., Baumann, A., & Löschinger, D. (2016). *Psychologie im Umweltschutz, Handbuch zur Förderung nachhaltigen Handelns*. Oekom Verlag. https://doi.org/10.14512/9783960061182

Harteis, C., Bauer, J., & Heid, H. (2006). Der Umgang mit Fehlern als Merkmal betrieblicher Fehlerkultur und Voraussetzung für Professional Learning. *Swiss Journal of Educational Research*, *28*(1), 111–130. https://doi.org/10.24452/sjer.28.1.4721

Heckhausen, J., & Heckhausen, H. (Eds.). (2018). *Motivation und Handeln*. Springer. https://doi.org/10.1007/978-3-662-53927-9

Heinrichs, H., & Michelsen, G. (Eds.). (2014). *Nachhaltigkeitswissenschaften*. Springer. https://doi.org/10.1007/978-3-642-25112-2

Heller, J. (Ed.). (2019). *Resilienz für die VUCA-Welt: Individuelle und organisationale Resilienz entwickeln*. Springer Fachmedien Wiesbaden. https://doi.org/10.1007/978-3-658-21044-1

Hendriks, P. (1999). Why share knowledge? The influence of ICT on the motivation for knowledge sharing. *Knowledge and Process Management*, *6*(2), 91–100. https://doi.org/10.1002/(SICI)1099-1441(199906)6:2<91::AID-KPM54>3.0.CO;2-M

Hunecke, M. (2022). *Psychologie der Nachhaltigkeit*. Oekom Verlag.

IDG project initiators. (2021). *Inner development goals: Background, method and IDG framework*. https://innerdevelopmentgoals.org/framework/

International Commission on the Futures of Education. (2021). *Reimagining our futures together: A new social contract for education.* UNESCO. https://doi.org/10. 54675/ASRB4722

Itzek-Greulich, H., & Vollmer, C. (2017). Emotional and motivational outcomes of lab work in the secondary intermediate track: The contribution of a science center outreach lab: Effects of lab work on student emotions. *Journal of Research in Science Teaching, 54*(1), 3–28. https://doi.org/10.1002/tea.21334

Jenny, G. J., Bauer, G. F., Forbech Vinje, H., Vogt, K., & Torp, S. (2017). The application of salutogenesis to work. In M. B. Mittelmark, S. Sagy, M. Eriksson, G. F. Bauer, J. M. Pelikan, B. Lindström, & G. A. Espnes (Eds.), *The handbook of salutogenesis* (pp. 195–210). Springer International Publishing. https://doi.org/10. 1007/978-3-319-04600-6

Kagan, S., Hauerwaas, A., Helldorff, S., & Weisenfeld, U. (2020). Jamming sustainable futures: Assessing the potential of design thinking with the case study of a sustainability jam. *Journal of Cleaner Production, 251*, 119595. https://doi.org/10. 1016/j.jclepro.2019.119595

Kangas, M. (2010a). Creative and playful learning: Learning through game co-creation and games in a playful learning environment. *Thinking Skills and Creativity, 5*(1), 1–15. https://doi.org/10.1016/j.tsc.2009.11.001

Kangas, M. (2010b). *The school of the future: Theoretical and pedagogical approaches for creative and playful learning environments.* University of Lapland.

Keller, L. (2017). »Sustainable development? – Let us change concepts!" theoretical and practical contributions to the transformation of society. In *Science, knowledge, and education from a geographer's perspective [Habilitation].* University of Innsbruck.

Kelly, R. (2016). *Creative development. Transforming education through design thinking, innovation, and invention.* Brush Education Inc.

Kohl, K., Hopkins, C., Barth, M., Michelsen, G., Dlouhá, J., Razak, D. A., Abidin Bin Sanusi, Z., & Toman, I. (2022). A whole-institution approach towards sustainability: A crucial aspect of higher education's individual and collective engagement with the SDGs and beyond. *International Journal of Sustainability in Higher Education, 23*(2), 218–236. https://doi.org/10.1108/IJSHE-10-2020-0398

Kolb, M., Fröhlich, L., & Schmidpeter, R. (2017). Implementing sustainability as the new normal: Responsible management education – From a private business school's perspective. *International Journal of Management in Education, 15*(2), 280–292. https://doi.org/10.1016/j.ijme.2017.03.009

Kuckartz, U. (2014). *Mixed methods: Methodologie, Forschungsdesign und Analyseverfahren.* Springer Verlag.

Leal Filho, W., Azeiteiro, U. M., Alves, F., & Molthan-Hill, P. (Hrsg.). (2017). *Handbook of theory and practice of sustainable development in higher education* (Vol. 4). Springer International Publishing. https://doi.org/10.1007/978-3-319-47877-7

Macharis, C., & Kerret, D. (2019). The 5E model of environmental engagement: Bringing sustainability change to higher education through positive psychology. *Sustainability, 11*(1), 241. https://doi.org/10.3390/su11010241

Martiskainen, M., & Sovacool, B. K. (2021). Mixed feelings: A review and research agenda for emotions in sustainability transitions. *Environmental Innovation and Societal Transitions, 40*, 609–624. https://doi.org/10.1016/j.eist.2021.10.023

Matthews, J., & Wrigley, C. (2017). Design and design thinking in business and management higher education. *Journal of Learning Design, 10*(1), 41–54. https://doi.org/10.5204/jld.v9i3.294

Mayer, C.-H. (2020). Positive Fehlerkultur als Ressource. *Schmerzmedizin, 36*(4), 62–67. https://doi.org/10.1007/s00940-020-1739-4

Mayr, H. (2023). Promoting education for sustainable development using blended learning and digital tools: Two university courses, one case study. In L. Keller, G. Michelsen, M. Dür, S. Bachri, & M. Zint (Eds.), *Digialization, new media, and education for sustainable development* (pp. 187–208). IGI Global. https://doi.org/10.4018/978-1-7998-5033-5.ch013

Mayr, H., Oberauer, K., & Parth, S. (2023). Jamming für eine bessere Welt! Global Goals Design Jam: Anwendung des Design-Thinking-Ansatzes, um Lösungen im Kontext der 17 Ziele für eine nachhaltige Entwicklung zu entwickeln. Ein Unterrichtsbeispiel. *GW-Unterricht, 1*, 61–79. https://doi.org/10.1553/gw-unterricht169s61

Mayr, H., & Vollmer, C. (2023). Intrinsic motivation for change with the global goals design jam – Testing its effectiveness with a mixed methods design. In *Thinking skills and creativity.* Manuscript accepted for publication.

Mayr, H., & Vollmer, C. (2024). Fostering interest in sustainable development with the Global Goals Design Jam–Testing its effectiveness with a mixed methods design. *Thinking Skills and Creativity, 51*, 101449.

McLaughlin, J. E., Chen, E., Lake, D., Guo, W., Skywark, E. R., Chernik, A., & Liu, T. (2022). Design thinking teaching and learning in higher education: Experiences across four universities. *PLoS One, 17*(3), e0265902. https://doi.org/10.1371/journal.pone.0265902

Meinel, C., & von Thienen, J. (2016). Design thinking. *Informatik-Spektrum, 39*(4), 310–314. https://doi.org/10.1007/s00287-016-0977-2

Micheli, P., Wilner, S. J. S., Bhatti, S. H., Mura, M., & Beverland, M. B. (2018). Doing design thinking: Conceptual review, synthesis, and research agenda: Doing design thinking. *Journal of Product Innovation Management, 36*(2), 124–148. https://doi.org/10.1111/jpim.12466

Michelsen, G. (2014). Bildung für eine nachhaltige Entwicklung. In H. Heinrichs (Ed.), *Nachhaltigkeitswissenschaften* (pp. 567–594). Springer Spektrum. https://link.springer.com/10.1007/978-3-658-23230-6_42

Nørgård, R. T., Toft-Nielsen, C., & Whitton, N. (2017). Playful learning in higher education: Developing a signature pedagogy. *International Journal of Play, 6*(3), 272–282. https://doi.org/10.1080/21594937.2017.1382997

OECD. (2019). *Learning compass 2030. OECD future of education and skills 2030. Conceptual learning framework.* https://www.oecd.org/education/2030-project/teaching-and-learning/learning/learning-compass-2030/OECD_Learning_Compass_2030_Concept_Note_Series.pdf

Ohio Department of Education. (2016). *Partnership for 21st century skills. Core content integration.* www.p21.org

Oser, F., Hascher, T., & Spychiger, M. (1999). Lernen aus Fehlern. Zur Psychologie des „negativen" Wissens. In W. Althof (Ed.), *Fehlerwelten: Vom Fehlermachen und Lernen aus Fehlern. Beiträge und Nachträge zu einem interdisziplinären Symposium aus Anlass des 60. Geburtstags von Fritz Oser* (pp. 11–41). Springer Fachmedien Wiesbaden.

Painter-Morland, M. (2015). Philosophical assumptions undermining responsible management education. *The Journal of Management Development, 34*(1), 61–75. https://doi.org/10.1108/JMD-06-2014-0060

Pande, M., & Bharathi, S. V. (2020). Theoretical foundations of design thinking – A constructivism learning approach to design thinking. *Thinking Skills and Creativity, 36,* 100637. https://doi.org/10.1016/j.tsc.2020.100637

Pekrun, R., Goetz, T., Frenzel, A. C., Barchfeld, P., & Perry, R. P. (2011). Measuring emotions in students' learning and performance: The Achievement Emotions Questionnaire (AEQ). *Contemporary Educational Psychology, 36*(1), 36–48. https://doi.org/10.1016/j.cedpsych.2010.10.002

Plass, J. L., Homer, B. D., & Kinzer, C. K. (2014). Playful learning: An integrated design framework. *White Paper, 2,* 2014.

Poleac, D. (2022, May). Responsive design thinking: Transitioning from human-centered to a planetary-centric approach to innovation. Principles and perspectives. In A. L. Negruşa & M. M. Coroş (Eds.), *Remodelling Businesses for Sustainable Development: 2nd International Conference on Modern Trends in Business, Hospitality, and Tourism,* Cluj-Napoca, Romania, 2022. Springer International Publishing. https://doi.org/10.1007/978-3-031-19656-0

Pretorius, R. W., Carow, S., Wilson, G., & Schmitz, P. (2021). Using real-world engagements for sustainability learning in ODeL in the Global South: Challenges and opportunities. *International Journal of Sustainability in Higher Education, 22*(6), 1316–1335. https://doi.org/10.1108/IJSHE-08-2020-0287

Randler, C., Hummel, E., Gläser-Zikuda, M., Vollmer, C., Bogner, F. X., & Mayring, P. (2011). Reliability and validation of a short scale to measure situational emotions in science education. *International Journal of Environmental & Science Education, 6*(4), 359–370.

Ray, S. K. S. (2023). Moving towards agile leadership to help organizations succeed. *IUP Journal of Soft Skills, 17*(1), 5–17.

Rice, L. (2009). Playful learning. *Journal for Education in the Built Environment, 4*(2), 94–108. https://doi.org/10.11120/jebe.2009.04020094

Rieckmann, M. (2018). Learning to transform the world: Key competencies in education for sustainable development. *Issues and trends in education for sustainable development, 39,* 39–59.

Rifkin, J. (2022). *Das Zeitalter der Resilienz: Leben neu denken auf einer wilden Erde.* Frankfurt.

Rodríguez Aboytes, J. G., & Barth, M. (2020). Transformative learning in the field of sustainability: A systematic literature review (1999–2019). *International Journal of Sustainability in Higher Education, 21*(5), 993–1013. https://doi.org/10.1108/IJSHE-05-2019-0168

Ryan, R. M., & Deci, E. L. (2000). Self-determination theory and the facilitation of intrinsic motivation, social development, and well-being. *American Psychologist, 55*(1), 68.

Schäfer, B. (1983). Semantische Differential Technik. In H. Feger & J. Bredenkamp (Eds.), *Enzyklopädie der Psychologie. Band 2: Datenerhebung* (pp. 154–221). Verlag für Psychologie Dr. C. J. Hogrefe.

Scheer, A., Noweski, C., & Meinel, C. (2012). Transforming constructivist learning into action: Design thinking in education. *Design and Technology Education: An International Journal, 17*(3), 8–19.

Schmidt, S. J. (2019). Embracing and harnessing the intimate connection between emotion and cognition to help students learn. *Journal of Food Science Education, 18*(4), 87–96. https://doi.org/10.1111/1541-4329.12167

Schneider, C. R., Zaval, L., & Markowitz, E. M. (2021). Positive emotions and climate change. *Current Opinion in Behavioral Sciences, 42*, 114–120. https://doi.org/10.1016/j.cobeha.2021.04.009

Schulten, M. L. (2017). Assoziationen vergleichen mit dem Semantischen Differential. *Methoden empirischer Forschung in der Musikpädagogik. Eine anwendungsbezogene Einführung*, 121–130.

Seligman, M. (2012). *Flourish-Wie Menschen aufblühen: Die positive Psychologie des gelingenden Lebens.* Kösel-Verlag.

Singer-Brodowski, M. (2016). Transformative Bildung durch transformatives Lernen. Zur Notwendigkeit der erziehungswissenschaftlichen Fundierung einer neuen Idee. *Zeitschrift für internationale Bildungsforschung und Entwicklungspädagogik, 39*(1), 13–17. https://doi.org/10.25656/01:15443

Stickdorn, M., Hormess, M. E., Lawrence, A., & Schneider, J. (2018). *This is service design doing: Applying service design thinking in the real world.* O'Reilly Media, Inc.

Stoltenberg, U., & Burandt, S. (2014). Bildung für nachhaltige Entwicklung. In H. Heinrichs & G. Michelsen (Eds.), *Nachhaltigkeitswissenschaften* (pp. 557–594). Springer Verlag.

Talgorn, E., & Ullerup, H. (2023). Invoking 'empathy for the planet' through participatory ecological storytelling: From human-centered to planet-centered design. *Sustainability, 15*(10), 7794. https://doi.org/10.3390/su15107794

Tang, T., Vezzani, V., & Eriksson, V. (2020). Developing critical thinking, collective creativity skills and problem solving through playful design jams. *Thinking Skills and Creativity, 37*, 100696. https://doi.org/10.1016/j.tsc.2020.100696

Tironi, M., Albornoz, C., & Chilet, M. (2022). Problematizing human-centred design: Notes on planet-oriented design. *Disegno Industriale / Industrial Design, 01*(77). https://doi.org/10.30682/diid7722c

UN Global Compact. (2007). *The principles for responsible management education.* https://d306pr3pise04h.cloudfront.net/docs/news_events%2F8.1%2FGC_Summit_Report_07.pdf

UNESCO. (2013). *Positionspapier »Zukunftsstrategie BNE 2015+«.* Deutsche UNESCO-Kommission e.V. (Stand: November 2013).

UNESCO. (2019). *Framework for the implementation of education for sustainable development (ESD) beyond 2019* [Proposal for a framework for ESD]. Paris. https://unesdoc.unesco.org/ark:/48223/pf0000370215

UNESCO. (2020). *Education for sustainable development: A roadmap.* UNESCO. https://doi.org/10.54675/YFRE1448

UNESCO. (n.d.). *Education for sustainable development for 2030 toolbox.* Paris. https://en.unesco.org/themes/education-sustainable-development/toolbox

United Nations. (1992). *Agenda 21.* Rio de Janeiro.

United Nations. (2002). *Resolution adopted by the general assembly. United Nations decade of education for sustainable development.* https://digitallibrary.un.org/record/482207/files/A_RES_57_254-EN.pdf?ln=zh_CN

United Nations. (2015). *Transforming our world: The 2030 agenda for sustainable development.* United Nations, Department of Economic and Social Affairs.

van der Linden, S. (2015). Intrinsic motivation and pro-environmental behaviour. *Nature Climate Change, 5*(7), 612–613. https://doi.org/10.1038/nclimate2669

Vare, P., Millican, R., & de Vries, G. (2018). A rounder sense of purpose: Towards a pedagogy for transformation. In P. Bamber (Ed.), *Research in action special* (Vol. 4, pp. 18–22). https://aroundersenseofpurpose.eu/

Vare, P., & Scott, W. (2007). Learning for a change: Exploring the relationship between education and sustainable development. *Journal of Education for Sustainable Development, 1*(2), 191–198. https://doi.org/10.1177/097340820700100209

Waidelich, L., Richter, A., Kolmel, B., & Bulander, R. (2018, June). Design thinking process model review. In *2018 IEEE international conference on engineering, technology and innovation (ICE/ITMC)* (pp. 1–9). IEEE. https://doi.org/10.1109/ICE.2018.8436281

Wals, A. E. J. (2011). Learning our way to sustainability. *Journal of Education for Sustainable Development, 5*(2), 177–186. https://doi.org/10.1177/097340821100500208

Weinert, F. E. (2001). Vergleichende Leistungsmessung in Schulen - Eine umstrittene Selbstverständlichkeit. In F. E. Weinert, (Hrsg.), *Leistungsmessungen in Schulen* (pp. 17–32). Basel.

Whitton, N. (2018). Playful learning: Tools, techniques, and tactics. *Research in Learning Technology, 26*(0). https://doi.org/10.25304/rlt.v26.2035

Wiek, A., Withycombe, L., & Redman, C. L. (2011). Key competencies in sustainability: A reference framework for academic program development. *Sustainability Science, 6*(2), 203–218. https://doi.org/10.1007/s11625-011-0132-6

Willems, A. S. (2011). *Bedingungen des situationalen Interesses im Mathematikunterricht: Eine mehrebenenanalytische Perspektive.* Waxmann Verlag.

Zelenski, J. M., & Desrochers, J. E. (2021). Can positive and self-transcendent emotions promote pro-environmental behavior? *Current Opinion in Psychology, 42,* 31–35. https://doi.org/10.1016/j.copsyc.2021.02.009

Part 3

Inspiration From Innovative Business Practices

Chapter 9

Sharing Economy and Its Potential to Achieve SDG 12: The Fashion Sharing Platform Case

Kristina Steinbiß[a] and Elisabeth Fröhlich[b]

[a]Reutlingen University, Germany
[b]ISPIRA Think Tank for Sustainable Supply Chains, Germany

Abstract

The fast fashion industry is one of the most polluting industries. For this reason, the industry should look into new circular business models in order to reduce its material footprint as well as the amount of waste produced. This article focuses on the question of how the sharing economy, as one possible circular business model, can contribute to achieving Sustainable Development Goal 12 (SDG 12) "Ensuring Sustainable Consumption and Production." After a brief introduction to SDG 12, a short outline of the current development of the sharing economy in the fast fashion sector is given. To develop consumer buying behavior toward environmental sustainability, it is important to understand their motives. Utilitarian and hedonic motives are examined in order to determine to what extent they can positively influence buying intention and thus the acceptance of fashion sharing platforms. The database gathered through a master thesis is used to investigate the specific influence these motives have on buying intention. To increase the acceptance and thus the use of fashion sharing platforms, recommendations for action are developed in the final step of this chapter throughout the five steps of the buying cycle model. Circular business models will play a key role in the context of sustainable transformation in the future. Therefore, it is particularly important to derive concrete recommendations for action based on research in order to get the ecological footprint of environmentally harmful industries – such as the fast fashion industry – under control.

Innovation in Responsible Management Education, 221–239
Copyright © 2024 Kristina Steinbiß and Elisabeth Fröhlich
Published under exclusive licence by Emerald Publishing Limited
doi:10.1108/978-1-83549-464-620241013

Keywords: SDG 12; sharing platforms; fashion industry; sustainable consumer buying behavior; circular business models; utilitarian motivation; hedonic motivation; buying cycle model

Introduction

The growing success of fast fashion over the past 20 years has led consumers to view clothing as disposable. The rise of social media and technological advancements has exacerbated this trend. Consumers want to dress differently every day to stay hip and be respected by their peers. In order to follow the latest trends, it has become inevitable to buy clothes from fast fashion brands, which have a huge negative impact on society and the environment. The overconsumption and overproduction of inexpensively manufactured clothing create tons of waste, water pollution, and carbon emissions every year (Assoune, 2023). Clothing is an essential part of our lives. However, due to the mass consumption of fast fashion products, more and more garments end up in the trash. The throwaway culture has worsened progressively over the last few years. At present, many items are worn only seven to 10 times before being tossed. That is a decline of more than 35% in just 15 years (Earth.Org, 2023).

Sharing economy business models have gained significant importance in recent years (Martos-Carrión & Miguel, 2022). Renting and selling clothes that are no longer needed or wanted has become a way to dress more diversely and sustainably. The purpose of this paper is to identify new ways of shaping sustainable consumer buying behavior by referring to corresponding sub targets of Sustainable Development Goal 12 (SDG 12) (UN, 2023).

The research question on which this article is based discusses how the sharing economy can contribute to achieving SDG 12 with a focus on the enhancement of utilitarian and hedonic customer value. The article adopts the following structure: A short introduction of SDG 12 and the current development of the sharing economy in the fast fashion sector are given. This includes an overview of today's best-known and most widely used sharing platforms. In order to influence consumer behavior, it is important to understand their motives. This is achieved in Chapter 3, where purchasing motives are analyzed and categorized into utilitarian and hedonic motives. The methodology in Chapter 4 sets out a research framework using a regression analysis to investigate the influence those motives have on the purchase intention of fashion sharing platforms. To increase the use of fashion sharing platforms and thus contribute to the targets of SDG 12, recommendations for action are developed in the fifth section. A future outlook rounds off the chapter.

SDG 12 and the Sharing Economy

SDG 12, Ensuring Sustainable Consumption and Production Patterns (UN, 2023), is one of the major targets of the Agenda 2030 aiming to reduce the environmental impact of unsustainable global industries, including the fast fashion industry. With the rise of the fast fashion industry, the amount of clothes made and discarded has dramatically increased. Textile consumption per person needs 400 m² of land, 9 m³ of water, and 391 kg of raw materials. This leads to a carbon footprint of 270 kg per person (per year) in the European Union (numbers are from 2020), which makes the fast fashion industry one of the main contributors to global warming and climate change (European Parliament, 2023). The Fashion Transparency Index (Fashion Revolution, 2023) included a so-called "de-growth" commitment in its latest report. Yet 99% of all fashion brands interviewed are unwilling to publish a statement about their commitment to reduce the number of new products manufactured. All these realities call for new business models – such as sharing platforms – to sustainably change and shape consumer buying behavior to make the fashion industry less harmful to the environment.

SDG 12: Ensuring Sustainable Consumption and Production Patterns

"SDG 12 calls for a comprehensive set of actions from businesses, policy-makers and consumers to adapt to sustainable practices. It envisions sustainable production and consumption based on advanced technological capacity, resource efficiency and reduced global waste" (Eurostat, 2023). This chapter focuses on the "planet" part of the Agenda 2030 and will identify different measures for the fast fashion industry throughout the buying cycle model to manage a more efficient use of resources and actions against climate change. SDG 12 covers 11 sub targets and 13 aligned indicators. The sub targets 12.A (support of developing countries), 12.B (sustainable tourism), and 12.C (restructuring taxation) will not be considered, as these goals cannot be influenced by fashion companies themselves. UNStats (2023) offers metadata sheets where more detailed information can be found. Out of the eight remaining sub targets, this chapter is focusing on four:

(1) *Sub target 12.1* deals with the implementation of a 10-year sustainable consumption and production framework. This framework aims to achieve a better quality of life by reducing the waste footprint in the respective country by optimizing natural resource efficiency and reducing use of toxic materials. This sub target is based on the indicator "number of countries developing, adopting, or implementing the shift to sustainable consumption and production" (Our World in Data, 2023). A map published by Our World in Data (2023) shows the countries which have already announced a sustainable consumption and production national action plan. As one can learn from this map, only a few countries that play a major role in the textile industry have so far introduced this action plan. The implementation of circular business models can give those countries an additional impetus to establish concrete measures to implement this SDG 12 framework. The authors have decided not to address sub target 12.5. "substantially reduce waste generation" in this chapter, as waste management is also part of sub target 12.1.

(2) *Sub target 12.2*, Sustainable management and use of natural resources includes three indicators. "Material Footprint (MF) is the attribution of global material extraction to domestic final demand of a country. The total material footprint is the sum of the weight of the used biomass, fossil fuels, metal ores, and non-metal ores" (Our World in Data, 2023). This indicator is currently only retrievable as a global estimate. The other indicators are domestic material consumption per capita and per GDP. It is important to understand that this indicator, which tracks the amount of materials directly consumed in a country, is measured on the basis of material production figures and not consumption. That is one of the major reasons why the Fashion Transparency Index (2023) includes the "de-growth" statement in its latest report. As was made clear in the introduction to this chapter, the fashion industry suffers from an immensely high material footprint. For this reason, sub target 12.2 was chosen for this paper to show which measures can be selected throughout the buying cycle model in order to significantly reduce the material footprint through the introduction of fashion sharing platforms.

(3) The first indicator "international agreements on hazardous waste" as part of *sub target 12.4* "responsible management of chemicals and waste" reports the share of relevant information that has been filed to international organizations, e.g., Montreal Protocol, Rotterdam Convention, Basel Convention or Stockholm Convention (Our World in Data, 2023). The second indicator focuses on the amount of hazardous waste generated and, more importantly, how companies manage and dispose of this waste, which is harmful to the environment and human health. Our World in Data (2023) visualizes the hazardous waste produced per capita in 2021. Unfortunately, similar to sub target 12.1, this map lacks this important information for those countries in which textiles are heavily produced. This paper therefore discusses various measures that a company can implement in order to achieve more sustainable consumer purchasing behavior.

(4) And finally, this paper addresses *sub target 12.8* "promote universal understanding of sustainable lifestyle." Indicator 12.8.1 (understanding of sustainable lifestyle) is defined as the "extent to which global citizenship education and education for sustainable development are mainstreamed in national education policies; curricula; teacher education; and student assessment" (Our World in Data, 2023). The main reason for tackling this sub target is based on the opinion of the authors that education is not only the task of society and educational institutions. This paper illustrates that companies can also provide an understanding of a sustainable lifestyle throughout the buying cycle model through appropriate communication policy measures. The detailed description of the sub targets is particularly relevant for deriving managerial implications in the further course of this chapter.

As the previous remarks make clear, there is little concrete data and information on how to achieve SDG 12 within the fashion industry. For this reason, it is important that innovative circular business models are introduced to the fashion industry as a major potential strategy helping to tackle the challenges identified in the context of the fashion industry's ecological footprint.

Sharing Economy in the Fashion Industry

The *circular economy* opens up completely new perspectives for the fashion industry. Circular business models aim to maximize the value of resources. Companies that adopt a circular economy approach benefit from reduced dependence on scarce resources and increased operational efficiency. This paper focuses in particular on the reuse and remanufacturing aspects of the circular economy, which creates many new touchpoints on the buying cycle model. In this way, the use of fashion sharing platforms can help to reduce the large material footprint and the high level of pollution in the fashion industry (Fröhlich & Steinbiß, 2020).

As stated previously, circular economy is a major driver for solving the environmental issues raised by the fashion industry, and includes five different "business models" (OECD, 2018). "Circular supply models" replace common materials derived from new raw materials with bio-based, recovered, renewable, or recycled materials. "Resource recovery models" process waste, e.g., from the textile industry, into secondary raw materials in order to avoid the incineration or storage of waste in landfills. Extending the lifespan of products that have already been produced to reduce and slow down the resource extraction, and thus the generation of waste, is the major task of "product life extension models." "Product service system models" sell services, not products, in order to promote more efficient product use and thus a more economical use of natural resources through environmentally friendly product design. The focus of this paper lies on *sharing models* that enable the shared use of underutilized products. The aim of the sharing economy is therefore to reduce the demand for new products and the raw materials they contain. In fact, it has opened a new pathway to deal with capitalism and modern consumerism, driven by the "global financial and economic crises and paired with the urgent need for sustainable resource usage" (Argaval & Steinmetz, 2019).

Building on new technologies such as Web 2.0, a *sharing economy* business model is defined as a peer-to-peer activity. Access to goods and services is governed by a community (e.g., platform) (Argaval & Steinmetz, 2019). Sharing economy is a very broad term that encompasses various concepts, such as collaborative consumption or economy, peer-to-peer economy or maker movement. It can therefore be described as a disruptive socioeconomic system that can pose a major challenge to established economic models (Wruk et al., 2019), such as the fashion industry. Sharing models focus on hyper-consumption and private property in order to implement innovative business models that reduce the ecological footprint by combining collaborative principles and the potential of the internet (Martos-Carrión & Miguel, 2022). The sharing economy aims to redistribute existing goods among the population to maximize their functionality.

Sharing economy platforms allow users to exchange their belongings with others (not necessarily for free) and thus develop new patterns of consumption (Dolnicar, 2021). Accordingly, a considerable number of everyday goods, such as toys, construction tools, sports equipment, cars, etc., are passed on from user to user, significantly reducing the number of new products purchased (Martos-Carrión & Miguel, 2022).

The constant reduction of transaction costs in e-commerce and logistics processes means that the potential scope of application of sharing models is constantly increasing. This not only benefits the areas of transportation, tourism, accommodation, and entertainment with Uber and Airbnb, two sharing models that everyone is familiar with, but also the fashion industry. "Rent the Runway" (https://www.renttherunway.com/) from the US is one of the most famous pioneers in this sector. The introduction of a sharing economy model in the luxury fashion market has fundamentally changed the consumption of famous luxury brands. "Le Tote" (https://letote.com) entered the online clothing rental market with different business models, initially introducing the monthly subscription clothing rental business model to successfully target different customer segments. "Tulerie" (https://tulerie.com) has also introduced a clothing exchange model to the market known as a "peer-to-peer rental clothing community." This trend toward fashion sharing platforms has now spread globally, such as "LENA The Fashion Library" (https://lena-library.com) in the Netherlands, "Lookerio" (https://lookiero.de) in Germany, "airCloset" (https://www.air-closet.com/) in Japan and "Designer 24" (https://www.designer-24.com/) in the United Arab Emirates. According to the taxonomy of the collaborative economy, fashion sharing platforms follow two business models: the rental of fashion products and the second-hand sale or exchange of these (part of market redistribution) (Owyang et al., 2014).

Buying Motivations

As this article evaluates the extent to which sharing economy can contribute to achieving SDG 12, it is first necessary to analyze the reasons for consumption – the buying motivations. Only if they are covered by the sharing economy will it be possible to establish a positive link to the targets and sub targets of SDG 12.

Buying motivations are defined as "the drivers of behavior that bring consumers to the marketplace to satisfy their internal needs (Jin & Kim, 2003)." With regard to the satisfaction of needs, Hirschman and Holbrook (1982) describe consumers as either "problem solvers" or as individuals seeking "fun, fantasy, arousal, sensory stimulation, and enjoyment." This dichotomy has been represented in the literature by themes of shopping as work versus the festive, more enjoyable perspective on shopping as fun (Childersa et al., 2001). This dual characterization of motivations is consistent with the perspective taken to elaborate on the impact of sharing economy on SDG 12.

The focus of this study will be on buying motivations as the key indicators to predict consumer purchase intention. Fischbein and Ajzen (1975) pointed out that purchase intention is an individual's subjective probability of engaging in certain behavior. As purchase intention is regarded to be the most accurate prefactor for marketers to predict consumer purchase behavior, this paper will follow Assael's statement (2001): If the consumers' perceived value of a product is higher, the willingness to purchase the product is also greater. In summary, as a basis for further investigation on sharing economy and SDG 12, this study will focus on purchase intention under the influence of utilitarian and hedonic value factors.

Utilitarian Motivation

The utilitarian dimension of consumption value is related to functional, non-sensory attributes, and functional expectations of customers (Batra & Ahtola, 1990). It refers to a rational, planned, and goal-oriented shopping behavior (Scarpi, 2020) as well as considering risk reduction strategies and achieving information search goals (Hamid et al., 2019). This implies that consumers who act for utilitarian motives try to find the right product without spending a lot of time on searching and evaluating alternatives in the process (Indrawati et al., 2022). Babin et al. (1994) defined utilitarian shopping motivation as acquiring the benefit of the product needed, or acquiring the product more effortlessly. Hence, from the perspective of utilitarian motivation toward the usefulness of time and cost reduction using fashion sharing platforms, two categories of main influence are to be investigated: cost savings and product selection.

Hedonic Motivation

Hedonic shopping motivation is based on psychological needs (Widago & Roz, 2021) and presents behavior that is related to fun, amusement, fantasy, and the sensorial stimuli aspects of consumption (Babin et al., 1994). Consumer value is based on the feelings and experiences they retain from shopping activities. For this reason, hedonic motives are all about pleasure, luxury, and solace. They are mainly intrinsically based upon self-interested needs, curiosity, entertainment, and self-expression (Indrawati et al., 2022) and are further emphasized by considering shopping with family or friends as a socializing and bonding activity (Timothy, 2005) with a focus on interactions (To et al., 2007). As a second aspect that shapes the hedonic motives, value is seen as the consumer's perception of bargaining and negotiating with others (Arnold & Reynolds, 2003). Hence, from the perspective of hedonic motivation toward the use of fashion sharing platforms, two categories of main influence are to be investigated: social interaction and value.

As both utilitarian and hedonic motives are relevant to consumer behavior in the purchasing process, the following section will analyze whether this relevance also applies to the willingness of consumers to use fashion sharing platforms.

Database

According to the previously provided information, sharing clothes via online platforms has not yet become the mainstream, as most consumers are particularly unfamiliar with models such as monthly rentals and clothing exchanges. In order to enhance the use of fashion sharing platforms as one aspect of collaborative consumption, the empirical information collected by a master thesis submitted at CBS International Business School, Cologne dealing with the topic "The effects of fashion sharing platform factors on consumers' purchase intention" (Ping-Yu, 2022) serves as a data basis to deduct the managerial implications provided in section 5 of this paper. The focus of the thesis lies on explaining the importance of hedonic and utilitarian motives to enhance the purchase intention of sharing platforms in the fashion industry. The empirical data collected on the basis of a regression analysis is used as the fundamental input for developing the implications in section 5 of this paper. Various marketing measures are identified along the five steps of the buying cycle model that enable the achievement of the previously discussed sub targets of SDG 12. The empirical findings of the master thesis relevant to this paper are compiled in the following two sections "Research Frame and Hypothesis" and "Research Design and Data Analysis."

Research Frame and Hypothesis

From the perspective of utilitarian motives, two variables are investigated: cost saving by reducing expenditure on product cost and browsing cost, and product selection by having a larger and more diversified product selection available. From the perspective of hedonic motives, the focus is also on two variables – social interaction and value. In theory, both dimensions partly have a more comprehensive number of variables (To et al., 2007). However, in this study, only the most relevant variables for shaping customer behavior toward the use of fashion sharing will be investigated. In conclusion, the research model on hand, shown in Fig. 9.1, includes seven criteria: cost saving, product selection, and

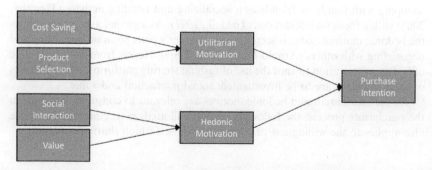

Fig. 9.1.　Research Structure. *Source:* Own illustration.

social interaction as independent variables and utilitarian motivation, hedonic motivation, and purchase intention as dependent variables.

Based on the literature and according to the conceptual research frame, six hypotheses are derived.

H1. Cost saving has a significant positive influence on the utilitarian motivation in the context of fashion sharing platform shopping.

H2. Product selection has a significant positive influence on the utilitarian motivation in the context of fashion sharing platform shopping.

H3. Social interaction has a significant positive influence on the hedonic motivation in the context of fashion sharing platform shopping.

H4. Value has a significant positive influence on the hedonic motivation in the context of fashion sharing platform shopping.

H5. Hedonic motivation has a significant positive influence on the purchase intention in the context of fashion sharing platform shopping.

H6. Utilitarian motivation has a significant positive influence on the purchase intention in the context of fashion sharing platform shopping.

Research Design and Data Analysis

To measure the relevance of the conceptual research model, an online questionnaire on a Likert five-point scale has been conducted. The study collected responses from consumers older than 16 years from Germany in September and October 2022. The questionnaire asked respondents about their fashion sharing motives and behavior in line with eight categories. The first category covered basic information of respondents, while the following categories addressed their view on the importance of all seven criteria taken from the research frame. 66 online questionnaires were distributed in a pretest, and 290 online questionnaires were received as the final sample.

In order to test the fit and validity of the model, the descriptive statistical analysis of sample structure and reliability analysis was performed with SPSS 26 statistical software. Discriminant validity, the confirmatory factor analysis (CFA) and path analysis in the structural equation modeling (SEM) was performed with AMOS version 23.

According to the results of the analysis, the majority of respondents were female (171 respondents, 59%), the main age group ranged from 16 to 24 years (148 respondents, 51%), and students were the most represented employment status (169 respondents, 58.3%). The majority of monthly budgets for the purchase of clothing is below 20% (70 respondents, 24.1%), followed by 60–80% (69 respondents, 23.8%). Hence, the monthly budget for buying clothes in this study is less than 100 euros (156 respondents, 53.8%). 51% of the 290 respondents already had experience in apparel sharing while 49% of the respondents never used a fashion sharing offer. Respondents with experience of clothes sharing most often bought second-hand clothes (113 respondents, 75%) and most frequently used clothing sharing platforms (63 respondents, 42%).

A descriptive statistical analysis on a five-point Likert scale was used to calculate the mean and standard deviation of all variables. In order to ensure a better readability, the measured items of each dimension were shortened into succinct aspects. Fig. 9.2 shows the results of the study.

As the standard deviation of cost saving, product selection, value, utilitarian motivation, and purchase intention is between 0.715 and 1.108, it is shown that the views of respondents on these dimensions were relatively consistent. The average score of the items is between 3.93 and 4.2, showing that participants see them as "important to very important" factors while shopping on fashion sharing platforms. As the standard deviation of social interaction and hedonic motivation range between 0.058 and 0.072, it is also shown that the views of respondents on these two dimensions were relatively consistent. However, the average score of these two items is between 3.73 and 3.96, indicating that the participants see both dimensions as "neutral to important" factors. Hence, it can be said that practical considerations are still more important than the pleasure and experience of shopping on fashion sharing platforms.

As a second step, structural equation modeling was conducted to investigate the relationship between the different factors. In this study, t-value was used to test the significance of the beta coefficient, and the higher the t-value, the more significant it is. Fig. 9.3 is to be read as the beta coefficient between cost saving and utilitarian motivation is 0.419, the t value is 5.47, and $p < 0.001$, reaching a statistically significant level. Therefore "cost saving" has a positive and direct

Item	Mean	Standard Devination
Cost Saving		
CS 1: Save money	4.14	0.946
CS2: Cheaper purchases	4.20	0.897
CS3: Competitive price	4.16	0.854
CS4: Less spending	4.17	0.857
Product Selection		
PS1: Assess multiple brands	3.98	0.947
PS2: Wide range of products offered	4.13	1.108
PS3: Favorable selection of products	4.00	1.064
PS4: Higher variety of prodcts	4.03	1.052
PS5: Easily avaiable	4.03	1.091
Social Interaction		
SI1: Exchange information with friends	3.87	0.057
SI2: Development friendship	3.73	0.072
SI3: Extend personal relationship	3.76	0.068
SI4: Share Experiences	3.92	0.061
Value		
V1: Discount	4.05	0.93
V2: Bargain	3.99	1.009
V3: Special offer	4.05	1.009
V4: Get discout by bargaining	3.93	1.042

Item	Mean	Standard Devination
Utilitarian Motivation		
UM1: Price-Quality-Equivation	4.14	0.915
UM2: Good economic value	4.20	1.025
UM3: Save time	4.16	1.103
UM4: Easy to find	4.17	1.079
Hedonic Motivation		
HM1: Fun	3.85	0.058
HM2: Enjoyable	3.96	0.069
HM3: Own sake	3.82	0.068
HM4: Adventure	3.78	0.065
HM5: Keep up with trends	3.90	0.069
Purchase Intention		
PI1: Willingness	4.11	0.715
PI2: Need	3.95	1.049
PI3: High possibility	3.98	1.060
PI4: Future intention	4.09	0.914
PI5: Recommendation	4.04	0.927
PI6: Continually usage	4.15	0.944

Fig. 9.2.   Mean and Standard Deviation of Each Dimension. *Source: Own illustration.*

Hypothesis	Path	Relationship	Beta coefficient	P value	S.E.	T value	Significance
H1	Cost Saving > Utilitarian Motivation	positive	0.419	***	0.089	5.470	Significant
H2	Product selection > Utilitarian Motivation	positive	0.394	***	0.063	5.637	Significant
H3	Social Interaction > Hedonic Motivation	positive	0.257	0.005	0.104	2.844	Significant
H4	Value > Hedonic Motivation	positive	0.361	***	0.126	3.827	Significant
H5	Utilitarian Motivation > Purchase Intention	positive	0.625	***	0.063	10.194	Significant
H6	Hedonic Motivation > Purchase Intention	positive	0.200	***	0.056	3.872	Significant

Note: *** $p<0.001$

Fig. 9.3.   Hypothesis Test. *Source:* Own illustration.

impact on "utilitarian motivation." As Fig. 9.3 reveals, the study clearly shows that the relationships between all factors investigated had a positive and significant impact to fulfill either utilitarian or hedonic motivations and using fashion sharing platforms.

To summarize, this study has applied the sharing economy model to the apparel sector. After summarizing the database by analyzing the correlation between the four factors of consumption on utilitarian motivation, hedonic motivation, and purchase intention, it can be said that the use of sharing economy models in the fashion industry has a high potential to positively impact the environment and thus the achievement of SDG 12.

Managerial Implications for the Fast Fashion Industry Based on SDG 12

The rapid development of science and technology combined with the customers' increasing awareness of ecological issues has given a major boost to sharing economy business models. New fashion sharing models have also emerged in the textile industry, spreading from the United States to the rest of the world. Although, fashion sharing platforms are not yet very popular, its positive impact on environmental and social challenges should not be underestimated. Therefore, the development of clothing sharing opportunities has to be taken seriously. For this reason, this section attempts to develop some ideas throughout the buying cycle model (Foscht et al., 2017) that provide guidance to companies from the fashion industry on how the empirical findings of this paper can be translated into concrete communicative measures toward the end consumer in order to successfully achieve the chosen sub targets of SDG 12. It should be added at this point that the sub goal 12.1. was chosen intentionally, even if it refers to country indicators. The more fashion sharing platforms are accepted by consumers, the more likely SDG 12.1 will be achieved. This will also enable the fast fashion industry to establish "sustainable consumption and production frameworks."

As stated before, the so-called "buying cycle model" (Foscht et al., 2017) is used to translate the results of the data-based part into concrete recommendations for action. The focus here is on using the individual stages of the buying process model to show how the acceptance and use of fashion sharing platforms can be improved. In this model, the buyer progresses through the five phases of problem recognition, information search, evaluation of alternatives, purchase decision, and postpurchase evaluation. The buying process starts with problem recognition, when a problem or need arises. In the second phase of the buying process, the potential buyer wants to obtain information on which products are best for satisfying their needs. The aim here is to get to know the potential products and brands and, above all, their characteristics. In phase three, which is referred to as the evaluation of alternatives, the previously determined product or brand information is analyzed. Consumers process the information very differently. If the evaluation of the alternatives leads to a purchase intention, two external influences impact the actual purchase decision. Firstly, the "attitudes of peers" and secondly, "unforeseen situational factors." The final step (postpurchase phase) is of particular importance in marketing, especially if the product is to be needed or purchased again by the end consumer. Concepts such as customer satisfaction and loyalty (Reichheld & Markey, 2011) come into play.

Problem Recognition

Recognizing one's own needs and thus the existing problem is reflected the most critical step in the consumer buying process. If customers do not recognize their needs properly, they usually do not consider buying the product at all. It is therefore very important to make the use of fashion sharing platforms as simple and attractive as possible, which directly applies to the utilitarian motivation. On the one hand, awareness of fashion sharing platforms is still very low, on the other hand, there is little knowledge among consumers about the ecological added value when using this new business model. In order to provide customers with a cheap and simple first-time-shopping experience, it is proposed to offer "new customer discounts" or "quick orders", e.g., without having to fill out time-consuming user profiles, which again relates to the utilitarian motivation of cost saving. Offering consumers quick and easy access to use the different fashion sharing models in order to experience the product or service first-hand makes problem recognition much easier. Communicatively emphasizing the low entry threshold is the key success factor in this first step of the consumer buying process. Traditional marketing strategies mostly focus on emphasizing the benefits of the product itself. However, if this cannot be "simply experienced", the probability that the innovative concept of fashion sharing platforms will be tested is relatively low. The previous chapters have illustrated the potential of fashion sharing platforms to achieve sub targets 12.2, 12.4, and 12.8 of SDG 12. If fashion companies do not succeed in convincing consumers of those benefits, such as reducing the material footprint, waste or carbon footprint, when using sharing models, consumers will never use them to satisfy their needs. Awareness building is therefore the first important step in the buying cycle model. Sub target 12.8 covers the educational approach, whereby communicative measures play an important role to enable customers to understand their needs properly and support them in showing new and innovative buying behavior. Therefore, fashion sharing platforms go for qualitative instead of quantitative growth, which requires new communicative marketing concepts.

Information Search

In this step of the buying cycle model, consumers evaluate and decide on the basis of past experience. Among other things, they ask for recommendations from family or friends or research online for helpful information that makes decision-making easier. As awareness and acceptance of fashion sharing platforms is still low, it makes sense to maintain the concept of low entry thresholds to stimulate the utilitarian motivation. These measures push consumption by keeping registration and usage costs as low as possible (cost savings). In addition, it should also be ensured that the user interface is easy to understand and utilize. With regard to promotional messages, the "user's recommendation" approach should be adopted when introducing the range of offers on a fashion sharing platform. This aspect addresses the second part of utilitarian motivation – product selection. The motto "Sharing brings joy" shows how a variety of fashionable clothing styles can be created by mixing and matching used or rented clothes and accessories. It is important to convey that the desire to be able to dress fashionably according to current trends can also be satisfied with offers from sharing platforms. It is also necessary to highlight the environmental benefits of using the platform by e.g., emphasizing that renting and sharing clothes is very environmentally friendly. Creating advertisements in this context is usually not an easy task. At this stage, customers need to quickly understand, but also experience, the difference between fashion sharing platforms and fast fashion brands. The use of youtubers or having your own customers report on their experiences in short commercials could be promising communicative measures. This enables a meaningful combination of relevant information and the "emotional" element of wanting to dress fashionably or being "hip." The second argument of the previous sentence refers to the hedonic motivation, which at the same time supports the achievement of sub target 12.8. To attain a quick and easy understanding of the advantages of sharing fashion, platforms must take on the role of an educator. This requires a communication concept that is based on facts, but at the same time uses innovative measures to disseminate information. This indirectly supports the two sub targets 12.2 and 12.4. If end consumers develop an understanding that it is possible to dress fashionably with used or rented fashion products and that they will not lose the recognition of their peer group, but on the contrary, even gain recognition, the material footprint, the huge amount of waste and the use of chemicals in the fashion industry can be significantly reduced.

Evaluation of Alternatives

In the "evaluation of alternatives" step, consumers asses the value and benefits of all products considered in order to make an appropriate purchase decision. This phase relates primarily to the hedonic buying motive, in particular to self-interested needs. This "self-interest" can be used to influence environmentally friendly behavior. One strategy is to emphasize the self-benefits associated with consuming a given sustainable product. Self-efficacy includes the belief that the individual can engage in the required actions and that the behavior performed will have the intended effect (Steinbiß & Fröhlich, 2021). Fashion sharing platforms should therefore emphasize design and versatility to give customers the feeling that the offerings are constantly updated, even though they are second-hand items. One such element of versatility could be that the fashion items on offer are available in all sizes. This should be communicated prominently on the platform in order to dispel the preconception that only the "usual" sizes are available on such fashion platforms. The end consumer is surprised by the continuous redesign of the platform with new offers, products, and fashion styles, thus satisfying the hedonic buying motive. However, it must be made clear that a wide range of products is also conducive to the utilitarian motivation and thus also increases the acceptance of fashion sharing platforms. In order to clearly differentiate itself from fast fashion products, the ecological advantages of renting (used) clothing should be particularly emphasized on the product page. Compared to buying fast fashion products, the environmental impact of one's own consumer behavior is significantly reduced. In addition, providers of fashion sharing platforms can also highlight that a defined percentage of sales is donated to support environmental protection or charitable organizations. This phase, like the one discussed above, therefore indirectly supports the achievement of sub targets 12.2 and 12.4. The more confident consumers are about the ecological added value of such fashion sharing platforms, the more likely it is that environmental pollution – from waste to the utilization of chemicals – will be reduced. Donations from providers of fashion platforms can also be used to take measures to improve working conditions in the fast fashion industry, as well as to make processes safer and more efficient.

Purchase Decision

This phase is about buying intention, which is also the focus of the empirical study. Once a purchase decision has been made, it makes sense to continue working with influencers or youtubers in order to further strengthen the acceptance of fashion sharing platforms and thus encourage more sustainable purchasing behavior. Advertising measures can, for example, focus on pieces of clothing that can be combined with already existing items, accessories, cosmetics, and other fashion elements. It is made clear that you can enrich your life with just a few new pieces of clothing and thus make a valuable contribution to achieving ecological targets. In this step of the buying cycle model, the hedonic motivation is addressed very clearly. This is particularly important, because under no circumstances should the impression be created that you are sacrificing anything by buying on fashion sharing platforms. By emphasizing the high quality of the borrowed or used garments, this impression can be easily avoided.

On the contrary, by using sharing models, the egoistic orientation in the context of the Value-Belief-Norm Theory (VBN) (Stern, 2000) can be considered. "VBN theory posits that values are deeply rooted and established early in an individual's life. Three types of value orientation are included: egoistic concern for own welfare), altruistic (concern of the welfare of others), and biospheric (concern for non-human aspects of the environment)" (Ciocirlan et al., 2020). This is particularly relevant when fashion providers try to shape the purchasing behavior of their customers in a more sustainable way (Steinbiß & Fröhlich, 2022). One proposed communicative measure is to set up a blog or an Instagram-like story (e.g., https://fogsmagazin.com/sharing-is-caring/) on the fashion sharing platform. After all, giving customers inspiration for renting or sharing garments is more credible and down-to-earth compared to official brand ambassadors. This step in the buying cycle model therefore also addresses sub target 12.8. in terms of establishing a more sustainable lifestyle. This phase is thus more focused on hedonic motivation to ensure that purchases on fashion sharing platforms consider the egoistic orientation of purchasing behavior. This ensures that consumers adopt a more ecologically sustainable purchasing behavior with regard to fashion products and thus also contribute to the two selected sub targets 12.2 and 12.4 in the long run.

Postpurchase Evaluation

The buying cycle model concludes with the "postpurchase evaluation" phase. In this step, the main aim is to persuade customers who have used a fashion sharing platform for the first time to continue shopping on this platform. In this phase, the utilitarian motivation comes to the fore again. The cost-saving aspect is addressed, e.g., by not charging shipping costs for repeat purchases. At the same time, by using the fashion sharing platform, the lower environmental impact can be calculated (addresses sub targets 12.2 and 12.4) and converted into a reward like a shopping voucher. This voucher can then be cashed in on the next purchase. Historical consumption data should be continuously analyzed in order to meet the utilitarian motivation of product selection. On this basis, desired fashion styles and suitable sizes can be recommended. Customers who shop regularly or spend more than a certain amount can be notified preferentially and have the right to rent new products before all other customers. In addition, the characteristics can be used to segment consumers with various clothing styles. Different sales weeks can be organized according to the preferences of the final consumers, reflecting the preferred fashion styles of the individual consumer segments. In this way, the utilitarian aspect of product selection can be considered based on easier availability, a greater variety of products offered and a favorable selection of products, which are particularly important for the accepted use of fashion sharing platforms. If providers of fashion sharing platforms succeed in keeping the repurchase

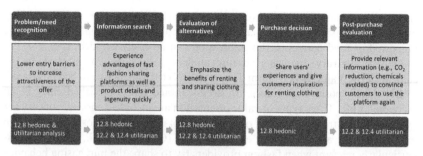

Fig. 9.4.   Managerial Implications and SDG 12. *Source:* Own
illustration.

rate high, this will have a particularly positive effect on the two sub targets 12.2
and 12.4. The decreasing production figures for fashion products reduce the
material footprint and also the waste rate. In summary, the raised repurchase rate
also achieves sub target 12.8, as the more consumers use fashion sharing platforms, the more recognized the use of this new business model becomes. The fast
fashion industry can thus take a significant step toward ecological sustainability.

Fig. 9.4 summarizes the statements made succinctly and concisely. It is
apparent that companies can activate the willingness to use sharing platforms
throughout the entire purchasing process and thus enhance the achievement of the
chosen sub targets of SDG 12.

Conclusion and Outlook

This study has shown that there are various options to shape customer behavior
to become more sustainable throughout the entire purchasing process and thus
fulfill the sub targets of SDG 12, having an impact on sustainable consumption
and production as the overall SDG 12 target.

The focus of this chapter is on the sharing economy in the fashion industry as a
new concept to consume more sustainably. This chapter deliberately does not
refer to overconsumption, as it does not intend to take a moral view on this topic.
Rather, it aims to show that the introduction of circular business models – in this
case sharing platforms – encourages a change in consumer buying behavior
toward sustainability. If the fashion industry succeeds in realizing the business
implications discussed in this article, customers will begin to question their
motives and recognize sustainable consumption options. Schroer (2022) stated
that not living better but living differently is on the agenda as a real revolution in
view of the massive planetary threats (p. 589). Taking this statement to heart, the
authors have derived recommendations for action for fashion companies that will
change consumer behavior toward a different, more sustainable life. So, customers will hopefully move from buying new to reusing. The recently published
UNEP study (2023) – *How the world can end plastic pollution* – argues that the

"reuse strategy" offers the greatest opportunity to stop pollution. What applies to the plastics industry also applies to the fashion industry.

Among other things, the need for companies to embrace this business model can be further supported by looking at the "neo-ecology" megatrend analyzed by the Zukunftsinstitut (2023). It reflects a new, environmentally conscious set of consumer values that extends into all areas of everyday life by changing consumer behavior and fundamentally realigning corporate action. As such, the sharing economy is an important aspect of this neo-ecology trend. "Using instead of owning" might be the motto of a new generation of consumers. The more individual ownership recedes into one's mindset and renting becomes the norm, and the more trends such as "minimalism", "zero waste", and "beyond plastic" create new markets, the more it becomes obvious that future economy will follow new criteria based on purpose and sustainability (Zukunftsinstitut, 2023).

References

Argaval, N., & Steinmetz, R. (2019). Sharing economy: A systematic literature review. *International Journal of Innovation and Technology Management, 16*(6), 1–17. https://doi.org/10.1142/S0219877019300027

Arnold, M., & Reynolds, K. (2003). Hedonic shopping motivations. *Journal of Retailing, 79*(2), 77–95. https://doi.org/10.1016/S0022-4359(03)00007-1

Assael, H. (2001). *Consumer behavior and marketing action* (6th ed.). Thomson Learning.

Assoune, A. (2023). Top 5 sustainable fashion documentations you need to watch. https://www.panaprium.com/blogs/i/sustainable-fashion-documentaries. Accessed on October 30, 2023.

Babin, B. J., Darden, W. R., & Griffin, M. (1994). Work and/or fun: Measuring hedonic and utilitarian shopping value. *Journal of Consumer Research, 20*(4), 644–656. https://doi.org/10.1086/209376

Batra, R., & Ahtola, O. T. (1990). Measuring the hedonic and utilitarian sources of consumer attitudes. *Marketing Letters, 2*(2), 159–170. https://doi.org/10.1007/BF00436035

Childersa, T. L., Carrb, C. L., Peckc, J., & Carsond, S. (2001). Hedonic and utilitarian motivations for online retail shopping behavior. *Journal of Retailing, 77*, 511–535. https://doi.org/10.1016/S0022-4359(01)00056-2

Ciocirlan, C. E., Gregory-Smith, D., Manika, D., & Wells, V. (2020). Using values, beliefs, and norms to predict conserving behaviors in organizations. *European Management Review, 17*(2), 543–558. https://doi.org/10.1111/emre.12388

Dolnicar, S. (2021). Sharing economy and peer-to-peer accommodation – A perspective paper. *Tourism Review, 76*(1), 34–37. https://doi.org/10.1108/TR-05-2019-0197

Earth.Org. (2023). 10 concerning fast fashion waste statistics. https://earth.org/statistics-about-fast-fashion-waste/. Accessed on November 10, 2023.

European Parliament. (2023). The impact of textile production and waste on the environment. https://www.europarl.europa.eu/news/en/headlines/society/20201208STO93327/the-impact-of-textile-production-and-waste-on-the-environment-infographics. Accessed on October 30, 2023.

Eurostat. (2023). *SDG 12 sustainable consumption and production.* https://ec.europa.eu/eurostat/statistics-explained/index.php?title=SDG_12_-_Responsible_consum-ption_and_production. Accessed on October 30, 2023.

Fashion Revolution. (2023). Fashion transparency index. https://issuu.com/fashionrevolution/docs/fashion_transparency_index_2023_pages. Accessed on October 30, 2023.

Fischbein, M. A., & Ajzen, I. (1975). *Belief, attitude, intention, and behavior: An introduction to theory and research.* Addison-Wesley.

Foscht, T., Swoboda, B., & Schramm-Klein, H. (2017). *Käuferverhalten* (5th ed.). Springer. https://doi.org/10.1007/978-3-658-17465-1_3

Fröhlich, E., & Steinbiß, K. (2020). Circular economy applies to beauty industry. In W. Filho, P. Gökçin Özuyar, A. Azul, L. Brandli, & T. Wall (Eds.), *Encyclopedia of the UN sustainable development goals: SDG 12* (pp. 1–11). https://doi.org/10.1007/978-3-319-71062-4_119-1

Hamid, N. A. A., Cheun, C. H., Abdullah, N. H., Ahmad, M. F., & Ngadiman, Y. (2019). Does persuasive e-commerce website Influence users' acceptance and online buying behaviour? The findings of the largest e-commerce website in Malaysia, lecture notes in information systems and organization. In Y. Baghdadi & A. Harfouche (Eds.), *ICT for a better life and a better world,* (pp. 263–279).

Hirschman, E. C., & Holbrook, M. B. (1982). Hedonic consumption: Emerging concepts, methods and propositions. *Journal of Marketing, 46*(3), 92–101. https://doi.org/10.1177/002224298204600314

Indrawati, I., Ramantaoki, G., Widarmanit, T., Aziz, I. A., & Khan, F. U. (2022). Utilitarian, hedonic, and self-esteem motives in online shopping. *Spanish Journal of Marketing – ESIC, 26*(2), 231–246. https://doi.org/10.1108/SJME-06-2021-0113

Jin, B., & Kim, J. (2003). A typology of Korean discount shoppers: Shopping motives, store attributes, and outcomes. *International Journal of Service Industry Management, 14*(4), 396–419. https://doi.org/10.1108/09564230310489240

Martos-Carrión, E., & Miguel, C. (2022). Sharing economy: History, definitions, and related concepts. The sharing economy: Perspectives, opportunities, and challenges (Chapter 2). In B. Taheri, R. Rahimi, & D. Buhalis (Eds.), *The sharing economy in the tourism industry.* Goodfellow Publishers. https://doi.org/10.23912/9781915097064-5094

OECD. (2018). *Business models for the circular economy: Opportunities and challenges from a policy perspective, policy highlights.* OECD Publishing.

Our world in Data. (2023). *Sustainable development goal 12 – Ensure sustainable consumption and production patterns.* https://ourworldindata.org/sdgs/responsible-consumption-production. Accessed on November 04, 2023.

Owyang, J., Samuel, A., Grenville, A. (2014). *Sharing is the new buying: How to win in the collaborative economy.* https://de.slideshare.net/jeremiah_owyang/sharing newbuying. Accessed on November 05, 2024.

Ping-Yu, H. (2022). *The effects of fashion sharing platform factors on consumers' purchase items.* Master Thesis, CBS International Business School, Cologne.

Reichheld, F. F., & Markey, R. (2011). *The ultimate question 2.0: How net promoter companies thrive in a customer-driven world* (Revised and expanded edition). Harvard Business School Press.

Scarpi, D. (2020). *Hedonism, utilitarianism, and consumer behavior. Exploring the consequences of customer orientation.* https://doi.org/10.1007/978-3-030-43876-0

Schroer, M. (2022). *Geosoziologie. Die Erde als Raum des Lebens.* Suhrkamp.

Steinbiß, K., & Fröhlich, E. (2021). Zur Steuerung nachhaltigen Konsums: Die Entwicklung einer nachhaltigen Customer Journey. In W. Wellbrock & D. Ludin (Eds.), *Nachhaltiger Konsum* (pp. 129–145). Springer. https://doi.org/10.1007/978-3-658-33353-9_8

Steinbiß, K., & Fröhlich, E. (2022). Die Verpackung als Enabler für nachhaltige Kundenerlebnisse. *PraxisWISSEN Marketing, 1*(2022), 21–32. https://doi.org/10.15459/95451.15

Stern, P. C. (2000). Towards a coherent theory of environmentally significant behavior. *Journal of Social Issues, 56*(3), 407–427. https://doi.org/10.1111/0022-4537.00175

Timothy, D. J. (2005). *Shopping tourism, retailing and leisure.* Channel View Publications. https://doi.org/10.21832/9781873150610

To, P. L., Liao, C., & Lin, T. H. (2007). Shopping motivations on internet: A study based on utilitarian and hedonic value. *Technovation, 27*(12), 774–787. https://doi.org/10.1016/j.technovation.2007.01.001

UN. (2023). *SDG 12: Responsible consumption and production.* https://sdgs.un.org/goals/goal12. Accessed on October 30, 2023.

UNEP. (2023). *Turning off the Tap – How the world can end plastic pollution and create a circular economy.* Version 2, Nairobi. https://wedocs.unep.org/bitstream/handle/20.500.11822/42277/Plastic_pollution.pdf?sequence=3

UNStats. (2023). *SDG indicators: Metadata repository.* https://unstats.un.org/sdgs/metadata/?Text=&Goal=12&Target. Accessed on November 04, 2023.

Widago, B., & Roz, K. (2021). Hedonic shopping motivation and impulse buying: The effect of website quality on customer satisfaction. *The Journal of Asian Finance, Economics and Business, 8*(1), 395–405. https://doi.org/10.13106/jafeb.2021.vol8.no1395

Wruk, D., Oberberg, A., & Maurer, I. (2019). Introduction: Perspectives on the sharing economy. In D. Wruk, A. Oberberg, & I. Maurer (Eds.), *Perspectives on the sharing economy* (pp. 1–29). Cambridge Scholars Publishing.

Zukunftsinstitut. (2023). *Megatrend Neo-Ökologie.* Zukunftsreport 2023. https://www.zukunftsinstitut.de/dossier/megatrend-neo-oekologie/

Chapter 10

A Framework of Personal Resilience of SME Owners

Anita Zehrer, Lisa Marx and Gundula Glowka

MCI | The Entrepreneurial School, Austria

Abstract

Every organization must deal with new challenges such as automation, digitization, or structural transformation, which requires a highly resilient and engaged workforce to stay competitive. Strong leadership in a firm and specific abilities of the leader are necessary to manage uncertainties and to be able to react to certain changes. Various studies regarding organizations and resilience focus on large enterprises, while studies on small- and medium-sized enterprises (SMEs) are lacking. SMEs account for 99.6% of all companies in Austria and are largely run by entrepreneurial owners and their families. Based on transformational theory, the theory of resilience as well as positive psychology, we investigate five SME owners and their personal resilience in an exploratory study. The owners were selected by purposive sampling with the aim to develop a framework with recommended actions for the personal resilience of SME leaders.

Keywords: Resilience; family firm; owner; SME; leaders

Introduction

Various studies on resilience focus on large enterprises. Research on resilience in small- and medium-sized enterprises (SMEs) is lacking due to fewer resources in terms of financial, human resources, and political aspects (Branicki et al., 2017). Especially for small firms, it is tough to deal with change and transformation, but in previous years, they not only represented underlying resilience but also showed how flexible and adaptable they can be (Smallbone et al., 2012). Especially, SME owners need to show high resilience, as changes affect them even more than larger firms (Linnenluecke, 2017). Given their ownership structure, i.e., being owned by

Innovation in Responsible Management Education, 241–265

Copyright © 2024 Anita Zehrer, Lisa Marx and Gundula Glowka

Published under exclusive licence by Emerald Publishing Limited

doi:10.1108/978-1-83549-464-620241014

the family, these businesses are hit not only in the business space but also in the family space, given the ambidexterity of family and business. Iborra et al. (2020) found that ambidexterity has a positive impact on the resilience of SMEs, when they face internal or external contingencies. However, they outline the missing qualitative approach on various "How" – questions in terms of how to improve ambidexterity in SMEs and how to become resilient (Iborra et al., 2020).

Recent studies investigated how organizations respond to adversity (Williams et al., 2017), how resilience and demographic characteristics predict distress during a crisis (Kimhi et al., 2020) or in general, outlined resilience as an important factor in personal well-being and job performance (Pink et al., 2021). Another stream of literature investigated the COVID-19 pandemic's impact on work routines; this condition forced companies to adapt quickly and also challenged resilience (Guzzo et al., 2021; Kniffin et al., 2021). Nevertheless, none of them explored how personal resilience can be developed in the context of SMEs and this specific ownership situation, where the CEO is also the owner of the business. Therefore, we pose the following research question: *How can SME owners develop personal resilience?*

Thus, drawing from transformational theory as well as positive psychology, this chapter investigates resilience via five in-depth semi-structured interviews conducted with Austrian SME owners to build a framework for personal resilience development.

In the following, the literature review focuses on SME owner and their characteristics. Therefore, we first give an introduction on how SMEs are structured before discussing transformational leadership and positive psychology as well as personal well-being and owner-specific characteristics. Then, this chapter gives an introduction to resilience and its importance for SME owners and presents a qualitative exploratory study.

Literature Review

Small- and Medium-Sized Enterprises (SMEs)

Gelinas and Bigras (2004) emphasize that the structures of SMEs are often not as complex as in large organizations. On the one hand, the flatter structure can spare difficulties when implementing new processes and products (Gelinas & Bigras, 2004). On the other hand, Yew Wong and Aspinwall (2004) outline the shorter and often more direct line in communicating, as well as the resulting, more agile incorporation of new business tasks. Due to the less complex structure of the firm (Gelinas & Bigras, 2004), owners can keep a tighter relationship and overview the individual tasks of their firm; they are more directly involved in operational tasks (Cragg et al., 2011). Also, since the owner of SMEs family firms is involved with their own capital (Bharati & Chaudhury, 2009), this leads to a higher risk adversity and deeper thoughts about decisions, in comparison to CEOs of larger organizations (Leyden & Link, 2004).

Due to the smaller company size, SMEs mostly keep their business within the same geographical area to keep a better relationship with their direct business partners such as suppliers and partners (Heidt et al., 2019). Also, customers are often treated differently in SMEs, since they are more dependent on their customers and need to make sure to keep in touch and encourage word of mouth (Yew Wong & Aspinwall, 2004). However, SMEs also face a number of challenges: Sullivan-Taylor and Branicki (2011) diagnosed resource scarcity, not only covering the technological aspect but also the complexity to receive financial support, and the limited number of human resources. When SMEs face a decision, they need to think if they can afford to invest or hire new employees and have to consider potential risks (e.g., cash-flow difficulties), unlike larger firms (Heidt et al., 2019). Especially since the COVID-19 pandemic, uncertainty is an even stronger topic and demands to adapt even quicker (Altig et al., 2020).

Transformational Leadership

The transformational theory or relationship theory of leadership has its emphasis on intrinsic motivation and characterizes the leader as a person who wants to get the best out of followers (Hunt et al., 1988). Bass and Riggio (2006) explain transformational leaders as personalities who want to bring out the best in their workforce. They try to motivate them to use their full potential and have higher standards for themselves. They tend to have less employee turnover and higher satisfaction rates. Transformational leadership is especially needed in times of change to bring people on board and create a vision they can identify with (de Clercq & Belausteguigoitia, 2017). Moreover, it contributes to a more resilient workforce with a higher level of positive effect (Sommer et al., 2015).

Avolio et al. (1999) named four components that usually make a transformational leader, which can also be seen in owners. First, leaders show charisma, which falls under the factor of *idealized influence.* Charisma outlines the competence of a leader to positively influence their followers with their behavior and convince or influence them to a certain extent. They also build up an emotional connection to their workforce and outline the skill of being a role model, someone to follow and identify with (Judge & Piccolo, 2004). Conveying an inspiring vision that employees want to achieve is the core of *inspirational motivation,* the second component. The ulterior motive of the leader is to put optimism first and give confidence to the workforce by delegating responsibility and laying meaning into their tasks to boost the confidence of the followers and motivate them intrinsically (Connelly & Ruark, 2010). Creativity is always encouraged by transformational leaders and new ideas, or suggested improvements of followers are taken into consideration and questioned critically (Judge & Piccolo, 2004). This falls under the third dimension of *intellectual stimulation,* and to provide such, it is also important to live a positive culture of failure where employees are not afraid to come up with new ways of thinking and suggesting (Bass et al., 2003). Lastly, another item set that was identified is *individualized consideration.* This equally is focusing on the needs of each individuum and aims to activate the full potential of an employee. The concerns and needs of employees are heard by a transformational leader and to fulfill and cover them is always in the interest of the leader, who is acting as a mentor or coach (Jin et al., 2016). This is especially true for owners, who own their own businesses since they have a personal stake in their success, which creates a higher sense of responsibility and commitment (Blackburn et al., 2013).

Positive Psychology and Personal Well-Being

The study of positive psychology is important as well when it comes to being resilient (Ramlall et al., 2014; Youssef & Luthans, 2007). Seligman and Csikszentmihalyi (2000) investigated this field and described it as not just enduring and surviving in life but also flourishing. On a subjective level, the researchers explained positive psychology is about well-being, contentment, and satisfaction (in the past); flow and happiness (in the present); and hope and optimism (for the future). On the individual level, it is more about positive individual traits such as courage and perseverance (Seligman & Csikszentmihalyi, 2000). A study done by Raghunathan and Trope (2002) found that people with positive emotions can handle feedback, in this context negative feedback, better than people with negative emotions as a fundamental attitude, due to their mental stability. Additionally, Fredrickson (2001) outlined that the personal resources acquired under the use of positive emotions happen to be permanent and constitute a reserve, to which an individual can go back to in diverse situations. As the terminology of "flourishing" is widely used in this context (Bakker & Sanz-Vergel, 2013; Huppert, 2009; Lyngdoh et al., 2018; Tu et al., 2020), Fredrickson and Losada (2005) conceptualized four components of human flourishing. First, goodness explains the feeling of being happy, satisfied, or functioning in a superior way. Second, generativity refers more to the behavior of an individual and its flexibility but also the ability to broaden one's mindset. The third component is social and personal growth, and lastly, resilience is named in relation to coming back stronger from an adverse event. Shortly, it refers to a state where one not only feels good but also functions effectively (Demerouti et al., 2015). A study by Sonnentag and Grant (2012) outlines the importance of having time off after work to reflect, to develop other thoughts, to be mindful and, therefore, be able to process the things that happened during the day. Often, people are too stressed during the workday to realize their achievements and are missing a satisfactory feeling which can only be awakened with proper work-free time (van Hooff & de Pater, 2017).

By nourishing the positive emotions of oneself, individuals would be able to achieve psychological growth and as a result improve their personal well-being (Fredrickson, 2001). In a working context, there is a relation between the behavior toward job tasks, for example, setting a limit to how many tasks need to be done a day, the interaction with the working colleagues, or the attitude toward work in general – and the well-being of someone. The output is a higher work engagement (Demerouti et al., 2015; Malik & Garg, 2017; Xu et al., 2022). Diener (1984) introduced subjective well-being (SWB) and defined it with the same approach as the term happiness. On the one hand, the flatter structure can spare difficulties by implementing new processes and products (Gelinas & Bigras, 2004), overall life satisfaction, and low negative effect (Lyngdoh et al., 2018; Ryff, 2019). Lyubomirsky et al. (2005) concluded that happy people, as well as people with a positive mood in general, are not only more creative (Sweetman et al., 2010) but also are more solution-oriented than others. They also attribute success to those characteristics. Moreover, happiness contributes to satisfying relationships, a fulfilled job, and better mental and physical health as well as longevity (Lips-Wiersma & Wright, 2012; Lyubomirsky et al., 2005). Roche et al. (2014) focused their study on the state of acting mindfully as a leader, meaning to be more focused on the current experience and to be more aware of the present reality. Results have shown that it positively contributes to emotional well-being. When aware of being stronger and emotionally reactive, Xu and Jin (2022) suggest taking mindfulness-based courses to help with high levels of stress. Colbert et al. (2016) did a study on what influence work relationships have on the well-being of individuals. They concluded that those relationships, in a positive manner, play an important role in enhancing job satisfaction and imbuing the tasks undertaken with a heightened sense of significance. As a result, positive work relationships generate positive emotions and enhance not only work but also life satisfaction. This delineates advantages not only for the individual but also for the organization. Xu et al. (2022) critically reflected on the impact of support from family and friends in demanding situations in work life and emphasized the autonomy of leaders. Leaders need to be aware to which degree they occupy family support. Moreover, being emotionally supported is important and beneficial for the well-being of a leader, but involving the family in specific work situations is rather counterproductive and can be followed by relational tension between family members and the leader itself. As Kaluza et al. (2019, p. 34) stated, transformational leadership contributes to a leader's well-being (Bernerth & Hirschfeld, 2016, p. 706). Since a leader's behavior has a high impact on the workforce and the organization itself, they, therefore, outline the importance of leadership development programs as well as courses in general to ensure the health of a leader (Jin et al., 2016; Kaluza et al., 2019; Oh & Roh, 2022; Xu & Jin, 2022).

Resilience

Resilience theory roots in the individual and the upcoming risk factors that can be mentally disruptive. Looking into different characteristics, social and environmental factors, the goal is to find the differences between those who overcome adversity and those who don't (King et al., 2015). Child psychiatry was probably the first research field of interest for resilience. Back in the 1950s, Bowlby (1951) investigated childhood adversity. His work developed from early research on mental hygiene as well as child guidance movements. In the 1980s, scholars studied various protective factors that enhance the resilience of an individual, reduce the impact of risks, and see it positively as an opportunity to learn and grow (Rutter, 1987).

Already in the 1990s, Noe et al. (1990) investigated career motivation and determined resilience as one of its characteristics. It was defined as the ability to deal with challenging events, to be able to structure problems that occur at work, and maintain the existing performance level. Examples of such are coping with time pressure or being exposed to a lack of resources (Noe et al., 1990). In 2002, Luthans (2002, p. 702) defined resilience not only in the context of adversity but stated that resilience is "the capacity to rebound or bounce back from adversity, conflict, failure, or even positive events, progress, and increased responsibility." Bonanno (2004) counteracts the assumption that personal resilience is something rare and describes it as something common and rather potentially gained by every individual (Youssef & Luthans, 2007). He also distinguished it from the term recovery, as recovery often leads to the need of stepping away from daily life and undergoing treatment to get back on track. Resilience by contrast focuses on specific factors which protect a stable equilibrium and foster healthy personality traits that enhance positive outcomes (Bonanno, 2004).

Scholars started resilience research by investigating individuals, but current studies explore the resilience of communities, organizations, cultures, and economies alike (Linnenluecke, 2017) and also try to see the big picture and not only investigate specific factors but the whole process and mechanisms behind resilience (Kossek & Perrigino, 2016).

Kumpfer (2002, p. 183) created a resilience framework that includes internal, personal factors and processes as well as external, environmental factors that lead to a final outcome (see Fig. 10.1). Fig. 10.1 shows the starting point of the necessity and stimuli of resilience, namely specific stressors or challenges (Kumpfer, 2002). These can be several indicators as well as individual perceptions, but for example, in the working context, it might refer to various

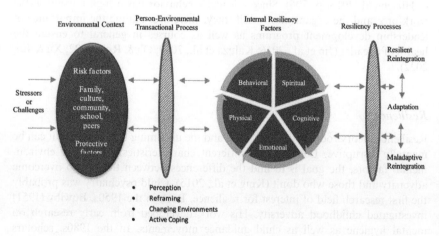

Fig. 10.1.   Resilience Framework. *Source:* Marx (2022, p. 26), based
on Kumpfer (2002, p. 185).

environmental demands which can be too much workload or too many working hours. It can also refer to emotional reactions to such demands or others. In general, the term stress relates to a process, having an effect on personal well-being (Ganster, 2008; Webster et al., 2010). Ranked next is the environmental context which consists of various risk and protective factors that are explained in detail in the first subcategory of this chapter on personal resilience. The topic of person-environmental interactional processes refers to processes between the individual and its environment that include perceiving, reframing when stressors or challenges occur, changing the environment, and actively coping. These actions can happen consciously or unconsciously by, for example, attending prevention programs or seeking a healthy surrounding and therefore reducing upcoming risk factors (Kumpfer, 2002). To cope, the cycle seen in Fig. 10.1 shows the different factors of characteristics and behaviors that will help the individual. Spiritual characteristics are also referred to as motivation and those factors that create direction for the individual. Examples are dreams and goals, purpose in life, hopefulness, optimism, determination, and perseverance (Kumpfer, 2002). Cognitive competencies help the person achieve their goals and dreams due to, e.g., intelligence, interpersonal awareness, and self-reflective skills (Kumpfer, 2002). Referring to those cognitive competencies, behavioral competencies are built on those and need not only thoughts but behavioral action such as social skills, problem-solving skills, or communication skills (Kumpfer, 2002). Regarding emotional characteristics, examples such as happiness, recognition of feelings, humor, and hopefulness are stated (Kumpfer, 2002). Lastly, physical well-being and competencies are mentioned, which refer to good health and health maintenance skills and are described in more detail in the topic of personal well-being of this chapter (Kumpfer, 2002).

The resiliency process is an interaction of the mentioned internal characteristics and the final outcome, meaning the individual had to deal with certain adverse aspects and needed to be able to bounce back through the interaction of their internal abilities and the final outcome of being resilient. Lastly, successful life adaption in stressful situations closes the resilience framework. This can also be predictive of future hurdles and a positive, resilient handling of such as the individual has already dealt with situations and is, therefore, prepared for further events (Kumpfer, 2002).

Resilience of SME Owners

Resilience involves two events. Firstly, adversity, and secondly, the urge for positive adaption (Malik & Garg, 2017). Fisher et al. (2018) differentiate between adversity on the one hand as a high-intensity circumstance, such as a crisis, and on the other hand as a high-frequent situation, such as stress at work (Hartmann et al., 2019). Positive adaption subsequently means the encompassed process that contributes to recovery (McLarnon & Rothstein, 2013). Resilience research started by defining risk factors that can trigger the need for resilience; however, scholars also defined some protective factors such as positive emotions and self-esteem, that protect an individual from such risks (King et al., 2015). Lyubomirsky et al. (2005) showed that the ability to cope in stressful times, meaning to be resilient, is necessary for long-term well-being in the private and business space. Tugade and Fredrickson (2004) stated further characteristics of resilient leaders such as optimistic thinking, energetic approaches to life, and openness to new experiences. Other factors are using humor or relaxation techniques to proactively cultivate positive emotions (Cooke et al., 2019). In the context of work, scholars outline the importance of a good communication base between leader and employee, through crisis as well as positive events. It is important to be transparent as a leader as well as an employee to give everyone the chance to adapt to a situation and obtain care and support (Agarwal, 2021; Tuan, 2022). Another finding, discovered by Kuntz et al. (2017), is the connection between receiving feedback on a regular basis and high levels of resilience, which outlines the importance of social support from work colleagues and/or employees. Sharing values among one another in the business as well as talking about stressful experiences also helps to foster resilience (Lamb & Cogan, 2016).

Masten and Reed (2002) outline three strategies to develop resilience:

(1) Risk-Focused Strategies – A risk factor is something connotated to a negative outcome in the future. It can be described as a measurable characteristic that happens to take place for an individual in a specific situation. Examples mentioned are stressful life events or conflicts, lack of communication, and stress in the work context. Therefore, strategies against those risk factors should reduce their likelihood to happen (Masten & Reed, 2002; Youssef & Luthans, 2007).

(2) Asset-Focused Strategies – These strategies aim to focus on the assets of an individual and deploy them to the right extent. Assets in the working context can not only be existing skills but also personality traits and social relationships. The focus lies on increasing success and building resilience (Youssef & Luthans, 2007). Those assets are also called protective factors (McLarnon & Rothstein, 2013).

(3) Process-Focused Strategies – All in all, it is not only about eliminating risks and adding assets but trying to influence processes for change, i.e., to focus on specific programs or practices that make an individual experience successful and stay motivated to continue and gain self-efficacy (Vanhove et al., 2015).

Methodology

To examine the personal resilience of SME owners, we made use of semi-structured problem-centered interviews. Qualitative research aims to receive deeper insights and gain information that is not obvious from the outside but can only be heard by directly speaking to the people (Bell et al., 2019). The approach offers the option to spontaneously deviate from an interview guideline to ask comprehension and in-depth questions or also vary the wording of the question suitable for the situation. Data were collected in April 2022 in the Tirol, Austria. Table 10.1 shows the characteristics of the five interviewees, who were all owners of family-run SMEs.

Before starting the qualitative content analysis according to Mayring (2016), the voice records were transcribed verbatim. The interviews lasted between 55 and 128 minutes. Text passages and statements were then assigned to specific categories (resulting in three main categories, see results). For coding, a coding guide was developed which included the categories and their definition, anchor samples, which have a prototypical function for the categories, as well as coding rules, to clearly identify which passages belong to the specific category (Mayring, 2016). The codes were inductively derived from the qualitative data and then aligned with theory. The coding scheme can be found in the appendix.

Results

The results will be described on the basis of the main categories: personal stressors, resiliency factors, and the resilience process (see appendix).

Personal Stressors

In this category, the respondents are talking about hurdles they currently face or had to deal with in the past to kick off the interview. A leader must deal with various challenges or stressors daily. Often, these are specific circumstances that the individual has to cope with: "We are currently confronted with a time where we are having major staffing difficulties because we are experiencing a high level of fluctuation. This means that some employees are leaving us, and often for reasons that are incomprehensible to us, that are incomprehensible to me as well. And that's a huge problem at the moment because it's not easy for us to fill these positions" (I1, 143–148). The interviewees also name change in leadership as a personal stressor: "So leadership in the past was much easier than leadership today. Because the young generation, you can no longer lead them the way you

Table 10.1. Overview of Interviewees.

Interviewee	Gender	Years in Position	SME Size	Industry
I1	Male	10	102	Software development
I2	Female	14	28	HR consulting
I3	Male	17	85	Technical device/ manufacturing
I4	Male	12	52	Cosmetics
I5	Female	20	120	Lightning industry

Source: Own illustration.

lead the 60- or 50-year-old generation" (I3, 74–77). Some challenges are related to lack of time: "Challenges are, when you have new employees, to have enough time for them. Getting them well acquainted with the topics. (. . .)" (I5, 154–156) and to make sure to have a proper work–life balance "I am personally challenged with my own time management" (I3, 219). This can have serious impacts for example lead to an "(. . .) increase in emotional pressure" (I2, 217–218).

Resiliency Factors

The factors and characteristics that are mentioned in the context of resiliency factors actively help the owners to cope in challenging times. This main category is divided into the following subcategories: spiritual, cognitive, behavioral, emotional, and physical factors (see Fig. 10.1).

Spiritual

Assigned to this category are all statements that refer to characteristics and actions that are linked to staying motivated as well as creating direction for the individual. Reminding oneself about what makes oneself happy or letting oneself stay positive: "A central point is certainly to say 'okay, I focus on what makes me happy, what I like to do, simply what is important to me and to see that I articulate the small, as well as the larger success stories'" (I2, 328–332). Something that was pointed out very clearly is the fact that it is constant work to stay motivated. "This includes, for example, not looking back too much. To have little self-pity. Little 'would I be, would I have,'. . ." (I4, 172–173), and that it starts from the moment they get up in the morning: "I have a motivational book, a success book, where I read every day, and then on each day sort of write my own passage to bring myself forward, to positively start my day" (I5, 189–192) or "At 6 o'clock in the morning I get up, then I meditate for about half an hour. That's mine. With affirmations, with strengthening" (I3, 246–247).

Cognitive

Under this category, we coded all statements regarding specific cognitive competencies, that help the owner to achieve their goals and dreams. "I just know what I can do as a human being, I know what my development is, I know what my aspiration is and I know exactly what my path looks like in my life" (I3, 70–72). What goes hand in hand with this is authenticity: ". . .that one is then still authentic. When I try things that someone practices who has a completely different style of leadership than I do, then it would no longer be authentic for me" (I4, 290–292). Being an owner means responsibility and sometimes rushed decisions: "So I have also learned to pause, think, come the next day with the answer, but not immediately, as one then often assesses the situation wrongly, or reacts too quickly and often gives the wrong answer" (I2, 263, 267). In general, it is about trying to stay calm and give challenging situations different perspectives, but also the topic of reflection appeals in this context. "That has a lot to do with self-reflection as well" (I5, 357).

Behavioral

Behavioral and social competencies are mainly actions, which are built on cognitive competencies and outline certain skills owners have or which actions they take to cope with specific situations. "I have always enjoyed taking on leadership responsibilities because I simply like people, I like offering solutions, and I have always had a very positive attitude towards interesting encounters" (I1, 81–84) or "I think I have realized, over the years, that I am good at talking to people. I can make very factual and objective/as far as that even exists (laughs), decisions and stand by them. I also take responsibility for the team, so I stand behind them. And I just realized that my opinion or my decisions are respected, are heard" (I4, 43–47). Another behavioral aspect of an owner is to try to develop strengths and accept weaknesses: "I think I am quite good when it comes to recognizing potential, so where are the strengths of the individual team members I've learned very well over the years that yes you can only strengthen strengths, and you can't try to make up for deficiencies by doing more work - that doesn't work..." (I1, 89–94), "...so for me this means not dwell on the weaknesses but really put the strengths in the foreground" (I4, 65–66).

Emotional

This subcategory covers specific characteristics and skills that describe a resilient owner on an emotional level. This has among other things to do with recognizing one's own feelings and seeing when something is too demanding. "To say 'ok, I'm not doing well at the moment, and I just have to deal with it now' and I am able to deal with it because I have created the base for it" (I5, 442–444). "So just to take oneself out on an emotional level and ask for help when needed" (I2, 254–265). "In very hot situations, I personally also take coaching. I am a coach myself, but I also make use of it myself. So, I say that I really let myself be accompanied externally" (I5, 171–174). "To be able to laugh about oneself here and there. So, I think humor relaxes, relieves, and is very important" (I3, 247–248). Also accepting situations that cannot be changed is mentioned: "So you don't have any influence on it and that's very important that you accept it at some point, that you say, 'ok this is Corona, and this is something, it doesn't help if I deal with it 24/7 now', it won't change the situation" (I1, 176–179). What was outlined as another helping approach is to "put the topic, one's own situation in comparison, I think that helps to gain a bit of distance" (I5, 206–208).

Physical

Physical well-being and physical competencies have a decisive influence on the resiliency of an owner. Statements that contribute to physical health are mentioned in this context. The purpose of physical competencies is to actively find the distance to work-related matters. "I very often go for a walk. I live in the country side, I live right by the forest, I'd say. I step outside and in 10 minutes I am in the forest. And that is the most important thing for me. I go home, change clothes and go into the forest. And there I go for half an hour, I mean, it can also be 2 hours. But during the week it is just rather short and I have learned that I am also able to distract myself also with short walks." (I4, 137, 143) or "Endurance sports is a must and climbing or other weight training, that's also, so to speak, 4 times a week sport, that's what I need as my personal balance" (I3, 310–312). To be physically fit is seen to be "a very important element" (I1, 163) to become resilient. Examples of various sports that were mentioned in the interviews are walking, climbing, endurance sports, yoga, tai chi, chi gong, weight training, and hiking. But not only physical sports belong to this category, as it refers to the health context in general: "It's very important to have a fantastic night's sleep, as studies have shown as well, sleep is necessary. This is particularly important in phases of increased workload" (I5, 134–136).

Resiliency Process

It became clear that the need for being resilient is something that is necessary on a regular basis: "One often wishes or imagines that it always goes linear and ideally upwards, but that's not how it is. Neither in my private life nor at work, it's just like a sine curve, I always say. Life is a constant up and down" (I3, 149–152). All interviewees were convinced that one needs to go through such hurdles, and that those occasions make oneself stronger for the future. "Everything that does not kill you makes you stronger and that's just true" (I1, 2013–204). It is about trusting the process and being convinced that better times are coming. This has to do with relying on one's abilities but also strengthening oneself to the extent that risk factors get minimized. However, there will always come unexpected challenges and situations where the individual will fail. It is about "standing up once more than falling down" (I3, 236–237). The interviewees talked about situations that first seemed hopeless but then developed to become something great and rewarding and opened up new opportunities. "Again, and again, you must find a new way and often you really find out in the next step what it was actually good for. And that it has had a very positive effect on everything that comes afterward" (I4, 355–358).

From an interview point of view, the owners seemed very self-reflective, and they see it as important to stay optimistic in daily business but not in an unrealistic way. They seemed to be keeping their eyes on the facts.

Interpretation

Since this chapter focuses on SMEs, various challenges in terms of SMEs and challenges that are coming up in an owner's daily life were addressed as a starting point for resilience. Theory (e.g., Sullivan-Taylor & Branicki, 2011) and the empirical findings overlap in this context as the interviewees of SME owners show that resource scarcity (human or financial resources) or uncertainties impact the company much harder compared to larger companies. Given that owners are usually also involved in operations, responsibilities as well as the pressure to succeed are often much higher. In the same way, as scholars like Bass et al. (2003) and Lord et al. (2017) define the shift in leadership in the last decades, the interviewees also mentioned their experiences in their changing behavior by leading different generations (Jin et al., 2016; Koeslag-Kreunen et al., 2018). This individualized consideration and conscientiousness in transformational leadership happen to be one of the big five personality traits that describe an individual as emotionally stable, persistent, and resilient (Benoliel & Somech, 2012).

Resilience is something that can be learned and needs a lot of dedication rather than being something rare, which is congruent with Bonanno (2004) and the empirical study: "So you don't get that in the cradle, it simply has to do with work and with attitude and taking oneself out of it here and there" (I1, 247–249).

As literature (Malik & Garg, 2017) outlined, resilience involves two events, namely adversity and the urge for positive adaption, which is congruent with the interviews. The interviews revealed that issues like resource scarcity, in terms of human or financial resources, have an impact on the company or the need for dealing with it much quicker due to uncertainties in SMEs compared to larger companies. In the same way, scholars like Bass et al. (2003) and Lord et al. (2017) define the shift in leadership in the last decades; also, the owners were talking about their experiences in their changing behavior by leading different generations. People used to need specific tasks and instructions, nowadays, leaders build the tasks of the employees around their strengths and try to encourage them, which, in transformational leadership is called individualized consideration (Jin et al., 2016).

As Fredrickson (2001) confirms, positive emotions build resilience in individuals and improve emotional well-being. All interviewed owners consider positive thinking and optimism as their basic attitudes and consider it inevitable for someone in a leading position who aims to become resilient. Other factors like humor (Cooke et al., 2019) can contribute to positive emotions too. During the conversations, the owners attached great importance to communication with their employees. Also, Tuan (2022) outlines the significance of a good communication base between leaders and employees. To have a connection with other individuals outlines another basic psychological need, namely relatedness (Ryan & Deci, 2008).

The keywords of intellectual stimulation stand for the actions a transformational leader takes and encourages (Bass et al., 2003). This dimension covers the fact that such leaders want their workforce to be creative and to come up with new ideas. Hereby, it is important to provide a positive error culture, which is also stated by the interviewees as an important point in their firm culture. A lot of risk factors and challenges were mentioned that speak to the need for resilience. Protective factors, like spending time with family and friends or talking to work colleagues to see you are not alone, can counteract those. This helped the leaders through tough times. Lamb and Cogan (2016) consider social support from work colleagues and sharing stressful experiences as a helpful tool to foster resilience. This additionally falls under the asset-focused strategy that is mentioned by Masten and Reed (2002), which covers social relationships as an asset that builds resilience.

Framework for Personal Resilience of SME Owners

The development of personal resilience is a process. In the context of SME leaders, it starts with personal challenges and stressors as well as challenges that are SME-related. The environmental context that includes protective factors such as family, friends, and work colleagues can help among others to counteract those. Further, person-environmental transactional processes, which refer to processes between the individual and their environment, consist of measures and programs from the company that support the leader and the important factor of communicating with the workforce and exchange openly on a regular basis. Not only external but also internal resiliency factors help to foster resilience and moreover are split into spiritual, cognitive, behavioral, emotional, and physical aspects that include skills, actions, and behaviors. Acting as an additional support system, intrinsic motivation, meaning to do something that brings joy, frames those five internal resiliency factors. Lastly, a resiliency process mostly refers to the fact that individuals have had to go through adversity to strengthen their resilience and prevent future hurdles. A synergy of all these components can result in a positive outcome – a resilient individual (see Fig. 10.2).

Implications for Theory and Practice

Pink et al. (2021, p. 789) already discovered resilience as an important factor in personal well-being and job performance. This is also resulting from this study but moreover shows the topic in a more concrete context, namely SME leaders and not online outlines THAT it is important but captures personal coping strategies of those and answers HOW it can be developed. Also, the study of Lombardi et al. (2021), which investigated the unfolding of resilient leadership in times of a pandemic, can be complemented. This present study shows what domains are having an impact on the learning process in the development of resilience. Further, some studies already explored the resilience of organizations (Williams et al., 2017) but mentioned the missing approach on how leaders build endowments that promote resilience in themselves and therefore impact the organization positively. This study fills this gap of research and suggests specific practices that can be found in the developed framework.

With regards to implications for practice, the awareness that resilience is a required tool for SME leaders as well as that it will gain even more importance in the future is a present topic. On the one hand, the framework can support leaders to develop personal resilience on their own as they can see the different components that need to be thought of. That they think stress triggers them personally as well as on an SME level. That they try to identify the protective factors that help them from an

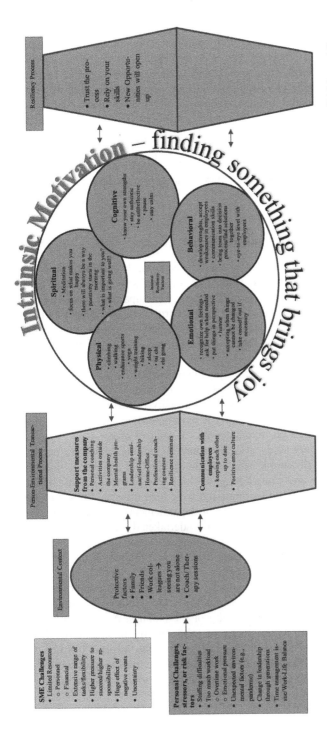

Fig. 10.2. Framework for Personal Resilience of SME Owners and Recommended Actions. *Source:* Marx (2022, p. 49).

environmental perspective. Further, that support measures from the company are going to be requested or self-organized, and that communication with their employees is encouraged. Other than that, with the help of the categorization of the five internal resiliency factors, one can make sure to cover all these aspects. To focus on their goals, identify their own strengths, make decisions together with the team, ask for help when needed and things get too much, and find physical activities that provide a work–life balance. On the other hand, it can also be a reference point for organizations to develop leadership programs that help to foster resilience by making sure to cover all the different components. They could provide seminars to identify their own stress triggers or programs to sharpen self-awareness and strengthen their own resources. Another example is that they could encourage leaders in physical activities and offer opportunities to relax.

Conclusions, Limitations, and Outlook

Building personal resilience is a gradual journey, particularly for SME owners. It initiates with confronting personal challenges and stressors, along with those specific to SMEs. The surrounding environment, encompassing protective elements like family, friends, and colleagues, plays a crucial role in mitigating these challenges. Resilience, however, extends beyond external factors; internal elements, categorized into spiritual, cognitive, behavioral, emotional, and physical aspects (encompassing skills, actions, and behaviors), contribute significantly. Intrinsic motivation, driven by a sense of joy in one's actions acts as an additional pillar, supporting these internal resilience factors. Ultimately, the resilience process indicates that owner-managers undergo adversity to fortify their resilience and preemptively tackle future obstacles. The harmonious integration of all these components culminates in a positive outcome – a resilient owner.

The current exploratory study also has some limitations, which we need to consider: First, the small sample size and the qualitative approach, thus the findings are exploratory and cannot be generalized (Saunders et al., 2012). Second, the interviews were held in German and were then translated into English, which could possibly change the meaning of the statements to a certain extent. Third, the lack of validity, since the study was undertaken during tough times – as the pandemic created a big shift in every company. Some of the interviewees mentioned that their answers would have looked very different if the interview would have been conducted 3 years ago.

Since the assumption exists that resilience will gain even more importance in the future, several options for future research arise. More interviews with owners could be conducted to increase the validity of the findings. A case study in an SME could be undertaken, with a focus on validating the findings through the involvement of additional stakeholders, beyond just the owners. Further, the study could be extended in a quantitative survey and also include leaders of larger companies to find out differences or overlaps across personal stressors, resilience factors, and processes.

In summary, the development of personal resilience is a multifaceted process for SME owners, involving the navigation of personal and SME-related challenges. Ultimately, the resilience process entails overcoming adversity, with a synergy of these components culminating in the emergence of a resilient owner-manager.

References

Agarwal, P. (2021). Shattered but smiling: Human resource management and the wellbeing of hotel employees during COVID-19. *International Journal of Hospitality Management, 93*, 1–10.

Altig, D., Baker, S., Barrero, J., Bloom, N., Bunn, P., Chen, S., Davis, S. J., Leather, J., Meyer, B. H., Mihaylov, E., Mizen, P., Parker, N., Renault, T., Smietanka, P., & Thwaites, G. (2020). Economic uncertainty before and during the Covid-19 pandemic. *Journal of Public Economics*, 1–13.

Avolio, B. J., Bass, B. M., & Jung, D. I. (1999). Re-examining the components of transformational and transactional leadership using the multifactor leadership. *Journal of Occupational and Organizational Psychology, 72*(4), 441–462.

Bakker, A. B., & Sanz-Vergel, A. I. (2013). Weekly work engagement and flourishing: The role of hindrance and challenge job demands. *Journal of Vocational Behavior, 83*(3), 397–409.

Bass, B. M., Avolio, B. J., Jung, D. I., & Berson, Y. (2003). Predicting unit performance by assessing transformational and transactional leadership. *Journal of Applied Psychology, 88*(2), 207–218.

Bass, B. M., & Riggio, R. E. (2006). *Transformational leadership*. Psychology Press.

Bell, E., Bryman, A., & Harley, B. (2019). *Business research methods*. Oxford University Press.

Benoliel, P., & Somech, A. (2012). The health and performance effects of participative leadership: Exploring the moderating role of the Big Five personality dimensions. *European Journal of Work & Organizational Psychology, 23*(2), 277–294.

Bernerth, J. B., & Hirschfeld, R. R. (2016). The subjective well-being of group leaders as explained by the quality of leader–member exchange. *The Leadership Quarterly, 27*(4), 697–710.

Bharati, P., & Chaudhury, A. (2009). SMEs and competitiveness: The role of information systems. *Management Science and Information Systems Faculty Publication Series, 15*, 1–10.

Blackburn, R. A., Hart, M., & Wainwright, T. (2013). Small business performance: Business, strategy and owner-manager characteristics. *Journal of Small Business and Enterprise Development, 20*(1), 8–27.

Bonanno, G. A. (2004). Loss, trauma, and human resilience: Have we underestimated the human capacity to thrive after extremely aversive events? *American Psychologist, 59*(1), 20–28.

Bowlby, J. (1951). Maternal care and mental health. *Social Service Review, 25*(3), 423–424.

Branicki, L. J., Sullivan-Taylor, B., & Livschitz, S. R. (2017). How entrepreneurial resilience generates resilient SMEs. *International Journal of Entrepreneurial Behavior & Research, 24*(7), 1244–1263.

Colbert, A. E., Bono, J. E., & Purvanova, R. K. (2016). Flourishing via workplace relationships: Moving beyond instrumental support. *Academy of Management Journal, 59*(4), 1–64.

Connelly, S., & Ruark, G. (2010). Leadership style and activating potential moderators of the relationships among leader emotional displays and outcomes. *The Leadership Quarterly, 21*(5), 745–764.

Cooke, F. L., Cooper, B., Bartram, T., Wang, J., & Mei, H. (2019). Mapping the relationships between high-performance work systems, employee resilience and engagement: A study of the banking industry in China. *International Journal of Human Resource Management, 30*(8), 1–37.

Cragg, P., Caldeira, M., & Ward, J. (2011). Organizational information systems competences in small and medium-sized enterprises. *Information & Management, 48*(8), 353–363.

de Clercq, D., & Belausteguigoitia, I. (2017). Mitigating the negative effect of perceived organizational politics on organizational citizenship behavior: Moderating roles of contextual and personal resources. *Journal of Management and Organization, 23*(5), 1–45.

Demerouti, E., Bakker, A. B., & Gevers, J. M. (2015). Job crafting and extra-role behavior: The role of work engagement and flourishing. *Journal of Vocational Behavior, 91*, 87–96.

Diener, E. (1984). Subjective well-being. *Psychological Bulletin, 95*(3), 542–575.

Fisher, D. M., Ragsdale, J. M., & Fisher, E. C. (2018). The importance of definitional and temporal issues in the study of resilience. *Applied Psychology, 68*(4), 583–620.

Fredrickson, B. L. (2001). The role of positive emotions in positive psychology: The broaden-and-build theory of positive emotions. *American Psychologist, 56*(3), 218–226.

Fredrickson, B. L., & Losada, M. F. (2005). Positive affect and the complex dynamics of human flourishing. *American Psychologist, 60*(7), 678–686.

Ganster, D. C. (2008). Measurement challenges for studying work-related stressors and strains. *Human Resource Management Review, 18*(4), 259–270.

Gelinas, R., & Bigras, Y. (2004). The characteristics and features of SMEs: Favorable or unfavorable o logistics integration? *Journal of Small Business Management, 42*(3), 263–278.

Guzzo, R. F., Wang, X., Madera, J. M., & Abbott, J. (2021). Organizational trust in times of COVID-19: Hospitality employees' affective responses to managers' communication. *International Journal of Hospitality Management, 93*, 1–11.

Hartmann, S., Weiss, M., Newman, A., & Hoegl, M. (2019). Resilience in the workplace: A multilevel review and synstudy. *Applied Psychology, 69*(3), 913–959.

Heidt, M., Gerlach, J. P., & Buxmann, P. (2019). Investigating the security divide between SME and large companies: How SME characteristics influence organizational IT security investments. *Information Systems Frontiers, 21*(6), 1285–1305.

Hunt, J. G., Tichy, N. M., & Devanna, M. A. (1988). The transformational leader. *Administrative Science Quarterly, 33*(1), 132–135.

Huppert, F. A. (2009). Psychological well-being: Evidence regarding its causes and consequences. *Applied Psychology: Health and Well-Being, 1*(2), 137–164.

Iborra, M., Safon, V., & Dolz, C. (2020). What explains the resilience of SMEs? Ambidexterity capability and strategic consistency. *Long Range Planning, 53*(6), 1–15.

Jin, S., Seo, M. G., & Shapiro, D. L. (2016). Do happy leaders lead better? Affective and attitudinal antecedents of transformational leadership. *The Leadership Quarterly, 27*(1), 64–84.

Judge, T. A., & Piccolo, R. F. (2004). Transformational and transactional leadership: A meta-analytic test of their relative validity. *Journal of Applied Psychology, 89*(5), 755–768.

Kaluza, A. J., Boer, D., Buengeler, C., & van Dick, R. (2019). Leadership behaviour and leader self-reported well-being: A review, integration and meta-analytic examination. *Work & Stress, 34*(1), 34–56.

Kimhi, S., Marciano, H., Eshel, Y., & Adini, B. (2020). Resilience and demographic characteristics predicting distress during the COVID-19 crisis. *Social Science & Medicine, 265*, 1–6.

King, D. D., Newman, A., & Luthans, F. (2015). Not if, but when we need resilience in the workplace. *Journal of Organizational Behavior, 37*(5), 782–786.

Kniffin, K. M., Narayanan, J., Anseel, F., Antonakis, J., Ashford, S. P., Bakker, A. B., Bamberger, P., Bapuji, H., Bhave, D. P., Choi, V. K., Creary, S. J., Demerouti, E., Flynn, F. J., Gelfand, M. J., Greer, L. L., Johns, G., Kesebir, S., Klein, P. G., Lee, S. Y., . . . Vugt, M. V. (2021). COVID-19 and the workplace: Implications, issues, and insights for future research and action. *American Psychologist, 76*(1), 63–77.

Koeslag-Kreunen, M., van den Bossche, P., Hoven, M., van der Klink, M., & Gijselaers, W. (2018). When leadership powers team learning: A meta-analysis. *Small Group Research, 49*(4), 475–513.

Kossek, E. E., & Perrigino, M. B. (2016). Resilience: A review using a grounded integrated occupational approach. *Academy of Management Annals, 10*(1), 727–797.

Kumpfer, K. L. (2002). Factors and processes contributing to resilience. In *Resilience and development* (pp. 179–224). Springer.

Kuntz, J., Connell, P., & Naswall, K. (2017). Workplace resources and employee resilience: The role of regulatory profiles. *Career Development International, 22*(4), 419–435.

Lamb, D., & Cogan, N. (2016). Coping with work-related stressors and building resilience in mental health workers: A comparative focus group study using interpretative phenomenological analysis. *Journal of Occupational and Organizational Psychology, 89*(3), 474–492.

Leyden, D. P., & Link, A. N. (2004). Transmission of risk-averse behavior in small firms. *Small Business Economics, 23*(3), 255–259.

Linnenluecke, M. K. (2017). Resilience in business and management research: A review of influential publications and a research agenda. *International Journal of Management Reviews, 19*(1), 4–30.

Lips-Wiersma, M., & Wright, S. (2012). Measuring the meaning of meaningful work. *Group & Organization Management, 37*(5), 655–685.

Lombardi, S., E Cunha, M. P., & Giustiniano, L. (2021). Improvising resilience: The unfolding of resilient leadership in COVID-19 times. *International Journal of Hospitality Management, 95*, 1–13.

Lord, R. G., Day, D. V., Zaccaro, S. J., Avolio, B. J., & Eagly, A. H. (2017). Leadership in applied psychology: Three waves of theory and research. *Journal of Applied Psychology, 102*(3), 434–451.

Luthans, F. (2002). The need for and meaning of positive organizational behavior. *Journal of Organizational Behavior, 23*(6), 695–706.

Lyngdoh, T., Liu, A. H., & Sridhar, G. (2018). Applying positive psychology to selling behaviors: A moderated–mediation analysis integrating subjective well-being, coping and organizational identity. *Journal of Business Research, 92,* 142–153.

Lyubomirsky, S., King, L., & Diener, E. (2005). The benefits of frequent positive affect: Does happiness lead to success? *Psychological Bulletin, 131*(6), 803–855.

Malik, P., & Garg, P. (2017). Learning organization and work engagement: The mediating role of employee resilience. *International Journal of Human Resource Management, 31*(8), 1–24.

Marx, L. (2022). *It's your job to make yourself happy. Developing personal resilience as a leader within an SME context.* MCI The Entrepreneurial School.

Masten, A. S., & Reed, M. G. J. (2002). Resilience in development. In C. R. Snyder & S. Lopez (Eds.), *Handbook of positive psychology* (pp. 74–88). Oxford University Press.

Mayring, P. (2016). *Einführung in die qualitative Sozialforschung: Eine Anleitung zu qualitativem Denken.* Beltz.

McLarnon, M. J. W., & Rothstein, M. G. (2013). Development and initial validation of the workplace resilience inventory. *Journal of Personnel Psychology, 12*(2), 63–73.

Noe, R. A., Noe, A. W., & Bachhuber, J. A. (1990). An investigation of the correlates of career motivation. *Journal of Vocational Behavior, 37*(3), 340–356.

Oh, S., & Roh, S. C. (2022). Intrinsic motivation for work activities is associated with empathy: Investigating the indirect relationship between intrinsic motivation for work activities and social support through empathy and prosocial behavior. *Personality and Individual Differences, 189,* 1–6.

Pink, J., Gray, N. S., O'Connor, C., Knowles, J. R., Simkiss, N. J., & Snowden, R. J. (2021). Psychological distress and resilience in first responders and health care workers during the COVID-19 pandemic. *Journal of Occupational and Organizational Psychology, 94*(4), 789–807.

Raghunathan, R., & Trope, Y. (2002). Walking the tightrope between feeling good and being accurate: Mood as a resource in processing persuasive messages. *Journal of Personality and Social Psychology, 83*(3), 510–525.

Ramlall, S. J., Al-Kahtani, A., & Damanhouri, H. (2014). Positive organizational behavior in the workplace: A cross-cultural perspective. *International Journal of Management & Information Systems, 18*(3), 149–154.

Roche, M., Haar, J. M., & Luthans, F. (2014). The role of mindfulness and psychological capital on the well-being of leaders. *Journal of Occupational Health Psychology, 19*(4), 1–14.

Rutter, M. (1987). Psychosocial resilience and protective mechanisms. *American Journal of Orthopsychiatry, 57*(3), 316–331.

Ryan, R. M., & Deci, E. L. (2008). A self-determination theory approach to psychotherapy: The motivational basis for effective change. *Canadian Psychology/ Psychologie Canadienne, 49*(3), 186–193.

Ryff, C. D. (2019). Entrepreneurship and eudaimonic well-being: Five venues for new science. *Journal of Business Venturing, 34*(4), 646–663.

Saunders, M., Lewis, P., & Thornhill, A. (2012). *Research methods for business students.* Pearson Education Limited.

Smallbone, D., Deakins, D., Battisti, M., & Kitching, J. (2012). Small business responses to a major economic downturn: Empirical perspectives from New

Zealand and the United Kingdom. *International Small Business Journal: Researching Entrepreneurship, 30*(7), 754–777.

Sommer, S. A., Howell, J. M., & Hadley, C. N. (2015). Keeping positive and building strength. *Group & Organization Management, 41*(2), 172–202.

Seligman, M. E. P., & Csikszentmihalyi, M. (2000). Positive psychology: An introduction. *American Psychologist, 55*(1), 5–14.

Sonnentag, S., & Grant, A. M. (2012). Doing good at work feels good at home, but not right away: When and why perceived prosocial impact predicts positive affect. *Personnel Psychology, 65*(3), 495–530.

Sullivan-Taylor, B., & Branicki, L. (2011). Creating resilient SMEs: Why one size might not fit all. *International Journal of Production Research, 49*(18), 5565–5579.

Sweetman, D., Luthans, F., Avey, J. B., & Luthans, B. C. (2010). Relationship between positive psychological capital and creative performance. *Canadian Journal of Administrative Sciences/Revue Canadienne Des Sciences de l'Administration, 28*(1), 4–13.

Tu, Y., Lu, X., Wang, S., & Liu, Y. (2020). When and why conscientious employees are proactive: A three-wave investigation on employees' conscientiousness and organizational proactive behavior. *Personality and Individual Differences, 159*, 1–6.

Tuan, L. T. (2022). Leader crisis communication and salesperson resilience in face of the COVID-19: The roles of positive stress mindset, core beliefs challenge, and family strain. *Industrial Marketing Management, 102*, 488–502.

Tugade, M. M., & Fredrickson, B. L. (2004). Resilient individuals use positive emotions to bounce back from negative emotional experiences. *Journal of Personality and Social Psychology, 86*(2), 320–333.

van Hooff, M. L. M., & de Pater, I. E. (2017). Let's have fun tonight: The role of pleasure in daily recovery from work. *Applied Psychology, 66*(3), 359–381.

Vanhove, A. J., Herian, M. N., Perez, A. L. U., Harms, P. D., & Lester, P. B. (2015). Can resilience be developed at work? A meta-analytic review of resilience-building programme effectiveness. *Journal of Occupational and Organizational Psychology, 89*(2), 1–31.

Webster, J. R., Beehr, T. A., & Christiansen, N. D. (2010). Toward a better understanding of the effects of hindrance and challenge stressors on work behavior. *Journal of Vocational Behavior, 76*(1), 68–77.

Williams, T. A., Gruber, D. A., Sutcliffe, K. M., Shepherd, D. A., & Zhao, E. Y. (2017). Organizational response to adversity: Fusing crisis management and resilience research streams. *The Academy of Management Annals, 11*(2), 733–769.

Xu, F., & Jin, L. (2022). Impact of daily entrepreneurial stressors on long-term transformational leader behaviors and well-being: Differences in experienced and nascent entrepreneurs. *Journal of Business Research, 139*, 280–291.

Xu, T., Yi, L. J., Liang, C. S., Gu L., Peng C., Chen, G. H., & Jiménez-Herrera, M. F. (2022). The impact of Mindfulness-Based Stress Reduction (MBSR) on psychological outcomes and quality of life in patients with lung cancer: A meta-analysis. *Frontiers in Psychology, 13*, 901247.

Yew Wong, K., & Aspinwall, E. (2004). Characterizing knowledge management in the small business environment. *Journal of Knowledge Management, 8*(3), 44–61.

Youssef, C. M., & Luthans, F. (2007). Positive organizational behavior in the workplace. *Journal of Management, 33*(5), 774–800.

Appendix

Table A1. Coding Scheme.

Content Analysis

Main Category	Sub Category	Definition	Anchor Example	Coding Rules
Personal stressors		An initiating event a person experiences that outlines the need of resilience	We are currently confronted with a time, where we are having major staffing difficulties because we are experiencing a high level of fluctuation. This means that some employees are leaving us, and often for reasons that are incomprehensible to us, that are incomprehensible to me as well. And that's a huge problem at the moment, because it's not easy for us to fill these positions (I1, 143–148).	Inclusion of all statements which bring hurdles to the leader and could cause the need for resilience.
Resiliency factors		Characteristics and behaviors that help the individual internally		Considering all statements that happen to help the individuum from the inside to cope
	Spiritual	Characteristics and actions that are referred to motivation and	A central point is certainly to say "okay, I focus on what makes me happy, what I like	Inclusion of all statements that create direction for the individual to

Table A1. *(Continued)*

Content Analysis

Main Category	Sub Category	Definition	Anchor Example	Coding Rules
		those factors that create direction for the individual	to do, simply what is important to me and see that I articulate the small, as well as the larger successes." But other than that, it's really constant work to maintain a positive attitude (I2, 328–333).	achieve where they want to go
	Cognitive	Competencies that help the individual to achieve their goals and dreams	I just know what I can do as a human being, I know what my development is, I know what my aspiration is and I know exactly how my path looks like in my life (I3, 70–72).	Inclusion of all statements that mention the cognitive competencies of an individual that help to achieve goals
	Behavioral	Skills, and mainly actions that are built on cognitive competencies.	I have always enjoyed taking on leadership responsibilities because I simply like people, I like offering solutions, and I have always had a very positive attitude toward interesting encounters (I1+D11, 81–84).	Inclusion of all statements that mention specific skills the leader has or which actions they take

(Continued)

Table A1. *(Continued)*

Main Category	Sub Category	Definition	Anchor Example	Coding Rules
Content Analysis				
	Emotional	Emotional characteristics and skills that characterize a resilient individual	To say "ok, I'm not doing well at the moment and I just have to deal with it now" and I am able deal with it, because I have created the base for it (I5, 442–444).	Considering all statements that describe specific emotional characteristics and skills
	Physical	Good health and health maintenance skills that help the individual with their resiliency	I very often go for a walk. I live in the country side, I live right by the forest, I'd say. I step outside and in 10 minutes I am in the forest. And that is the most important thing for me. I go home, change clothes and go into the forest. And there I go for half an hour, I mean, it can also be 2 hours. But during the week it is just rather short and I have learned that I am also able to distract myself also with short walks (I4, 137, 143).	Considering all statements that are mentioned, that contribute to the physical well-being of the individual

Table A1. *(Continued)*

Content Analysis

Main Category	Sub Category	Definition	Anchor Example	Coding Rules
Resiliency processes		Includes processes (recoveries), by which the individual had to deal with certain aspects, needed to be able to bounce back and therefore became more resilient in the long run.	One often wishes or imagines that it always goes linear and ideally upwards, but that's not how it is. Neither in my private life nor at work, it's just like a sine curve, I always say. Life is a constant up and down (I3, 149–152).	Considering all statements from former experiences (recoveries) that by looking back made the leader more resilient

Source: Own illustration.

Conclusion

Chapter 11

Innovation and Social Impact in Responsible Management Education

Desiree Wieser[a], Regina Obexer[a] and Alfred Rosenbloom[b]

[a]MCI | The Entrepreneurial School, Austria
[b]Dominican University, USA

Abstract

In the face of pressing global challenges, the role of educational institutions in fostering responsible management practices has never been more crucial. Drawing on the preceding chapters, this concluding contribution explores the nexus of innovation and social impact within the realm of responsible management education (RME), offering a synthesis of perspectives and strategies for driving positive change at micro-, meso-, and macro level. The authors argue that the frequent inertia of higher education institutions must be overcome with urgent action in reshaping curricula, teaching methodologies, and institutional policies to foster sustainable development and effect positive social impact. The chapter emphasizes the role of innovation in education and the development and diffusion of responsible business practices as a means to catalyze systemic change.

Keywords: Responsible management education; innovation; social impact; resilience; positive change

Articles about sustainability, responsible management, and ethical business conduct often start with listing the numerous crises that the world is facing as humanity finds itself in the middle of a historical transition. While this realization for many people can lead to paralysis and inaction (if not reaction), many of us have realized that we must act now if we want to have a world in which all people prosper and all forms of life flourish. Educational institutions, as major agents in forming our society, play a vital role in facilitating and accelerating this transition. At the same time, we have to admit that just like businesses and government institutions, universities and business schools are often overwhelmed with the

Innovation in Responsible Management Education, 269–276
doi:10.1108/978-1-83549-464-620241016

challenge of really instigating and driving the systemic changes required to put the world on a more sustainable trajectory, and often do not know where to start to take action in the first place. The chapters in this book provide a range of positive examples where individuals at different levels in management schools have not succumbed to paralysis and inaction, but have taken action, created opportunities, experimented with new ways of doing things, and have brought others along with them to champion change.

The goal of this final chapter, then, is to synthesize various paths along which positive action can be taken in responsible management education (RME). Our intent is to highlight aspects of social impact and innovation in RME as they are enacted through institutional policies, curriculum designs, teaching and learning methods, competence frameworks, and business practices described in the preceding chapters. We commence by defining what we mean by innovation and social impact in RME before delving into the individual chapters to discuss core messages on these issues. We conclude with a synthesis of the overall implications derived from these 11 chapters.

Let's start with *innovation*. In its essence, innovation combines two aspects, namely novelty and advancement. Novelty refers to the creation of something new and advancement to the change that results as a consequence of this new idea (Evans & Leppmann, 1970). According to Serdyukov (2017), the primary focus of innovation in education should be on teaching and learning theory and practice. Following this call, we define innovation in RME as the development, adoption, adaptation, and diffusion of responsibility in business education, which includes, for example, new ideas in curriculum design, new ways of teaching and learning, but also the reforming of institutional policies and frameworks. These novel approaches are influenced by and, in turn, impact the "real world" context of business practice and the economic, social, political and regulatory developments shaping it.

Social impact refers generally to the outcomes for society of a certain intervention, action, or measure that are ideally positive, but which may have negative unintended consequences. While a common definition of "social impact" in higher education has yet to emerge (Rawhouser et al., 2019), there is growing agreement that social impact must become an increasingly important goal for all organizations, as every organization can and should contribute to the overall well-being of society. In higher education, social impact has different labels, including Third Mission, Social Responsibility, Societal Impact, Community Engagement, etc. (Godonoga & Sporn, 2023).

Within the private sector, Polman and Winston (2021) capture the essence of social impact when they challenge every executive, every manager, every small business owner, and every entrepreneur to be "net positive," that is, to manage their business with the imperative to actively make the world a better place because one's business is in it. Visser (2022), with his holistic concept of thriving, embodies our other theme: Innovation. For Visser (2022), innovation is the singular force that drives positive, purposeful, system-wide regenerative change in nature, society, and the economy that enables the entire planet to prosper and flourish indefinitely (i.e., to thrive). Further, Carl and Menter (2021) discuss what impact universities' key activity areas, teaching, research, and knowledge as well as technological transfer have on firms' social engagement. They found that teaching shows the most effect by virtue of the impact that university alumni have when they enter the workforce.

Unfortunately, business school graduates have also been accused of being irresponsible business leaders, who engage in unsustainable and unethical business practices that have contributed to economic, societal, and environmental crises (Pless & Maak, 2011). Responsible management emerged as a collective acknowledgment that businesses *did* bear responsibility for these crises and that responsible leaders should take responsibility for positive as well as negative societal impacts caused by economic activity, while balancing stakeholders' economic, environment, and societal interests beyond traditional organizational borders (Laasch et al., 2020). This requires, as Patzer et al. (2018, p. 345) put it "that responsible leaders become conscious initiators and moderators of stakeholder dialogues." And yet, we see little progress and even decline in some sectors and places in the global effort to reach a more sustainable and equitable future (Leal Filho et al., 2023).

Against this background, it is legitimate that many scholars, but also practitioners, are questioning the role and social impact of RME's current model. Calls for more radical approaches are becoming more prominent (Laasch, 2024), where the role of education in preparing responsible leaders who contribute to the well-being of society and the environment are at the very center of management education. RME should aim to prioritize social and environmental considerations, preparing future leaders to not only make ethical, socially just and environmentally sustainable decisions, but also to question existing and invent new economic paradigms that support those decisions.

RME is believed to play a crucial role in shaping students' values, attitudes, and intentions, particularly in relation to corporate social responsibility (Haski-Leventhal, 2020). The United Nation's "Principles of Responsible Management Education" (PRME) provide a framework for integrating social responsibility, sustainability, and partnership values into management education (Tavanti, 2012; Morsing, 2022). However, while RME can enhance students' understanding and attitudes toward ethical decision-making and sustainability issues, it may not always lead to significant behavioral change (Zhang & Szerensci, 2023) or to positive social impact.

So, what we see is (a) a need for innovation in RME and (b) RME with tangible outcomes in terms of social impact and paradigmatic change. In the remainder of this concluding chapter, we discuss concepts of innovation and social impact by analyzing and synthesizing what the authors of the preceding 11 chapters say or infer about these concepts, but also critically questioning whether the strategies and approaches discussed go far enough.

The Macro Level: Underlying Values, Curricula, and Institutional Policies

We start with a critical view of the very foundation of the current economic system underlying much of today's business and management curricula, which still takes capitalism and its economic logic of growth, profit, and consumer primacy as given (Kim & Shinohara, Chapter 1). The question whether these prevailing principles, theories, and tenets are still suitable or indeed able to meet the needs of our postmodern society is becoming increasingly mute. To create the change makers of tomorrow, it is not enough to proceed as we have always done. When we ask what management education should be and should do, we have to look at the underlying assumptions and values underpinning it. By acknowledging the shortcomings of capitalism (Barney & Rangan, 2019) and ethical failures in management leadership (Ghoshal, 2005), higher education institutions and business schools can pave the way for the further development of management education and a successful transition into a more responsible and sustainable future.

Translating this into transformative curricula will require intelligent critique of current models and the co-creation of new models, resulting in strong forms of collaboration between current and emerging stakeholder groups, and the courage to face down those who profit from maintaining the status quo. The status quo often appears in the form of a "hidden curriculum" (Blasco, 2012), where underlying messages, behaviors, and values conveyed to student conflict with the RME core intention, or where curricular content in some subjects contradict those in RME classes (Fearon, Chapter 3).

The adoption of a competence-based approach across management disciplines to develop responsible and sustainable capabilities is a promising approach in this endeavor (Mach & Ebersberger, Chapter 2), as it becomes clear that new models and behaviors need to be cultivated. This involves educating learners in defining, applying, and negotiating sustainability values and responsible decision-making at the basic level. At the proficiency level, students should be trained to become active, encouraging them to engage in interventions toward positive social impact.

If business schools, and in a wider sense all higher education institution, are to question and change deeply held beliefs and engrained economic and social systems, they first must fully accept their crucial role in the transition process toward a more responsible and sustainable future. Unless institutions vigorously commit not only to aligning research and innovation with societal values to cultivating a generation of responsible leaders equipped to address pressing global challenges but also to rewarding such research, curriculum change may be indeed impossible. We adapt Davies et al.'s (2020) insight to RME by noting "[c]urrent institutional structures, that [value] short term research performance management and assessments...do not...lend themselves to long term, integrative, extensive theory building and testing work [which is at the core of responsible management]. Current research expectations mean [that management education's incentive structure] privileges short term, empirically driven, fragmented (journal article sized) chunks of research" (p. 2928) rather than more integrative, long-term, applied research required by RME.

Thus, it is time to take a step back, calling on the accountability of educational institutions to rethink their missions, policies, incentive structures, and strategies. Responsible Research & Innovation (RRI), for example, is an emerging and transformative policy framework for universities that provides a strategic approach to align research and innovation with societal values, needs, and expectations. Recognized as a catalyst for system change in higher education, RRI encourages universities to proactively address global, social challenges and engage in ethical governance and evaluation of research outcomes. RRI can serve as an institutional roadmap and a commitment that fosters a quadruple helix approach, going beyond the third mission, in strengthening relationships between academia, industry, public authorities, and civil society (Grammenou, Chapter 4). We note in passing that RRI overlaps significantly with the principles and goals of Responsible Research in Business Management (RRBM), the first principle of which is that management and business research must benefit society "whether a study is basic or applied, strategic or tactical, theoretical or empirical" (Bolton, 2022, p. 109).

The Micro Level: Teaching and Learning Approaches

A next question to answer, then, is how students learn best and which RME teaching methods are particularly valuable to instill in students a sense of social responsibility, a deep understanding of the interconnectedness between business, policy, and civil society, and the agency that they can affect change. Again, we are not there yet (Mason & Rosenbloom, 2023). Educators play a crucial role in this transformative process. Innovative educators, who are willing to experiment, to shift from traditional roles to become lead learners and, for example, community facilitators to guide students in how to work collectively to eventually master transformation, are key. Active participation in civil society initiatives and linking education to real-world issues can support the development of students' social integrity and responsibility, often overlooked in traditional business education. By connecting Sustainable Development Goals (SDGs) to practical experiences, students gain a broader understanding of systemic impacts and are empowered to effect positive change. For example, the immersion in local welfare situations can help students comprehend the social and environmental consequences of economic practices, promoting critical thinking and sustainable habits, such as reduced consumption and improved waste management (Kreikebaum & Singh, Chapter 6). Working closely with local entities is believed to enhance the relevance and effectiveness of educational initiatives, allowing students to experience firsthand what decision making and dealing with unexpected issues might be like. This approach can lead to innovations in management education that are contextually sensitive and tailored to unique cultural and societal aspects, thereby fostering students' soft skills and a more meaningful and sustainable impact on the local community (Mohan, Chapter 7).

At the same time, we need to equip students with imaginative and foresight capabilities to address complex challenges that lead to positive social change. Many scholars are highlighting the integration of futures thinking and artistic elements in this regard and have adopted a forward-looking perspective to fostering student creativity, vision, and adaptability (Bierwisch & Schmitz, Chapter 5). Also, play-based learning, which simultaneously enhances participant engagement while building a foundation of dynamic experiences for emerging and radically innovative solutions to global challenges, has been identified as an effective method in RME (Mayr & Baumgartner, Chapter 8). Various and diverse formats are conceivable in this light. Our view as well is to elevate nontraditional and dynamic formats, such as a more intentional and active integration of students into research conferences. Research conferences can be reshaped to be more inclusive and dynamic for students (e.g., dedicated agenda points, student participation in all sessions, etc.). Conferences can provide a safe platform for exchange and learning between juniors and experts, but even more so for the development of new ideas to generate and co-create real world impact.

The Context: Complexity of the Real World

The chapters in the final part of this volume draw our attention to the space where the agents of our educational endeavors, students and then alumni, eventually apply their learning and where social impact and innovation are enacted – the business world. These chapters shed light on different contexts, thereby highlighting the diversity of realities business education is challenged to prepare students for. However, what these chapters have in common is the complexity of 21st century business environment, the nature of local and global business drivers and their impacts, as well as a common human dimension which underlies the challenges and opportunities we observe and which provide a basis for social impact and innovation that goes beyond local fixes and isolated solutions. Similarly, across both chapters we observe a common theme of change, be it change that creates new, circular economic models that decrease pollution and resource exploitation (Steinbiß & Fröhlich, Chapter 09), or the necessary change in leadership models, competences, and mindsets needed by business leaders in this transitory state of uncertainty (Zehrer, Marx & Glowka, Chapter 10). Lastly, we note the common theme of resilience. When applied in the context of RME, resilience not only enables students to build skills and competences but also gives them the ability to overcome obstacles, deal with and learn from failure, and maintain a healthy sense of self-worth in adverse circumstances.

So, what is the essence, the message we need to take forward in order for this volume to drive change and fulfill its promise of creating social impact?

First, higher education institutions must grasp the intricate and multi-faceted nature of the challenges confronting society today. This entails removing blinders, acknowledging prevailing circumstances, embracing experiential learning – as often advocated in business schools – and actively engaging with these issues. Second, they must acknowledge the imperative for change within the educational landscape, while also cultivating and passing on the resilience necessary to navigate these challenges. Third, we should recognize that drawing lessons from real-world scenarios can catalyze innovations in curriculum design, as well as teaching and learning methodologies and vice versa. By implementing these measures, educational institutions can ultimately empower their graduates to evolve into responsible changemakers, enabling them to fulfill the profound and vital impact that we all aspire to witness.

References

Barney, J., & Rangan, S. (2019). Editors' comments: Why do we need a special issue on new theoretical perspectives on market-based economic systems? *Academy of Management Review, 44*(1), 1–5.

Blasco, M. (2012). Aligning the hidden curriculum of management education with PRME: An inquiry-based framework. *Journal of Management Education, 36*(3), 364–388. https://doi.org/10.1177/1052562911420213

Bolton, R. N. (2022). The convergence of sustainability and marketing: Transforming marketing to respond to a new world. *Australasian Marketing Journal, 30*(2), 107–112.

Carl, J., & Menter, M. (2021). The social impact of universities: Assessing the effects of the three university missions on social engagement. *Studies in Higher Education, 46*(5), 965–976. https://doi.org/10.1080/03075079.2021.1896803

Davies, I., Oates, C. J., Tynan, C., Carrigan, M., Casey, K., Heath, T., Henninger, C. E., Lichrou, M., McDonagh, P., McDonald, S., McKechnie, S., McLeay, F., O'Malley, L. & Wells, V. (2020). Seeking sustainable futures in marketing and consumer research. *European Journal of Marketing, 54*(11), 2911–2939.

Evans, R., & Leppmann, P. (1970). *Resistance to innovation in higher education.* Jossey-Bass Publishers Inc.

Ghoshal, S. (2005). Bad management theories are destroying good management practices. *The Academy of Management Learning and Education, 4*(1), 75–91.

Godonoga, A., & Sporn, B. (2023). The conceptualization of socially responsible universities in higher education research: A systematic literature review. *Studies in Higher Education, 48*(3), 445–459. https://doi.org/10.1080/03075079.2022.2145462

Haski-Leventhal, D. (2020). Responsible management education: The voice and perspective of students. In D. C. Moosmayer, O. Laasch, & C. Parkes (Eds.), *The SAGE handbook of responsible management learning and education* (pp. 28–41). SAGE Publications. https://doi.org/10.4135/9781526477187.n4

Laasch, O. (2024). Radicalizing managers' climate education: Getting beyond the bull**** fairy tale of eternal economic growth. *Journal of Management Education, 48*(1), 110–140. https://doi.org/10.1177/10525629231210524

Laasch, O., Suddaby, R., Freeman, R. E., & Jamali, D. (2020). Mapping the emerging field of responsible management: Domains, spheres, themes, and future research. In O. Laasch, R. Suddaby, R. E. Freeman, & D. Jamali (Eds.), *Research handbook of responsible management* (pp. 2–39). Edward Elgar Publishing.

Leal Filho, W., Trevisan, L. V., Rampasso, I. S., Anholon, R., Dinis, M. A. P., Brandli, L. L., & Mazutti, J. (2023). When the alarm bells ring: Why the UN sustainable development goals may not be achieved by 2030. *Journal of Cleaner Production, 407*, 137108.

Mason, G., & Rosenbloom, A. (2023). Poverty as a legitimate management topic: The student voice. *International Journal of Management in Education, 21*(3), 100841.

Morsing, M. (Ed.). (2022). *Responsible management education: The PRME global movement.* Taylor & Francis.

Patzer, M., Voegtlin, C., & Scherer, A. G. (2018). The normative justification of integrative stakeholder engagement: A Habermasian view on responsible leadership. *Business Ethics Quarterly, 28*(3), 325–354. https://doi.org/10.1017/beq.2017.33

Pless, N. M., & Maak, T. (2011). Responsible leadership: Pathways to the future. *Journal of Business Ethics*, *98*(November), 3–13. https://doi.org/10.1007/s10551-011-1114-4

Polman, P., & Winston, A. (2021). *Net positive: How courageous companies thrive by giving more than they take.* Harvard Business Press.

Rawhouser, H., Cummings, M., & Newbert, S. L. (2019). Social impact measurement: Current approaches and future directions for social entrepreneurship research. *Entrepreneurship: Theory and Practice*, *43*(1), 82–115.

Serdyukov, P. (2017). Innovation in education: What works, what doesn't, and what to do about it? *Journal of Research in Innovative Teaching & Learning*, *10*(1), 4–33.

Tavanti, M. (2012). Responsible management education in practice: The principles and processes for educating socially responsible and world engaged leaders. In *Handbook of research on teaching ethics in business and management education* (pp. 546–563). IGI Global.

Visser, W. (2022). *Thriving: The breakthrough movement to regenerate nature, society, and the economy.* Greenleaf Book Group.

Zhang, E. Y., & Szerencsi, A. (2023). Major shift or business as usual? An investigation on the impacts of responsible management education. *Journal of Education for Business*, *98*(1), 25–33.

Printed and bound by CPI Group (UK) Ltd, Croydon, CR0 4YY

18/12/2024